Page Controller (333): An object that handles a request for a specific page or action on a Web site.

Pessimistic Offline Lock (426): Prevents conflicts between concurrent business transactions by allowing only one business transaction at a time to access data.

Plugin (499): Links classes during configuration rather than compilation.

Query Object (316): An object that represents a database query.

Record Set (508): An in-memory representation of tabular data.

Registry (480): A well-known object that other objects can use to find common objects and services.

Remote Facade (388): Provides a coarse-grained facade on fine-grained objects to improve efficiency over a network.

Repository (322): Mediates between the domain and data mapping layers using a collection-like interface for accessing domain objects.

Row Data Gateway (152): An object that acts as a Gateway (466) to a single record in a data source. There is one instance per row.

Separated Interface (476): Defines an interface in a separate package from its implementation.

Serialized LOB (272): Saves a graph of objects by serializing them into a single large object (LOB), which it stores in a database field.

Server Session State (458): Keeps the session state on a server system in a serialized form.

Service Layer (133): Defines an application's boundary with a layer of services that establishes a set of available operations and coordinates the application's response in each operation.

Service Stub (504): Removes dependence upon problematic services during testing.

Single Table Inheritance (278): Represents an inheritance hierarchy of classes as a single table that has columns for all the fields of the various classes.

Special Case (496): A subclass that provides special behavior for particular cases.

Table Data Gateway (144): An object that acts as a Gateway (466) to a database table. One instance handles all the rows in the table.

Table Module (125): A single instance that handles the business logic for all rows in a database table or view.

Template View (350): Renders information into HTML by embedding markers in an HTML page.

Transaction Script (110): Organizes business logic by procedures where each procedure handles a single request from the presentation.

Transform View (361): A view that processes domain data element by element and transforms it into HTML.

Two Step View (365): Turns domain data into HTML in two steps: first by forming some kind of logical page, then rendering the logical page into HTML.

Unit of Work (184): Maintains a list of objects affected by a business transaction and coordinates the writing out of changes and the resolution of concurrency problems.

Value Object (486): A small simple object, like money or a date range, whose equality isn't based on identity.

Patterns of Enterprise Application Architecture

The Addison-Wesley Signature Series

The Addison-Wesley Signature Series provides readers with practical and authoritative information on the latest trends in modern technology for computer professionals. The series is based on one simple premise: great books come from great authors. Books in the series are personally chosen by expert advisors, world-class authors in their own right. These experts are proud to put their signatures on the covers, and their signatures ensure that these thought leaders have worked closely with authors to define topic coverage, book scope, critical content, and overall uniqueness. The expert signatures also symbolize a promise to our readers: you are reading a future classic.

THE ADDISON-WESLEY SIGNATURE SERIES
SIGNERS: KENT BECK & MARTIN FOWLER

Martin Fowler has been a pioneer of object technology in enterprise applications. His central concern is how to design software well. He focuses on getting to the heart of how to build enterprise software that will last well into the future. He is interested in looking behind the specifics of technologies to the patterns, practices, and principles that last for many years; these books should be usable a decade from now. Martin's criterion is that these are books he wished he could write.

Kent Beck has pioneered people-oriented technologies like JUnit, Extreme Programming, and patterns for software development. Kent is interested in helping teams do well by doing good — finding a style of software development that simultaneously satisfies economic, aesthetic, emotional, and practical constraints. His books focus on touching the lives of the creators and users of software.

TITLES IN THE SERIES

Patterns of Enterprise Application Architecture
Martin Fowler, ISBN: 0321127420

Beyond Software Architecture: Creating and Sustaining Winning Solutions
Luke Hohmann, ISBN: 0201775948

Test-Driven Development: By Example
Kent Beck, ISBN: 0321146530

Patterns of Enterprise Application Architecture

Martin Fowler

**With contributions from David Rice,
Matthew Foemmel, Edward Hieatt,
Robert Mee, and Randy Stafford**

♦♦Addison-Wesley

Boston • San Francisco • New York • Toronto • Montreal
London • Munich • Paris • Madrid
Capetown • Sydney • Tokyo • Singapore • Mexico City

The publisher offers discounts on this book when ordered in quantity for bulk purchases and special sales. For more information, please contact:

U.S. Corporate and Government Sales
(800) 382-3419
corpsales@pearsontechgroup.com

For sales outside of the U.S., please contact:

International Sales
(317) 581-3793
international@pearsontechgroup.com

Visit Addison-Wesley on the Web: www.awprofessional.com

Library of Congress Cataloging-in-Publication Data

Fowler, Martin, 1963-
 Patterns of enterprise application architecture / Martin Fowler.
 p. cm.
 Includes bibliographical references and index.
 ISBN 0-321-12742-0 (alk. paper)
 1. System design. 2. Computer architecture. 3. Application software—Development. 4. Business—Data processing. I. Title.

QA76.9.S88 F69 2003
005.1—dc21

2002027743

ISBN 0-321-12742-0
Text printed on recycled paper
 3 4 5 6 7 8 9 10—MA—07 06 05 04 03
Third printing, March 2003

For Denys William Fowler, 1922–2000
in memoriam

—Martin

Contents

Preface

In the spring of 1999 I flew to Chicago to consult on a project being done by ThoughtWorks, a small but rapidly growing application development company. The project was one of those ambitious enterprise application projects: a back-end leasing system. Essentially it deals with everything that happens to a lease after you've signed on the dotted line: sending out bills, handling someone upgrading one of the assets on the lease, chasing people who don't pay their bills on time, and figuring out what happens when someone returns the assets early. That doesn't sound too bad until you realize that leasing agreements are infinitely varied and horrendously complicated. The business "logic" rarely fits any logical pattern, because, after all, it's written by business people to capture business, where odd small variations can make all the difference in winning a deal. Each of those little victories adds yet more complexity to the system.

That's the kind of thing that gets me excited: how to take all that complexity and come up with a system of objects that can make the problem more tractable. Indeed, I believe that the primary benefit of objects is in making complex logic tractable. Developing a good *Domain Model (116)* for a complex business problem is difficult but wonderfully satisfying.

Yet that's not the end of the problem. Our domain model had to be persisted to a database, and, like many projects, we were using a relational database. We also had to connect this model to a user interface, provide support to allow remote applications to use our software, and integrate our software with third-party packages. All of this on a new technology called J2EE, which nobody in the world had any real experience in using.

Even though this technology was new, we did have the benefit of experience. I'd been doing this kind of thing for ages with C++, Smalltalk, and CORBA. Many of the ThoughtWorkers had a lot of experience with Forte. We already had the key architectural ideas in our heads, and we just had to figure out how to apply them to J2EE. Looking back on it three years later, the design is not perfect but it has stood the test of time pretty damn well.

That's the kind of situation this book was written for. Over the years I've seen many enterprise application projects. These projects often contain similar design ideas that have proven effective in dealing with the inevitable complexity that enterprise applications possess. This book is a starting point to capture these design ideas as patterns.

The book is organized in two parts, with the first part a set of narrative chapters on a number of important topics in the design of enterprise applications. These chapters introduce various problems in the architecture of enterprise applications and their solutions. However, they don't go into much detail on these solutions. The details of the solutions are in the second part, organized as patterns. These patterns are a reference, and I don't expect you to read them cover to cover. My intention is that you read the narrative chapters in Part 1 from start to finish to get a broad picture of what the book covers; then you dip into the patterns chapters of Part 2 as your interest and needs drive you. Thus, the book is a short narrative book and a longer reference book combined into one.

This is a book on enterprise application design. Enterprise applications are about the display, manipulation, and storage of large amounts of often complex data and the support or automation of business processes with that data. Examples include reservation systems, financial systems, supply chain systems, and many others that run modern business. Enterprise applications have their own particular challenges and solutions, and they are different from embedded systems, control systems, telecoms, or desktop productivity software. Thus, if you work in these other fields, there's nothing really in this book for you (unless you want to get a feel for what enterprise applications are like.) For a general book on software architecture, I'd recommend [POSA].

There are many architectural issues in building enterprise applications. I'm afraid this book can't be a comprehensive guide to them. In building software I'm a great believer in iterative development. At the heart of iterative development is the notion that you should deliver software as soon as you have something useful to the user, even if it's not complete. Although there are many differences between writing a book and writing software, this notion is one that I think the two share. That said, this book is an incomplete but (I trust) useful compendium of advice on enterprise application architecture. The primary topics I talk about are

- Layering of enterprise applications

- Structuring domain (business) logic

- Structuring a Web user interface

- Linking in-memory modules (particularly objects) to a relational database

- Handling session state in stateless environments

- Principles of distribution

The list of things I don't talk about is rather longer. I really fancied writing about organizing validation, incorporating messaging and asynchronous communication, security, error handling, clustering, application integration, architectural refactoring, structuring rich-client user interfaces, among other topics. However, because of space and time constraints and lack of cogitation, you won't find them in this book. I can only hope to see some patterns for this work in the near future. Perhaps I'll do a second volume someday and get into these topics, or maybe someone else will fill these and other gaps.

Of these, message-based communication is a particularly big issue. People who are integrating multiple applications are increasingly making use of asynchronous message-based communication approaches. There's much to be said for using them within an application as well.

This book is not intended to be specific for any particular software platform. I first came across these patterns while working with Smalltalk, C++, and CORBA in the late '80s and early '90s. In the late '90s I started to do extensive work in Java and found that these patterns applied well to both early Java/CORBA systems and later J2EE-based work. More recently I've been doing some initial work with Microsoft's .NET platform and find the patterns apply again. My ThoughtWorks colleagues have also introduced their experiences, particularly with Forte. I can't claim generality across all platforms that have ever been or will be used for enterprise applications, but so far these patterns have shown enough recurrence to be useful.

I have provided code examples for most of the patterns. My choice of language for them is based on what I think most readers are likely to be able to read and understand. Java is a good choice here. Anyone who can read C or C++ can read Java, yet Java is much less complex than C++. Essentially most C++ programmers can read Java but not vice versa. I'm an object bigot, so I inevitably lean to an OO language. As a result, most of the code examples are in Java. As I was working on the book, Microsoft started stabilizing its .NET environment, and its C# language has most of the same properties as Java for an author. So I did some of the code examples in C# as well, although that introduced some risk since developers don't have much experience with .NET and so the idioms for using it well are less mature. Both are C-based languages, so if you can read one you should be able to read both, even if you aren't deeply into that language or platform. My aim was to use a language that the largest amount of software developers can read, even if it's not their primary or preferred language. (My apologies to those who like Smalltalk, Delphi, Visual Basic, Perl, Python, Ruby, COBOL, or any other language. I know you think you know a better language than Java or C#. All I can say is I do, too!)

The examples are there for inspiration and explanation of the ideas in the patterns. They aren't canned solutions; in all cases you'll need to do a fair bit of work to fit them into your application. Patterns are useful starting points, but they are not destinations.

Who This Book Is For

I've written this book for programmers, designers, and architects who are building enterprise applications and who want to improve either their understanding of architectural issues or their communication about them.

I'm assuming that most of my readers will fall into two groups: those with modest needs who are looking to build their own software and readers with more demanding needs who will be using a tool. For those of modest needs, my intention is that these patterns should get you started. In many areas you'll need more than the patterns will give you, but I'll provide you more of a headstart in this field than I got. For tool users I hope this book will give you some idea of what's happening under the hood and also help you choose which of the tool-supported patterns to use. Using, say, an object-relational mapping tool still means that you have to make decisions about how to map certain situations. Reading the patterns should give you some guidance in making the choices.

There is a third category; those with demanding needs who want to build their own software. The first thing I'd say here is to look carefully at using tools. I've seen more than one project get sucked into a long exercise at building frameworks, which wasn't what the project was really about. If you're still convinced, go ahead. Remember in this case that many of the code examples in this book are deliberately simplified to help understanding, and you'll find you'll need to do a lot tweaking to handle the greater demands you face.

Since patterns are common solutions to recurring problems, there's a good chance that you have already come across some of them. If you've been working in enterprise applications for a while, you may well know most of them. I'm not claiming to present anything new in this book. Indeed, I claim the opposite—this is a book of (for our industry) old ideas. If you're new to this field, I hope the book will help you learn about these techniques. If you're familiar with the techniques, I hope the book will help you communicate and teach them to others. An important part of patterns is trying to build a common vocabulary, so you can say that this class is a *Remote Facade (388)* and other designers will know what you mean.

Acknowledgments

As with any book, what's written here has a great deal to do with the many people who have worked with me in various ways over the years. Lots of people have helped in lots of ways. Often I don't recall important things people said that went into this book, but I can acknowledge those contributions I do remember.

I'll start with my contributors. David Rice, a colleague of mine at Thought-Works, has made a huge contribution—a good tenth of the book. As we worked hard to hit the deadline (while he was also supporting a client), we had several late-night instant message conversations where he confessed to finally seeing why writing a book is both so hard and so compulsive.

Matt Foemmel is another ThoughtWorker, and although the Arctic will need air conditioning before he writes prose for fun, he's been a great contributor of code examples (as well as a very succinct critic of the book.) I was pleased that Randy Stafford contributed *Service Layer (133)* as he's been such a strong advocate for it. I'd also like to thank Edward Hieatt and Rob Mee for their contribution, which arose from Rob's noticing a gap while he was doing his review of the text. He became my favorite reviewer: Not only does he notice something missing, he helps write a section to fix it!

As usual, I owe more than I can say to my first-class panel of official reviewers:

John Brewer	Rob Mee
Kyle Brown	Gerard Meszaros
Jens Coldewey	Dirk Riehle
John Crupi	Randy Stafford
Leonard Fenster	David Siegel
Alan Knight	Kai Yu

I could almost list the ThoughtWorks telephone directory here, for so many of my colleagues have helped this project by talking over their designs and experiences with me. Many patterns formed in my mind because I had the opportunity to talk with the many talented designers we have, so I have little choice but to thank the whole company.

Kyle Brown, Rachel Reinitz, and Bobby Woolf have gone out of their way to have long and detailed review sessions with me in North Carolina. Their fine-tooth comb has injected all sorts of wisdom, not including this particularly heinous mixed metaphor. In particular I've enjoyed several long telephone calls with Kyle that contributed more than I can list.

Early in 2000 I prepared a talk for Java One with Alan Knight and Kai Yu that was the earliest genesis of this material. As well as thanking them for their help in that, I should also thank Josh Mackenzie, Rebecca Parsons, and Dave Rice for helping me refine these talks, and the ideas, later on. Jim Newkirk did a great deal in helping me get used to the new world of .NET.

I've learned a lot from the many people working in this field with whom I've had good conversations and collaborations. In particular I'd like to thank Colleen Roe, David Muirhead, and Randy Stafford for sharing their work on the Foodsmart example system at Gemstone. I've also had great conversations at the Crested Butte workshop that Bruce Eckel has hosted and must thank all the people who attended that event in the last couple of years. Joshua Kerievsky didn't have time to do a full review, but he was an excellent patterns consultant.

As usual, I had the remarkable help of the UIUC reading group with their unique brand of no-holds-barred audio reviews. My thanks to: Ariel Gertzenstein, Bosko Zivaljevic , Brad Jones, Brian Foote, Brian Marick, Federico Balaguer, Joseph Yoder, John Brant, Mike Hewner, Ralph Johnson, and Weerasak Witthawaskul.

Dragos Manolescu, an ex-UIUC hitman, got his own group together to give me feedback. My thanks to Muhammad Anan, Brian Doyle, Emad Ghosheh, Glenn Graessle, Daniel Hein, Prabhaharan Kumarakulasingam, Joe Quint, John Reinke, Kevin Reynolds, Sripriya Srinivasan, and Tirumala Vaddiraju.

Kent Beck has given me more good ideas than I can remember. But I do remember that he came up with the name for *Special Case (496)*. Jim Odell was responsible for getting me into the world of consulting, teaching, and writing—no acknowledgment will ever do his help justice.

As I was writing this book, I put drafts on the Web. During this time many people sent me e-mails pointing out problems, asking questions, or talking about alternatives. These people include Michael Banks, Mark Bernstein, Graham Berrisford, Bjorn Beskow, Bryan Boreham, Sean Broadley, Peris Brodsky, Paul Campbell, Chester Chen, John Coakley, Bob Corrick, Pascal Costanza, Andy Czerwonka, Martin Diehl, Daniel Drasin, Juan Gomez Duaso, Don Dwiggins, Peter Foreman, Russell Freeman, Peter Gassmann, Jason Gorman, Dan Green,

Lars Gregori, Rick Hansen, Tobin Harris, Russel Healey, Christian Heller, Richard Henderson, Kyle Hermenean, Carsten Heyl, Akira Hirasawa, Eric Kaun, Kirk Knoernschild, Jesper Ladegaard, Chris Lopez, Paolo Marino, Jeremy Miller, Ivan Mitrovic, Thomas Neumann, Judy Obee, Paolo Parovel, Trevor Pinkney, Tomas Restrepo, Joel Rieder, Matthew Roberts, Stefan Roock, Ken Rosha, Andy Schneider, Alexandre Semenov, Stan Silvert, Geoff Soutter, Volker Termath, Christopher Thames, Volker Turau, Knut Wannheden, Marc Wallace, Stefan Wenig, Brad Wiemerslage, Mark Windholtz, Michael Yoon.

There are many others who gave input whose names I either never knew or can't remember, but my thanks is no less heartfelt.

My biggest thanks is, as ever, to my wife Cindy, whose company I appreciate much more than anyone can appreciate this book.

Colophon

This is the first book that I wrote using XML and related technologies. The master text was written as a series of XML documents using trusty TextPad. I also used a home-grown DTD. While I was working I used XSLT to generate the web pages for the HTML site. For the diagrams I relied on my old friend Visio using Pavel Hruby's wonderful UML templates (much better than those that come with the tool. I have a link on my Web site if you want them.) I wrote a small program that automatically imported the code examples into the output, which saved me from the usual nightmare of code cut and paste. For my first draft I tried XSL-FO with Apache FOP. At the time it wasn't quite up to the job, so for later work I wrote scripts in XSLT and Ruby to import the text into FrameMaker.

I used several open source tools while working on this book—in particular, JUnit, NUnit, ant, Xerces, Xalan, Tomcat, Jboss, Ruby, and Hsql. My thanks to the many developers of these tools. There was also a long list of commercial tools. In particular, I relied on Visual Studio for .NET and on IntelliJ's wonderful Idea—the first IDE that's excited me since Smalltalk—for Java.

The book was acquired for Addison Wesley by Mike Hendrickson who, assisted by Ross Venables, has supervised its publication. I started work on the manuscript in November 2000 and released the final draft to production in June 2002. As I write this, the book is due for release in November 2002 at OOPSLA.

Sarah Weaver was the production editor, coordinating the editing, composition, proofreading, indexing, and production of final files. Dianne Wood was the copy editor, carrying out the tricky job of cleaning up my English without introducing any untoward refinement. Kim Arney Mulcahy composed the book into the design you see here, cleaned up the diagrams, set the text in Sabon, and prepared the final Framemaker files for the printer. The text design is based on the format we used for *Refactoring*. Cheryl Ferguson proofread the pages and ferreted out any errors that had slipped through the cracks. Irv Hershman prepared the index.

About the Cover Picture

During the couple of years I spent writing this book a more significant construction project was going on in Boston. The Leonard P. Zakim Bunker Hill Bridge (try fitting that name on a road sign) will replace the ugly double-decker that now carries Interstate 93 over the Charles River. The Zakim bridge is a cable-stayed bridge, a style that hasn't been widely used in the U.S. so far, but is very popular in Europe. The Zakim bridge isn't particularly long, but it is the world's widest cable-stayed bridge and also the first U.S. cable-stayed bridge to have an asymmetric design. It's a very beautiful bridge, but that doesn't stop me from teasing Cindy about Henry Petroski's conjecture that we are due for a major failure in a cable-stayed bridge soon.

Martin Fowler, Melrose, Massachusetts, August 2002
http://martinfowler.com

Introduction

In case you haven't realized it, building computer systems is hard. As the complexity of the system gets greater, the task of building the software gets exponentially harder. As in any profession, we can progress only by learning, both from our mistakes and from our successes. This book represents some of this learning written in a form that I hope will help you to learn these lessons quicker than I did, or to communicate to others more effectively than I did before I boiled these patterns down.

In this introduction I want to set the scope of the book and provide some of the background that will underpin its ideas.

Architecture

The software industry delights in taking words and stretching them into a myriad of subtly contradictory meanings. One of the biggest sufferers is "architecture." I tend to look at "architecture" as one of those impressive-sounding words, used primarily to indicate that we're talking something that's important. But I'm pragmatic enough not to let my cynicism get in the way of attracting people to my book. :-)

"Architecture" is a term that lots of people try to define, with little agreement. There are two common elements: One is the highest-level breakdown of a system into its parts; the other, decisions that are hard to change. It's also increasingly realized that there isn't just one way to state a system's architecture; rather, there are multiple architectures in a system, and the view of what is architecturally significant is one that can change over a system's lifetime.

From time to time Ralph Johnson has a truly remarkable posting on a mailing list, and he did one on architecture just as I was finishing the draft of this book. In this posting he brought out the point that architecture is a subjective thing, a shared understanding of a system's design by the expert developers on a

1

project. Commonly this shared understanding is in the form of the major components of the system and how they interact. It's also about decisions, in that it's the decisions that developers wish they could get right early on because they're perceived as hard to change. The subjectivity comes in here as well because, if you find that something is easier to change than you once thought, then it's no longer architectural. In the end architecture boils down to the important stuff—whatever that is.

In this book I present my perception of the major parts of an enterprise application and of the decisions I wish I could get right early on. The architectural pattern I like the most is that of layers, which I describe more in Chapter 1. This book is thus about how you decompose an enterprise application into layers and how these layers work together. Most nontrivial enterprise applications use a layered architecture of some form, but in some situations other approaches, such as pipes and filters, are valuable. I don't go into those situations, focusing instead on the context of a layered architecture because it's the most widely useful.

Some of the patterns in this book can reasonably be called architectural, in that they represent significant decisions about these parts; others are more about design and help you to realize that architecture. I don't make any strong attempt to separate the two, since what is architectural or not is so subjective.

Enterprise Applications

Lots of people write computer software, and we call all of it software development. However, there are distinct kinds of software out there, each of which has its own challenges and complexities. This comes out when I talk with some of my friends in the telecom field. In some ways enterprise applications are much easier than telecoms software—we don't have very hard multithreading problems, and we don't have hardware and software integration. But in other ways it's much tougher. Enterprise applications often have complex data—and lots of it—to work on, together with business rules that fail all tests of logical reasoning. Although some techniques and patterns are relevant for all kinds of software, many are relevant for only one particular branch.

In my career I've concentrated on enterprise applications, so my patterns here are all about that. (Other terms for enterprise applications include "information systems" or, for those with a long memory, "data processing.") But what do I mean by the term "enterprise application"? I can't give a precise definition, but I can give some indication of my meaning.

I'll start with examples. Enterprise applications include payroll, patient records, shipping tracking, cost analysis, credit scoring, insurance, supply chain, accounting, customer service, and foreign exchange trading. Enterprise applications don't include automobile fuel injection, word processors, elevator controllers, chemical plant controllers, telephone switches, operating systems, compilers, and games.

Enterprise applications usually involve **persistent data**. The data is persistent because it needs to be around between multiple runs of the program—indeed, it usually needs to persist for several years. Also during this time there will be many changes in the programs that use it. It will often outlast the hardware that originally created much of it, and outlast operating systems and compilers. During that time there'll be many changes to the structure of the data in order to store new pieces of information without disturbing the old pieces. Even if there's a fundamental change and the company installs a completely new application to handle a job, the data has to be migrated to the new application.

There's usually **a lot of data**—a moderate system will have over 1 GB of data organized in tens of millions of records—so much that managing it is a major part of the system. Older systems used indexed file structures such as IBM's VSAM and ISAM. Modern systems usually use databases, mostly relational databases. The design and feeding of these databases has turned into a subprofession of its own.

Usually many people **access data concurrently**. For many systems this may be less than a hundred people, but for Web-based systems that talk over the Internet this goes up by orders of magnitude. With so many people there are definite issues in ensuring that all of them can access the system properly. But even without that many people, there are still problems in making sure that two people don't access the same data at the same time in a way that causes errors. Transaction manager tools handle some of this burden, but often it's impossible to hide this from application developers.

With so much data, there's usually **a lot of user interface screens** to handle it. It's not unusual to have hundreds of distinct screens. Users of enterprise applications vary from occasional to regular, and normally they will have little technical expertise. Thus, the data has to be presented lots of different ways for different purposes. Systems often have a lot of batch processing, which is easy to forget when focusing on use cases that stress user interaction.

Enterprise applications rarely live on an island. Usually they need to **integrate with other enterprise applications** scattered around the enterprise. The various systems are built at different times with different technologies, and even the collaboration mechanisms will be different: COBOL data files, CORBA, messaging systems. Every so often the enterprise will try to integrate its different systems using a common communication technology. Of course, it hardly ever finishes the job, so there are several different unified integration schemes in place at once. This gets even worse as businesses seek to integrate with their business partners as well.

Even if a company unifies the technology for integration, they run into problems with differences in business process and **conceptual dissonance** with the data. One division of the company may think a customer is someone with whom it has a current agreement; another division also counts those that had a contract but don't any longer; another counts product sales but not service sales. That may sound easy to sort out, but when you have hundreds of records in which every field can have a subtly different meaning, the sheer size of the problem becomes a challenge—even if the only person who knows what the field really means is still with the company. (And, of course, all of this changes without warning.) As a result, data has to be constantly read, munged, and written in all sorts of different syntactic and semantic formats.

Then there's the matter of what comes under the term "business logic." I find this a curious term because there are few things that are less logical than business logic. When you build an operating system you strive to keep the whole thing logical. But business rules are just given to you, and without major political effort there's nothing you can do to change them. You have to deal with a haphazard array of strange conditions that often interact with each other in surprising ways. Of course, they got that way for a reason: Some salesman negotiated to have a certain yearly payment two days later than usual because that fit with his customer's accounting cycle and thus won a couple of million dollars in business. A few thousand of these one-off special cases is what leads to the **complex business "illogic"** that makes business software so difficult. In this situation you have to organize the business logic as effectively as you can, because the only certain thing is that the logic will change over time.

For some people the term "enterprise application" implies a large system. However, it's important to remember that not all enterprise applications are large, even though they can provide a lot of value to the enterprise. Many people assume that, since small systems aren't large, they aren't worth bothering with, and to some degree there's merit here. If a small system fails, it usually makes less noise than a big system. Still, I think such thinking tends to short-change the cumulative effect of many small projects. If you can do things that improve small projects, then that cumulative effect can be very significant on an enterprise, particularly since small projects often have disproportionate value. Indeed, one of the best things you can do is turn a large project into a small one by simplifying its architecture and process.

Kinds of Enterprise Application

When we discuss how to design enterprise applications, and what patterns to use, it's important to realize that enterprise applications are all different and that different problems lead to different ways of doing things. I have a set of alarm bells that go off when people say, "Always do this." For me much of the challenge (and interest) in design is in knowing about alternatives and judging the trade-offs of using one alternative over another. There is a large space of alternatives to choose from, but here I'll pick three points on this very big plane.

Consider a B2C (business to customer) online retailer: People browse and—with luck and a shopping cart—buy. For such a system we need to be able to handle a very high volume of users, so our solution needs to be not only reasonably efficient in terms of resources used but also scalable so that you can increase the load by adding more hardware. The domain logic for such an application can be pretty straightforward: order capturing, some relatively simple pricing and shipping calculations, and shipment notification. We want anyone to be able access the system easily, so that implies a pretty generic Web presentation that can be used with the widest possible range of browsers. Data source includes a database for holding orders and perhaps some communication with an inventory system to help with availability and delivery information.

Contrast this with a system that automates the processing of leasing agreements. In some ways this is a much simpler system than the B2C retailer's because there are many fewer users—no more than a hundred or so at one time. Where it's more complicated is in the business logic. Calculating monthly bills on a lease, handling events such as early returns and late payments, and validating data as a lease is booked are all complicated tasks, since much of the leasing industry's competition comes in the form of little variations over deals done in the past. A complex business domain such as this is challenging because the rules are so arbitrary.

Such a system also has more complexity in the user interface (UI). At the least this means a much more involved HTML interface with more, and more complex, screens. Often these systems have UI demands that lead users to want a more sophisticated presentation than a HTML front end allows, so a more conventional rich-client interface is needed. A more complex user interaction also leads to more complicated transaction behavior: Booking a lease may take an hour or two, during which time the user is in a logical transaction. We also see a complex database schema with perhaps two hundred tables and connections to packages for asset valuation and pricing.

A third example point is a simple expense-tracking system for a small company. Such a system has few users and simple logic and can easily be made accessible across the company with an HTML presentation. The only data source is a few tables in a database. As simple as it is, a system like this is not devoid of a challenge. You have to build it very quickly and you have to bear in mind that it may grow as people want to calculate reimbursement checks, feed them into the payroll system, understand tax implications, provide reports for the CFO, tie into airline reservation Web services, and so on. Trying to use the architecture for either of the other two example systems will slow down the development of this one. If a system has business benefits (as all enterprise applications should), delaying those benefits costs money. However, you don't want to make decisions now that will hamper future growth. But if you add flexibility now and get it wrong, the complexity added for flexibility's sake may actually make it harder to evolve in the future and may delay deployment and thus delay the benefit. Although such systems may be small, most enterprises have a lot of them so the cumulative effect of an inappropriate architecture can be significant.

Each of these three enterprise application examples has difficulties, and they are different difficulties. As a result you can't come up with a single architecture that will be right for all three. Choosing an architecture means that you have to understand the particular problems of your system and choose an appropriate design based on that understanding. That's why in this book I don't give a single solution for your enterprise needs. Instead, many of the patterns are about choices and alternatives. Even when you choose a particular pattern, you'll have to modify it to meet your demands. You can't build enterprise software without thinking, and all any book can do is give you more information to base your decisions on.

If this applies to patterns, it also applies to tools. Although it obviously makes sense to pick as small a set of tools as you can to develop applications, you also have to recognize that different tools are best for different purposes. Beware of using a tool that is really suited for a different kind of application—it may hinder more than help.

Thinking About Performance

Many architectural decisions are about performance. For most performance issues I prefer to get a system up and running, instrument it, and then use a disciplined optimization process based on measurement. However, some architectural decisions affect performance in a way that's difficult to fix with later optimization. And even when it is easy to fix, people involved in the project worry about these decisions early.

It's always difficult to talk about performance in a book such as this. The reason that it's so difficult is that any advice about performance should not be treated as fact until it's measured on your configuration. Too often I've seen designs used or rejected because of performance considerations, which turn out to be bogus once somebody actually does some measurements on the real setup used for the application.

I give a few guidelines in this book, including minimizing remote calls, which has been good performance advice for quite a while. Even so, you should verify every tip by measuring on your application. Similarly there are several occasions where code examples in this book sacrifice performance for understandability. Again it's up to you to apply the optimizations for your environment. Whenever you do a performance optimization, however, you must measure both before and after, otherwise, you may just be making your code harder to read.

There's an important corollary to this: A significant change in configuration may invalidate any facts about performance. Thus, if you upgrade to a new version of your virtual machine, hardware, database, or almost anything else, you must redo your performance optimizations and make sure they're still helping. In many cases a new configuration can change things. Indeed, you may find that an optimization you did in the past to improve performance actually hurts performance in the new environment.

Another problem with talking about performance is the fact that many terms are used in an inconsistent way. The most noted victim of this is "scalability," which is regularly used to mean half a dozen different things. Here are the terms I use.

Response time is the amount of time it takes for the system to process a request from the outside. This may be a UI action, such as pressing a button, or a server API call.

Responsiveness is about how quickly the system acknowledges a request as opposed to processing it. This is important in many systems because users may become frustrated if a system has low responsiveness, even if its response time is good. If your system waits during the whole request, then your responsiveness and response time are the same. However, if you indicate that you've received the request before you complete, then your responsiveness is better. Providing a progress bar during a file copy improves the responsiveness of your user interface, even though it doesn't improve response time.

Latency is the minimum time required to get any form of response, even if the work to be done is nonexistent. It's usually the big issue in remote systems. If I ask a program to do nothing, but to tell me when it's done doing nothing, then I should get an almost instantaneous response if the program runs on my laptop. However, if the program runs on a remote computer, I may get a few seconds just because of the time taken for the request and response to make their way across the wire. As an application developer, I can usually do nothing to improve latency. Latency is also the reason why you should minimize remote calls.

Throughput is how much stuff you can do in a given amount of time. If you're timing the copying of a file, throughput might be measured in bytes per second. For enterprise applications a typical measure is transactions per second (tps), but the problem is that this depends on the complexity of your transaction. For your particular system you should pick a common set of transactions.

In this terminology **performance** is either throughput or response time—whichever matters more to you. It can sometimes be difficult to talk about performance when a technique improves throughput but decreases response time, so it's best to use the more precise term. From a user's perspective responsiveness may be more important than response time, so improving responsiveness at a cost of response time or throughput will increase performance.

Load is a statement of how much stress a system is under, which might be measured in how many users are currently connected to it. The load is usually a context for some other measurement, such as a response time. Thus, you may say that the response time for some request is 0.5 seconds with 10 users and 2 seconds with 20 users.

Load sensitivity is an expression of how the response time varies with the load. Let's say that system A has a response time of 0.5 seconds for 10 through 20 users and system B has a response time of 0.2 seconds for 10 users that rises to 2 seconds for 20 users. In this case system A has a lower load sensitivity than system B. We might also use the term **degradation** to say that system B degrades more than system A.

Efficiency is performance divided by resources. A system that gets 30 tps on two CPUs is more efficient than a system that gets 40 tps on four identical CPUs.

The **capacity** of a system is an indication of maximum effective throughput or load. This might be an absolute maximum or a point at which the performance dips below an acceptable threshold.

Scalability is a measure of how adding resources (usually hardware) affects performance. A scalable system is one that allows you to add hardware and get a commensurate performance improvement, such as doubling how many servers you have to double your throughput. **Vertical scalability, or scaling up,** means adding more power to a single server, such as more memory. **Horizontal scalability, or scaling out,** means adding more servers.

The problem here is that design decisions don't affect all of these performance factors equally. Say we have two software systems running on a server: Swordfish's capacity is 20 tps while Camel's capacity is 40 tps. Which has better performance? Which is more scalable? We can't answer the scalability question from this data, and we can only say that Camel is more efficient on a single server. If we add another server, we notice that swordfish now handles 35 tps and camel handles 50 tps. Camel's capacity is still better, but Swordfish looks like it may scale out better. If we continue adding servers we'll discover that Swordfish gets 15 tps per extra server and Camel gets 10. Given this data we can say that Swordfish has better horizontal scalability, even though Camel is more efficient for less than five servers.

When building enterprise systems, it often makes sense to build for hardware scalability rather than capacity or even efficiency. Scalability gives you the option of better performance if you need it. Scalability can also be easier to do. Often designers do complicated things that improve the capacity on a particular hardware platform when it might actually be cheaper to buy more hardware. If Camel has a greater cost than Swordfish, and that greater cost is equivalent to a couple of servers, then Swordfish ends up being cheaper even if you only need 40 tps. It's fashionable to complain about having to rely on better hardware to make our software run properly, and I join this choir whenever I have to upgrade my laptop just to handle the latest version of Word. But newer hardware is often cheaper than making software run on less powerful systems. Similarly, adding more servers is often cheaper than adding more programmers—providing that a system is scalable.

Patterns

Patterns have been around for a long time, so part of me doesn't want to regurgitate their history yet another time. Still, this is an opportunity for me to provide my view of patterns and what makes them a worthwhile approach to describing design.

There's no generally accepted definition of a pattern, but perhaps the best place to start is Christopher Alexander, an inspiration for many pattern enthusiasts: "Each pattern describes a problem which occurs over and over again in our environment, and then describes the core of the solution to that problem, in such a way that you can use this solution a million times over, without ever doing it the same way twice" [Alexander et al.]. Alexander is an architect, so he was talking about buildings, but the definition works pretty nicely for software as well. The focus of the pattern is a particular solution, one that's both common and effective in dealing with one or more recurring problems. Another way of looking at it is that a pattern is a chunk of advice and the art of creating patterns is to divide up many pieces of advice into relatively independent chunks so that you can refer to them and discuss them more or less separately.

A key part of patterns is that they're rooted in practice. You find patterns by looking at what people do, observing things that work, and then looking for the "core of the solution." It isn't an easy process, but once you've found some good patterns they become a valuable thing. For me their value lies in being able to create a book that serves as a reference. You don't need to read all of this book, or all of any patterns book, to find it useful. You just need to read enough to have a sense of what the patterns are, what problems they solve, and how they solve them. You don't need to know all the details but just enough so that if you run into one of the problems you can find the pattern in the book. Only then do you need to really understand the pattern in depth.

Once you need the pattern, you have to figure out how to apply it to your circumstances. A key thing about patterns is that you can never just apply the solution blindly, which is why pattern tools have been such miserable failures. I like to say that patterns are "half baked," meaning that you always have to finish them off in the oven of your own project. Every time I use a pattern I tweak it a little here and a little there. You see the same solution many times over, but it's never exactly the same.

Each pattern is relatively independent, but patterns aren't isolated from each other. Often one pattern leads to another or one occurs only if another is around. Thus, you'll usually only see *Class Table Inheritance (285)* if there's a *Domain Model (116)* in your design. The boundaries between the patterns are naturally fuzzy, but I've tried to make each pattern as self-standing as I can. If someone says "Use a *Unit of Work (184)*," you can look it up and see how to apply it without having to read the entire book.

If you're an experienced designer of enterprise applications, you'll probably find that most of these patterns are familiar to you. I hope you won't be too disappointed (I did try to warn you in the Preface). Patterns aren't original ideas; they're very much observations of what happens in the field. As a result, we pattern authors don't say we "invented" a pattern but rather that we "discovered" one. Our role is to note the common solution, look for its core, and then write down the resulting pattern. For an experienced designer, the value of the pattern is not that it gives you a new idea; the value lies in helping you communicate your idea. If you and your colleagues all know what a *Remote Facade (388)* is, you can communicate a lot by saying, "This class is a *Remote Facade.*" It also allows you to say to someone newer, "Use a *Data Transfer Object* for this," and they can come to this book to look it up. The result is that patterns create a vocabulary about design, which is why naming is such an important issue.

While most of these patterns are truly for enterprise applications, those in the base patterns chapter (Chapter 18) are more general and localized. I include them because I refer to them in discussions of the enterprise application patterns.

The Structure of the Patterns

Every author has to choose his pattern form. Some base their forms on a classic patterns book such as [Alexander et al.], [Gang of Four], or [POSA]. Others make up their own. I've long wrestled with what makes the best form. On the one hand I don't want something as small as the GOF form; on the other hand I need to have sections that support a reference book. So this is what I've used for this book.

The first item is the name of the pattern. Pattern names are crucial, because part of the purpose of patterns is to create a vocabulary that allows designers to communicate more effectively. Thus, if I tell you my Web server is built around a *Front Controller (344)* and a *Transform View (361)* and you know these patterns, you have a very clear idea of my web server's architecture.

Next are two items that go together: the intent and the sketch. The intent sums up the pattern in a sentence or two; the sketch is a visual representation of the pattern, often but not always a UML diagram. The idea is to create a brief reminder of what the pattern is about so you can quickly recall it. If you already "have the pattern," meaning that you know the solution even if you don't know the name, then the intent and the sketch should be all you need to know what the pattern is.

The next section describes a motivating problem for the pattern. This may not be the only problem that the pattern solves, but it's one that I think best motivates the pattern.

How It Works describes the solution. In here I put a discussion of implementation issues and variations that I've come across. The discussion is as independent as possible of any particular platform—where there are platform-specific sections I've indented them so you can see them and easily skip over them. Where useful I've put in UML diagrams to help explain them.

When to Use It describes when the pattern should be used. Here I talk about the trade-offs that make you select this solution compared to others. Many of the patterns in this book are alternatives; such *Page Controller (333)* and *Front Controller (344)*. Few patterns are always the right choice, so whenever I find a pattern I always ask myself, "When would I not use this?" That question often leads me to alternative patterns.

The *Further Reading* section points you to other discussions of this pattern. This isn't a comprehensive bibliography. I've limited my references to pieces that I think are important in helping you understand the pattern, so I've eliminated any discussion that I don't think adds much to what I've written and of course I've eliminated discussions of patterns I haven't read. I also haven't mentioned items that I think are going to be hard to find, or unstable Web links that I fear may disappear by the time you read this book.

I like to add one or more *examples*. Each one is a *simple* example of the pattern in use, illustrated with some code in Java or C#. I chose those languages because they seem to be languages that the largest number of professional programmers can read. It's absolutely essential to understand that the example is not the pattern. When you use the pattern, it won't look exactly like this example so don't treat it as some kind of glorified macro. I've deliberately kept the example as simple as possible so you can see the pattern in as clear a form as I can imagine. All sorts of issues are ignored that will become important when you use it, but these will be particular to your own environment. This is why you always have to tweak the pattern.

One of the consequences of this is that I've worked hard to keep each example as simple as I can, while still illustrating its core message. Thus, I've often chosen an example that's simple and explicit, rather than one that demonstrates how a pattern works with the many wrinkles required in a production system. It's a tricky balance between simple and simplistic, but it's also true that too many realistic yet peripheral issues can make it harder to understand the key points of a pattern.

This is also why I've gone for simple independent examples instead of a connected running examples. Independent examples are easier to understand in isolation, but give less guidance on how you put them together. A connected example shows how things fit together, but it's hard to understand any one pattern without understanding all the others involved in the example. While in theory it's possible to produce examples that are connected yet understandable independently, doing so is very hard—or at least too hard for me—so I chose the independent route.

The code in the examples is written with a focus on making the ideas understandable. As a result several things fall aside—in particular, error handling, which I don't pay much attention to since I haven't developed any patterns in this area yet. They are there purely to illustrate the pattern. They are not intended to show how to model any particular business problem.

For these reasons the code isn't downloadable from my Web site. Each code example in this book is surrounded with too much scaffolding to simplify the basic ideas so they're worth anything in a production setting.

Not all the sections appear in all the patterns. If I couldn't think of a good example or motivation text, I left it out.

Limitations of These Patterns

As I indicated in the Preface, this collection of patterns is by no means a comprehensive guide to enterprise application development. My test for this book is not whether it's complete but merely if it's useful. The field is too big for one mind, let alone one book.

The patterns here are all ones that I've seen in the field, but I'm not going to claim I completely understand all of their ramifications and interrelationships. This book reflects my current understanding, and that understanding has developed as I've been writing the book. I expect it will continue to evolve long after this book has turned into paper. One certainty of software development is that it never stands still.

As you consider using the patterns, never forget that they're a starting point, not a final destination. There's no way that any author can see all the many variations that software projects have. I've written these patterns to help provide a beginning, so you can read about lessons that I, and the people I've observed, have learned from doing and struggling. You'll have your own struggles on top of these. Always remember that every pattern is incomplete and that you have the responsibility, and the fun, of completing it in the context of your own system.

PART 1

The Narratives

Chapter 1

Layering

Layering is one of the most common techniques that software designers use to break apart a complicated software system. You see it in machine architectures, where layers descend from a programming language with operating system calls into device drivers and CPU instruction sets, and into logic gates inside chips. Networking has FTP layered on top of TCP, which is on top of IP, which is on top of ethernet.

When thinking of a system in terms of layers, you imagine the principal subsystems in the software arranged in some form of layer cake, where each layer rests on a lower layer. In this scheme the higher layer uses various services defined by the lower layer, but the lower layer is unaware of the higher layer. Furthermore, each layer usually hides its lower layers from the layers above, so layer 4 uses the services of layer 3, which uses the services of layer 2, but layer 4 is unaware of layer 2. (Not all layering architectures are opaque like this, but most are—or rather most are mostly opaque.

Breaking down a system into layers has a number of important benefits.

- You can understand a single layer as a coherent whole without knowing much about the other layers. You can understand how to build an FTP service on top of TCP without knowing the details of how ethernet works.

- You can substitute layers with alternative implementations of the same basic services. An FTP service can run without change over ethernet, PPP, or whatever a cable company uses.

- You minimize dependencies between layers. If the cable company changes its physical transmission system, providing they make IP work, we don't have to alter our FTP service.

- Layers make good places for standardization. TCP and IP are standards because they define how their layers should operate.

- Once you have a layer built, you can use it for many higher-level services. Thus, TCP/IP is used by FTP, telnet, SSH, and HTTP. Otherwise, all of these higher-level protocols would have to write their own lower-level protocols.

17

Layering is an important technique, but there are downsides.

- Layers encapsulate some, but not all, things well. As a result you sometimes get cascading changes. The classic example of this in a layered enterprise application is adding a field that needs to display on the UI, must be in the database, and thus must be added to every layer in between.

- Extra layers can harm performance. At every layer things typically need to be transformed from one representation to another. However, the encapsulation of an underlying function often gives you efficiency gains that more than compensate. A layer that controls transactions can be optimized and will then make everything faster.

But the hardest part of a layered architecture is deciding what layers to have and what the responsibility of each layer should be.

The Evolution of Layers in Enterprise Applications

Although I'm too young to have done any work in the early days of batch systems, I don't sense that people thought much of layers in those days. You wrote a program that manipulated some form of files (ISAM, VSAM, etc.), and that was your application. No layers need apply.

The notion of layers became more apparent in the '90s with the rise of **client–server** systems. These were two-layer systems: The client held the user interface and other application code, and the server was usually a relational database. Common client tools were VB, Powerbuilder, and Delphi. These made it particularly easy to build data-intensive applications, as they had UI widgets that were aware of SQL. Thus you could build a screen by dragging controls onto a design area and then using property sheets to connect the controls to the database.

If the application was all about the display and simple update of relational data, then these client–server systems worked very well. The problem came with domain logic: business rules, validations, calculations, and the like. Usually people would write these on the client, but this was awkward and usually done by embedding the logic directly into the UI screens. As the domain logic got more complex, this code became very difficult to work with. Furthermore, embedding logic in screens made it easy to duplicate code, which meant that simple changes resulted in hunting down similar code in many screens.

An alternative was to put the domain logic in the database as stored procedures. However, stored procedures gave limited structuring mechanisms, which again led to awkward code. Also, many people liked relational databases because

SQL was a standard that would allow them to change their database vendor. Despite the fact that few people actually did this, many liked having the option to change vendors without too high a porting cost. Because they are all proprietary, stored procedures removed that option.

At the same time that client–server was gaining popularity, the object-oriented world was rising. The object community had an answer to the problem of domain logic: Move to a three-layer system. In this approach you have a presentation layer for your UI, a domain layer for your domain logic, and a data source. This way you could move all of that intricate domain logic out of the UI and put it into a layer where you could structure it properly with objects.

Despite this, the object bandwagon made little headway. The truth was that many systems were simple, or at least started that way. And although the three-layer approach had many benefits, the tooling for client–server was compelling if your problem was simple. The client–server tools also were difficult, or even impossible, to use in a three-layer configuration.

I think the seismic shock here was the rise of the Web. Suddenly people wanted to deploy client–server applications with a Web browser. However, if all your business logic was buried in a rich client, then all your business logic needed to be redone to have a Web interface. A well-designed three-layer system could just add a new presentation layer and be done with it. Furthermore, with Java we saw an unashamedly object-oriented language hit the mainstream. The tools that appeared to build Web pages were much less tied to SQL and thus more amenable to a third layer.

When people discuss layering, there's often some confusion over the terms *layer* and *tier*. Often the two are used as synonyms, but most people see *tier* as implying a physical separation. Client–server systems are often described as two-tier systems, and the separation is physical: The client is a desktop and the server is a server. I use *layer* to stress that you don't have to run the layers on different machines. A distinct layer of domain logic often runs on either a desktop or the database server. In this situation you have two nodes but three distinct layers. With a local database I can run all three layers on a single laptop, but there will still be three distinct layers.

The Three Principal Layers

For this book I'm centering my discussion around an architecture of three primary layers: presentation, domain, and data source. (I'm following the names used in [Brown et al.]). Table 1.1 summarizes these layers.

Presentation logic is about how to handle the interaction between the user and the software. This can be as simple as a command-line or text-based menu

Table 1.1 *Three Principal Layers*

Layer	Responsibilities
Presentation	Provision of services, display of information (e.g., in Windows or HTML, handling of user request (mouse clicks, keyboard hits), HTTP requests, command-line invocations, batch API)
Domain	Logic that is the real point of the system
Data Source	Communication with databases, messaging systems, transaction managers, other packages

system, but these days it's more likely to be a rich-client graphics UI or an HTML-based browser UI. (In this book I use **rich client** to mean a Windows/Swing/fat-client UI, as opposed to an HTML browser.) The primary responsibilities of the presentation layer are to display information to the user and to interpret commands from the user into actions upon the domain and data source.

Data source logic is about communicating with other systems that carry out tasks on behalf of the application. These can be transaction monitors, other applications, messaging systems, and so forth. For most enterprise applications the biggest piece of data source logic is a database that is primarily responsible for storing persistent data.

The remaining piece is the **domain logic**, also referred to as business logic. This is the work that this application needs to do for the domain you're working with. It involves calculations based on inputs and stored data, validation of any data that comes in from the presentation, and figuring out exactly what data source logic to dispatch, depending on commands received from the presentation.

Sometimes the layers are arranged so that the domain layer completely hides the data source from the presentation. More often, however, the presentation accesses the data store directly. While this is less pure, it tends to work better in practice. The presentation may interpret a command from the user, use the data source to pull the relevant data out of the database, and then let the domain logic manipulate that data before presenting it on the glass.

A single application can often have multiple packages of each of these three subject areas. An application designed to be manipulated not only by end users through a rich-client interface but also through a command line would have two presentations: one for the rich-client interface and one for the command line. Multiple data source components may be present for different databases, but would be particularly for communication with existing packages. Even the domain may be broken into distinct areas relatively separate from each other. Certain data source packages may only be used by certain domain packages.

So far I've talked about a user. This naturally raises the question of what happens when there is no a human being driving the software. This could be something new and fashionable like a Web service or something mundane and useful like a batch process. In the latter case the user is the client program. At this point it becomes apparent that there is a lot of similarity between the presentation and data source layers in that they both are about connection to the outside world. This is the logic behind Alistair Cockburn's *Hexagonal Architecture* pattern [wiki], which visualizes any system as a core surrounded by interfaces to external systems. In *Hexagonal Architecture* everything external is fundamentally an outside interface, and thus it's a symmetrical view rather than my asymmetric layering scheme.

I find this asymmetry useful, however, because I think there is a good distinction to be made between an interface that you provide as a service to others and your use of someone else's service. Driving down to the core, this is the real distinction I make between presentation and data source. Presentation is an external interface for a service your system offers to someone else, whether it be a complex human or a simple remote program. Data source is the interface to things that are providing a service to you. I find it beneficial to think about these differently because the difference in clients alters the way you think about the service.

Although we can identify the three common responsibility layers of presentation, domain, and data source for every enterprise application, how you separate them depends on how complex the application is. A simple script to pull data from a database and display it in a Web page may all be one procedure. I would still endeavor to separate the three layers, but in that case I might do it only by placing the behavior of each layer in separate subroutines. As the system gets more complex, I would break the three layers into separate classes. As complexity increased I would divide the classes into separate packages. My general advice is to choose the most appropriate form of separation for your problem but make sure you do some kind of separation—at least at the subroutine level.

Together with the separation, there's also a steady rule about dependencies: The domain and data source should never be dependent on the presentation. That is, there should be no subroutine call from the domain or data source code into the presentation code. This rule makes it easier to substitute different presentations on the same foundation and makes it easier to modify the presentation without serious ramifications deeper down. The relationship between the domain and the data source is more complex and depends upon the architectural patterns used for the data source.

One of the hardest parts of working with domain logic seems to be that people often find it difficult to recognize what is domain logic and what is other forms of logic. An informal test I like is to imagine adding a radically different layer to an application, such as a command-line interface to a Web application. If there's any functionality you have to duplicate in order to do this, that's a sign of where domain logic has leaked into the presentation. Similarly, do you have to duplicate logic to replace a relational database with an XML file?

A good example of this is a system I was told about that contained a list of products in which all the products that sold over 10 percent more than they did the previous month were colored in red. To do this the developers placed logic in the presentation layer that compared this month's sales to last month's sales and if the difference was more than 10 percent, they set the color to red.

The trouble is that that's putting domain logic into the presentation. To properly separate the layers you need a method in the domain layer to indicate if a product has improving sales. This method does the comparison between the two months and returns a Boolean value. The presentation layer then simply calls this Boolean method and, if true, highlights the product in red. That way the process is broken into its two parts: deciding whether there is something highlightable and choosing how to highlight.

I'm uneasy with being overly dogmatic about this. When reviewing this book, Alan Knight commented that he was "torn between whether just putting that into the UI is the first step on a slippery slope to hell or a perfectly reasonable thing to do that only a dogmatic purist would object to." The reason we are uneasy is because it's both!

Choosing Where to Run Your Layers

For most of this book I will be talking about logical layers—that is, dividing a system into separate pieces to reduce the coupling between different parts of a system. Separation between layers is useful even if the layers are all running on one physical machine. However, there are places where the physical structure of a system makes a difference.

For most IS applications the decision is whether to run processing on a client, on a desktop machine, or on a server.

Often the simplest case is to run everything on servers. An HTML front end that uses a Web browser is a good way to do this. The great advantage of running on the server is that everything is easy to upgrade and fix because it's in a limited amount of places. You don't have to worry about deployment to many desktops and keeping them all in sync with the server. You don't have to worry about compatibilities with other desktop software.

The general argument in favor of running on a client turns on responsiveness or disconnected operation. Any logic that runs on the server needs a server roundtrip to respond to anything the user does. If the user wants to fiddle with things and see immediate feedback, that roundtrip gets in the way. It also needs a network connection to run. The network may like to be everywhere, but as I type this it isn't at 31,000 feet. It may be everywhere soon, but there are people who want to do work now without waiting for wireless coverage to reach Dead End Creek. Disconnected operation brings particular challenges, and I'm afraid I decided to put those out of the scope of this book.

With those general forces in place, we can look at the options layer by layer. The data source pretty much always runs only on servers. The exception is where you might duplicate server functionality onto a suitably powerful client, usually when you want disconnected operation. In this case changes to the data source on the disconnected client need to be synchronized with the server. As I mentioned earlier, I decided to leave those issues to another day—or another author.

The decision of where to run the presentation depends mostly on what kind of user interface you want. Running a rich client pretty much means running the presentation on the client. Running a Web interface pretty much means running on the server. There are exceptions—for one, remote operation of client software (such as X servers in the Unix world) running a Web server on the desktop—but these exceptions are rare.

If you're building a B2C system, you have no choice. Any Tom, Dick, or Harriet can be connecting to your servers and you don't want to turn anyone away because they insist on doing their online shopping with a TRS-80. In this case you do all processing on the server and offer up HTML for the browser to deal with. Your limitation with the HTML option is that every bit of decision making needs a roundtrip from the client to the server, and that can hurt responsiveness. You can reduce some of the lag with browser scripting and downloadable applets, but they reduce your browser compatibility and tend to add other headaches. The more pure HTML you can go, the easier life is.

That ease of life is appealing even if every one of your desktops is lovingly hand-built by your IS department. Keeping clients up to date and avoiding compatibility errors with other software are problems even simple rich-client systems have.

The primary reason that people want a rich-client presentation is that some tasks are complicated for users to do and, to have a usable application, they'll need more than what a Web GUI can give. Increasingly, however, people are getting used to ways to make Web front ends more usable, and that reduces the need for a rich client presentation. As I write this I'm very much in favor of the Web presentation if you can and the rich client if you must.

This leaves us with the domain logic. You can run business logic all on the server or all on the client, or you can split it. Again, all on the server is the best choice for ease of maintenance. The demand to move it to the client is for either responsiveness or disconnected use.

If you have to run some logic on the client, you can consider running all of it there—at least that way it's all in one place. Usually this goes hand in hand with a rich client—running a Web server on a client machine isn't going to help responsiveness much, although it can be a way to deal with disconnected operation. In this case you can still keep your domain logic in separate modules from the presentation, with either a *Transaction Script (110)* or a *Domain Model (116)*. The problem with putting all the domain logic on the client is that you have more to upgrade and maintain.

Splitting across both the desktop and the server sounds like the worst of both worlds because you don't know where any piece of logic may be. The main reason to do it is that you have only a small amount of domain logic that needs to run on the client. The trick then is to isolate this piece of logic in a self-contained module that isn't dependent on any other part of the system. That way you can run that module on the client or the server. This will require a good bit of annoying jiggery-pokery, but it's a good way of doing the job.

Once you've chosen your processing nodes, you should try to keep all the code in a single process, either on one node or copied on several nodes in a cluster. Don't try to separate the layers into discrete processes unless you absolutely have to. Doing that will both degrade performance and add complexity, as you have to add things like *Remote Facades (388)* and *Data Transfer Objects (401)*.

It's important to remember that many of these things are what Jens Coldewey refers to as **complexity boosters**—distribution, explicit multithreading, paradigm chasms (such as object/relational), multiplatform development, and extreme performance requirements (such as more than 100 transactions per second). All of these carry a high cost. Certainly there are times when you have to do it, but never forget that each one carries a charge both in development and in on-going maintenance.

Chapter 2

Organizing Domain Logic

In organizing domain logic I've separated it into three primary patterns: *Transaction Script (110)*, *Domain Model (116)*, and *Table Module (125)*.

The simplest approach to storing domain logic is the *Transaction Script (110)*. A *Transaction Script (110)* is essentially a procedure that takes the input from the presentation, processes it with validations and calculations, stores data in the database, and invokes any operations from other systems. It then replies with more data to the presentation, perhaps doing more calculation to help organize and format the reply. The fundamental organization is of a single procedure for each action that a user might want to do. Hence, we can think of this pattern as being a script for an action, or business transaction. It doesn't have to be a single inline procedure of code. Pieces get separated into subroutines, and these subroutines can be shared between different *Transaction Scripts (110)*. However, the driving force is still that of a procedure for each action, so a retailing system might have *Transaction Scripts (110)* for checkout, for adding something to the shopping cart, for displaying delivery status, and so on.

A *Transaction Script (110)* offers several advantages:

- It's a simple procedural model that most developers understand.

- It works well with a simple data source layer using *Row Data Gateway (152)* or *Table Data Gateway (144)*.

- It's obvious how to set the transaction boundaries: Start with opening a transaction and end with closing it. It's easy for tools to do this behind the scenes.

Sadly, there are also plenty of disadvantages, which tend to appear as the complexity of the domain logic increases. Often there will be duplicated code as several transactions need to do similar things. Some of this can be dealt with by factoring out common subroutines, but even so much of the duplication is tricky to remove and harder to spot. The resulting application can end up being quite a tangled web of routines without a clear structure.

Of course, complex logic is where objects come in, and the object-oriented way to handle this problem is with a *Domain Model (116)*. With a *Domain Model (116)* we build a model of our domain which, at least on a first approximation, is organized primarily around the nouns in the domain. Thus, a leasing system would have classes for lease, asset, and so forth. The logic for handling validations and calculations would be placed into this domain model, so shipment object might contain the logic to calculate the shipping charge for a delivery. There might still be routines for calculating a bill, but such a procedure would quickly delegate to a *Domain Model (116)* method.

Using a *Domain Model (116)* as opposed to a *Transaction Script (110)* is the essence of the paradigm shift that object-oriented people talk about so much. Rather than one routine having all the logic for a user action, each object takes a part of the logic that's relevant to it. If you're not used to a *Domain Model (116)*, learning to work with one can be very frustrating as you rush from object to object trying to find where the behavior is.

It's hard to capture the essence of the difference between the two patterns with a simple example, but in the discussions of the patterns I've tried to do that by building a simple piece of domain logic both ways. The easiest way to see the difference is to look at sequence diagrams for the two approaches (Figures 2.1 and 2.2). The essential problem is that different kinds of product have different algorithms for recognizing revenue on a given contract (see Chapter 9, page 109, for more background). The calculation method has to determine what kind of product a given contract is for, apply the correct algorithm, and

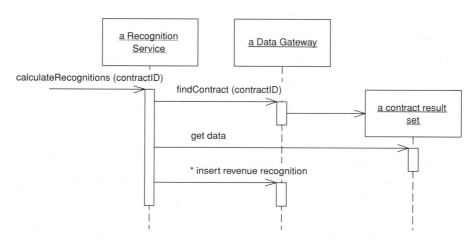

Figure 2.1 *A Transaction Script's (110) way of calculating revenue recognitions.*

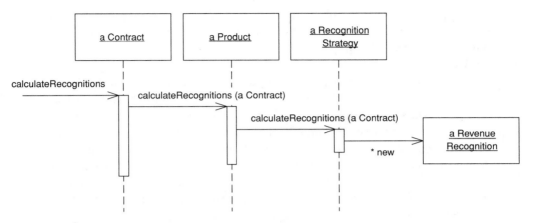

Figure 2.2 *A* Domain Model's *(116)* way of calculating revenue recognitions.

then create revenue recognition objects to capture the results of the calculation. (For simplicity I'm ignoring the database interaction issues.)

In Figure 2.1, *Transaction Script's (110)* method does all the work. The underlying objects are just *Table Data Gateways (144)*, and all they do is pass data to the transaction script.

In contrast, Figure 2.2 shows multiple objects, each forwarding part of the behavior to another until a strategy object creates the results.

The value of a *Domain Model (116)* lies in the fact that once you've gotten used to things, there are many techniques that allow you to handle increasingly complex logic in a well-organized way. As we get more and more algorithms for calculating revenue recognition, we can add these by adding new recognition strategy objects. With *Transaction Script (110)* we're adding more conditions to the conditional logic of the script. Once your mind is as warped to objects as mine is, you'll find you prefer a *Domain Model (116)* even in fairly simple cases.

The costs of a *Domain Model (116)* come from the complexity of using it and the complexity of your data source layer. It takes time for people new to rich object models to get used to a rich *Domain Model (116)*. Often developers may need to spend several months working on a project that uses this pattern before their paradigms are shifted. However, when you're used to *Domain Model (116)* you're usually infected for life and it becomes easy to work with in the future—that's how object bigots like me are made. However, a significant minority of developers seem to be unable to make the shift.

Even once you've made the shift, you still have to deal with the database mapping. The richer your *Domain Model (116)*, the more complex your mapping to a relational database (usually with *Data Mapper (165)*). A sophisticated data source layer is much like a fixed cost—it takes a fair amount of money (if you buy) or time (if you build) to get a good one, but once you have it you can do a lot with it.

There's a third choice for structuring domain logic, *Table Module (125)*. At very first blush the *Table Module (125)* looks like a *Domain Model (116)* since both have classes for contracts, products, and revenue recognitions. The vital difference is that a *Domain Model (116)* has one instance of contract for each contract in the database whereas a *Table Module (125)* has only one instance. A *Table Module (125)* is designed to work with a *Record Set (508)*. Thus, the client of a contract *Table Module (125)* will first issue queries to the database to form a *Record Set (508)* and will create a contract object and pass it the *Record Set (508)* as an argument. The client can then invoke operations on the contract to do various things (Figure 2.3). If it wants to do something to an individual contract, it must pass in an ID.

A *Table Module (125)* is in many ways a middle ground between a *Transaction Script (110)* and a *Domain Model (116)*. Organizing the domain logic around tables rather than straight procedures provides more structure and makes it easier to find and remove duplication. However, you can't use a number of the techniques that a *Domain Model (116)* uses for finer grained structure of the logic, such as inheritance, strategies, and other OO patterns.

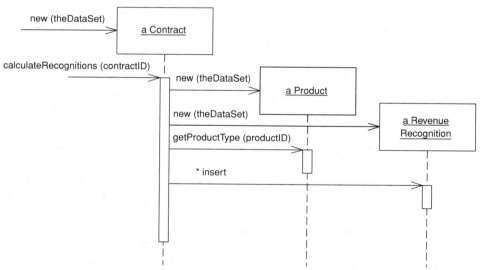

Figure 2.3 *Calculating revenue recognitions with a* Table Module (125).

The biggest advantage of a *Table Module (125)* is how it fits into the rest of the architecture. Many GUI environments are built to work on the results of a SQL query organized in a *Record Set (508)*. Since a *Table Module (125)* also works on a *Record Set (508)*, you can easily run a query, manipulate the results in the *Table Module (125)*, and pass the manipulated data to the GUI for display. You can also use the *Table Module (125)* on the way back for further validations and calculations. A number of platforms, particularly Microsoft's COM and .NET, use this style of development.

Making a Choice

So, how do you choose between the three patterns? It's not an easy choice, and it very much depends on how complex your domain logic is. Figure 2.4 is one of those nonscientific graphs that really irritate me in PowerPoint presentations because they have utterly unquantified axes. However, it helps to visualize my sense of how the three compare. With simple domain logic the *Domain Model (116)* is less attractive because the cost of understanding it and the complexity of

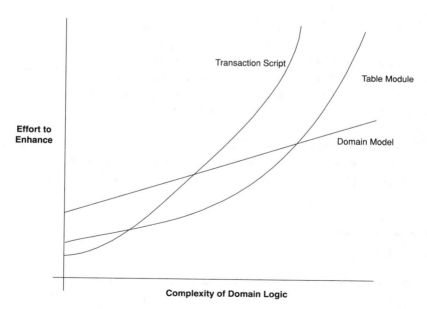

Figure 2.4 *A sense of the relationships between complexity and effort for different domain logic styles.*

the data source add a lot of effort to developing it that won't be paid back. Nevertheless, as the complexity of the domain logic increases, the other approaches tend to hit a wall where adding more features becomes exponentially more difficult.

Your problem, of course, is to figure out where on that *x* axis your application lies. The good news is that I can say that you should use a *Domain Model (116)* whenever the complexity of your domain logic is greater than 7.42. The bad news is that nobody knows how to measure the complexity of domain logic. In practice, then, all you can do is find some experienced people who can do an initial analysis of the requirements and make a judgment call.

There are some factors that alter the curves a bit. A team that's familiar with *Domain Model (116)* will lower the initial cost of using this pattern. It won't lower it to same starting point as the others because of the data source complexity. Still, the better the team is, the more I'm inclined to use a *Domain Model (116)*.

The attractiveness of a *Table Module (125)* depends very much on the support for a common *Record Set (508)* structure in your environment. If you have an environment like .NET or Visual Studio, where lots of tools work around a *Record Set (508)*, then that makes a *Table Module (125)* much more attractive. Indeed, I don't see a reason to use *Transaction Scripts (110)* in a .NET environment. However, if there's no special tooling for *Record Sets (508)*, I wouldn't bother with *Table Module (125)*.

Once you've made it, your decision isn't completely cast in stone, but it is more tricky to change. So it's worth some upfront thought to decide which way to go. If you find you went the wrong way, then, if you started with *Transaction Script (110)*, don't hesitate to refactor toward *Domain Model (116)*. If you started with *Domain Model (116)*, however, going to *Transaction Script (110)* is usually less worthwhile unless you can simplify your data source layer.

These three patterns are not mutually exclusive choices. Indeed, it's quite common to use *Transaction Script (110)* for some of the domain logic and *Table Module (125)* or *Domain Model (116)* for the rest.

Service Layer

A common approach in handling domain logic is to split the domain layer in two. A *Service Layer (133)* is placed over an underlying *Domain Model (116)* or *Table Module (125)*. Usually you only get this with a *Domain Model (116)* or *Table Module (125)* since a domain layer that uses only *Transaction Script*

(110) isn't complex enough to warrant a separate layer. The presentation logic interacts with the domain purely through the *Service Layer (133)*, which acts as an API for the application.

As well as providing a clear API, the *Service Layer (133)* is also a good spot to place such things as transaction control and security. This gives you a simple model of taking each method in the *Service Layer (133)* and describing its transactional and security characteristics. A separate properties file is a common choice for this, but .NET's attributes provide a nice way of doing it directly in the code.

When you see a *Service Layer (133)*, a key decision is how much behavior to put in it. The minimal case is to make the *Service Layer (133)* a facade so that all of the real behavior is in underlying objects and all the *Service Layer (133)* does is forward calls on the facade to lower-level objects. In that case the *Service Layer (133)* provides an API that's easier to use because it's typically oriented around use cases. It also makes a convenient point for adding transactional wrappers and security checks.

At the other extreme, most business logic is placed in *Transaction Scripts (110)* inside the *Service Layer (133)*. The underlying domain objects are very simple; if it's a *Domain Model (116)* it will be one-to-one with the database and you can thus use a simpler data source layer such as *Active Record (160)*.

Midway between these alternatives is a more even mix of behavior: the **controller-entity** style. This name comes from a common practice influenced heavily by [Jacobson et al.]. The point here is to have logic that's particular to a single transaction or use case placed in *Transaction Scripts (110)*, which are commonly referred to as controllers or services. These are different controllers to the input controller in *Model View Controller (330)* or *Application Controller (379)* that we'll meet later, so I use the term **use-case controller**. Behavior that's used in more than one use case goes on the domain objects, which are called entities.

Although the controller-entity approach is a common one, it's not one that I've ever liked much. The use case controllers, like any *Transaction Script (110)*, tend to encourage duplicate code. My view is that, if you decide to use a *Domain Model (116)* at all, you really should go whole hog and make it dominant. The one exception to this is if you've started with a design that uses *Transaction Script (110)* with *Row Data Gateway (152)*. Then it makes sense to move duplicated behavior to the *Row Data Gateways (152)*, which will turn them into a simple *Domain Model (116)* using *Active Record (160)*. However, I wouldn't start that way. I would only do that to improve a design that's showing cracks.

I'm saying not that you should never have service objects that contain business logic, but that you shouldn't necessarily make a fixed layer of them.

Procedural service objects can sometimes be a very useful way to factor logic, but I tend to use them as needed rather than as an architectural layer.

My preference is thus to have the thinnest *Service Layer (133)* you can, if you even need one. My usual approach is to assume that I don't need one and only add it if it seems that the application needs it. However, I know many good designers who always use a *Service Layer (133)* with a fair bit of logic, so feel free to ignore me on this one. Randy Stafford has had a lot of success with a rich *Service Layer (133)*, which is why I asked him to write the *Service Layer (133)* pattern for this book.

Chapter 3

Mapping to Relational Databases

The role of the data source layer is to communicate with the various pieces of infrastructure that an application needs to do its job. A dominant part of this problem is talking to a database, which, for the majority of systems built today, means a relational database. Certainly there's still a lot of data in older data storage formats, such as mainframe ISAM and VSAM files, but most people building systems today worry about working with a relational database.

One the biggest reasons for the success of relational databases is the presence of SQL, a mostly standard language for database communication. Although SQL is full of annoying and complicated vendor-specific enhancements, its core syntax is common and well understood.

Architectural Patterns

The first set of patterns comprises the architectural patterns, which drive the way in which the domain logic talks to the database. The choice you make here is far-reaching for your design and thus difficult to refactor, so it's one that you should pay some attention to. It's also a choice that's strongly affected by how you design your domain logic.

Despite SQL's widespread use in enterprise software, there are still pitfalls in using it. Many application developers don't understand SQL well and, as a result, have problems defining effective queries and commands. Although various techniques exist for embedding SQL in a programming language, they're all somewhat awkward. It would be better to access data using mechanisms that fit in with the application development langauge. Database administrations (DBAs) also like to get at the SQL that accesses a table so that they can understand how best to tune it and how to arrange indexes.

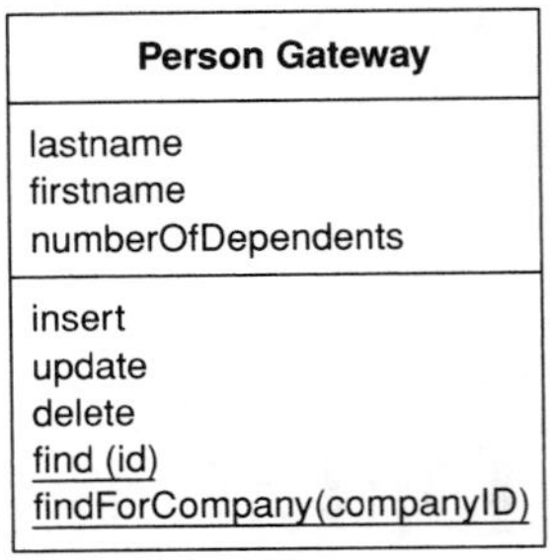

Person Gateway
lastname
firstname
numberOfDependents
insert
update
delete
find (id)
findForCompany(companyID)

Figure 3.1 *A* Row Data Gateway (152) *has one instance per row returned by a query.*

For these reasons, it's wise to separate SQL access from the domain logic and place it in separate classes. A good way of organizing these classes is to base them on the table structure of the database so that you have one class per database table. These classes then form a *Gateway (466)* to the table. The rest of the application needs to know nothing about SQL, and all the SQL that accesses the database is easy to find. Developers who specialize in the database have a clear place to go.

There are two main ways in which you can use a *Gateway (466)*. The most obvious is to have an instance of it for each row that's returned by a query (Figure 3.1). This *Row Data Gateway (152)* is an approach that naturally fits an object-oriented way of thinking about the data.

Many environments provide a *Record Set (508)*—that is, a generic data structure of tables and rows that mimics the tabular nature of a database. Because a *Record Set (508)* is a generic data structure, environments can use it in many parts of an application. It's quite common for GUI tools to have controls that work with a *Record Set (508)*. If you use a *Record Set (508)*, you only need a single class for each table in the database. This *Table Data Gateway (144)* (see Figure 3.2) provides methods to query the database that return a *Record Set (508)*.

Person Gateway
find (id) : RecordSet
findWithLastName(String) : RecordSet
update (id, lastname, firstname, numberOfDependents)
insert (lastname, firstname, numberOfDependents)
delete (id)

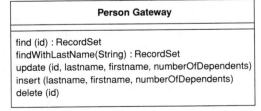

Figure 3.2 *A* Table Data Gateway (144) *has one instance per table.*

Even for simple applications I tend to use one of the gateway patterns. A glance at my Ruby and Python scripts will confirm this. I find the clear separation of SQL and domain logic to be very helpful.

The fact that *Table Data Gateway (144)* fits very nicely with *Record Set (508)* makes it the obvious choice if you are using *Table Module (125)*. It's also a pattern you can use to think about organizing stored procedures. Many designers like to do all of their database access through stored procedures rather than through explicit SQL. In this case you can think of the collection of stored procedures as defining a *Table Data Gateway (144)* for a table. I would still have an in-memory *Table Data Gateway (144)* to wrap the calls to the stored procedures, since that keeps the mechanics of the stored procedure call encapsulated.

If you're using *Domain Model (116)*, some further options come into play. Certainly you can use a *Row Data Gateway (152)* or a *Table Data Gateway (144)* with a *Domain Model (116)*. For my taste, however, that can be either too much indirection or not enough.

In simple applications the *Domain Model (116)* is an uncomplicated structure that actually corresponds pretty closely to the database structure, with one domain class per database table. Such domain objects often have only moderately complex business logic. In this case it makes sense to have each domain object be responsible for loading and saving from the database, which is *Active Record (160)* (see Figure 3.3). Another way to think of the *Active Record (160)* is that you start with a *Row Data Gateway (152)* and then add domain logic to the class, particularly when you see repetitive code in multiple *Transaction Scripts (110)*.

In this kind of situation the added indirection of a *Gateway (466)* doesn't provide a great deal of value. As the domain logic gets more complicated and you begin moving toward a rich *Domain Model (116)*, the simple approach of an *Active Record (160)* starts to break down. The one-to-one match of domain

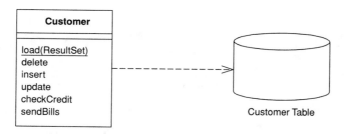

Figure 3.3 *In the* Active Record (160) *a customer domain object knows how to interact with database tables.*

classes to tables starts to fail as you factor domain logic into smaller classes. Relational databases don't handle inheritance, so it becomes difficult to use strategies [Gang of Four] and other neat OO patterns. As the domain logic gets feisty, you want to be able to test it without having to talk to the database all the time.

All of these forces push you to in'direction as your *Domain Model (116)* gets richer. In this case the *Gateway (466)* can solve some problems, but it still leaves you with the *Domain Model (116)* coupled to the schema of the database. As a result there's some transformation from the fields of the *Gateway (466)* to the fields of the domain objects, and this transformation complicates your domain objects.

A better route is to isolate the *Domain Model (116)* from the database completely, by making your indirection layer entirely responsible for the mapping between domain objects and database tables. This *Data Mapper (165)* (see Figure 3.4) handles all of the loading and storing between the database and the *Domain Model (116)* and allows both to vary independently. It's the most complicated of the database mapping architectures, but its benefit is complete isolation of the two layers.

I don't recommend using a *Gateway (466)* as the primary persistence mechanism for a *Domain Model (116)*. If the domain logic is simple and you have a close correspondence between classes and tables, *Active Record (160)* is the simple way to go. If you have something more complicated, *Data Mapper (165)* is what you need.

These patterns aren't entirely mutually exclusive. In much of this discussion we're thinking of the primary persistence mechanism, by which we mean how you save the data in some kind of in-memory model to the database. For that you'll pick one of these patterns; you don't want to mix them because that ends up getting very messy. Even if you're using *Data Mapper (165)* as your primary persistence mechanism, however, you may use a data *Gateway (466)* to wrap tables or services that are being treated as external interfaces.

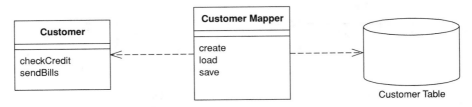

Figure 3.4 *A Data Mapper (165) insulates the domain objects and the database from each other.*

In my discussion of these ideas, both here and in the patterns themselves, I tend to use the word "table." However, most of these techniques can apply equally well to views, queries encapsulated through stored procedures, and commonly used dynamic queries. Sadly, there isn't a widely used term for table/view/query/stored procedure, so I use "table" because it represents a tabular data structure. I usually think of views as virtual tables, which is of course how SQL thinks of them too. The same syntax is used for querying views as for querying tables.

Updating obviously is more complicated with views and queries, as you can't always update a view directly but instead have to manipulate the tables that underlie it. In this case encapsulating the view/query with an appropriate pattern is a very good way to implement that update logic in one place, which makes using the views both simpler and more reliable.

One of the problems with using views and queries in this way is that it can lead to inconsistencies that may surprise developers who don't understand how a view is formed. They may perform updates on two different structures, both of which update the same underlying tables where the second update overwrites an update made by the first. Providing that the update logic does proper validation, you shouldn't get inconsistent data this way, but you may surprise your developers.

I should also mention the simplest way of persisting even the most complex *Domain Model (116)*. During the early days of objects many people realized that there was a fundamental "impedance mismatch" between objects and relations. Thus, there followed a spate of effort on object-oriented databases, which essentially brought the OO paradigm to disk storage. With an OO database you don't have to worry about mapping. You work with a large structure of interconnected objects, and the database figures out when to move objects on or off disks. Also, you can use transactions to group together updates and permit sharing of the data store. To programmers this seems like an infinite amount of transactional memory that's transparently backed by disk storage.

The chief advantage of OO databases is that they improve productivity. Although I'm not aware of any controlled tests, anecdotal observations put the effort of mapping to a relational database at around a third of programming effort—a cost that continues during maintenance.

Most projects don't use OO databases, however. The primary reason against them is risk. Relational databases are a well-understood and proven technology backed by big vendors who have been around a long time. SQL provides a relatively standard interface for all sorts of tools. (If you're concerned about performance, all I can say is that I haven't seen any conclusive data comparing the performance of OO against that of relational systems.)

Even if you can't use an OO database, you should seriously consider buying an O/R mapping tool if you have a *Domain Model (116)*. While the patterns in this book will tell you a lot about how to build a *Data Mapper (165)*, it's still a complicated endeavor. Tool vendors have spent many years working on this problem, and commercial O/R mapping tools are much more sophisticated than anything that can reasonably be done by hand. While the tools aren't cheap, you have to compare their price with the considerable cost of writing and maintaining such a layer yourself.

There are moves to provide an OO-database-style layer that can work with relational databases. JDO is such a beast in the Java world, but it's still too early to tell how they'll work out. I haven't had enough experience with them to draw any conclusions for this book.

Even if you do buy a tool, however, it's a good idea to be aware of these patterns. Good O/R tools give you a lot of options in mapping to a database, and these patterns will help you understand when to use the different choices. Don't assume that a tool makes all the effort go away. It makes a big dent, but you'll still find that using and tuning an O/R tool takes a small but significant chunk of work.

The Behavioral Problem

When people talk about O/R mapping, they usually focus on the structural aspects—how you relate tables to objects. However, I've found that the hardest part of the exercise is its architectural and behavioral aspects. I've already talked about the main architectural approaches; the next thing to think about is the behavioral problem.

That behavioral problem is how to get the various objects to load and save themselves to the database. At first sight this doesn't seem to be much of a problem. A customer object can have load and save methods that do this task. Indeed, with *Active Record (160)* this is an obvious route to take.

If you load a bunch of objects into memory and modify them, you have to keep track of which ones you've modified and make sure to write all of them back out to the database. If you only load a couple of records, this is easy. As you load more and more objects it gets to be more of an exercise, particularly when you create some rows and modify others since you'll need the keys from the created rows before you can modify the rows that refer to them. This is a slightly tricky problem to solve.

As you read objects and modify them, you have to ensure that the database state you're working with stays consistent. If you read some objects, it's important to ensure that the reading is isolated so that no other process changes any of the objects you've read while you're working on them. Otherwise, you could have inconsistent and invalid data in your objects. This is the issue of concurrency, which is a very tricky problem to solve; we'll talk about this in Chapter 5.

A pattern that's essential to solving both of these problems is *Unit of Work (184)*. A *Unit of Work (184)* keeps track of all objects read from the database, together with all objects modified in any way. It also handles how updates are made to the database. Instead of the application programmer invoking explicit save methods, the programmer tells the unit of work to commit. That unit of work then sequences all of the appropriate behavior to the database, putting all of the complex commit processing in one place. *Unit of Work (184)* is an essential pattern whenever the behavioral interactions with the database become awkward.

A good way of thinking about *Unit of Work (184)* is as an object that acts as the controller of the database mapping. Without a *Unit of Work (184)*, typically the domain layer acts as the controller; deciding when to read and write to the database. The *Unit of Work (184)* results from factoring the database mapping controller behavior into its own object.

As you load objects, you have to be wary about loading the same one twice. If you do that, you'll have two in-memory objects that correspond to a single database row. Update them both, and everything gets very confusing. To deal with this you need to keep a record of every row you read in an *Identity Map (195)*. Each time you read in some data, you check the *Identity Map (195)* first to make sure that you don't already have it. If the data is already loaded, you can return a second reference to it. That way any updates will be properly coordinated. As a benefit you may also be able to avoid a database call since the *Identity Map (195)* also doubles as a cache for the database. Don't forget, however, that the primary purpose of an *Identity Map (195)* is to maintain correct identities, not to boost performance.

If you're using a *Domain Model (116)*, you'll usually arrange things so that linked objects are loaded together in such a way that a read for an order object loads its associated customer object. However, with many objects connected together any read of any object can pull an enormous object graph out of the database. To avoid such inefficiencies you need to reduce what you bring back yet still keep the door open to pull back more data if you need it later on. *Lazy Load (200)* relies on having a placeholder for a reference to an object. There are several variations on the theme, but all of them have the object reference modified so that, instead of pointing to the real object, it marks a placeholder. Only if you try to follow the link does the real object get pulled in from the database. Using *Lazy Load (200)* at suitable points, you can bring back just enough from the database with each call.

Reading in Data

When reading in data I like to think of the methods as **finders** that wrap SQL select statements with a method-structured interface. Thus, you might have methods such as find(id) or findForCustomer(customer). Clearly these methods can get pretty unwieldy if you have 23 different clauses in your select statements, but these are, thankfully, rare.

Where you put the finder methods depends on the interfacing pattern used. If your database interaction classes are table based—that is, you have one instance of the class per table in the database—then you can combine the finder methods with the inserts and updates. If your interaction classes are row based—that is, you have one interaction class per row in the database—this doesn't work.

With row-based classes you can make the find operations static, but doing so will stop you from making the database operations substitutable. This means that you can't swap out the database for testing purposes with *Service Stub (504)*. To avoid this problem the best approach is to have separate finder objects. Each finder class has many methods that encapsulate a SQL query. When you execute the query, the finder object returns a collection of the appropriate row-based objects.

One thing to watch for with finder methods is that they work on the database state, not the object state. If you issue a query against the database to find all people within a club, remember that any person objects you've added to the club in memory won't get picked up by the query. As a result it's usually wise to do queries at the beginning.

When reading in data, performance issues can often loom large. This leads to a few rules of thumb.

Try to pull back multiple rows at once. In particular, never do repeated queries on the same table to get multiple rows. It's almost always better to pull back too much data than too little (although you have to be wary of locking too many rows with pessimistic concurrency control). Therefore, consider a situation where you need to get 50 people that you can identify by a primary key in your domain model, but you can only construct a query such that you get 200 people, from which you'll do some further logic to isolate the 50 you need. It's usually better to use one query that brings back unnecessary rows than to issue 50 individual queries.

Another way to avoid going to the database more than once is to use joins so that you can pull multiple tables back with a single query. The resulting record set looks odd but can really speed things up. In this case you may have a *Gate-*

way (466) that has data from multiple joined tables, or a *Data Mapper (165)* that loads several domain objects with a single call.

However, if you're using joins, bear in mind that databases are optimized to handle up to three or four joins per query. Beyond that, performance suffers, although you can restore a good bit of this with cached views.

Many optimizations are possible in the database. These things involve clustering commonly referenced data together, careful use of indexes, and the database's ability to cache in memory. These are outside the scope of this book but inside the scope of a good DBA.

In all cases you should profile your application with your specific database and data. General rules can guide your thinking, but your particular circumstances will always have their own variations. Database systems and application servers often have sophisticated caching schemes, and there's no way I can predict what will happen for your application. For every rule of thumb I've used, I've heard of surprising exceptions, so set aside time to do performance profiling and tuning.

Structural Mapping Patterns

When people talk about object-relational mapping, mostly what they mean is these kinds of structural mapping patterns, which you use when mapping between in-memory objects and database tables. These patterns aren't usually relevant for *Table Data Gateway (144)*, but you may use a few of them if you use *Row Data Gateway (152)* or *Active Record (160)*. You'll probably need to use all of them for *Data Mapper (165)*.

Mapping Relationships

The central issue here is the different way in which objects and relations handle links, which leads to two problems. First there's a difference in representation. Objects handle links by storing references that are held by the runtime of either memory-managed environments or memory addresses. Relational databases handle links by forming a key into another table. Second, objects can easily use collections to handle multiple references from a single field, while normalization forces all relation links to be single valued. This leads to reversals of the data structure between objects and tables. An order object naturally has a collection of line item objects that don't need any reference back to the order. However, the table structure is the other way around—the line item must include a foreign key reference to the order since the order can't have a multi-valued field.

The way to handle the representation problem is to keep the relational identity of each object as an *Identity Field (216)* in the object, and to look up these values to map back and forth between the object references and the relational keys. It's a tedious process but not that difficult once you understand the basic technique. When you read objects from the disk you use an *Identity Map (195)* as a lookup table from relational keys to objects. Each time you come across a foreign key in the table, you use *Foreign Key Mapping (236)* (see Figure 3.5) to wire up the appropriate inter-object reference. If you don't have the key in the *Identity Map (195)*, you need to either go to the database to get it or use a *Lazy Load (200)*. Each time you save an object, you save it into the row with the right key. Any inter-object reference is replaced with the target object's ID field.

On this foundation the collection handling requires a more complex version of *Foreign Key Mapping (236)* (see Figure 3.6). If an object has a collection, you need to issue another query to find all the rows that link to the ID of the source object (or you can now avoid the query with *Lazy Load (200)*). Each object that comes back gets created and added to the collection. Saving the collection involves saving each object in it and making sure it has a foreign key to the source object. This gets messy, especially when you have to detect objects added or removed from the collection. This can get repetitive when you get the hang of it, which is why some form of metadata-based approach becomes an obvious move for larger systems (I'll elaborate on that later). If the collection

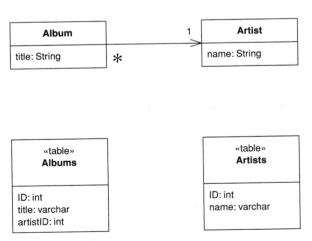

Figure 3.5 *Use a* Foreign Key Mapping (236) *to map a single-valued field.*

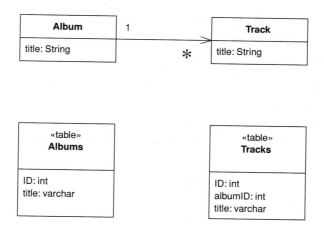

Figure 3.6 *Use a* Foreign Key Mapping (236) *to map a collection field.*

objects aren't used outside the scope of the collection's owner, you can use *Dependent Mapping (262)* to simplify the mapping.

A different case comes up with a many-to-many relationship, which has a collection on both ends. An example is a person having many skills and each skill knowing the people who use it. Relational databases can't handle this directly, so you use an *Association Table Mapping (248)* (see Figure 3.7) to create a new relational table just to handle the many-to-many association.

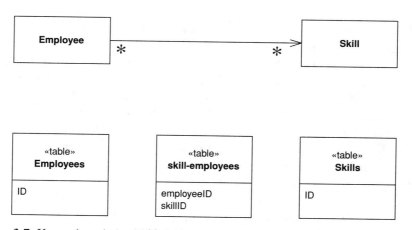

Figure 3.7 *Use an* Association Table Mapping (248) *to map a many-to-many association.*

When you're working with collections, a common gotcha is to rely on the ordering within the collection. In OO languages it's common to use ordered collections such as lists and arrays—indeed, it often makes testing easier. Nevertheless, it's very difficult to maintain an arbitrarily ordered collection when saved to a relational database. For this reason it's worth considering using unordered sets for storing collections. Another option is to decide on a sort order whenever you do a collection query, although that can be quite expensive.

In some cases referential integrity can make updates more complex. Modern systems allow you to defer referential integrity checking to the end of the transaction. If you have this capability, there's no reason not to use it. Otherwise, the database will check on every write. In this case you have to be careful to do your updates in the right order. How to do this is out of the scope of this book, but one technique is to do a topological sort of your updates. Another is to hardcode which tables get written in which order. This can sometimes reduce deadlock problems inside the database that cause transactions to roll back too often.

Identity Field (216) is used for inter-object references that turn into foreign keys, but not all object relationships need to be persisted that way. Small *Value Objects (486)*, such as date ranges and money objects clearly shouldn't be represented as their own table in the database. Instead, take all the fields of the *Value Object (486)* and embed them into the linked object as a *Embedded Value (268)*. Since *Value Objects (486)* have value semantics, you can happily create them each time you get a read and you don't need to bother with an *Identity Map (195)*. Writing them out is also easy—just dereference the object and spit out its fields into the owning table.

You can do this kind of thing on a larger scale by taking a whole cluster of objects and saving them as a single column in a table as a *Serialized LOB (272)*. LOB stands for "Large OBject," which can be either binary (BLOB) textual (CLOB—Character Large OBject). Serializing a clump of objects as an XML document is an obvious route to take for a hierarchic object structure. This way you can grab a whole bunch of small linked objects in a single read. Often databases perform poorly with small highly interconnected objects—where you spend a lot of time making many small database calls. Hierarchic structures such as org charts and bills of materials are where a *Serialized LOB (272)* can save a lot of database roundtrips.

The downside is that SQL isn't aware of what's happening, so you can't make portable queries against the data structure. Again, XML may come to the rescue here, allowing you to embed XPath query expressions within SQL calls, although the embedding is largely nonstandard at the moment. As a result *Serialized LOB (272)* is best used when you don't want to query for the parts of the stored structure.

Usually a *Serialized LOB (272)* is best for a relatively isolated group of objects that make part of an application. If you use it too much, it ends up turning your database into little more than a transactional file system.

Inheritance

In the above hierarchies I'm talking about compositional hierarchies, such as a parts tree, which relational system traditionally do poorly. There's another kind of hierarchy that causes relational headaches: a class hierarchy linked by inheritance. Since there's no standard way to do inheritance in SQL, we again have a mapping to perform. For any inheritance structure there are basically three options. You can have a one table for all the classes in the hierarchy: *Single Table Inheritance (278)* (see Figure 3.8); one table for each concrete class: *Concrete Table Inheritance (293)* (see Figure 3.9); or one table per class in the hierarchy; *Class Table Inheritance (285)* (see Figure 3.10).

The trade-offs are all between duplication of data structure and speed of access. *Class Table Inheritance (285)* is the simplest relationship between the classes and the tables, but it needs multiple joins to load a single object, which usually reduces performance. *Concrete Table Inheritance (293)* avoids the joins, allowing you pull a single object from one table, but it's brittle to changes. With any change to a superclass you have to remember to alter all the tables (and the

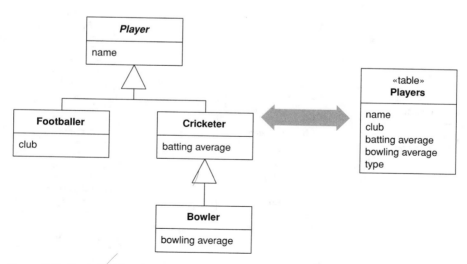

Figure 3.8 Single Table Inheritance (278) *uses one table to store all the classes in a hierarchy.*

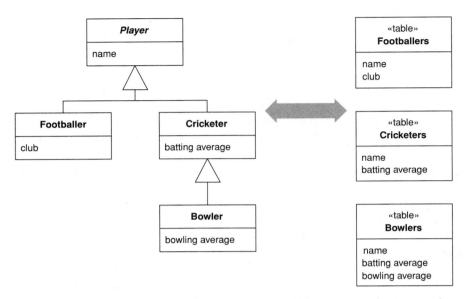

Figure 3.9 Concrete Table Inheritance (293) *uses one table to store each concrete class in a hierarchy.*

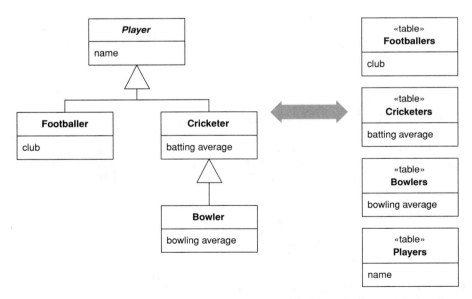

Figure 3.10 Class Table Inheritance (285) *uses one table for each class in a hierarchy.*

mapping code). Altering the hierarchy itself can cause even bigger changes. Also, the lack of a superclass table can make key management awkward and get in the way of referential integrity, although it does reduce lock contention on the super-class table. In some databases *Single Table Inheritance (278)*'s biggest downside is wasted space, since each row has to have columns for all possible subtypes and this leads to empty columns. However, many databases do a very good job of compressing wasted table space. Another problem with *Single Table Inheritance (278)* is its size, making it a bottleneck for accesses. Its great advantage is that it puts all the stuff in one place, which makes modification easier and avoids joins.

The three options aren't mutually exclusive, and in one hierarchy you can mix patterns. For instance, you could have several classes pulled together with *Single Table Inheritance (278)* and use *Class Table Inheritance (285)* for a few unusual cases. Of course, mixing patterns adds complexity.

There's no clearcut winner here. You need to take into account your own cir-cumstances and preferences, much as with all the rest of these patterns. My first choice tends to be *Single Table Inheritance (278)*, as it's easy to do and is resil-ient to many refactorings. I tend to use the other two as needed to help solve the inevitable issues with irrelevant and wasted columns. Often the best is to talk to the DBAs; they often have good advice as to the sort of access that makes the most sense for the database.

All the examples just described, and in the patterns, use single inheritance. Although multiple inheritance is becoming less fashionable these days and most languages are increasingly avoiding it, the issue still appears in O/R mapping when you use interfaces, as in Java and .NET. The patterns here don't go into this topic specifically, but essentially you cope with multiple inheritance using varia-tions of the trio of inheritance patterns. *Single Table Inheritance (278)* puts all superclasses and interfaces into the one big table, *Class Table Inheritance (285)* makes a separate table for each interface and superclass, and *Concrete Table Inheritance (293)* includes all interfaces and superclasses in each concrete table.

Building the Mapping

When you map to a relational database, there are essentially three situations that you encounter:

- You choose the schema yourself.

- You have to map to an existing schema, which can't be changed.

- You have to map to an existing schema, but changes to it are negotiable.

The simplest case is where you're doing the schema yourself and have little to moderate complexity in your domain logic, resulting in a *Transaction Script (110)* or *Table Module (125)* design. In this case you can design the tables around the data using classic database design techniques. Use a *Row Data Gateway (152)* or *Table Data Gateway (144)* to pull the SQL away from the domain logic.

If you're using a *Domain Model (116)*, you should beware of a design that looks like a database design. In this case build your *Domain Model (116)* without regard to the database so that you can best simplify the domain logic. Treat the database design as a way of persisting the objects' data. *Data Mapper (165)* gives you the most flexibility here, but it's more complex. If a database design isomorphic to the *Domain Model (116)* makes sense, you might consider an *Active Record (160)* instead.

Although building the model first is a reasonable way of thinking about it, this advice only applies within short iterative cycles. Spending six months building a database-free *Domain Model (116)* and then deciding to persist it once you're done is highly risky. The danger is that the resulting design will have crippling performance problems that take too much refactoring to fix. Instead, build up the database with each iteration, of no more than six weeks in length and preferably fewer. That way you'll get rapid and continuous feedback about how your database interactions work in practice. Within any particular task you should think about the *Domain Model (116)* first, but integrate each piece of *Domain Model (116)* in the database as you go.

When the schema's already there, your choices are similar but the process is slightly different. With simple domain logic you build *Row Data Gateway (152)* or *Table Data Gateway (144)* classes that mimic the database, and layer domain logic on top of that. With more complex domain logic you'll need a *Domain Model (116)*, which is highly unlikely to match the database design. Therefore, gradually build up the *Domain Model (116)* and include *Data Mappers (165)* to persist the data to the existing database.

Double Mapping

Occasionally I run into situations where the same kind of data needs to be pulled from more than one source. There may be multiple databases that hold the same data but have small differences in the schema because of some copy and paste reuse. (In this situation the amount of annoyance is inversely proportional to the amount of the difference.) Another possibility is using different mechanisms, storing the data sometimes in a database and sometimes in messages. You may want to pull similar data from both XML messages, CICS transactions, and relational tables.

The simplest option is to have multiple mapping layers, one for each data source. However, if data is very similar this can lead to a lot of duplication. In this situation you might consider a two-step mapping scheme. The first step converts data from the in-memory schema to a logical data store schema. The logical data store schema is designed to maximize the similarities in the data source formats. The second step maps from the logical data store schema to the actual physical data store schema. This second step contains the differences.

The extra step only pays for itself when you have many commonalities, so you should use it when you have similar but annoyingly different physical data stores. Treat the mapping from the logical data store to the physical data store as a *Gateway (466)* and use any of the mapping techniques to map from the application logic to the logical data store.

Using Metadata

In this book most of my examples use handwritten code. With simple and repetitive mapping this can lead to code that's simple and repetitive—and repetitive code is a sign of something wrong with the design. There's much you can do by factoring out common behaviors with inheritance and delegation—good, honest OO practices—but there's also a more sophisticated approach using *Metadata Mapping (306)*.

Metadata Mapping (306) is based on boiling down the mapping into a metadata file that details how columns in the database map to fields in objects. The point of this is that once you have the metadata you can avoid the repetitive code by using either code generation or reflective programming.

Using metadata buys you a lot of expressiveness from a little metadata. One line of metadata can say something like

```
<field name = customer targetClass = "Customer", dbColumn = "custID", targetTable = "customers"
lowerBound = "1" upperBound = "1" setter = "loadCustomer"/>
```

From that you can define the read and write code, automatically generate ad hoc joins, do all of the SQL, enforce the multiplicity of the relationship, and even do fancy things like computing write orders under the presence of referential integrity. This is why commercial O/R mapping tools tend to use metadata.

When you use *Metadata Mapping (306)* you have the necessary foundation to build queries in terms of in-memory objects. A *Query Object (316)* allows you to build your queries in terms of in-memory objects and data in such a way that developers don't need to know either SQL or the details of the relational schema. The *Query Object (316)* can then use the *Metadata Mapping (306)* to translate expressions based on object fields into the appropriate SQL.

Take this far enough and you can form a *Repository (322)* that largely hides the database from view. Any queries to the database can be made as *Query Objects (316)* against a *Repository (322)*, and developers can't tell whether the objects were retrieved from memory or from the database. *Repository (322)* works well with rich *Domain Model (116)* systems.

Despite the many advantages of metadata, in this book I've focused on hand-written examples because I think they're easier to understand first. Once you get the hang of the patterns and can handwrite them for your application, you'll be able to figure out how to use metadata to make matters easier.

Database Connections

Most database interfaces rely on some kind of database connection object to act as the link between application code and the database. Typically a connection must be opened before you can execute commands against the database. Indeed, usually you need an explicit connection to create and execute a command. The whole time you execute the command this same connection must be open. Queries return a *Record Set (508)*. Some interfaces provide for disconnected *Record Sets (508)*, which can be manipulated after the connection is closed. Other interfaces provide only connected *Record Sets (508)*, implying that the connection must remain open while the *Record Set (508)* is manipulated. If you're running inside a transaction, usually the transaction is bound to a particular connection and the connection must remain open while it is taking place.

In many environments it's expensive to create a connection, which makes it worthwhile to create a connection pool. In this situation developers request a connection from the pool and release it when they're done, instead of creating and closing the connection. Most platforms these days give you pooling, so you'll rarely have to do it yourself. If you do have to do it yourself, first check to see if pooling actually does help performance. Increasingly environments make it quicker to create a new connection so there's no need to pool.

Environments that give you pooling often put it behind an interface that looks like creating a new connection. That way you don't know whether you're getting a brand new connection or one allocated from a pool. That's a good thing, as the choice to pool or not is properly encapsulated. Similarly, closing the connection may not actually close it but just return it to the pool for someone else to use. In this discussion I'll use "open" and "close," which you can substitute for "getting" from the pool and "releasing" back to the pool.

Expensive to create or not, connections need management. Since they're expensive resources to manage, they must be closed as soon as you're done using them. Furthermore, if you're using a transaction, usually you need to ensure that every command inside a particular transaction goes with the same connection.

The most common advice is to get a connection explicitly, using a call to a pool or connection manager, and then supply it to each database command you want to make. Once you're done with the connection, close it. This advice leads to a couple of issues: making sure you have the connection everywhere you need it and ensuring that you don't forget to close it at the end.

To ensure that you have a connection where you need it there are two choices. One is to pass the connection around as an explicit parameter. The problem with this is that the connection gets added to all sorts of method calls where its only purpose is to be passed to some other method five layers down the call stack. Of course, this is the situation to bring out *Registry (480)*. Since you don't want multiple threads using the same connection, you'll want a thread-scoped *Registry (480)*.

If you're half as forgetful as I am, explicit closing isn't such a good idea. It's just too easy to forget to do it when you should. You also can't close the connection with every command because you may be running inside a transaction and the closing will usually cause the transaction to roll back.

Like a connection, memory is a resource that needs to be freed up when you're not using it. Modern environments these days provide automatic memory management and garbage collection, so one way to ensure that connections are closed is to use the garbage collector. In this approach either the connection itself or some object that refers to it closes the connection during garbage collection. The good thing about this is that it uses the same management scheme that's used for memory and so it's both convenient and familiar. The problem is that the close of the connection only happens when the garbage collector actually reclaims the memory, and this can be quite a bit later than when the connection lost its last reference. As a result unreferenced connections may sit around a while before they're closed. Whether this is a problem or not depends very much on your specific environment.

On the whole I don't like relying on garbage collection. Other schemes— even explicit closing—are better. Still, garbage collection makes a good backup in case the regular scheme fails. After all, it's better to have the connections close eventually than to have them hanging around forever.

Since connections are so tied to transactions, a good way to manage them is to tie them to a transaction. Open a connection when you begin a transaction, and close it when you commit or roll back. Have the transaction know what connection it's using so you can ignore the connection completely and just deal with the transaction. Since the transaction's completion has a visible effect, it's easier to remember to commit it and to spot if you forget. A *Unit of Work (184)* makes a natural fit to manage both the transaction and the connection.

If you do things outside of a transaction, such as reading immutable data, you use a fresh connection for each command. Pooling can deal with any issues in creating short-lived connections.

If you're using a disconnected *Record Set (508)*, you can open a connection to put the data in the record set and close it while you manipulate the *Record Set (508)* data. Then, when you're done with the data, you can open a new connection, and transaction, to write the data out. If you do this, you'll need to worry about the data being changed while the *Record Set (508)* was being manipulated. This is a topic I'll talk about with concurrency control.

The specifics of connection management are very much a feature of your database interaction software, so the strategy you use is often dictated by your environment.

Some Miscellaneous Points

You'll notice that some of the code examples use select statements in the form select * from while others use named columns. Using select * can have serious problems in some database drivers, which break if a new column is added or a column is reordered. Although more modern environments don't suffer from this, it's not wise to use select * if you're using positional indices to get information from columns, as a column reorder will break code. It's okay to use column name indices with a select *, and indeed column name indices are clearer to read; however, column name indices may be slower, although that probably won't make much difference given the time for the SQL call. As usual, measure to be sure.

If you do use column number indices, you need to make sure that the accesses to the result set are very close to the definition of the SQL statement so they don't get out of sync if the columns are reordered. Consequently, if you're using *Table Data Gateway (144)*, you should use column name indices as the result set is used by every piece of code that runs a find operation on the gateway. As a result it's usually worth having simple create/read/update/delete test cases for each database mapping structure you use. This will help catch cases when your SQL gets out of sync with your code.

It's always worth making the effort to use static SQL that can be precompiled, rather than dynamic SQL that has to be compiled each time. Most platforms give you a mechanism for precompiling SQL. A good rule of thumb is to avoid using string concatenation to put together SQL queries.

Many environments give you the ability to batch multiple SQL queries into a single database call. I haven't done that for these examples, but it's certainly a tactic you should use in production code. How you do it varies with the platform.

For connections in these examples, I just conjure them up with a call to a "DB" object, which is a *Registry (480)*. How you get a connection will depend on your environment so you'll substitute this with whatever you need to do. I haven't involved transactions in any of the patterns other than those on concurrency. Again, you'll need to mix in whatever your environment needs.

Further Reading

Object-relational mapping is a fact of life for most people, so it's no surprise that there's been a lot written on the subject. The surprise is that there isn't a single coherent, complete, and up-to-date book, which is why I've devoted so much of this one to this tricky yet interesting subject.

The nice thing about database mapping is that there's a lot of ideas out there to steal from. The most victimized intellectual banks are [Brown and Whitenack], [Ambler], [Yoder], and [Keller and Coldewey]. I'd certainly urge you to have a good surf through this material to supplement the patterns in this book.

Chapter 4

Web Presentation

One of the biggest changes to enterprise applications in the last few years has been the rise of Web-browser-based user interfaces. They bring with them a lot of advantages: no client software to install, a common UI approach, and easy universal access. Also, many environments make it easy to build a Web app.

Preparing a Web app begins with the server software itself. Usually this has some form of configuration file that indicates which URLs are to be handled by which programs. Often a single Web server can handle many kinds of programs. These programs may be dynamic and can be added to a server by placing them in an appropriate directory. The Web server's job is to interpret the URL of a request and hand over control to a Web server program. There are two main forms of structuring a program in a Web server: as a script or as a server page.

The script form is a program, usually with functions or methods to handle the HTTP call. Examples include CGI scripts and Java servlets. The program text can do pretty much anything a program can do, and the script can be broken down into subroutines, and can create and use other services. It gets data from the Web page by examining the HTTP request object, which is a string. In some environments it does this by regular expression searching of the request string—Perl's ease of doing this makes it a popular choice for CGI scripts. Other platforms, such as Java servlets, do this parsing for the programmer, which allows the programmer to access the information from the request through a keyword interface. This at least means less regular expressions to mess with. The output of the Web server is another string—the response—which the script can write to using the usual write stream operations in the language.

Writing an HTML response through stream commands is uncomfortable for programmers, and nearly impossible for nonprogrammers, who would otherwise be comfortable preparing HTML pages. This has led to the idea of server pages, where the program is structured around the returning text page. You write the return page in HTML and insert into the HTML scriptlets of code to execute at certain points. Examples of this approach include PHP, ASP, and JSP.

The server page approach works well when there's little processing of the response, such as "Show me the details of album # 1234." Things get a lot more messy when you have to make decisions based on the input, such as different display formats for classical and jazz albums.

Because the script style works best for interpreting the request and the server page style works best for formatting a response, there's the obvious option to use a script for request interpretation and a server page for response formatting. This separation is in fact an old idea that first surfaced in user interfaces with the pattern *Model View Controller (330)*. Combine it with the essential notion that nonpresentation logic should be factored out and we have a very good fit for the concepts of this pattern.

Model View Controller (330) (see Figure 4.1) is a widely referenced pattern but one that's often misunderstood. Indeed, before Web apps appeared on the scene, most presentations of *Model View Controller (330)* I sat through would get it wrong. A main reason for the confusion was the use of the word "controller." Controller is used in a number of different contexts, and I've usually found it used in a different way to that described in *Model View Controller (330)*. As a result I prefer to use the term **input controller** for the controller in *Model View Controller (330)*.

A request comes in to an input controller, which pulls information off the request. It then forwards the business logic to an appropriate model object. The model object talks to the data source and does everything indicated by the request as well as gather information for the response. When it's done it returns control to the input controller, which looks at the results and decides which view is needed to display the response. It then passes control, together with the response data, to the view. The input controller's handoff to the view often isn't always a straight call but often involves forwarding with the data placed in an agreed place on some form of HTTP session object that's shared between the input controller and the view.

The first, and most important, reason for applying *Model View Controller (330)* is to ensure that the models are completely separated from the Web presentation. This makes it easier to modify the presentation as well as easier to add additional presentations later. Putting the processing into separate *Transaction Script (110)* or *Domain Model (116)* objects will make it easier to test them as well. This is particularly important if you're using a server page as your view.

At this point we come to a second use of the word "controller." A lot of user-interface designs separate the presentation objects from the domain objects with an intermediate layer of *Application Controller (379)* objects. The purpose of an *Application Controller (379)* is to handle the flow of an application,

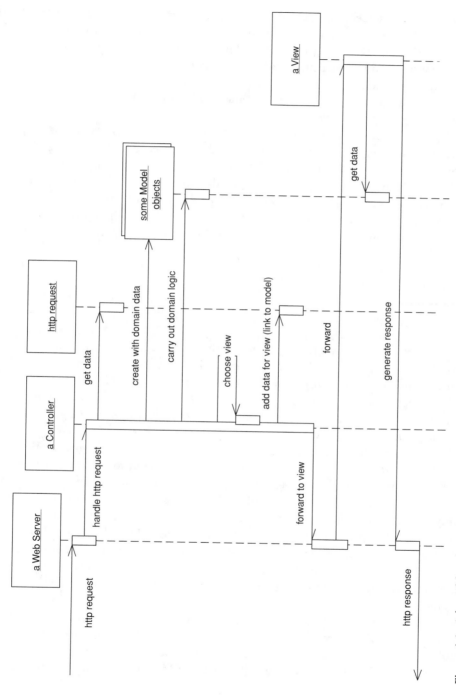

Figure 4.1 *A broad-brush picture of how the model, view, and input controller roles work together in a Web server. The controller handles the request, gets the model to do the domain logic, and then gets the view to create a response based on the model.*

deciding which screens should appear in which order. It may appear as part of the presentation layer, or you can think of it as a separate layer that mediates between the presentation and domain layers. *Application Controllers (379)* may be written to be independent of any particular presentation, in which case they can be reused between presentations. This works well if you have different presentations with the same basic flow and navigation, although often it's best to give different presentations a different flow.

Not all systems need an *Application Controller (379)*. They're useful if your system has a lot of logic about the order of screens and the navigation between them. They're also useful if you haven't got a simple mapping between your pages and the actions on the domain. But if someone can pretty much see any screen in any order, you'll probably have little need for an *Application Controller (379)*. A good test is this: If the machine is in control of the screen flow, you need an *Application Controller (379)*; if the user is in control, you don't.

View Patterns

On the view side there are three patterns to think about: *Transform View (361)*, *Template View (350)*, and *Two Step View (365)*. These give rise to essentially two choices: whether to use *Transform View (361)* or *Template View (350)*, and whether either of them uses one stage or a *Two Step View (365)*. The basic patterns for *Transform View (361)* and *Template View (350)* are single stage. *Two Step View (365)* is a variation you can apply to either.

I'll start with the choice between *Template View (350)* and *Transform View (361)*. *Template View (350)* allows you write the presentation in the structure of the page and embed markers into the page to indicate where dynamic content needs to go. Quite a few popular platforms are based on this pattern, many of which are the server pages technologies (ASP, JSP, PHP) that allow you to put a full programming language into the page. This clearly provides a lot of power and flexibility; sadly, it also leads to very messy code that's difficult to maintain. As a result if you use server page technology you must be very disciplined to keep programming logic out of the page structure, often by using a helper object.

The *Transform View (361)* uses a transform style of program. The usual example is XSLT. This can be very effective if you're working with domain data that's in XML format or can easily be converted to it. An input controller picks the appropriate XSLT stylesheet and applies it to XML gleaned from the model.

If you use procedural scripts as your view, you can write the code in the style of either *Transform View (361)* or *Template View (350)* or in some interesting mix of the two. I've noticed that most scripts follow one of these two patterns as their main form.

The second decision is whether to be single stage (see Figure 4.2) or to use *Two Step View (365)*. A single-stage view mostly has one view component for each screen in the application. The view takes domain oriented data and renders it in HTML. I say "mostly" because similar logical screens may share views. Even so, most of the time you can think of it as one view per screen.

A two-stage view (Figure 4.3) breaks this process into two stages, producing a logical screen from the domain data and then rendering it in HTML. There's one first-stage view for each screen but only one second-stage view for the whole application.

The advantage of the *Two Step View (365)* is that it puts the decision of what HTML to use in a single place. This makes global changes to the HTML easy since there's only one object to alter in order to alter every screen on the site. Of course, you only get that advantage if your logical presentation stays the same, so it works best with sites where different screens use the same basic layout. Highly design intensive sites won't be able to come up with a good logical screen structure.

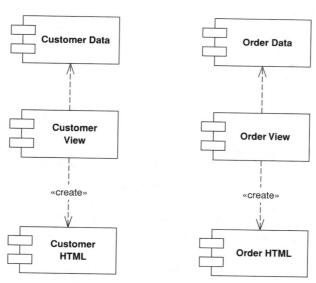

Figure 4.2 *A single-stage view.*

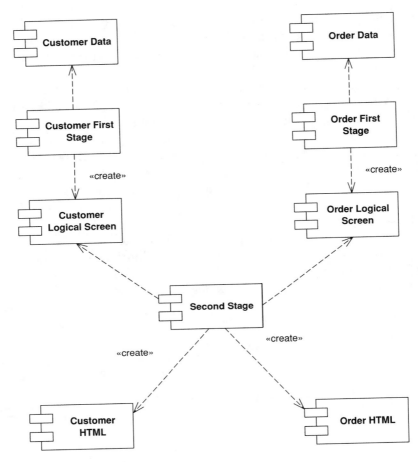

Figure 4.3 *A two-stage view.*

Two Step View (365) works even better if you have a Web application where its services are being used by multiple front-end customers, such as multiple airlines fronting the same basic reservation system. Within the limits of the logical screen, each front end can have a different appearance by using a different second stage. In a similar way you can use a *Two Step View (365)* to handle different output devices, with separate second stages for a regular Web browser and for a palmtop. Again, the limitation is that you can have the two share a common logical screen, which may not be possible if the UIs are very different, such as in a browser and a cell phone.

Input Controller Patterns

There are two patterns for the input controller. The most common is an input controller object for every page on your Web site. In the simplest case this *Page Controller (333)* can be a server page itself, combining the roles of view and input controller. In many implementations it makes things easier to split the input controller into a separate object. The input controller can then create appropriate models to do the processing and instantiate a view to return the result. Often you'll find that there isn't quite a one-to-one relationship between *Page Controllers (333)* and views. A more precise thought is that you have a *Page Controller (333)* for each action, where an action is a button or link. Most of the time the actions correspond to pages, but occasionally they don't—such as a link that may go to a couple of different pages depending some condition.

With any input controller there are two responsibilities—handling the HTTP request and deciding what to do with it—and it often makes sense to separate them. A server page can handle the request, delegating a separate helper object to decide what to do with it. *Front Controller (344)* goes further in this separation by having only one object handling all requests. This single handler interprets the URL to figure out what kind of request it's dealing with and creates a separate object to process it. In this way you can centralize all HTTP handling within a single object, avoiding the need to reconfigure the Web server whenever you change the action structure of the site.

Further Reading

Most books on Web server technologies provide a chapter or two on good server designs, although these are often buried in the technological descriptions. An excellent discussion of Java Web design is Chapter 9 of [Brown et al.]. The best source for further patterns is [Alur et al.]; most of these patterns can be used in non-Java situations. I stole the terminology on separating input and application controllers from [Knight and Dai].

Chapter 5

Concurrency

by Martin Fowler and David Rice

Concurrency is one of the most tricky aspects of software development. Whenever you have multiple processes or threads manipulating the same data, you run into concurrency problems. Just thinking about concurrency is hard since it's difficult to enumerate the possible scenarios that can get you into trouble. Whatever you do, there always seems to be something you miss. Furthermore, concurrency is hard to test for. We're great fans of a large body of automated tests acting as a foundation for software development, but it's hard to get tests to give us the security we need for concurrency problems.

One of the great ironies of enterprise application development is that few branches of software development use concurrency more yet worry about it less. The reason enterprise developers can get away with a naive view of concurrency is transaction managers. Transactions provide a framework that helps avoid many of the most tricky aspects of concurrency in an enterprise application. As long as you do all your data manipulation within a transaction, nothing really bad will happen to you.

Sadly, this doesn't mean we can ignore concurrency problems completely, for the primary reason that many interactions with a system can't be placed within a single database transaction. This forces us to manage concurrency in situations where data spans transactions. The term we use is **offline concurrency**, that is, concurrency control for data that's manipulated during multiple database transactions.

The second area where concurrency rears its ugly head for enterprise developers is application servers—supporting multiple threads in an application server system. We've spent much less time on this because dealing with it is much simpler. Indeed, you can use server platforms that take care of much of it for you.

Sadly, to understand these issues, you need to understand at least some of the general concurrency concepts. So we begin this chapter by going over

63

these issues. We don't pretend that this chapter is a general treatment of concurrency in software development—for that we'd need at least a complete book. What this chapter does is introduce concurrency issues for enterprise application development. Once we've done that we'll introduce the patterns for handling offline concurrency and say our brief words on application server concurrency.

In much of this chapter we'll illustrate the ideas with examples from an area that we hope you are very familiar with—the source code control systems used by teams to coordinate changes to a code base. We do this because it's relatively easy to understand as well as well as familiar. After all, if you aren't familiar with source code control systems, you really shouldn't be developing enterprise applications.

Concurrency Problems

We'll start by going through the essential problems of concurrency. We call them essential because they're the fundamental problems that concurrency control systems try to prevent. They aren't the only problems of concurrency, because the control mechanisms often create a new set of problems in their solutions! However, they do focus on the essential point of concurrency control.

Lost updates are the simplest idea to understand. Say Martin edits a file to make some changes to the checkConcurrency method—a task that takes a few minutes. While he's doing this David alters the updateImportantParameter method in the same file. David starts and finishes his alteration very quickly, so quickly that, even though he starts after Martin, he finishes before him. This is unfortunate. When Martin read the file it didn't include David's update, so when Martin writes the file it writes over the version that David updated and David's update is lost forever.

An **inconsistent read** occurs when you read two things that are correct pieces of information but not correct at the same time. Say Martin wishes to know how many classes are in the concurrency package, which contains two subpackages for locking and multiphase. Martin looks in the locking package and sees seven classes. At this point he gets a phone call from Roy on some abstruse question. While Martin's answering the phone, David finishes dealing with that pesky bug in the four-phase lock code and adds two classes to the locking package and three classes to the five that were in the multiphase package. His phone call over, Martin looks in the multiphase package to see how many classes there are and sees eight, producing a grand total of fifteen.

Sadly, fifteen classes was never the right answer. The correct answer was twelve before David's update and seventeen afterward. Either answer would have been correct, even if not current, but fifteen was never correct. This problem is called an inconsistent read because the data that Martin read was inconsistent.

Both of these problems cause a failure of **correctness** (or safety), and they result in incorrect behavior that would not have occurred without two people trying to work with the same data at the same time. However, if correctness were the only issue, these problems wouldn't be that serious. After all, we can arrange things so that only one of us can work the data at one time. While this helps with correctness, it reduces the ability to do things concurrently. The essential problem of any concurrent programming is that it's not enough to worry about correctness; you also have to worry about **liveness**: how much concurrent activity can go on. Often people need to sacrifice some correctness to gain more liveness, depending on the seriousness and likelihood of the failures and the need for people to work on their data concurrently.

These aren't all the problems you get with concurrency, but we think of these as the basic ones. To solve them we use various control mechanisms. Alas, there's no free lunch. The solutions introduce problems of their own, although these problems are less serious than the basic ones. Still, this does bring up an important point: If you can tolerate the problems, you can avoid any form of concurrency control. This is rare, but occasionally you find circumstances that permit it.

Execution Contexts

Whenever processing occurs in a system, it occurs in some context and usually in more than one. There's no standard terminology for execution contexts, so here we'll define the ones that we're assuming in this book.

From the perspective of interacting with the outside world, two important contexts are the request and the session. A **request** corresponds to a single call from the outside world which the software works on and for which it optionally sends back a response. During a request the processing is largely in the server's court and the client is assumed to wait for a response. Some protocols allow the client to interrupt a request before it gets a response, but this is fairly rare. More often a client may issue another request that may interfere with one it just sent. So a client may ask to place an order and then issue a separate request to cancel that order. From the client's view the two requests may be obviously connected, but depending on your protocol that may not be so obvious to the server.

A **session** is a long-running interaction between a client and a server. It may consists of a single request, but more commonly it consists of a series of requests that the user regards as a consistent logical sequence. Commonly a session will begin with a user logging in and doing various bits of work that may involve issuing queries and one or more business transactions (to be discussed shortly). At the end of the session the user logs out, or he may just go away and assume that the system interprets that as logging out.

Server software in an enterprise application sees both requests and sessions from two angles, as the server from the client and as the client to other systems. Thus, you'll often see multiple sessions: HTTP sessions from the client and database sessions with various databases.

Two important terms from operating systems are processes and threads. A **process** is a, usually heavyweight, execution context that provides a lot of isolation for the internal data it works on. A **thread** is a lighter-weight active agent that's set up so that multiple threads can operate in a single process. People like threads because they support multiple requests within a single process—which is good utilization of resources. However, threads usually share memory, and such sharing leads to concurrency problems. Some environments allow you to control what data a thread may access, allowing you to have **isolated threads** that don't share memory.

The difficulty with execution contexts comes when they don't line up as well as we might like. In theory each session would have an exclusive relationship with a process for its whole lifetime. Since processes are properly isolated from each other, this would help reduce concurrency conflicts. Currently we don't know of any server tools that allow you to work this way. A close alternative is to start a new process for each request, which was the common mode for early Perl Web systems. People tend to avoid that now because starting processes tie up a lot of resources, but it's quite common for systems to have a process handle only one request at a time—and that can save many concurrency headaches.

When you're dealing with databases there's another important context—a **transaction**. Transactions pull together several requests that the client wants treated as if they were a single request. They can occur from the application to the database (a system transaction) or from the user to an application (a business transaction). We'll dig into these terms more later on.

Isolation and Immutability

The problems of concurrency have been around for a while, and software people have come up with various solutions. For enterprise applications two solutions are particularly important: isolation and immutability.

Concurrency problems occur when more than one active agent, such as a process or thread, has access to the same piece of data. One way to deal with this is isolation: Partition the data so that any piece of it can only be accessed by one active agent. Processes work like this in operating system memory: The operating system allocates memory exclusively to a single process, and only that process can read or write the data linked to it. Similarly you find file locks in many popular productivity applications. If Martin opens a file, nobody else can open it. They may be allowed to open a read-only copy of the file as it was when Martin started, but they can't change it and they don't get to see the file between his changes.

Isolation is a vital technique because it reduces the chance of errors. Too often we've seen people get themselves into trouble because they use a technique that forces everyone to worry about concurrency all the time. With isolation you arrange things so that the programs enters an isolated zone, within which you don't have to worry about concurrency. Good concurrency design is thus to find ways of creating such zones and to ensure that as much programming as possible is done in one of them.

You only get concurrency problems if the data you're sharing can be modified. So one way to avoid concurrency conflicts is to recognize **immutable** data. Obviously we can't make all data immutable, as the whole point of many systems is data modification. But by identifying some data as immutable, or at least immutable almost all the time, we can relax our concurrency concerns for it and share it widely. Another option is to separate applications that are only reading data, and have them use copied data sources, from which we can then relax all concurrency controls.

Optimistic and Pessimistic Concurrency Control

What happens when we have mutable data that we can't isolate? In broad terms there are two forms of concurrency control that we can use: optimistic and pessimistic.

Let's suppose that Martin and David both want to edit the Customer file at the same time. With **optimistic locking** both of them can make a copy of the file and edit it freely. If David is the first to finish, he can check in his work without trouble. The concurrency control kicks in when Martin tries to commit his changes. At this point the source code control system detects a conflict between Martin's changes and David's changes. Martin's commit is rejected and it's up to him to figure out how to deal with the situation. With **pessimistic locking** whoever checks out the file first prevents anyone else from editing it. So if Martin is first to check out, David can't work with the file until Martin is finished with it and commits his changes.

A good way of thinking about this is that an optimistic lock is about conflict detection while a pessimistic lock is about conflict prevention. As it turns out real source code control systems can use either type, although these days most source code developers prefer to work with optimistic locks. (There is a reasonable argument that says that optimistic locking isn't really locking, but we find the terminology too convenient, and widespread, to ignore.)

Both approaches have their pros and cons. The problem with the pessimistic lock is that it reduces concurrency. While Martin is working on a file he locks it, so everybody else has to wait. If you've worked with pessimistic source code control mechanisms, you know how frustrating this can be. With enterprise data it's often worse because, if someone is editing data, nobody else is allowed to read it, let alone edit it.

Optimistic locks allow people to make much better progress, because the lock is only held during the commit. The problem with them is what happens when you get a conflict. Essentially everybody after David's commit has to check out the version of the file that David checked in, figure out how to merge their changes with David's changes, and then check in a newer version. With source code this happens not to be too difficult. Indeed, in many cases the source code control system can automatically do the merge for you, and even when it can't automerge, tools can make it much easier to see the differences. But business data is usually too difficult to automerge, so often all you can do is throw away everything and start again.

The essence of the choice between optimistic and pessimistic locks is the frequency and severity of conflicts. If conflicts are sufficiently rare, or if the consequences are no big deal, you should usually pick optimistic locks because they give you better concurrency and are usually easier to implement. However, if the results of a conflict are painful for users, you'll need to use a pessimistic technique instead.

Neither of these approaches is exactly free of problems. Indeed, by using them you can easily introduce problems that cause almost as much trouble as the basic concurrency problems that you're trying to solve in the first place. We'll leave a detailed discussion of these ramifications to a proper book on concurrency, but here are a few highlights to bear in mind.

Preventing Inconsistent Reads

Consider this situation. Martin edits the Customer class, which makes calls on the Order class. Meanwhile David edits the Order class and changes the interface. David compiles and checks in; Martin then compiles and checks in. Now the shared code is broken because Martin didn't realize that the Order class was altered underneath him. Some source code control systems will spot this inconsistent read, but others require some kind of manual discipline to enforce consistency, such as updating your files from the trunk before you check in.

In essence this is the inconsistent read problem, and it's often easy to miss because most people tend to focus on lost updates as the essential problem in concurrency. Pessimistic locks have a well-worn way of dealing with this problem through read and write locks. To read data you need a read (or shared) lock; to write data you need a write (or exclusive) lock. Many people can have read locks on the data at one time, but if anyone has a read lock nobody can get a write lock. Conversely, once somebody has a write lock, then nobody else can have any lock. With this system you can avoid inconsistent reads with pessimistic locks.

Optimistic locks usually base their conflict detection on some kind of version marker on the data. This can be a timestamp or a sequential counter. To detect lost updates the system checks the version marker of your update with the version marker of the shared data. If they're the same, the system allows the update and updates the version marker.

Detecting an inconsistent read is essentially similar: In this case every bit of data that was read also needs to have its version marker compared with the shared data. Any differences indicate a conflict.

Controlling access to every bit of data that's read often causes unnecessary problems due to conflicts or waits on data that doesn't actually matter that much. You can reduce this burden by separating out data you've *used* from data you've merely read. With a pick list of products it doesn't matter if a new product appears in it after you start your changes. But a list of charges that you're summarizing for a bill may be more important. The difficulty is that this requires some careful analysis of what it's used for. A zip code in a customer's address may seem innocuous, but, if a tax calculation is based on where somebody lives, that address has to be controlled for concurrency. As you can see, figuring out what you need to control and what you don't is an involved exercise whichever form of concurrency control you use.

Another way to deal with inconsistent read problems is to use **Temporal Reads**. These prefix each read of data with some kind of timestamp or immutable label, and the database returns the data as it was according to that time or label. Very few databases have anything like this, but developers often come across this in source code control systems. The problem is that the data source needs to provide a full temporal history of changes, which takes time and space to process. This is reasonable for source code but both more difficult and more expensive for databases. You may need to provide this capability for specific areas of your domain logic: see [Snodgrass] and [Fowler TP] for ideas on how to do that.

Deadlocks

A particular problem with pessimistic techniques is **deadlock**. Say Martin starts editing the Customer file and David starts editing the Order file. David realizes that to complete his task he needs to edit the Customer file too, but Martin has a lock on it so he has to wait. Then Martin realizes he has to edit the Order file, which David has locked. They are now deadlocked—neither can make progress until the other completes. Described like this, deadlocks sound easy to prevent, but they can occur with many people involved in a complex chain, and that makes them more tricky.

There are various techniques you can use to deal with deadlocks. One is to have software that can detect a deadlock when it occurs. In this case you pick a **victim,** who has to throw away his work and his locks so the others can make progress. Deadlock detection is very difficult and causes pain for victims. A similar approach is to give every lock a time limit. Once you hit that limit you lose your locks and your work—essentially becoming a victim. Timeouts are easier to implement than a deadlock detection mechanism, but if anyone holds locks for a while some people will be victimized when there actually is no deadlock present.

Timeouts and detection deal with a deadlock when it occurs, other approaches try to stop deadlocks occurring at all. Deadlocks essentially occur when people who already have locks try to get more (or to upgrade from read to write locks.) Thus, one way of preventing them is to force people to acquire all their locks at once at the beginning of their work and then prevent them gaining more.

You can force an order on how everybody gets locks. An example might be to always get locks on files in alphabetical order. This way, once David had a lock on the Order file, he can't try to get a lock on the Customer file because it's earlier in the sequence. At that point he essentially becomes a victim.

You can also make it so that, if Martin tries to acquire a lock and David already has one, Martin automatically becomes a victim. It's a drastic technique, but it's simple to implement. And in many cases such a scheme works just fine.

If you're very conservative, you can use multiple schemes. For example, you force everyone to get all their locks at the beginning, but add a timeout in case something goes wrong. That may seem like using a belt and braces, but such conservatism is often wise with deadlocks because they are pesky things that are easy to get wrong.

It's very easy to think you have a deadlock-proof scheme and then find some chain of events you didn't consider. As a result we prefer very simple and conservative schemes for enterprise application development. They may cause unnecessary victims, but that's usually much better than the consequences of missing a deadlock scenario.

Transactions

The primary tool for handling concurrency in enterprise applications is the transaction. The word "transaction" often brings to mind an exchange of money or goods. Walking up to an ATM machine, entering your PIN, and withdrawing cash is a transaction. Paying the $3 toll at the Golden Gate Bridge is a transaction. Buying a beer at the local pub is a transaction.

Looking at typical financial dealings such as these provides a good definition for the term. First, a transaction is a bounded sequence of work, with both start and endpoints well defined. An ATM transaction begins when the card is inserted and ends when cash is delivered or an inadequate balance is discovered. Second, all participating resources are in a consistent state both when the transaction begins and when the transaction ends. A man purchasing a beer has a few bucks less in his wallet but has a nice pale ale in front of him. The sum value of his assets hasn't changed. It's the same for the pub—pouring free beer would be no way to run a business.

In addition, each transaction must complete on an all-or-nothing basis. The bank can't subtract from an account holder's balance unless the ATM machine actually delivers the cash. While the human element might make this last property optional during the above transactions, there is no reason software can't make a guarantee on this front.

ACID

Software transactions are often described in terms of the **ACID** properties:

- **Atomicity**: Each step in the sequence of actions performed within the boundaries of a transaction must complete successfully or all work must roll back. Partial completion is not a transactional concept. Thus, if Martin is transferring some money from his savings to his checking account and the server crashes after he's withdrawn the money from his savings, the system behaves as if he never did the withdrawal. Committing says both things occurred; a roll back says neither occurred. It has to be both or neither.

- **Consistency:** A system's resources must be in a consistent, noncorrupt state at both the start and the completion of a transaction.

- **Isolation:** The result of an individual transaction must not be visible to any other open transactions until that transaction commits successfully.

- **Durability:** Any result of a committed transaction must be made permanent. This translates to "Must survive a crash of any sort."

Transactional Resources

Most enterprise applications run into transactions in terms of databases. But there are plenty of other things that can be controlled using transactions, such as message queues, printers, and ATMs. As a result, technical discussions of transactions use the term "transactional resource" to mean anything that's transactional—that is, that uses transactions to control concurrency. "Transactional resource" is a bit of a mouthful, so we just use "database," since that's the most common case. But when we say "database," the same applies for any other transactional resource.

To handle the greatest throughput, modern transaction systems are designed to keep transactions as short as possible. As a result the general advice is to never make a transaction span multiple requests. A transaction that spans multiple requests is generally known as a **long transaction**.

For this reason a common approach is to start a transaction at the beginning of a request and complete it at the end. This **request transaction** is a nice simple model, and a number of environments make it easy to do declaratively, by just tagging methods as transactional.

A variation on this is to open a transaction as late as possible. With a **late transaction** you may do all the reads outside it and only open it up when you do updates. This has the advantage of minimizing the time spent in a transaction. If there's a lengthy time lag between the opening of the transaction and the first write, this may improve liveness. However, this means that you don't have any concurrency control until you begin the transaction, which leaves you open to inconsistent reads. As a result it's usually not worth doing this unless you have very heavy contention or you're doing it anyway because of business transactions that span multiple requests (which is the next topic).

When you use transactions, you need be somewhat aware of what exactly is being locked. For many database actions the transaction system locks the rows involved, which allows multiple transactions to access the same table. However, if a transaction locks a lot of rows in a table, then the database has more locks than it can handle and escalates the locking to the entire table—locking out other transactions. This **lock escalation** can have a serious effect on concurrency, and it's particularly why you shouldn't have some "object" table for data at the domain's *Layer Supertype (475)* level. Such a table is a prime candidate for lock escalation, and locking that table shuts everybody else out of the database.

Reducing Transaction Isolation for Liveness

It's common to restrict the full protection of transactions so that you can get better liveness. This is particularly the case when it comes to handling isolation. If you have full isolation, you get serializable transactions. Transactions are **serializable** if they can be executed concurrently and you get a result that's the same as you get from some sequence of executing the transactions serially. Thus, if we take our earlier example of Martin counting his files, serializability guarantees that he gets a result that corresponds to completing his transaction either entirely before David's transaction starts (twelve) or entirely after David's finishes (seventeen). Serializability can't guarantee which result, as in this case, but at least it guarantees a correct one.

Most transactional systems use the SQL standard which defines four levels of isolation. Serializable is the strongest level, and each level below allows a particular kind of inconsistent read to enter the picture. We'll explore these with the example of Martin counting files while David modifies them. There are two packages: locking and multiphase. Before David's update there are seven files in the locking package and five in the multiphase package; after his update there are nine in the locking package and eight in the multiphase package. Martin looks at the locking package and David then updates both; then Martin looks at the multiphase package.

If the isolation level is serializable, the system guarantees that Martin's answer is either twelve or seventeen, both of which are correct. Serializability can't guarantee that every run through this scenario will give the same result, but it always gets either the number before David's update or the number afterwards.

The first isolation level below serializable is **repeatable read**, which allows **phantoms**. Phantoms occur when you add some elements to a collection and the reader sees only some of them. The case here is that Martin looks at the files in the locking package and sees seven. David then commits his transaction, after which Martin looks at the multiphase package and sees eight. Hence, Martin gets an incorrect result. Phantoms occur because they are valid for some of Martin's transaction but not all of it, and they're always things that are inserted.

Next down the list is the isolation level of **read committed,** which allows **unrepeatable reads**. Imagine that Martin looks at a total rather than the actual files. An unrepeatable read allows him to read a total of seven for locking. Next David commits; then he reads a total of eight for multiphase. It's called an unrepeatable read because, if Martin were to reread the total for the locking package after David committed, he would get the new number of nine. His original read of seven can't be repeated after David's update. It's easier for databases to spot unrepeatable reads than phantoms, so the repeatable read gives you more correctness than read committed but less liveness.

The lowest level of isolation is **read uncommitted**, which allows **dirty reads**. At read uncommitted you can read data that another transaction hasn't actually committed yet. This causes two kinds of errors. Martin might look at the locking package when David adds the first of his files but before he adds the second. As a result he sees eight files in the locking package. The second kind of error comes if David adds his files but then rolls back his transaction—in which case Martin sees files that were never really there.

Table 5.1 lists the read errors caused by each isolation level.

To be sure of correctness you should always use the serializable isolation level. The problem is that choosing serializable really messes up the liveness of a system, so much so that you often have to reduce serializability in order to increase throughput. You have to decide what risks you want take and make your own trade-off of errors versus performance.

You don't have to use the same isolation level for all transactions, so you should look at each transaction ande decide how to balance liveness versus correctness for it.

Business and System Transactions

What we've talked about so far, and most of what most people talk about, is what we call system transactions, or transactions supported by RDBMS systems and transaction monitors. A database transaction is a group of SQL com-

Table 5.1 *Isolation Levels and the Inconsistent Read Errors They Allow*

Isolation Level	Dirty Read	Unrepeatable Read	Phantom
Read Uncommitted	Yes	Yes	Yes
Read Committed	No	Yes	Yes
Repeatable Read	No	No	Yes
Serializable	No	No	No

mands delimited by instructions to begin and end it. If the fourth statement in the transaction results in an integrity constraint violation, the database must roll back the effects of the first three statements and notify the caller that the transaction has failed. If all four statements had completed successfully all would have been made visible to other users at the same time rather than one at a time. RDBMS systems and application server transaction managers are so commonplace that they can pretty much be taken for granted. They work well and are well understood by application developers.

However, a system transaction has no meaning to the user of a business system. To an online banking system user a transaction consists of logging in, selecting an account, setting up some bill payments, and finally clicking the OK button to pay the bills. This is what we call a **business transaction**, and that it displays the same ACID properties as a system transaction seems a reasonable expectation. If the user cancels before paying the bills, any changes made on previous screens should be canceled. Setting up payments shouldn't result in a system-visible balance change until the OK button is pressed.

The obvious answer to supporting the ACID properties of a business transaction is to execute the entire business transaction within a single system transaction. Unfortunately business transactions often take multiple requests to complete, so using a single system transaction to implement one results in a long system transaction. Most transaction systems don't work very efficiently with long transactions.

This doesn't mean that you should never use long transactions. If your database has only modest concurrency needs, you may well be able to get away with it. And if you can get away with it, we suggest you do it. Using a long transaction means you avoid a lot of awkward problems. However, the application won't be scalable because long transactions will turn the database into a major bottleneck. In addition, the refactoring from long to short transactions is both complex and not well understood.

For this reason many enterprise applications can't risk long transactions. In this case you have to break the business transaction down into a series of short transactions. This means that you are left to your own devices to support the ACID properties of business transactions between system transactions—a problem we call **offline concurrency**. System transactions are still very much part of the picture. Whenever the business transaction interacts with a transactional resource, such as a database, that interaction will execute within a system transaction in order to maintain the integrity of that resource. However, as you'll read below it's not enough to string together a series of system transactions to properly support a business transaction. The business application must provide a bit of glue between them.

Atomicity and durability are the ACID properties most easily supported for business transactions. Both are supported by running the commit phase of the business transaction, when the user hits Save within a system transaction. Before the session attempts to commit all its changes to the record set, it first opens a system transaction. The system transaction guarantees that the changes will commit as a unit and will be made permanent. The only potentially tricky part here is maintaining an accurate change set during the life of the business transaction. If the application uses a *Domain Model (116)*, a *Unit of Work (184)* can track changes accurately. Placing business logic in a *Transaction Script (110)* requires a manual tracking of changes, but that's probably not much of a problem as the use of transaction scripts implies rather simple business transactions.

The tricky ACID property to enforce with business transactions is isolation. Failures of isolation lead to failures of consistency. Consistency dictates that a business transaction not leave the record set in an invalid state. Within a single transaction the application's responsibility in supporting consistency is to enforce all available business rules. Across multiple transactions the application's responsibility is to ensure that one session doesn't step all over another session's changes, leaving the record set in the invalid state of having lost a user's work.

As well as the obvious problems of clashing updates, there are the more subtle problems of inconsistent reads. When data is read over several system transactions, there's no guarantee that it will be consistent. The different reads can even introduce data in memory that's sufficiently inconsistent to cause application failures.

Business transactions are closely tied to sessions. In the user's view each session is a sequence of business transactions (unless they're only reading data), so we usually make the assumption that all business transactions execute in a single client session. While it's certainly possible to design a system that has multiple sessions for one business transaction, that's a very good way of getting yourself badly confused—so we'll assume that you won't do that.

Patterns for Offline Concurrency Control

As much as possible, you should let your transaction system deal with concurrency problems. Handling concurrency control that spans system transactions plonks you firmly in the murky waters of dealing with concurrency yourself. This water is full of virtual sharks, jellyfish, piranhas, and other, less friendly creatures. Unfortunately, the mismatch between business and system transactions means you sometimes just have to wade in. The patterns that we've provided here are some techniques that we've found helpful in dealing with concurrency control that spans system transactions.

Remember that these are techniques you should only use if you have to. If you can make all your business transactions fit into a system transaction by ensuring that they fit within a single request, then do that. If you can get away with long transactions by forsaking scalability, then do that. By leaving concurrency control in the hands of your transaction software you'll avoid a great deal of trouble. These techniques are what you have to use when you can't do that. Because of the tricky nature of concurrency, we have to stress again that the patterns are a starting point, not a destination. We've found them useful, but we don't claim to have found a cure for all concurrency ills.

Our first choice for handling offline concurrency problems is *Optimistic Offline Lock (416)*, which essentially uses optimistic concurrency control across the business transactions. We like this as a first choice because it's an easier approach to program and yields the best liveness. The limitation of *Optimistic Offline Lock (416)* is that you only find out that a business transaction is going to fail when you try to commit it, and in some circumstances the pain of that late discovery is too much. Users may have put an hour's work into entering details about a lease, and if you get lots of failures users lose faith in the system. Your alternative is *Pessimistic Offline Lock (426)*, with which you find out early if you're in trouble but lose out because it's harder to program and it reduces your liveness.

With either of these approaches you can save considerable complexity by not trying to manage locks on every object. A *Coarse-Grained Lock (438)* allows you to manage the concurrency of a group of objects together. Another way you can make life easier for application developers is to use *Implicit Lock (449)*, which saves them from having to manage locks directly. Not only does this save work, it also avoids bugs when people forget—and these bugs are hard to find.

A common statement about concurrency is that it's a purely technical decision that can be decided on after requirements are complete. We disagree. The choice of optimistic or pessimistic controls affects the whole user experience of the system. An intelligent design of *Pessimistic Offline Lock (426)* needs a lot of input about the domain from the users of the system. Similarly domain knowledge is needed to choose good *Coarse-Grained Locks (438)*.

Futzing with concurrency is one of the most difficult programming tasks. It's very difficult to test concurrent code with confidence. Concurrency bugs are hard to reproduce and very difficult to track down. The patterns we've described have worked for us so far, but this is particularly difficult territory. If you need to go down this path, it's worth getting some experienced help. At the very least consult the books we mention at the end of this chapter.

Application Server Concurrency

So far we've talked about concurrency mainly in terms of multiple sessions running against a shared data source. Another form of concurrency is the process concurrency of the application server itself: How does that server handle multiple requests concurrently and how does this affect the design of the application on the server? The big difference from the other concurrency issues we've talked about so far is that application server concurrency doesn't involve transactions, so working with them means stepping away from the relatively controlled transactional world.

Explicit multithreaded programming, with locks and synchronization blocks, is complicated to do well. It's easy to introduce defects that are very hard to find—concurrency bugs are almost impossible to reproduce—resulting in a system that works correctly 99 percent of the time but throws random fits. Such software is incredibly frustrating to use and debug, so our policy is to avoid the need for explicit handling of synchronization and locks as much as possible. Application developers should almost never have to deal with these explicit concurrency mechanisms.

The simplest way to handle this is to use **process-per-session**, where each session runs in its own process. Its great advantage is that the state of each process is completely isolated from the other processes so application programmers don't have to worry at all about multithreading. As far as memory isolation goes, it's almost equally effective to have each request start a new process or to have one process tied to the session that's idle between requests. Many early Web systems would start a new Perl process for each request.

The problem with process-per-session is that it uses up a lot resources, since processes are expensive beasties. To be more efficient you can pool the processes, such that each one only handles a single request at one time but can handle multiple requests from different sessions in a sequence. This approach of pooled **process-per-request** will use many fewer processes to support a given number of sessions. Your isolation is almost as good: You don't have many of the nasty multithreading issues. The main problem over process-per-session is that you have to ensure that any resources used to handle a request are released at the end of the request. The current Apache mod-perl uses this scheme, as do a lot of serious large-scale transaction processing systems.

Even process-per-request will need many processes running to handle a reasonable load. You can further improve throughput by having a single process run multiple threads. With this **thread-per-request** approach, each request is handled by a single thread within a process. Since threads use much fewer server resources than a process, you can handle more requests with less hardware this way, so your server is more efficient. The problem with using thread-per-request is that there's no isolation between the threads and any thread can touch any piece of data that it can get access to.

In our view there's a lot to be said for using process-per-request. Although it's less efficient than thread-per-request, using process-per-request is equally scalable. You also get better robustness—if one thread goes haywire it can bring down an entire process, so using process-per-request limits the damage. Particularly with a less experienced team, the reduction of threading headaches (and the time and cost of fixing bugs) is worth the extra hardware costs. We find that few people actually do any performance testing to assess the relative costs of thread-per-request and process-per-request for their application.

Some environments provide a middle ground of allowing isolated areas of data to be assigned to a single thread. COM does this with the single-threaded apartment, and J2EE does it with Enterprise Java Beans (and will in the future with isolates). If your platform has something like this available, it can allow you to have your cake and eat it—whatever that means.

If you use thread-per-request, the most important thing is to create and enter an isolated zone where application developers can mostly ignore multithreaded issues. The usual way to do this is to have the thread create new objects as it starts handling the request and to ensure that these objects aren't put anywhere (such as in a static variable) where other threads can see them. That way the objects are isolated because other threads have no way of referencing them.

Many developers are concerned about creating new objects because they've been told that object creation is an expensive process. As a result they often pool objects. The problem with pooling is that you have to synchronize access to the pooled objects in some way. But the cost of object creation is very dependent on the virtual machine and memory management strategies. In modern environments object creation is actually pretty fast [Peckish]. (Off the top of your head: how many Java date objects do you think we can create in one second on Martin's 600Mhz P3 with Java 1.3? We'll tell you later.) Creating fresh objects for each session avoids a lot of concurrency bugs and can actually improve scalability.

While this tactic works in many cases, there are still some areas that developers need to avoid. One is static, class-based variables or global variables because any use of these has to be synchronized. This is also true of singletons.

If you need some kind of global memory, use a *Registry (480)*, which you can implement in such a way that it looks like a static variable but actually uses thread-specific storage.

Even if you're able to create objects for the session, and thus make a comparatively safe zone, some objects are expensive to create and thus need to be handled differently—the most common example of this is a database connection. To deal with this you can place these objects in an explicit pool where you acquire a connection while you need it and return it when done. These operations will need to be synchronized.

Further Reading

In many ways, this chapter only skims the surface of a much more complex topic. To investigate further we suggest starting with [Bernstein and Newcomer], [Lea], and [Schmidt et al.].

Chapter 6

Session State

When we talked about concurrency, we raised the issue of the difference between business and system transactions (Chapter 5, page 74). As well as affecting concurrency, this difference affects how to store the data that's used within a business transaction but isn't yet ready to be committed to the general database of record.

The differences between business and system transactions underlie much of the debate over stateless versus stateful sessions. There's been a lot written about this issue, but in my view the basic problem is often disguised behind the technical questions of stateless and stateful server systems. I think the fundamental issue is realizing that some sessions are inherently stateful and then deciding what to do about the state.

The Value of Statelessness

What do people mean by a stateless server? The whole point of objects, of course, is that they combine state (data) with behavior. A true stateless object is one with no fields. Such animals do show up from time to time, but frankly, they're pretty rare. Indeed, you can make a strong case that a stateless object is a bad design.

As it turns out, however, this isn't what most people mean when they talk about statelessness in a distributed enterprise application. When people refer to a stateless server they mean an object that doesn't retain state between requests. Such an object may well have fields, but when you invoke a method on a stateless server the values of the fields are undefined.

An example of a stateless server object might be one that returns a Web page telling you all about a book. You invoke a call on it by accessing a URL—the object might be an ASP document or a servlet. In the URL you supply an ISBN number that the server uses to generate the HTTP reply. During the interaction the server object might stash the book's ISBN, title, and price in fields when it gets them back from the database, before it generates the HTML; maybe it does some business logic to determine which complimentary reviews to show the user. Once it's done its job, however, these values become useless. The next ISBN is a whole new story, and the server object will probably reinitialize to clear out any old values to avoid mistakes.

Now imagine that you want to keep track of all the ISBNs visited by a particular client IP address. You can keep this in a list maintained by the server object. However, this list must persist between requests and thus you have a stateful server object. The shift from stateless to stateful is much more than three or four letters at the end of the word. For many people stateful servers are nothing short of disastrous. Why is this?

The primary issue is one of server resources. Any stateful server object needs to keep all its state while waiting for a user to ponder a Web page. A stateless server object, however, can process other requests from other sessions. Here's a completely unrealistic yet helpful thought experiment. We have a hundred people who want to know about books, and processing a request about a book takes one second. Each person makes one request every ten seconds, and all requests are perfectly balanced. If we want to track a user's requests with a stateful server object, we must have one server object per user: one hundred objects. But 90 percent of the time these objects are sitting around doing nothing. If we forgo the ISBN tracking and just use stateless server objects to respond to requests, we can get away with only ten server objects fully employed all the time.

The point is that, if we have no state between method calls, it doesn't matter which object services the request, but if we do store state we need to always get the same object. Statelessness allows us to pool our objects so that we need fewer objects to handle more users. The more idle users we have, the more valuable stateless servers are. As you can imagine, stateless servers are very useful on high-traffic Web sites. Statelessness also fits in well with the Web since HTTP is a stateless protocol.

So everything should be stateless, right? Well, it would be if it could be. The problem is that many client interactions are inherently stateful. Consider the shopping cart metaphor that fuels a thousand e-commerce applications. The user's interaction involves browsing several books and picking which ones to buy. The shopping cart needs to be remembered for the user's entire session. Essentially we have a stateful business transaction, which implies that the session has to be stateful. If I only look at books and don't buy anything, my session is stateless, but if I buy, it's stateful. We can't avoid the state unless we stay poor; instead, we have to decide what to do with it. The good news is that we can use a stateless server to implement a stateful session; the interesting news is that we may not want to.

Session State

The details of the shopping cart are **session state**, meaning that the data in the cart is relevant only to that particular session. This state is within a business transaction, which means that it's separated from other sessions and their business transactions. (I'll continue to assume for this discussion that each business transaction runs in one session only and that each session does only one business transaction at any one time). Session state is distinct from what I call **record data**, which is the long-term persistent data held in the database and visible to all sessions. Session state needs to be committed to become record data.

Since session state is within a business transaction, it has many of the properties that people usually think of with transactions, such as ACID (atomicity, consistency, isolation, and durability). The consequences of this are not always understood.

One interesting consequence is the effect on consistency. While the customer is editing an insurance policy, the current state of the policy may not be legal. The customer alters a value, uses a request to send this to the system, and the system replies indicating invalid values. Those values are part of the session state, but they aren't valid. Session state is often like this—it isn't going to match the validation rules while it's being worked on; it will only when the business transaction commits.

The biggest issue with session state is dealing with isolation. With many fingers in the pot, a number of things can happen while a customer is editing a policy. The most obvious is two people editing the policy at the same time. But it's not just changes that are a problem. Consider that there are two records, the policy itself and the customer record. The policy has a risk value that depends partially on the zip code in the customer record. The customer begins by editing the policy and after ten minutes does something that opens the customer record so he can see the zip code. However, during that time someone else has changed the zip code and the risk value—leading to an inconsistent read. See page 76 for advice on how to deal with this.

Not all data held by the session counts as session state. The session may cache some data that doesn't really need to be stored between requests but is stored to improve performance. Since you can lose the cache without losing correct behavior, this is different from session state, which must be stored between requests for correct behavior.

Ways to Store Session State

So, how do you store session state once you know you have to have it? I divide the options into three blurred but basic choices.

Client Session State (456) stores the data on the client. There are several ways to do this: encoding data in a URL for a Web presentation, using cookies, serializing the data into some hidden field on a Web form, and holding the data in objects on a rich client.

Server Session State (458) may be as simple as holding the data in memory between requests. Usually, however, there's a mechanism for storing the session state somewhere more durable as a serialized object. The object can be stored on the application server's local file system, or it can be placed in a shared data source. This could be a simple database table with a session ID as a key and a serialized object as a value.

Database Session State (462) is also server-side storage, but it involves breaking up the data into tables and fields and storing it in the database much as you would store more lasting data.

There are quite a few issues involved in the choice of option. First off, I'll talk about bandwidth needs between the client and the server. Using *Client Session State (456)* means that session data needs to be transferred across the wire with every request. If we're talking about only a few fields, this is no big deal, but larger amounts of data result in bigger transfers. In one application this data amounted to about a megabyte or, as one of our team put it, three Shakespeare plays worth. Admittedly, we were using XML between the two, which is not the most compact of data transmission forms, but even so there was a lot of data to work with.

Of course, some data will need to be transferred because it has to be seen on the presentation. But using *Client Session State (456)* implies that with every request you have to transfer all the data the server uses for it, even if it isn't needed by the client for display. All in all this means that you don't want to use *Client Session State (456)* unless the amount of session state you need to store is pretty small. You also have to worry about security and integrity. Unless you encrypt the data, you have to assume that any malicious user could edit your session data, which might lead you to a whole new version of "name your own price."

Session data has to be isolated. In most cases what's going on in one session shouldn't affect what's going on in another. If we book a flight itinerary there should be no effect on any other user until the flight is confirmed. Indeed, part of the meaning of session data is that it's unseen to anything outside the session. This becomes a tricky issue if you use *Database Session State (462)*, because you have to work hard to isolate the session data from the record data that sits in the database.

If you have a lot of users, you'll want to consider clustering to improve your throughput. In this case you'll want to think about whether you need session migration. **Session migration** allows a session to move from server to server as one server handles one request and other servers take on the others. Its opposite is **server affinity**, which forces one server to handle all requests for a particular session. Server migration leads to a better balancing of your servers, particularly if your sessions are long. However, that can be awkward if you're using *Server Session State (458)* because often only the machine that handles the session can easily find that state.There are ways around that— ways that blur the lines between *Database Session State (462)* and *Server Session State (458)*.

Server affinity can lead to bigger problems than you might initially think. In trying to guarantee server affinity, the clustering system can't always inspect the calls to see which session they're part of. As a result, it will increase the affinity so all calls from one client go to the same application server. Often this is done by the client's IP address. If the client is behind a proxy, that could mean that many clients are all using the same IP address and are thus tied to a particular server. This can get pretty bad if you see most of your traffic handled by one server that bags the IP address for AOL!

If the server is going to use the session state, it needs to get it into a form that can be used quickly. If you use *Server Session State (458)*, the session state is pretty much there. If you use *Client Session State (456)*, it's there, but often needs to be put into the form you want. If you use *Database Session State (462)*, you need to go to the database to get it (and maybe do some transforming as well). This implies that each approach can have different effects on the system's responsiveness. The size and complexity of the data will have an effect on this time.

If you have a public retail system, you probably don't have that much data going into each session, but you do have a lot of mostly idle users. For that reason *Database Session State (462)* can work nicely in performance terms. For a leasing system you run the risk of schlepping masses of data in and out of the database with each request. That's when *Server Session State (458)* can give you better performance.

One of the big bugbears in many systems is when a user cancels a session and says forget it. This is particularly awkward with B2C applications because the user usually doesn't actually say forget it, it just disappears and doesn't come back. *Client Session State (456)* certainly wins here because you can forget about that user easily. In the other approaches you need to be able to clean out session state when you realize it's canceled, as well as set up a system that allows you to cancel after some timeout period. Good implementations of *Server Session State (458)* allow you to do this with an automatic timeout.

As well as what happens when a user cancels, consider what happens when a system cancels: A client can crash, a server can go south, and a network connection can disappear into the ether. *Database Session State (462)* can usually cope with all three pretty well. *Server Session State (458)* may or may not survive, depending on whether the session object is backed up to a nonvolatile store and where that store is kept. *Client Session State (456)* won't survive a client crash, but should survive the rest going down.

Don't forget the development effort involved in these patterns. Usually the *Server Session State (458)* is the easiest on development resources, particularly if you don't have to persist the session state between requests. *Database Session State (462)* and *Client Session State (456)* will usually involve code to transform from a database or transport format to the form that the session objects will use. That extra time means that you aren't able to build as many features as quickly with as you would with *Server Session State (458)*, particularly if the data is complex. On first sight *Database Session State (462)* might not seem that complex if you've already got to map to database tables, but the extra development effort comes in keeping all the other uses of the database isolated from the session data.

The three approaches aren't mutually exclusive. You can use a mix of two or three of them to store different parts of the session state. This usually makes things more complicated, however, as you're never sure which part of the state goes in what part of the system. Nevertheless, if you use something other than *Client Session State (456)*, you'll have to keep at least a session identifier in *Client Session State (456)* even if the rest of the state is held using the other patterns.

My preference is for *Server Session State (458)*, particularly if the memento is stored remotely so it can survive a server crash. I also like *Client Session State (456)* for session IDs and for session data that's very small. I don't like *Database Session State (462)* unless you need failover and clustering and if you can't store remote mementos or if isolation between sessions isn't an issue for you.

Chapter 7

Distribution Strategies

Objects have been around for a while, and sometimes it seems that, ever since they were created, folks have wanted to distribute them. However, distribution of objects, or indeed of anything else, has a lot more pitfalls than many people realize [Waldo et al.], especially when they're under the influence of vendors' cozy brochures. This chapter is about some of these hard lessons—lessons I've seen many of my clients learn the hard way.

The Allure of Distributed Objects

There is a recurring presentation that I used to see two or three times a year during design reviews. Proudly the system architect of a new OO system lays out his plan for a new distributed object system—let's pretend it's a some kind of ordering system. He shows me a design that looks rather like Figure 7.1. With separate remote objects for customers, orders, products, and deliveries. Each one is a separate component that can be placed on a separate processing node.

I ask, "Why do you do this?"

"Performance, of course," the architect replies, looking at me a little oddly. "We can run each component on a separate box. If one component gets too busy we add extra boxes for it so we can load-balance our application." The look is now curious as if he wonders if I really know anything about real distributed object stuff at all.

Meanwhile I'm faced with an interesting dilemma. Do I just say out and out that this design sucks like an inverted hurricane and get shown the door immediately? Or do I slowly try to show my client the light? The latter is more remunerative but much tougher since the client is usually very pleased with his architecture, and it takes a lot to give up on a fond dream.

So assuming you haven't shown this book the door I guess you'll want to know why this distributed architecture sucks. After all, many tool vendors will

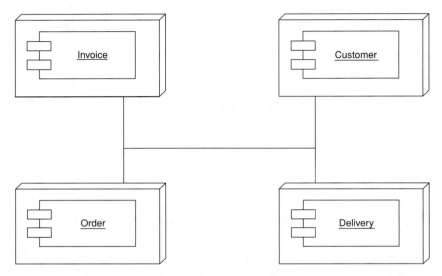

Figure 7.1 *Distributing an application by putting different components on different nodes (not recommended!)*

tell you that the whole point of distributed objects is that you can take a bunch of objects and position them as you like on processing nodes. Also, their powerful middleware provides transparency. Transparency allows objects to call each other within a process or between a process without having to know if the callee is in the same process, in another process, or on another machine.

Transparency is valuable, but while many things can be made transparent in distributed objects, performance isn't usually one of them. Although our prototypical architect was distributing objects the way he was for performance reasons, in fact his design will usually cripple performance, make the system much harder to build and deploy, or, usually, do both.

Remote and Local Interfaces

The primary reason that the distribution by class model doesn't work has to do with a fundamental fact of computers. A procedure call within a process is very, very fast. A procedure call between two separate processes is orders of magnitude slower. Make that a process running on another machine and you can add another order of magnitude or two, depending on the network topography involved.

As a result, the interface for an object to be used remotely must be different from that for an object used locally within the same process.

A local interface is best as a fine-grained interface. Thus, if I have an address class, a good interface will have separate methods for getting the city, getting the state, setting the city, setting the state, and so forth. A fine-grained interface is good because it follows the general OO principle of lots of little pieces that can be combined and overridden in various ways to extend the design into the future.

A fine-grained interface doesn't work well when it's remote. When method calls are slow, you want to obtain or update the city, state, and zip in one call rather than three. The resulting interface is coarse-grained, designed not for flexibility and extendibility but for minimizing calls. Here you'll see an interface along the lines of get-address details and update-address details. It's much more awkward to program to, but for performance you need to have it.

Of course, what vendors will tell you is that there's no overhead to using their middleware for remote and local calls. If it's a local call, it's done with the speed of a local call. If it's a remote call it's done more slowly. Thus, you only pay the price of a remote call when you need one. This much is, to some extent, true, but it doesn't avoid the essential point that any object that may be used remotely should have a coarse-grained interface while every object that isn't used remotely should have a fine-grained interface. Whenever two objects communicate you have to choose which to use. If the object could ever be in separate processes you have to use the coarse-grained interface and pay the cost of the harder programming model. Obviously, it only makes sense to pay that cost when you need to, and so you need to minimize the amount of inter-process collaborations.

For these reasons you can't just take a group of classes that you design in the world of a single process, throw CORBA or some such at them, and come up with a distributed model. Distribution design is more than that. If you base your distribution strategy on a classes, you'll end up with a system that does a lot of remote calls and thus needs awkward coarse-grained interfaces. In the end, even with coarse-grained interfaces on every remotable class, you'll still end up with too many remote calls and a system that's awkward to modify as a bonus.

Hence, we get to my **First Law of Distributed Object Design:** Don't distribute your objects!

How, then, do you effectively use multiple processors? In most cases the way to go is clustering (see Figure 7.2). Put all the classes into a single process and then run multiple copies of that process on the various nodes. That way each process uses local calls to get the job done and thus does things faster. You can

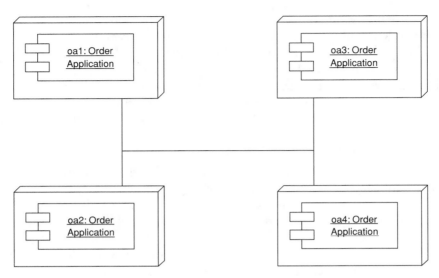

Figure 7.2 *Clustering involves putting several copies of the same application on different nodes.*

also use fine-grained interfaces for all the classes within the process and thus get better maintainability with a simpler programming model.

Where You Have to Distribute

So you want to minimize distribution boundaries and utilize your nodes through clustering as much as possible. The rub is that there are limits to that approach—that is, places where you need to separate the processes. If you're sensible, you'll fight like a cornered rat to eliminate as many of them as you can, but you won't eliminate them all.

- One obvious separation is between the traditional clients and servers of business software. PCs on users' desktops are different nodes to shared repositories of data. Since they're different machines you need separate processes that communicate. The client–server divide is a typical inter-process divide.

- A second divide often occurs between server-based application software (the application server) and the database. Of course, you don't have to do this. You can run all your application software in the database process itself using such things as stored procedures. But often that's not so practical, so you have to have separate processes. They may run on the same machine, but once you have separate processes you immediately have to have to pay most of the costs in remote calls. Fortunately, SQL is designed as a remote interface, so you can usually arrange things to minimize that cost.

- Another separation in process may occur in a Web system between the Web server and the application server. All things being equal it's best to run the Web and application servers in a single process, but all things aren't always equal.

- You may have to separate because of vendor differences. If you're using a software package, it will often run in its own process, so again you're distributing. At least a good package will have a coarse-grained interface.

- And finally there may be some genuine reason that you have to split your application server software. You should sell any grandparent you can get your hands on to avoid this, but cases do come up. Then you just have to hold your nose and divide your software into remote, coarse-grained components.

The overriding theme, in Colleen Roe's memorable phrase, is to be "parsimonious with object distribution." Sell your favorite grandma first if you possibly can.

Working with the Distribution Boundary

As you design your system you need to limit your distribution boundaries as much as possible, but where you have them you need to take them into account. Every remote call travels on the cyber equivalent of a horse and carriage. All sorts of places in the system will change shape to minimize remote calls. That's pretty much the expected price.

However, you can still design within a single process using fine-grained objects. The key is to use them internally and place coarse-grained objects at the distribution boundaries, whose sole role is to provide a remote interface to the fine-grained objects. The coarse-grained objects don't really do anything but delegate so they act as a facade for the fine-grained objects. This facade is there only for distribution purposes—hence the name *Remote Facade (388)*.

Using a *Remote Facade (388)* helps minimize the difficulties that the coarse-grained interface introduces. This way only the objects that really need a remote service get the coarse-grained method, and it's obvious to the developers that they're paying that cost. Transparency has its virtues, but you don't want to be transparent about a potential remote call.

By keeping the coarse-grained interfaces as mere facades, however, you allow people to use the fine-grained objects whenever they know they are running in the same process. This makes the whole distribution policy much more explicit. Hand in hand with *Remote Facade (388)* is *Data Transfer Object (401)*. Not only do you need coarse-grained methods, you also need to transfer coarse-grained objects. When you ask for an address, you need to send that information in one block. You usually can't send the domain object itself, because it's tied in a Web of fine-grained local inter-object references. So you take all the data that the client needs and bundle it in a particular object for the transfer— hence the term *Data Transfer Object (401)*. (Many people in the enterprise Java community use the term *value object* for this, but this causes a clash with other meanings of the term *Value Object (486)*). The *Data Transfer Object (401)* appears on both sides of the wire, so it's important that it not reference anything that isn't shared over the wire. This boils down to the fact that a *Data Transfer Object (401)* usually only references other *Data Transfer Objects (401)* and fundamental objects such as strings.

Another route to distribution is to have a broker that migrates objects between processes. The idea here is to use a *Lazy Load (200)* scheme where, instead of lazy reading from a database, you move objects across the wire. The hard part of this is ensuring that you don't end up with lots of remote calls. I haven't seen anyone try this in an application, but some O/R mapping tools (e.g., TOPLink) have this facility, and I've heard some good reports about it.

Interfaces for Distribution

Traditionally the interfaces for distributed components have been based on remote procedure calls, either with global procedures or as methods on objects. In the last couple of years, however, we've begun to see interfaces based on XML over HTTP. SOAP is probably going to be the most common form of this interface, but many people have experimented with it for some years.

XML-based HTTP communication is handy for several reasons. It easily allows a lot of data to be sent, in structured form, in a single roundtrip. Since remote calls need to be minimized, that's a good thing. The fact that XML is a common format with parsers available in many platforms allows systems built on very different platforms to communicate, as does the fact that HTTP is pretty universal these days. The fact that XML is textual makes it easy to see what's going across the wire. HTTP is also easy to get through firewalls when security and political reasons often make it difficult to open up other ports.

Even so, an object-oriented interface of classes and methods has value too. Moving all the transferred data into XML structures and strings can add a considerable burden to the remote call. Certainly applications have seen a significant performance improvement by replacing an XML-based interface with a remote call. If both sides of the wire use the same binary mechanism, an XML interface doesn't buy you much other than a jazzier set of acronyms. If you have two systems built with the same platform, then you're better off using the remote call mechanism built into that platform. Web services become handy when you want different platforms to talk to each other. My attitude is to use XML Web services only when a more direct approach isn't possible.

Of course, you can have the best of both worlds by layering an HTTP interface over an object-oriented interface. All calls to the Web server are translated by it into calls on an underlying object-oriented interface. To an extent this gives you the best of both worlds, but it does add complexity since you'll need both the Web server and the machinery for a remote OO interface. Therefore, you should only do this if you need an HTTP as well as a remote OO API or if the facilities of the remote OO API for security and transaction handling make it easier to deal with these issues than using non-remote objects.

In my discussions here I've assumed a synchronous, RPC-based interface. However, although that's what I've described, I actually don't think it's always the best way of handling a distributed system. Increasingly, my preference is for a message-based approach that's inherently asynchronous. Digging into patterns for message-based work is a sizable topic on its own, and that's why I ducked out of it for this book. I hope such a book will appear in the near future, but for the moment all I can do is urge you to look at asynchronous, message-based approaches. In particular I think they're the best use of Web services, even though most of the examples published so far are synchronous.

Chapter 8

Putting It All Together

So far these narratives have looked at one aspect of a system and explored the various options for handling it. Now it's time to sweep everything together and start to answer the tricky question of what patterns to use when designing an enterprise application.

The advice in this chapter is in many ways a repeat of the advice given in earlier chapters. I must admit that I've wondered whether this chapter was needed. However, I felt it was good to put all the discussion in context now that, I hope, you have at least an outline of the full scope of the patterns in this book.

As I write this, I'm very conscious of the limitations of my advice. Frodo said in *Lord of the Rings*, "Go not to the Elves for counsel, for they will say both no and yes." While I'm not claiming any immortal knowledge, I certainly understand their answer that advice is often a dangerous gift. If you're reading this to make architectural decisions for your project, you know far more about your project than I do. One of the biggest frustrations in being a pundit is that people often come up to me at a conference or send an e-mail message asking for advice on their architectural or process decisions. There's no way you can give particular advice on the basis of a five-minute description. I write this chapter with even less knowledge of your predicament.

So, read this chapter in the spirit in which it's presented. I don't know all the answers, and I certainly don't know your questions. Use this advice to prod your thinking, but don't use it as a replacement for your thinking. In the end you have to make, and live with, the decisions yourself.

One good thing is that your decisions are not cast forever in stone. Architectural refactoring is hard, and we're still ignorant of its full costs, but it isn't impossible. Here the best advice I can give is that, even if you dislike the full story of extreme programming [Beck XP], you should still consider seriously three technical practices: continuous integration [Fowler CI], test driven development [Beck TDD], and refactoring [Fowler Refactoring]. These won't be a panacea, but they'll make it much easier for you to change your mind when you discover you need to. And you will need to, unless you're either more fortunate, or more skillful, than anyone I've met to date.

Starting with the Domain Layer

The start of the process is deciding which domain logic approach to go with. The three main contenders are *Transaction Script (110)*, *Table Module (125)*, and *Domain Model (116)*.

As I indicated in Chapter 2 (page 25), the strongest force that drives you through this trio is the complexity of the domain logic, something currently impossible to quantify, or even qualify, with any degree of precision. But other factors also play in the decision, in particular, the difficulty of the connection with a database.

The simplest of the three patterns is *Transaction Script (110)*. It fits with the procedural model that most people are still comfortable with. It nicely encapsulates the logic of each system transaction in a comprehensible script. And it's easy to build on top of a relational database. Its great failing is that it doesn't deal well with complex business logic, being particularly susceptible to duplicate code. If you have a simple catalog application with little more than a shopping cart running off a basic pricing structure, then *Transaction Script (110)* will fill the bill perfectly. However, as your logic gets more complicated your difficulties multiply exponentially.

At the other end of the scale is the *Domain Model (116)*. Hard-core object bigots like myself will have an application no other way. After all, if an application is simple enough to write with *Transaction Scripts (110)*, why should our immense intellects bother with such an unworthy problem? Also, my experiences lead me to have no doubt that with really complex domain logic nothing can handle this hell better than a rich *Domain Model (116)*. Once you get used to working with a *Domain Model (116)* even simple problems can be tackled with ease.

Yet the *Domain Model (116)* has its faults. High on the list is the difficulty of learning how to use a domain model. Object bigots often look down their noses at people who just don't get objects, but the consequence is that a *Domain Model (116)* requires skill if it's to be done well—done poorly it's a disaster. The second big difficulty of a *Domain Model (116)* is its connection to a relational database. Of course, a real object zealot finesses this problem with the subtle flick of an object database. But for many, mostly nontechnical, reasons an object database isn't a possible choice for enterprise applications. The result is the messy relational database connection. Let's face it, object models and relational models don't fit well together. The complexity of many of the O/R mapping patterns I describe is the result.

Table Module (125) represents an attractive middle ground between these poles. It can handle domain logic better than *Transaction Scripts (110)*. Also, while it can't touch a real *Domain Model (116)* on handling complex domain logic, it fits really well with a relational database—and many other things too. If you have an environment such as .NET, where many tools orbit around the all-seeing *Record Set (508)*, then *Table Module (125)* works nicely by playing to the strengths of the relational database and yet representing a reasonable factoring of the domain logic.

In this argument we see that the tools you have also affect your architecture. Sometimes you're able to choose the tools based on the architecture, and in theory that's the way you should go. In practice, however, you often have to match your architecture to your tools. Of the three patterns *Table Module (125)* is the one whose star rises the most when you have tools that match it. It's a particularly strong choice for .NET environments, since so much of the platform is geared around *Record Set (508)*.

If you read the discussion of domain logic in Chapter 2, much of this will seem familiar. Yet I think it's worth repeating here because I really do think this is the central decision. From here we go downward to the database layer, but now the decisions are shaped by the context of your domain layer choice.

Down to the Data Source Layer

Once you've chose your domain layer, you have to figure out how to connect it to your data sources. Your decisions are based on your domain layer choice, so I'll tackle this in separate sections, driven by that choice.

Data Source for *Transaction Script (110)*

The simplest *Transaction Scripts (110)* contain their own database logic, but I avoid that even in the simplest cases. Separating the database delimits two parts that make sense as separate, so I make the separation even in the simplest applications. The database patterns to choose from here are *Row Data Gateway (152)* and *Table Data Gateway (144)*.

The choice between the two depends much on the facilities of your implementation platform and on where you expect the application to go in the future. With a *Row Data Gateway (152)* each record is read into an object with a clear and explicit interface. With *Table Data Gateway (144)* you may have less code to write since you don't need all the accessor code to get at the data, but you end up with a much more implicit interface that relies on accessing a record set structure that's little more than a glorified map.

The key decision, however, lies in the rest of your platform. Having a platform that provides a lot of tools that work well with *Record Set (508)*, particularly UI tools or transactional disconnected record sets, tilts you decisively in the direction of a *Table Data Gateway (144)*.

You usually don't need any of the other O/R mapping patterns in this context. The structural mapping issues are pretty much absent since the in-memory structure maps to the database structure so well. You might consider a *Unit of Work (184)*, but usually it's easy to keep track of what's changed in the script. You don't need to worry about most concurrency issues because the script often corresponds almost exactly to a system transaction. Thus, you can just wrap the whole script in a single transaction. The common exception is where one request pulls data back for editing and the next request tries to save the changes. In this case *Optimistic Offline Lock (416)* is almost always the best choice. Not only is it easier to implement, it also usually fits users' expectations and avoids the problem of a hanging session leaving all sorts of things locked.

Data Source *Table Module (125)*

The main reason to choose *Table Module (125)* is the presence of a good *Record Set (508)* framework. In this case you'll want a database mapping pattern that works well with *Record Sets (508)*, and that leads you inexorably toward *Table Data Gateway (144)*. These two patterns fit together as if it were a match made in heaven.

There's not really anything else you need to add on the data source side with this pattern. In the best cases the *Record Set (508)* has some kind of concurrency control mechanism built in, which effectively turns it into a *Unit of Work (184)*, further reducing hair loss.

Data Source for *Domain Model (116)*

Now things get interesting. In many ways the big weakness of *Domain Model (116)* is that the connection to the database is complicated. The degree of complication depends on the complexity of this pattern.

If your *Domain Model (116)* is fairly simple, say a couple of dozen classes that are pretty close to the database, then an *Active Record (160)* makes sense.

If you want to decouple things a bit, you can use either *Table Data Gateway (144)* or *Row Data Gateway (152)* to do that. Whether you separate or not isn't a huge deal either way.

As things get more complicated, you'll need to consider *Data Mapper (165)*. This is the approach that delivers on the promise of keeping your *Domain Model (116)* as independent as possible of all the other layers. But *Data Mapper (165)* is also the most complicated one to implement. Unless you either have a strong team or you can find some simplifications that make the mapping easier to do, I'd strongly suggest getting a mapping tool.

Once you choose *Data Mapper (165)* most of the patterns in the O/R mapping section come into play. In particular I heartily recommend *Unit of Work (184)*, which acts as a focal point for concurrency control.

The Presentation Layer

In many ways the presentation is relatively independent of the choice of the lower layers. Your first question is whether to provide a rich-client interface or an HTML browser interface. A rich client will give you a nicer UI, but then you need a certain amount of control and deployment of your clients. My preference is to pick an HTML browser if you can get away with it and a rich client if that's not possible. Rich clients will usually take more effort to program, but that's because they tend to be more sophisticated, not so much because of the inherent complexities of the technology.

I haven't explored any rich-client patterns in this book, so if you choose one I don't really have anything further to say.

If you go the HTML route, you have to decide how to structure your application. I certainly recommend the *Model View Controller (330)* as the underpinning for your design. That done, you're left with two decisions, one for the controller and one for the view.

Your tooling may well make your choice for you. If you use Visual Studio, the easiest way to go is *Page Controller (333)* and *Template View (350)*. If you use Java, you have a choice of Web frameworks to consider. Popular at the moment is Struts, which will lead you to a *Front Controller (344)* and a *Template View (350)*.

Given a freer choice, I'd recommend *Page Controller (333)* if your site is more document oriented, particularly if you have a mix of static and dynamic pages. More complex navigation and UI lead you toward a *Front Controller (344)*.

On the view front the choice between *Template View (350)* and *Transform View (361)* depends on whether your team uses server pages or XSLT in programming. *Template Views (350)* have the edge at the moment, although I rather like the added testability of *Transform View (361)*. If you have the need to display a common site with multiple looks and feels, you should consider *Two Step View (365)*.

How you communicate with the lower layers depends on what kind of layers they are and whether they're always going to be in the same process. My preference is to have everything run in one process if you can—that way you don't have to worry about slow inter-process calls. If you can't do that, you should wrap your domain layer with *Remote Facade (388)* and use *Data Transfer Object (401)* to communicate to the Web server.

Some Technology-Specific Advice

In most of this book I'm trying to bring out the common experience of doing projects on many different platforms. Experience with Forte, CORBA, and Smalltalk translates very effectively into developing with Java and .NET. The only reason I've concentrating on Java and .NET environments is that they look like the most common platforms for enterprise application development in the future. (Although I'd like to see the dynamically typed scripting languages, in particular Python and Ruby, give them a run for their money.)

In this section I want to apply the above advice to these two platforms. As soon as I do this, though, I'm in danger of dating myself. Technologies change much more rapidly than these patterns, so as you read remember that I'm writing in early 2002, when everyone is saying that economic recovery is just around the corner.

Java and J2EE

Currently the big debate in the Java world is exactly how valuable Enterprise Java Beans are. After as many final drafts as The Who had farewell concerts, the EJB 2.0 specification has finally appeared. But you don't *need* EJB to build a good J2EE application, despite what EJB vendors tell you. You can do a great deal with POJOs (plain old Java objects) and JDBC.

The design alternatives for J2EE vary in terms of the patterns you're using, and again they break out by domain logic.

If you use *Transaction Script (110)* on top of some form of *Gateway (466)*, the common approach with EJB at the moment is to use session beans as a *Transaction Script (110)* and entity beans as a *Row Data Gateway (152)*. This is a pretty reasonable architecture if your domain logic is sufficiently modest.

However, one problem with such a beany approach is that it's hard to get rid of the EJB server if you find you don't need it and you don't want to cough up the license fees. The non-EJB approach is a POJO for the *Transaction Script (110)* on top of either a *Row Data Gateway (152)* or a *Table Data Gateway (144)*. If JDBC 2.0 row sets get more acceptance, that's a reason to use them as *Record Sets (508)* and that leads to a *Table Data Gateway (144)*.

If you're using a *Domain Model (116)*, the current orthodoxy is to use entity beans. If your *Domain Model (116)* is pretty simple and matches your database well, doing that makes reasonable sense and your entity beans will then be *Active Records (160)*. It's still good practice to wrap your entity beans with session beans acting as *Remote Facades (388)* (although you can also think of CMP as a *Data Mapper (165)*). However, if your *Domain Model (116)* is more complex, you want it to be entirely independent of the EJB structure so that you can write, run, and test your domain logic without having to deal with the vagaries of the EJB container. In that model I would use POJOs for the *Domain Model (116)* and wrap them with session beans acting as *Remote Facades (388)*. If you choose not to use EJB, I would run the whole app in the Web server and avoid any remote calls between presentation and domain. If you're using POJO *Domain Model (116)*, I would also use POJOs for the *Data Mappers (165)*—either using an O/R mapping tool or rolling something myself if I felt up to it.

If you use entity beans in any context, avoid giving them a remote interface. I never understood the point of giving entity beans a remote interface in the first place. Entity beans are usually used as *Domain Models (116)* or as *Row Data Gateways (152)*. In either case they need a fine-grained interface to play those roles well. As I hope I've drilled into your psyche, however, that a remote interface must always be coarse-grained, so keep your entity beans local only. (The exception to this is the *Composite Entity* pattern from [Alur et al.], which is a different way of using entity beans and not one I find very useful.)

At the moment the *Table Module (125)* isn't common in the Java world. It will be interesting to see if more tooling surrounds the JDBC row set—if it does this pattern could become a viable approach. In this case the POJO approach fits best, although you can also wrap the *Table Module (125)* with session beans acting as *Remote Facades (388)* and returning *Record Sets (508)*.

.NET

Looking at .NET, Visual Studio, and the history of application development in the Microsoft world, the dominant pattern is *Table Module (125)*. Although object bigots tend to dismiss this as meaning only that Microsofties don't get objects, *Table Module (125)* does present a valuable compromise between *Transaction Script (110)* and *Domain Model (116)*, with an impressive set of tools that take advantage of the ubiquitous data set acting as a *Record Set (508)*

As a result *Table Module (125)* has to be the default choice for this platform. Indeed, I see no point at all in using *Transaction Scripts (110)* except in the very simplest of cases, and even then they should act on and return data sets.

This doesn't mean that you can't use *Domain Model (116)*. Indeed, you can build a *Domain Model (116)* just as easily in .NET as you can in any other OO environment. However, the tools don't give you the extra help they do for *Table Modules (125)*, so I would tolerate more complexity before I felt the need to shift to a *Domain Model (116)*.

The current hype in .NET is all about Web services, but I wouldn't use Web services inside an application, I'd use them, as in Java, as a presentation to allow applications to integrate. There's no real reason to make the Web server and the domain logic into separate processes in a .NET application, so *Remote Facade (388)* is less useful here.

Stored Procedures

There's usually a fair bit of debate over stored procedures. They're often the fastest way to do things since they run in the same process as your database and thus reduce the laggardly remote calls. However, most stored procedure environments don't give you good structuring mechanisms for your stored procedures, and stored procedures will lock you into a particular database vendor. (A nice way to avoid these problems is Oracle's approach of allowing you to run Java applications inside your database process; this is equivalent to putting your whole domain logic layer inside the database. For the moment this still leaves you with some vendor lockin, but it at least reduces porting costs.)

For the reasons of modularity and portability a lot of people avoid using stored procedures for business logic. I tend to side with that view unless there's a strong performance gain to be had, which, to be fair, there often is. In that case I take a method from the domain layer and happily move it into a stored procedure. I do this only on clear performance problem areas, treating it as an optimization step rather than as an architectural principle. ([Nilsson] presents a good argument for using stored procedures more widely.)

A common way of using stored procedures is to control access to a database, along the lines of a *Table Data Gateway (144)*. I don't have any strong feelings about whether or not to do this, and from what I've seen there's no strong reasons either way. In any case I prefer to isolate the database access with the same patterns, whether database access is through stored procedures or more regular SQL.

Web Services

As I write this, the general consensus among pundits is that Web services will make reuse a reality and drive system integrators out of business, but I'm not holding my breath. Within these patterns Web services don't play a huge role because they're about application integration rather than application construction. You shouldn't try to break up a single application into Web services that talk to each other unless you really need to. Rather, build your application and expose various parts of it as Web services, treating those Web services as *Remote Facades (388)*. Above all, don't let all the buzz about how easy it is to build Web services make you forget about the First Law of Distributed Object Design (page 89) .

Although most published examples I've seen use Web services synchronously, rather like an XML RPC call, I prefer them as asynchronous and message based. While I don't have any patterns for that here (this book is big enough as it is), I expect that we'll see some patterns for asynchronous messaging in the next few years.

Other Layering Schemes

I've built my discussion around three primary layers, but my approach to layering isn't the only one that makes sense. Other good architectural books have layering schemes, and they all have value. It's worth looking at these other schemes and comparing them to what I have here. You may find they make more sense for your application.

First up is what I'll call the Brown model, which is discussed in [Brown et al.] (see Table 8.1). This model has five layers: presentation, controller/mediator, domain, data mapping, and data source. Essentially it places additional mediating layers between the basic three layers. The controller/mediator mediates between the presentation and domain layers, while the data mapping layer mediates between the domain and data source layers.

I find that the mediating layers are useful some of the time but not all of the time, so I describe them in terms of patterns. The *Application Controller (379)* is the mediator between the presentation and domain, and the *Data Mapper (165)* is the mediator between the data source and the domain. For organizing this

Table 8.1 *Brown Layers*

Brown	Fowler
Presentation	Presentation
Controller/mediator	Presentation (*Application Controller (379)*)
Domain	Domain
Data mapping	Data source (*Data Mapper (165)*)
Data source	Data source

book, I've described *Application Controller (379)* in the presentation section (Chapter 14) and *Data Mapper (165)* in the data source section (Chapter 10).

For me, then, the addition of mediating layers, frequently but not always useful, represents an optional extra in the design. My approach is to always think of the three base layers, see if any of them is getting too complex, and if so add the mediating layer to separate the functionality.

Another good layering scheme for J2EE appears in CoreJ2EE patterns [Alur et al.] (see Table 8.2). Here the layers are client, presentation, business, integration, and resource. Simple correspondences exist for the business and integration layers. The resource layer comprises external services that the integration layer connects to. The main difference is that they split the presentation layer between the part that runs on the client (client) and the part that runs on a server (presentation). This is often a useful split, but again it's not one that's needed all the time.

The Microsoft DNA architect [Kirtland] defines three layers: presentation, business, and data access, that correspond pretty directly to the three layers I

Table 8.2 *Core J2EE Layers*

Core J2EE	Fowler
Client	Presentation that runs on client (e.g., rich-client systems)
Presentation	Presentation that runs on server (e.g., HTTP handlers, server pages)
Business	Domain
Integration	Data source
Resource	External resource that data source communicates with

Table 8.3 *Microsoft DNA Layers*

Microsoft DNA	Fowler
Presentation	Presentation
Business	Domain
Data access	Data source

use here (see Table 8.3). The biggest shift occurs in the way that data is passed up from the data access layers. In Microsoft DNA all the layers operate on record sets that result from SQL queries issued by the data access layer. This introduces an apparent coupling in that both the business and the presentation layers know about the database.

The way I look at this is that in DNA the record set acts as a *Data Transfer Object (401)* between layers. The business layer can modify the record set on its way up to the presentation or even create one itself (that is rare). Although this form of communication is in many ways unwieldy, it has the big advantage of allowing the presentation to use data-aware GUI controls, even on data that's been modified by the business layer.

In this case the domain layer is structured in the form of *Table Modules (125)* and the data source layer uses *Table Data Gateways (144)*.

[Marinescu] has five layers (see Table 8.4). The presentation is split into two layers, reflecting the separation of an *Application Controller (379)*. The domain is also split, with a *Service Layer (133)* built on a *Domain Model (116)*, reflecting the common idea of splitting a domain layer into two parts. This is a common approach, reinforced by the limitations of EJB as a *Domain Model (116)* (see page 118).

Table 8.4 *Marinescu Layers*

Marinescu	Fowler
Presentation	Presentation
Application	Presentation (*Application Controller (379)*)
Services	Domain (*Service Layer (133)*)
Domain	Domain (*Domain Model (116)*)
Persistence	Data source

The idea of splitting a services layer from a domain layer is based on a separation of workflow logic from pure domain logic. The services layer typically includes logic that's particular to a single use case and also some communication with other infrastructures, such as messaging. Whether to have separate services and domain layers is a matter some debate. I tend to look as it as occasionally useful rather than mandatory, but designers I respect disagree with me on this.

[Nilsson] uses one of the more complex layering schemes (see Table 8.5). Mapping to this scheme is made a bit more complex by the fact that Nilsson uses stored procedures extensively, and encourages domain logic in them for performance reasons. I'm uncomfortable with putting domain logic in stored procedures, as it can make an application much harder to maintain. On occasion, however, it's a valuable optimization technique. Nilsson's stored procedure layers contain both data source and domain logic.

Like [Marinescu], Nilsson uses separate application and domain layers for domain logic. He suggests that you can skip the domain layer in a small system, which is similar to my view that a *Domain Model (116)* is less worthwhile for smaller systems.

Table 8.5 *Nilsson Layers*

Nilsson	Fowler
Consumer	Presentation
Consumer helper	Presentation (*Application Controller (379)*)
Application	Domain (*Service Layer (133)*)
Domain	Domain (*Domain Model (116)*)
Persistence access	Data source
Public stored procedures	Data source (may include some domain)
Private stored procedures	Data source (may include some domain)

PART 2

The Patterns

Chapter 9

Domain Logic Patterns

Transaction Script

Organizes business logic by procedures where each procedure handles a single request from the presentation.

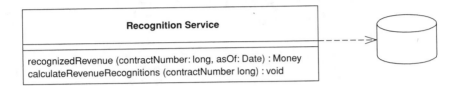

Most business applications can be thought of as a series of transactions. A transaction may view some information as organized in a particular way, another will make changes to it. Each interaction between a client system and a server system contains a certain amount of logic. In some cases this can be as simple as displaying information in the database. In others it may involve many steps of validations and calculations.

A *Transaction Script* organizes all this logic primarily as a single procedure, making calls directly to the database or through a thin database wrapper. Each transaction will have its own *Transaction Script*, although common subtasks can be broken into subprocedures.

How It Works

With *Transaction Script* the domain logic is primarily organized by the transactions that you carry out with the system. If your need is to book a hotel room, the logic to check room availability, calculate rates, and update the database is found inside the Book Hotel Room procedure.

For simple cases there isn't much to say about how you organize this. Of course, as with any other program you should structure the code into modules in a way that makes sense. Unless the transaction is particularly complicated, that won't be much of a challenge. One of the benefits of this approach is that you don't need to worry about what other transactions are doing. Your task is to get the input, interrogate the database, munge, and save your results to the database.

Where you put the *Transaction Script* will depend on how you organize your layers. It may be in a server page, a CGI script, or a distributed session object. My preference is to separate *Transaction Scripts* as much as you can. At the very least put them in distinct subroutines; better still, put them in classes separate from those that handle presentation and data source. In addition, don't have any calls from the *Transaction Scripts* to any presentation logic; that will make it easier to modify the code and test the *Transaction Scripts*.

You can organize your *Transaction Scripts* into classes in two ways. The most common is to have several *Transaction Scripts* in a single class, where each class defines a subject area of related *Transaction Scripts*. This is straightforward and the best bet for most cases. The other way is to have each *Transaction Script* in its own class (Figure 9.1), using the Command pattern [Gang of Four]. In this case you define a supertype for your commands that specifies some execute method in which *Transaction Script* logic fits. The advantage of this is that it allows you to manipulate instances of scripts as objects at runtime, although I've rarely seen a need to do this with the kinds of systems that use *Transaction Scripts* to organize domain logic. Of course, you can ignore classes completely in many languages and just use global functions. However, you'll often find that instantiating a new object helps with threading issues as it makes it easier to isolate data.

I use the term *Transaction Script* because most of the time you'll have one *Transaction Script* for each database transaction. This isn't a 100 percent rule, but it's true to the first approximation.

When to Use It

The glory of *Transaction Script* is its simplicity. Organizing logic this way is natural for applications with only a small amount of logic, and it involves very little overhead either in performance or in understanding.

As the business logic gets more complicated, however, it gets progressively harder to keep it in a well-designed state. One particular problem to watch for

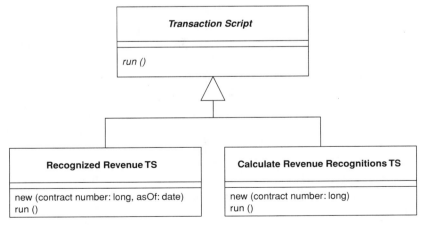

Figure 9.1 *Using commands for* Transaction Script.

is its duplication between transactions. Since the whole point is to handle one transaction, any common code tends to be duplicated.

Careful factoring can alleviate many of these problems, but more complex business domains need to build a *Domain Model (116)*. A *Domain Model (116)* will give you many more options in structuring the code, increasing readability and decreasing duplication.

It's hard to quantify the cutover level, especially when you're more familiar with one pattern than the other. You can refactor a *Transaction Script* design to a *Domain Model (116)* design, but it's a harder change than it otherwise needs to be. Therefore, an early shot is often the best way to move forward.

However much of an object bigot you become, don't rule out *Transaction Script*. There are a lot of simple problems out there, and a simple solution will get you up and running much faster.

The Revenue Recognition Problem

For this pattern, and others that talk about domain logic, I'm going to use the same problem as an illustration. To avoid typing the problem statement several times, I'm just putting it in here.

Revenue recognition is a common problem in business systems. It's all about when you can actually count the money you receive on your books. If I sell you a cup of coffee, it's a simple matter: I give you the coffee, I take your money, and I count the money to the books that nanosecond. For many things it gets complicated, however. Say you pay me a retainer to be available that year. Even if you pay me some ridiculous fee today, I may not be able to put it on my books right away because the service is to be performed over the course of a year. One approach might be to count only one-twelfth of that fee for each month in the year, since you might pull out of the contract after a month when you realize that writing has atrophied my programming skills.

The rules for revenue recognition are many, various, and volatile. Some are set by regulation, some by professional standards, and some by company policy. Revenue tracking ends up being quite a complex problem.

I don't fancy delving into the complexity right now, so instead we'll imagine a company that sells three kinds of products: word processors, databases, and spreadsheets. According to the rules, when you sign a contract for a word processor you can book all the revenue right away. If it's a spreadsheet, you can book one-third today, one-third in sixty days, and one-third in ninety days. If it's a database, you can book one-third today, one-third in thirty days, and one-third in sixty days. There's no basis for these rules other than my own fevered imagination. I'm told that the real rules are equally rational.

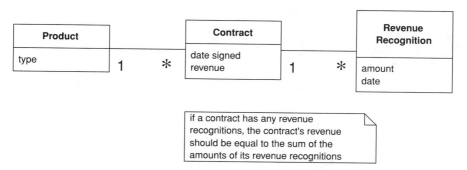

Figure 9.2 *A conceptual model for simplified revenue recognition. Each contract has multiple revenue recognitions that indicate when the various parts of the revenue should be recognized.*

Example: Revenue Recognition (Java)

This example uses two transaction scripts: one to calculate the revenue recognitions for a contract and one to tell how much revenue on a contract has been recognized by a certain date. The database structure has three tables: one for the products, one for the contracts, and one for the revenue recognitions.

```
CREATE TABLE products (ID int primary key, name varchar, type varchar)
CREATE TABLE contracts (ID int primary key, product int, revenue decimal, dateSigned date)
CREATE TABLE revenueRecognitions (contract int, amount decimal, recognizedOn date,
                        PRIMARY KEY (contract, recognizedOn))
```

The first script calculates the amount of recognition due by a particular day. I can do this in two stages: In the first I select the appropriate rows in the revenue recognitions table; in the second I sum up the amounts.

Many *Transaction Script* designs have *scripts* that operate directly on the database, putting SQL code in the procedure. Here I'm using a simple *Table Data Gateway (144)* to wrap the SQL queries. Since this example is so simple, I'm using a single gateway rather than one for each table. I can define an appropriate find method on the gateway.

```
class Gateway...

    public ResultSet findRecognitionsFor(long contractID, MfDate asof) throws SQLException{
        PreparedStatement stmt = db.prepareStatement(findRecognitionsStatement);
        stmt.setLong(1, contractID);
        stmt.setDate(2, asof.toSqlDate());
        ResultSet result = stmt.executeQuery();
        return result;
    }
```

```
private static final String findRecognitionsStatement =
    "SELECT amount " +
    "  FROM revenueRecognitions " +
    "  WHERE contract = ? AND recognizedOn <= ?";
private Connection db;
```

I then use the script to sum up based on the result set passed back from the gateway.

class RecognitionService...

```
public Money recognizedRevenue(long contractNumber, MfDate asOf) {
    Money result = Money.dollars(0);
    try {
        ResultSet rs = db.findRecognitionsFor(contractNumber, asOf);
        while (rs.next()) {
            result = result.add(Money.dollars(rs.getBigDecimal("amount")));
        }
        return result;
    } catch (SQLException e) {throw new ApplicationException (e);
    }
}
```

When the calculation is as simple as this, you can replace the in-memory script with a call to a SQL statement that uses an aggregate function to sum the amounts.

For calculating the revenue recognitions on an existing contract, I use a similar split. The script on the service carries out the business logic.

class RecognitionService...

```
public void calculateRevenueRecognitions(long contractNumber) {
    try {
        ResultSet contracts = db.findContract(contractNumber);
        contracts.next();
        Money totalRevenue = Money.dollars(contracts.getBigDecimal("revenue"));
        MfDate recognitionDate = new MfDate(contracts.getDate("dateSigned"));
        String type = contracts.getString("type");
        if (type.equals("S")){
            Money[] allocation = totalRevenue.allocate(3);
            db.insertRecognition
                (contractNumber, allocation[0], recognitionDate);
            db.insertRecognition
                (contractNumber, allocation[1], recognitionDate.addDays(60));
            db.insertRecognition
                (contractNumber, allocation[2], recognitionDate.addDays(90));
        } else if (type.equals("W")){
            db.insertRecognition(contractNumber, totalRevenue, recognitionDate);
        } else if (type.equals("D")) {
            Money[] allocation = totalRevenue.allocate(3);
            db.insertRecognition
                (contractNumber, allocation[0], recognitionDate);
```

```
        db.insertRecognition
            (contractNumber, allocation[1], recognitionDate.addDays(30));
        db.insertRecognition
            (contractNumber, allocation[2], recognitionDate.addDays(60));
    }
  } catch (SQLException e) {throw new ApplicationException (e);
  }
}
```

Notice that I'm using *Money (488)* to carry out the allocation. When splitting an amount three ways it's very easy to lose a penny.

The *Table Data Gateway (144)* provides support on the SQL. First there's a finder for a contract.

```
class Gateway...

    public ResultSet findContract (long contractID) throws SQLException{
        PreparedStatement stmt = db.prepareStatement(findContractStatement);
        stmt.setLong(1, contractID);
        ResultSet result = stmt.executeQuery();
        return result;
    }
    private static final String findContractStatement =
        "SELECT * " +
        "  FROM contracts c, products p " +
        "  WHERE ID = ? AND c.product = p.ID";
```

And secondly there's a wrapper for the insert.

```
class Gateway...

    public void insertRecognition (long contractID, Money amount, MfDate asof) throws SQLException {
        PreparedStatement stmt = db.prepareStatement(insertRecognitionStatement);
        stmt.setLong(1, contractID);
        stmt.setBigDecimal(2, amount.amount());
        stmt.setDate(3, asof.toSqlDate());
        stmt.executeUpdate();
    }
    private static final String insertRecognitionStatement =
        "INSERT INTO revenueRecognitions VALUES (?, ?, ?)";
```

In a Java system the recognition service might be a regular class or a session bean.

As you compare this to the example in *Domain Model (116)*, unless your mind is as twisted as mine, you'll probably be thinking that this is much simpler. The harder thing to imagine is what happens as the rules get more complicated. Typical revenue recognition rules get very involved, varying not just by product but also by date (if the contract was signed before April 15 this rule applies . . .). It's difficult to keep a coherent design with *Transaction Script* once things get that complicated, which is why object bigots like me prefer using a *Domain Model (116)* in these circumstances.

Domain Model

An object model of the domain that incorporates
both behavior and data.

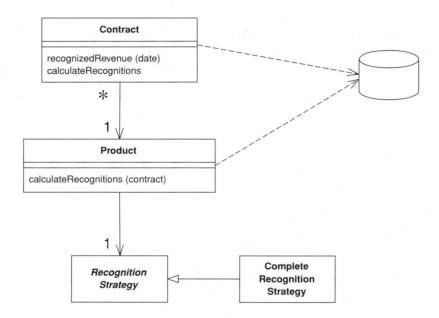

At its worst business logic can be very complex. Rules and logic describe many different cases and slants of behavior, and it's this complexity that objects were designed to work with. A *Domain Model* creates a web of interconnected objects, where each object represents some meaningful individual, whether as large as a corporation or as small as a single line on an order form.

How It Works

Putting a *Domain Model* in an application involves inserting a whole layer of objects that model the business area you're working in. You'll find objects that mimic the data in the business and objects that capture the rules the business uses. Mostly the data and process are combined to cluster the processes close to the data they work with.

An OO domain model will often look similar to a database model, yet it will still have a lot of differences. A *Domain Model* mingles data and process, has multivalued attributes and a complex web of associations, and uses inheritance.

As a result I see two styles of *Domain Model* in the field. A simple *Domain Model* looks very much like the database design with mostly one domain object for each database table. A rich *Domain Model* can look different from the database design, with inheritance, strategies, and other [Gang of Four] patterns, and complex webs of small interconnected objects. A rich *Domain Model* is better for more complex logic, but is harder to map to the database. A simple *Domain Model* can use *Active Record (160)*, whereas a rich *Domain Model* requires *Data Mapper (165)*.

Since the behavior of the business is subject to a lot of change, it's important to be able to modify, build, and test this layer easily. As a result you'll want the minimum of coupling from the *Domain Model* to other layers in the system. You'll notice that a guiding force of many layering patterns is to keep as few dependencies as possible between the domain model and other parts of the system.

With a *Domain Model* there are a number of different scopes you might use. The simplest case is a single-user application where the whole object graph is read from a file and put into memory. A desktop application may work this way, but it's less common for a multitiered IS application simply because there are too many objects. Putting every object into memory consumes too much memory and takes too long. The beauty of object-oriented databases is that they give the impression of doing this while moving objects between memory and disk.

Without an OO database you have to do this yourself. Usually a session will involve pulling in an object graph of all the objects involved in it. This will certainly not be all objects and usually not all the classes. Thus, if you're looking at a set of contracts you might pull in only the products referenced by contracts within your working set. If you're just performing calculations on contracts and revenue recognition objects, you may not pull in any product objects at all. Exactly what you pull into memory is governed by your database mapping objects.

If you need the same object graph between calls to the server, you have to save the server state somewhere, which is the subject of the section on saving server state (page 81).

A common concern with domain logic is bloated domain objects. As you build a screen to manipulate orders you'll notice that some of the order behavior is only needed only for it. If you put these responsibilities on the order, the risk is that the Order class will become too big because it's full of responsibilities that are only used in a single use case. This concern leads people to consider whether some responsibility is general, in which case it should sit in the order class, or specific, in which case it should sit in some usage-specific class, which might be a *Transaction Script (110)* or perhaps the presentation itself.

The problem with separating usage-specific behavior is that it can lead to duplication. Behavior that's separated from the order is harder to find, so people tend to not see it and duplicate it instead. Duplication can quickly lead to more complexity and inconsistency, but I've found that bloating occurs much less frequently than predicted. If it does occur, it's relatively easy to see and not difficult to fix. My advice is not to separate usage-specific behavior. Put it all in the object that's the natural fit. Fix the bloating when, and if, it becomes a problem.

Java Implementation

There's always a lot of heat generated when people talk about developing a *Domain Model* in J2EE. Many of the teaching materials and introductory J2EE books suggest that you use entity beans to develop a domain model, but there are some serious problems with this approach, at least with the current (2.0) specification.

Entity beans are most useful when you use Container Managed Persistence (CMP). Indeed, I would say there's little point in using entity beans without CMP. However, CMP is a limited form of object-relational mapping, and it can't support many of the patterns that you need in a rich *Domain Model*.

Entity beans can't be re-entrant. That is, if you call out from one entity bean into another object, that other object (or any object it calls) can't call back into the first entity bean. A rich *Domain Model* often uses re-entrancy, so this is a handicap. It's made worse by the fact that it's hard to spot re-entrant behavior. As a result, some people say that one entity bean should never call another. While this avoids re-entrancy, it very much cripples the advantages using a *Domain Model*.

A *Domain Model* should use fine-grained objects with fine-grained interfaces. Entity beans may be remotable (prior to version 2.0 they had to be). If you have remote objects with fine-grained interfaces you get terrible performance. You can avoid this problem quite easily by only using local interfaces for your entity beans in a *Domain Model*.

To run with entity beans you need a container and a database connected. This will increase build times and also increase the time to do test runs since the tests have to execute against a database. Entity beans are also tricky to debug.

The alternative is to use normal Java objects, although this often causes a surprised reaction—it's amazing how many people think that you can't run regular Java objects in an EJB container. I've come to the conclusion that people forget about regular Java objects because they haven't got a fancy name. That's why, while preparing for a talk in 2000, Rebecca Parsons, Josh Mackenzie, and I gave them one: POJOs (plain old Java objects). A POJO domain model is easy to put together, is quick to build, can run and test outside an EJB container, and is independent of EJB (maybe that's why EJB vendors don't encourage you to use them).

My view on the whole is that using entity beans as a *Domain Model* works if you have pretty modest domain logic. If so, you can build a *Domain Model* that has a simple relationship with the database: where there's mostly one entity bean class per database table. If you have a richer domain logic with inheritance, strategies, and other more sophisticated patterns, you're better off with a POJO domain model and *Data Mapper (165)*, using a commercial tool or with a homegrown layer.

The biggest frustration for me with the use of EJB is that I find a rich *Domain Model* complicated enough to deal with, and I want to keep as independent as possible from the details of the implementation environment. EJB forces itself into your thinking about the *Domain Model*, which means that I have to worry about both the domain and the EJB environment.

When to Use It

If the *how* for a *Domain Model* is difficult because it's such a big subject, the *when* is hard because of both the vagueness and the simplicity of the advice. It all comes down to the complexity of the behavior in your system. If you have complicated and everchanging business rules involving validation, calculations, and derivations, chances are that you'll want an object model to handle them. On the other hand, if you have simple not-null checks and a couple of sums to calculate, a *Transaction Script (110)* is a better bet.

One factor that comes into this is comfortable used the development team is with domain objects. Learning how to design and use a *Domain Model* is a significant exercise—one that has led to many articles on the "paradigm shift" of objects use. It certainly takes practice and coaching to get used to a *Domain Model*, but once used to it I've found that few people want to go back to a *Transaction Script (110)* for any but the simplest problems.

If you're using *Domain Model*, my first choice for database interaction is *Data Mapper (165)*. This will help keep your *Domain Model* independent from the database and is the best approach to handle cases where the *Domain Model* and database schema diverge.

When you use *Domain Model* you may want to consider *Service Layer (133)* to give your *Domain Model* a more distinct API.

Further Reading

Almost any book on OO design will talk about *Domain Models*, since most of what people refer to as OO development is centered around their use.

If you're looking for an introductory book on OO design, my current favorite is [Larman]. For examples of *Domain Model* take a look at [Fowler AP].

[Hay] also gives good examples in a relational context. To build a good *Domain Model* you should have an understanding of conceptual thinking about objects. For this I've always liked [Martin and Odell]. For an understanding of the patterns you'll see in a rich *Domain Model*, or any other OO system, you must read [Gang of Four].

Eric Evans is currently writing a book [Evans] on building *Domain Models*. As I write this I've seen only an early manuscript, but it looks very promising.

Example: Revenue Recognition (Java)

One of the biggest frustrations of describing a *Domain Model* is the fact that any example I show is necessarily simple so you can understand it; yet that simplicity hides the *Domain Model's* strength. You only appreciate these strengths when you have a really complicated domain.

But even if the example can't do justice to why you would want a *Domain Model*, at least it will give you a sense of what one can look like. Therefore, I'm using the same example (page 112) that I used for *Transaction Script (110)*, a little matter of revenue recognition.

An immediate thing to notice is that every class, in this small example (Figure 9.3) contains both behavior and data. Even the humble Revenue Recognition class contains a simple method to find out if that object's value is recognizable on a certain date.

```
class RevenueRecognition...

    private Money amount;
    private MfDate date;
    public RevenueRecognition(Money amount, MfDate date) {
        this.amount = amount;
        this.date = date;
    }
    public Money getAmount() {
        return amount;
    }
    boolean isRecognizableBy(MfDate asOf) {
        return asOf.after(date) || asOf.equals(date);
    }
```

Calculating how much revenue is recognized on a particular date involves both the contract and revenue recognition classes.

```
class Contract...

    private List revenueRecognitions = new ArrayList();
    public Money recognizedRevenue(MfDate asOf) {
        Money result = Money.dollars(0);
        Iterator it = revenueRecognitions.iterator();
```

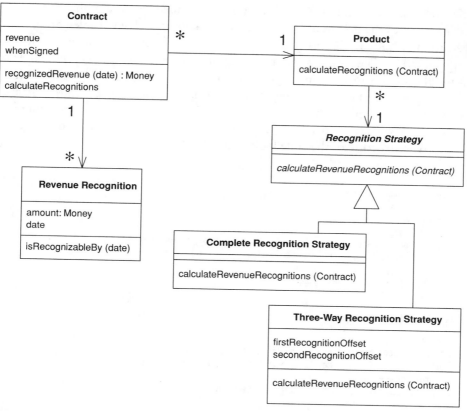

Figure 9.3 *Class diagram of the example classes for a Domain Model.*

```
while (it.hasNext()) {
    RevenueRecognition r = (RevenueRecognition) it.next();
    if (r.isRecognizableBy(asOf))
        result = result.add(r.getAmount());
}
return result;
}
```

A common thing you find in *domain model*s is how multiple classes interact to do even the simplest tasks. This is what often leads to the complaint that with OO programs you spend a lot of time hunting around from class to class trying to find them. There's a lot of merit to this complaint. The value comes as the decision on whether something is recognizable by a certain date gets more complex and as other objects need to know. Containing the behavior on the object that needs to know avoids duplication and reduces coupling between the different objects.

Looking at calculating and creating these revenue recognition objects further demonstrates the notion of lots of little objects. In this case the calculation and creation begin with the customer and are handed off via the product to a strategy hierarchy. The strategy pattern [Gang of Four] is a well-known OO pattern that allows you to combine a group of operations in a small class hierarchy. Each instance of product is connected to a single instance of recognition strategy, which determines which algorithm is used to calculate revenue recognition. In this case we have two subclasses of recognition strategy for the two different cases. The structure of the code looks like this:

```
class Contract...

    private Product product;
    private Money revenue;
    private MfDate whenSigned;
    private Long id;
    public Contract(Product product, Money revenue, MfDate whenSigned) {
        this.product = product;
        this.revenue = revenue;
        this.whenSigned = whenSigned;
    }
```

```
class Product...

    private String name;
    private RecognitionStrategy recognitionStrategy;
    public Product(String name, RecognitionStrategy recognitionStrategy) {
        this.name = name;
        this.recognitionStrategy = recognitionStrategy;
    }
    public static Product newWordProcessor(String name) {
        return new Product(name, new CompleteRecognitionStrategy());
    }
    public static Product newSpreadsheet(String name) {
        return new Product(name, new ThreeWayRecognitionStrategy(60, 90));
    }
    public static Product newDatabase(String name) {
        return new Product(name, new ThreeWayRecognitionStrategy(30, 60));
    }
```

```
class RecognitionStrategy...

    abstract void calculateRevenueRecognitions(Contract contract);
```

```
class CompleteRecognitionStrategy...
    void calculateRevenueRecognitions(Contract contract) {
        contract.addRevenueRecognition(new RevenueRecognition(contract.getRevenue(),
                                                      contract.getWhenSigned()));
    }
```

```
class ThreeWayRecognitionStrategy...

    private int firstRecognitionOffset;
    private int secondRecognitionOffset;
    public ThreeWayRecognitionStrategy(int firstRecognitionOffset,
                    int secondRecognitionOffset)
    {
        this.firstRecognitionOffset = firstRecognitionOffset;
        this.secondRecognitionOffset = secondRecognitionOffset;
    }
    void calculateRevenueRecognitions(Contract contract) {
        Money[] allocation = contract.getRevenue().allocate(3);
        contract.addRevenueRecognition(new RevenueRecognition
            (allocation[0], contract.getWhenSigned()));
        contract.addRevenueRecognition(new RevenueRecognition
            (allocation[1], contract.getWhenSigned().addDays(firstRecognitionOffset)));
        contract.addRevenueRecognition(new RevenueRecognition
            (allocation[2], contract.getWhenSigned().addDays(secondRecognitionOffset)));
    }
```

The great value of the strategies is that they provide well-contained plug points to extend the application. Adding a new revenue recognition algorithm involves creating a new subclass and overriding the calculateRevenueRecognitions method. This makes it easy to extend the algorithmic behavior of the application.

When you create products, you hook them up with the appropriate strategy objects. I'm doing this in my test code.

```
class Tester...

    private Product word = Product.newWordProcessor("Thinking Word");
    private Product calc = Product.newSpreadsheet("Thinking Calc");
    private Product db = Product.newDatabase("Thinking DB");
```

Once everything is set up, calculating the recognitions requires no knowledge of the strategy subclasses.

```
class Contract...

    public void calculateRecognitions() {
        product.calculateRevenueRecognitions(this);
    }
```

```
class Product...

    void calculateRevenueRecognitions(Contract contract) {
        recognitionStrategy.calculateRevenueRecognitions(contract);
    }
```

The OO habit of successive forwarding from object to object moves the behavior to the object most qualified to handle it, but it also resolves much of the conditional behavior. You'll notice that there are no conditionals in this calculation. You set up the decision path when you create the products with the appropriate strategy. Once everything is wired together like this, the algorithms just follow the path. Domain models work very well when you have similar conditionals because the similar conditionals can be factored out into the object structure itself. This moves complexity out of the algorithms and into the relationships between objects. The more similar the logic, the more you find the same network of relationships used by different parts of the system. Any algorithm that's dependent on the type of recognition calculation can follow this particular network of objects.

Notice in this example that I've shown nothing about how the objects are retrieved from, and written to, the database. This is for a couple of reasons. First, mapping a *Domain Model* to a database is always somewhat hard, so I'm chickening out and not providing an example. Second, in many ways the whole point of a *Domain Model* is to hide the database, both from upper layers and from people working the *Domain Model* itself. Thus, hiding it here reflects what it's like to actually program in this environment.

Table Module

*A single instance that handles the business logic for
all rows in a database table or view.*

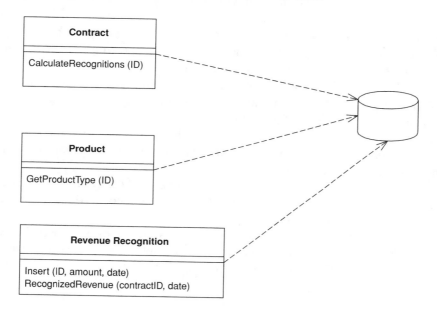

One of the key messages of object orientation is bundling the data with the behavior that uses it. The traditional object-oriented approach is based on objects with identity, along the lines of *Domain Model (116)*. Thus, if we have an Employee class, any instance of it corresponds to a particular employee. This scheme works well because once we have a reference to an employee, we can execute operations, follow relationships, and gather data on him.

One of the problems with *Domain Model (116)* is the interface with relational databases. In many ways this approach treats the relational database like a crazy aunt who's shut up in an attic and whom nobody wants to talk about. As a result you often need considerable programmatic gymnastics to pull data in and out of the database, transforming between two different representations of the data.

A *Table Module* organizes domain logic with one class per table in the database, and a single instance of a class contains the various procedures that will act on the data. The primary distinction with *Domain Model (116)* is that, if you have many orders, a *Domain Model (116)* will have one order object per order while a *Table Module* will have one object to handle all orders.

Table Module

How It Works

The strength of *Table Module* is that it allows you to package the data and behavior together and at the same time play to the strengths of a relational database. On the surface *Table Module* looks much like a regular object. The key difference is that it has no notion of an identity for the objects it's working with. Thus, if you want to obtain the address of an employee, you use a method like `anEmployeeModule.getAddress(long employeeID)`. Every time you want to do something to a particular employee you have to pass in some kind of identity reference. Often this will be the primary key used in the database.

Usually you use *Table Module* with a backing data structure that's table oriented. The tabular data is normally the result of a SQL call and is held in a *Record Set (508)* that mimics a SQL table. The *Table Module* gives you an explicit method-based interface that acts on that data. Grouping the behavior with the table gives you many of the benefits of encapsulation in that the behavior is close to the data it will work on.

Often you'll need behavior from multiple *Table Modules* in order to do some useful work. Many times you see multiple *Table Modules* operating on the same *Record Set (508)* (Figure 9.4).

The most obvious example of *Table Module* is the use of one for each table in the database. However, if you have interesting queries and views in the database you can have *Table Modules* for them as well.

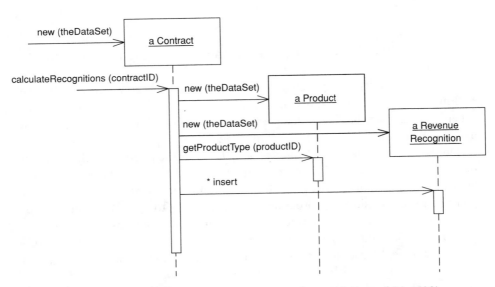

Figure 9.4 *Several* Table Modules *can collaborate with a single* Record Set (508).

The *Table Module* may be an instance or it may be a collection of static methods. The advantage of an instance is that it allows you to initialize the *Table Module* with an existing record set, perhaps the result of a query. You can then use the instance to manipulate the rows in the record set. Instances also make it possible to use inheritance, so we can write a rush contract module that contains additional behavior to the regular contract.

The *Table Module* may include queries as factory methods. The alternative is a *Table Data Gateway (144)*, but the disadvantage of this is having an extra *Table Data Gateway (144)* class and mechanism in the design. The advantage is that you can use a single *Table Module* on data from different data sources, since you use a different *Table Data Gateway (144)* for each data source.

When you use a *Table Data Gateway (144)* the application first uses the *Table Data Gateway (144)* to assemble data in a *Record Set (508)*. You then create a *Table Module* with the *Record Set (508)* as an argument. If you need behavior from multiple *Table Modules*, you can create them with the same *Record Set (508)*. The *Table Module* can then do business logic on the *Record Set (508)* and pass the modified *Record Set (508)* to the presentation for display and editing using the table-aware widgets. The widgets can't tell if the record

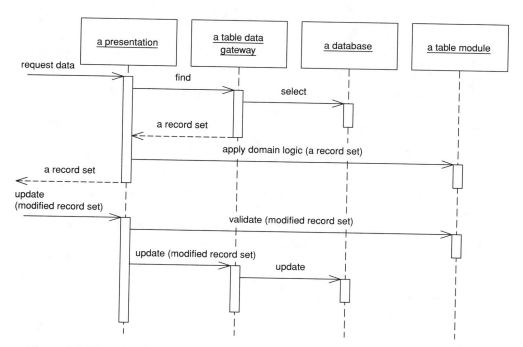

Figure 9.5 *Typical interactions for the layers around a* Table Module.

sets came directly from the relational database or if a *Table Module* manipulated the data on the way out. After modification in the GUI, the data set goes back to the *Table Module* for validation before it's saved to the database. One of the benefits of this style is that you can test the *Table Module* by creating a *Record Set (508)* in memory without going to the database.

The word "table" in the pattern name suggests that you have one *Table Module* per table in the database. While this is true to the first approximation, it isn't completely true. It's also useful to have a *Table Module* for commonly used views or other queries. Indeed, the structure of the *Table Module* doesn't really depend on the structure of tables in the database but more on the virtual tables perceived by the application, including views and queries.

When to Use It

Table Module is very much based on table-oriented data, so obviously using it makes sense when you're accessing tabular data using *Record Set (508)*. It also puts that data structure very much in the center of the code, so you also want the way you access the data structure to be fairly straightforward.

However, *Table Module* doesn't give you the full power of objects in organizing complex logic. You can't have direct instance-to-instance relationships, and polymorphism doesn't work well. So, for handling complicated domain logic, a *Domain Model (116)* is a better choice. Essentially you have to trade off *Domain Model (116)*'s ability to handle complex logic against *Table Module*'s easier integration with the underlying table-oriented data structures.

If the objects in a *Domain Model (116)* and the database tables are relatively similar, it may be better to use a *Domain Model (116)* that uses *Active Record (160)*. *Table Module* works better than a combination of *Domain Model (116)* and *Active Record (160)* when other parts of the application are based on a common table-oriented data structure. That's why you don't see *Table Module* very much in the Java environment, although that may change as row sets become more widely used.

The most well-known situation in which I've come across this pattern is in Microsoft COM designs. In COM (and .NET) the *Record Set (508)* is the primary repository of data in an application. Record sets can be passed to the UI, where data-aware widgets display information. Microsoft's ADO libraries give you a good mechanism to access the relational data as record sets. In this situation *Table Module* allows you to fit business logic into the application in a well-organized manner, without losing the way the various elements work on the tabular data.

Example: Revenue Recognition with a Table Module (C#)

Time to revisit the revenue recognition example (page 112) I used in the other domain modeling patterns, this time with a *Table Module*. To recap, our mission is to recognize revenue on orders when the rules vary depending on the product type. In this example we have different rules for word processors, spreadsheets, and databases.

Table Module is based on a data schema of some kind, usually a relational data model (although in the future we may well see an XML model used in a similar way). In this case I'll use the relational schema from Figure 9.6.

The classes that manipulate this data are in pretty much the same form; there's one *Table Module* class for each table. In the .NET architecture a data set object provides an in-memory representation of a database structure. It thus makes sense to create classes that operate on this data set. Each *Table Module* class has a data member of a data table, which is the .NET system class corresponding to a table within the data set. This ability to read a table is common to all *Table Modules* and so can appear in a *Layer Supertype (475)*.

```
class TableModule...

    protected DataTable table;
    protected TableModule(DataSet ds, String tableName) {
        table = ds.Tables[tableName];
    }
```

The subclass constructor calls the superclass constructor with the correct table name.

```
class Contract...

    public Contract (DataSet ds) : base (ds, "Contracts") {}
```

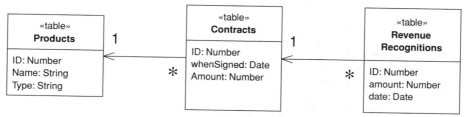

Figure 9.6 *Database schema for revenue recognition.*

This allows you to create a new *Table Module* just by passing in a data set to *Table Module*'s constructor

```
contract = new Contract(dataset);
```

which keeps the code that creates the data set away from the *Table Modules*, following the guidelines of ADO.NET.

A useful feature is the C# indexer, which gets to a particular row in the data table given the primary key.

class Contract...

```
public DataRow this [long key] {
get {
    String filter = String.Format("ID = {0}", key);
    return table.Select(filter)[0];
    }
}
```

The first piece of functionality calculates the revenue recognition for a contract, updating the revenue recognition tables accordingly. The amount recognized depends on the kind of product we have. Since this behavior mainly uses data from the contract table, I decided to add the method to the contract class.

class Contract...

```
public void CalculateRecognitions (long contractID) {
    DataRow contractRow = this[contractID];
    Decimal amount = (Decimal)contractRow["amount"];
    RevenueRecognition rr = new RevenueRecognition (table.DataSet);
    Product prod = new Product(table.DataSet);
    long prodID = GetProductId(contractID);
    if (prod.GetProductType(prodID) == ProductType.WP) {
        rr.Insert(contractID, amount, (DateTime) GetWhenSigned(contractID));
    } else if (prod.GetProductType(prodID) == ProductType.SS) {
        Decimal[] allocation = allocate(amount,3);
        rr.Insert(contractID, allocation[0], (DateTime) GetWhenSigned(contractID));
        rr.Insert(contractID, allocation[1], (DateTime)
            GetWhenSigned(contractID).AddDays(60));
        rr.Insert(contractID, allocation[2], (DateTime)
            GetWhenSigned(contractID).AddDays(90));
    } else if (prod.GetProductType(prodID) == ProductType.DB) {
        Decimal[] allocation = allocate(amount,3);
        rr.Insert(contractID, allocation[0], (DateTime) GetWhenSigned(contractID));
        rr.Insert(contractID, allocation[1], (DateTime)
            GetWhenSigned(contractID).AddDays(30));
        rr.Insert(contractID, allocation[2], (DateTime)
            GetWhenSigned(contractID).AddDays(60));
    } else throw new Exception("invalid product id");
}
private Decimal[] allocate(Decimal amount, int by) {
    Decimal lowResult = amount / by;
```

```
        lowResult = Decimal.Round(lowResult,2);
        Decimal highResult = lowResult + 0.01m;
        Decimal[] results = new Decimal[by];
        int remainder = (int) amount % by;
        for (int i = 0; i < remainder; i++) results[i] = highResult;
        for (int i = remainder; i < by; i++) results[i] = lowResult;
        return results;
    }
```

Usually I would use *Money (488)* here, but for variety's sake I'll show this using a decimal. I use an allocation method similar to the one I use for *Money (488)*.

To carry this out, we need some behavior that's defined on the other classes. The product needs to be able to tell us which type it is. We can do this with an enum for the product type and a lookup method.

```
    public enum ProductType {WP, SS, DB};

class Product...

    public ProductType GetProductType (long id) {
        String typeCode = (String) this[id]["type"];
        return (ProductType) Enum.Parse(typeof(ProductType), typeCode);
    }
```

GetProductType encapsulates the data in the data table. There's an argument for doing this for all columns of data, as opposed to accessing them directly as I did with the amount on the contract. While encapsulation is generally a Good Thing, I don't use it here because it doesn't fit with the assumption of the environment that different parts of the system access the data set directly. There's no encapsulation when the data set moves over to the UI, so column access functions only make sense when there's some additional functionality to be done, such as converting a string to a product type.

This is also a good time to mention that, although I'm using an untyped data set here because these are more common on different platforms, there's a strong argument (page 509) for using .NET's strongly typed data set.

The other additional behavior is inserting a new revenue recognition record.

```
class RevenueRecognition...

    public long Insert (long contractID, Decimal amount, DateTime date) {
        DataRow newRow = table.NewRow();
        long id = GetNextID();
        newRow["ID"] = id;
        newRow["contractID"] = contractID;
        newRow["amount"] = amount;
        newRow["date"]= String.Format("{0:s}", date);
        table.Rows.Add(newRow);
        return id;
    }
```

Again, the point of this method is less to encapsulate the data row and more to have a method instead of several lines of code that are repeated.

The second piece of functionality is to sum up all the revenue recognized on a contract by a given date. Since this uses the revenue recognition table it makes sense to define the method there.

class RevenueRecognition...

```
public Decimal RecognizedRevenue (long contractID, DateTime asOf) {
    String filter = String.Format("ContractID = {0} AND date <= #{1:d}#", contractID,asOf);
    DataRow[] rows = table.Select(filter);
    Decimal result = 0m;
    foreach (DataRow row in rows) {
        result += (Decimal)row["amount"];
    }
    return result;
}
```

This fragment takes advantage of the really nice feature of ADO.NET that allows you to define a where clause and then select a subset of the data table to manipulate. Indeed, you can go further and use an aggregate function.

class RevenueRecognition...

```
public Decimal RecognizedRevenue2 (long contractID, DateTime asOf) {
    String filter = String.Format("ContractID = {0} AND date <= #{1:d}#", contractID,asOf);
    String computeExpression = "sum(amount)";
    Object sum = table.Compute(computeExpression, filter);
    return (sum is System.DBNull) ? 0 : (Decimal) sum;
}
```

Service Layer

by Randy Stafford

Defines an application's boundary with a layer of services that establishes a set of available operations and coordinates the application's response in each operation.

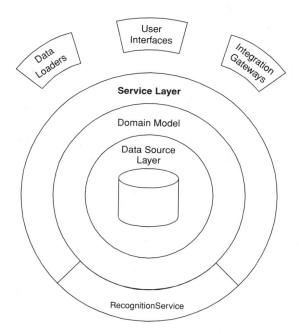

Enterprise applications typically require different kinds of interfaces to the data they store and the logic they implement: data loaders, user interfaces, integration gateways, and others. Despite their different purposes, these interfaces often need common interactions with the application to access and manipulate its data and invoke its business logic. The interactions may be complex, involving transactions across multiple resources and the coordination of several responses to an action. Encoding the logic of the interactions separately in each interface causes a lot of duplication.

A *Service Layer* defines an application's boundary [Cockburn PloP] and its set of available operations from the perspective of interfacing client layers. It encapsulates the application's business logic, controlling transactions and coordinating responses in the implementation of its operations.

How It Works

A *Service Layer* can be implemented in a couple of different ways, without violating the defining characteristics stated above. The differences appear in the allocation of responsibility behind the *Service Layer* interface. Before I delve into the various implementation possibilities, let me lay a bit of groundwork.

Kinds of "Business Logic" Like *Transaction Script (110)* and *Domain Model (116)*, *Service Layer* is a pattern for organizing business logic. Many designers, including me, like to divide "business logic" into two kinds: "domain logic," having to do purely with the problem domain (such as strategies for calculating revenue recognition on a contract), and "application logic," having to do with application responsibilities [Cockburn UC] (such as notifying contract administrators, and integrated applications, of revenue recognition calculations). Application logic is sometimes referred to as "workflow logic," although different people have different interpretations of "workflow."

Domain Models (116) are preferable to *Transaction Scripts (110)* for avoiding domain logic duplication and for managing complexity using classical design patterns. But putting application logic into pure domain object classes has a couple of undesirable consequences. First, domain object classes are less reusable across applications if they implement application-specific logic and depend on application-specific packages. Second, commingling both kinds of logic in the same classes makes it harder to reimplement the application logic in, say, a workflow tool if that should ever become desirable. For these reasons *Service Layer* factors each kind of business logic into a separate layer, yielding the usual benefits of layering and rendering the pure domain object classes more reusable from application to application.

Implementation Variations The two basic implementation variations are the domain facade approach and the operation script approach. In the **domain facade** approach a *Service Layer* is implemented as a set of thin facades over a *Domain Model (116)*. The classes implementing the facades don't implement any business logic. Rather, the *Domain Model (116)* implements all of the business logic. The thin facades establish a boundary and set of operations through which client layers interact with the application, exhibiting the defining characteristics of *Service Layer*.

In the **operation script** approach a *Service Layer* is implemented as a set of thicker classes that directly implement application logic but delegate to encapsulated domain object classes for domain logic. The operations available to clients of a *Service Layer* are implemented as scripts, organized several to a class defining a subject area of related logic. Each such class forms an application "service," and it's common for service type names to end with "Service." A *Service Layer* is comprised of these application service classes, which should extend a *Layer Supertype (475)*, abstracting their responsibilities and common behaviors.

To Remote or Not to Remote The interface of a *Service Layer* class is coarse grained almost by definition, since it declares a set of application operations available to interfacing client layers. Therefore, *Service Layer* classes are well suited to remote invocation from an interface granularity perspective.

However, remote invocation comes at the cost of dealing with object distribution. It likely entails a lot of extra work to make your *Service Layer* method signatures deal in *Data Transfer Objects (401)*. Don't underestimate the cost of this work, especially if you have a complex *Domain Model (116)* and rich editing UIs for complex update use cases! It's significant, and it's painful—perhaps second only to the cost and pain of object-relational mapping. Remember the First Law of Distributed Object Design (page 89).

My advice is to start with a locally invocable *Service Layer* whose method signatures deal in domain objects. Add remotability when you need it (if ever) by putting *Remote Facades (388)* on your *Service Layer* or having your *Service Layer* objects implement remote interfaces. If your application has a Web-based UI or a Web-services-based integration gateway, there's no law that says your business logic has to run in a separate process from your server pages and Web services. In fact, you can save yourself some development effort and runtime response time, without sacrificing scalability, by starting out with a colocated approach.

Identifying Services and Operations Identifying the operations needed on a *Service Layer* boundary is pretty straightforward. They're determined by the needs of *Service Layer* clients, the most significant (and first) of which is typically a user interface. Since a user interface is designed to support the use cases that actors want to perform with an application, the starting point for identifying *Service Layer* operations is the use case model and the user interface design for the application.

Disappointing as it is, many of the use cases in an enterprise application are fairly boring "CRUD" (create, read, update, delete) use cases on domain objects—create one of these, read a collection of those, update this other thing. My experience is that there's almost always a one-to-one correspondence between CRUD use cases and *Service Layer* operations.

The application's responsibilities in carrying out these use cases, however, may be anything but boring. Validation aside, the creation, update, or deletion of a domain object in an application increasingly requires notification of other people and other integrated applications. These responses must be coordinated, and transacted atomically, by *Service Layer* operations.

If only it were as straightforward to identify *Service Layer* abstractions to group related operations. There are no hard-and-fast prescriptions in this area; only vague heuristics. For a sufficiently small application, it may suffice to have but one abstraction, named after the application itself. In my experience larger applications are partitioned into several "subsystems," each of which includes a complete vertical slice through the stack of architecture layers. In this case I prefer one abstraction per subsystem, named after the subsystem. Other possibilities include abstractions reflecting major partitions in a domain model, if these are different from the subsystem partitions (e.g., ContractsService, ProductsService), and abstractions named after thematic application behaviors (e.g., RecognitionService).

Java Implementation

In both the domain facade approach and the operation script approach, a *Service Layer* class can be implemented as either a POJO (plain old Java object) or a stateless session bean. The trade-off pits ease of testing against ease of transaction control. POJOs might be easier to test, since they don't have to be deployed in an EJB container to run, but it's harder for a POJO *Service Layer* to hook into distributed container-managed transaction services, especially in interservice invocations. EJBs, on the other hand, come with the potential for container-managed distributed transactions but have to be deployed in a container before they can be tested and run. Choose your poison.

My preferred way of applying a *Service Layer* in J2EE is with EJB 2.0 stateless session beans, using local interfaces, and the operation script approach, delegating to POJO domain object classes. It's just so darned convenient to implement a *Service Layer* using stateless session bean, because of the distributed container-managed transactions provided by EJB. Also, with the local interfaces introduced in EJB 2.0, a *Service Layer* can exploit the valuable transaction services while avoiding the thorny object distribution issues.

On a related Java-specific note, let me differentiate *Service Layer* from the *Session Facade* pattern documented in the J2EE patterns literature [Alur et al.] and [Marinescu]. *Session Facade* was motivated by the desire to avoid the performance penalty of too many remote invocations on entity beans; it therefore prescribes facading entity beans with session beans. *Service Layer* is motivated instead by factoring responsibility to avoid duplication and promote reusability; it's an architecture pattern that transcends technology. In fact, the application boundary pattern [Cockburn PloP] that inspired *Service Layer* predates EJB by three years. *Session Facade* may be in the spirit of *Service Layer* but, as currently named, scoped, and presented, is not the same.

When to Use It

The benefit of *Service Layer* is that it defines a common set of application operations available to many kinds of clients and it coordinates an application's response in each operation. The response may involve application logic that needs to be transacted atomically across multiple transactional resources. Thus, in an application with more than one kind of client of its business logic, and complex responses in its use cases involving multiple transactional resources, it makes a lot of sense to include a *Service Layer* with container-managed transactions, even in an undistributed architecture.

The easier question to answer is probably when not to use it. You probably don't need a *Service Layer* if your application's business logic will only have one kind of client—say, a user interface—and its use case responses don't involve multiple transactional resources. In this case your Page Controllers can manually control transactions and coordinate whatever response is required, perhaps delegating directly to the Data Source layer.

But as soon as you envision a second kind of client, or a second transactional resource in use case responses, it pays to design in a *Service Layer* from the beginning.

Further Reading

There's not a great deal of prior art on *Service Layer*, whose inspiration is Alistair Cockburn's application boundary pattern [Cockburn PloP]. In the remotable services vein [Alpert, et al.] discuss the role of facades in distributed systems. Compare and contrast this with the various presentations of Session Facade [Alur et al.] and [Marinescu]. On the topic of application responsibilities that must be coordinated within *Service Layer* operations, Cockburn's description of use cases as a contract for behavior [Cockburn UC] is very helpful. An earlier background reference is the Fusion methodology's recognition of "system operations" [Coleman et al.].

Example: Revenue Recognition (Java)

This example continues the revenue recognition example of the *Transaction Script (110)* and *Domain Model (116)* patterns, demonstrating how *Service Layer* is used to script application logic and delegate for domain logic in a *Service Layer* operation. It uses the operation script approach to implement a *Service Layer*, first with POJOs and then with EJBs.

To make the demonstration we expand the scenario to include some application logic. Suppose the use cases for the application require that, when the revenue recognitions for a contract are calculated, the application must respond by sending an e-mail notification of that event to a designated contract administrator and by publishing a message using message-oriented middleware to notify other integrated applications.

We start by changing the RecognitionService class from the *Transaction Script (110)* example to extend a *Layer Supertype (475)* and to use a couple of *Gateways (466)* in carrying out application logic. This yields the class diagram of Figure 9.7. RecognitionService becomes a POJO implementation of a *Service Layer* application service, and its methods represent two of the operations available at the application's boundary.

The methods of the RecognitionService class script the application logic of the operations, delegating to domain object classes (of the example from *Domain Model (116)*) for domain logic.

```
public class ApplicationService {
   protected EmailGateway getEmailGateway() {
      //return an instance of EmailGateway
   }
   protected IntegrationGateway getIntegrationGateway() {
      //return an instance of IntegrationGateway
   }
}
public interface EmailGateway {
   void sendEmailMessage(String toAddress, String subject, String body);
}
public interface IntegrationGateway {
   void publishRevenueRecognitionCalculation(Contract contract);
}
public class RecognitionService
extends ApplicationService {
   public void calculateRevenueRecognitions(long contractNumber) {
      Contract contract = Contract.readForUpdate(contractNumber);
      contract.calculateRecognitions();
      getEmailGateway().sendEmailMessage(
         contract.getAdministratorEmailAddress(),
         "RE: Contract #" + contractNumber,
         contract + " has had revenue recognitions calculated.");
      getIntegrationGateway().publishRevenueRecognitionCalculation(contract);
   }
```

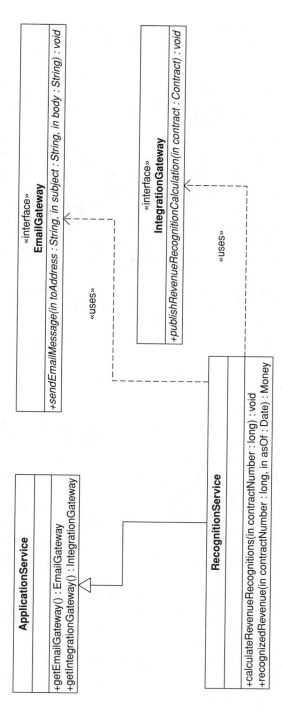

Figure 9.7 *RecognitionService POJO class diagram.*

```
public Money recognizedRevenue(long contractNumber, Date asOf) {
    return Contract.read(contractNumber).recognizedRevenue(asOf);
}
    }
```

Persistence details are again left out of the example. Suffice it to say that the Contract class implements static methods to read contracts from the Data Source layer by their numbers. One of these methods has a name revealing an intention to update the contract that's read, which allows an underlying *Data Mapper (165)* to register the read object(s) with for example, a *Unit of Work (184).*

Transaction control details are also left out of the example. The calculateRevenueRecognitions() method is inherently transactional because, during its execution, persistent contract objects are modified via addition of revenue recognitions; messages are enqueued in message-oriented middleware; and e-mail messages are sent. All of these responses must be transacted atomically because we don't want to send e-mail and publish messages to other applications if the contract changes fail to persist.

In the J2EE platform we can let the EJB container manage distributed transactions by implementing application services (and *Gateways (466)*) as stateless session beans that use transactional resources. Figure 9.8 shows the class diagram of a RecognitionService implementation that uses EJB 2.0 local interfaces and the "business interface" idiom. In this implementation a *Layer Supertype (475)* is still used, providing default implementations of the bean implementation class methods required by EJB, in addition to the application-specific methods. If we assume that the EmailGateway and IntegrationGateway interfaces are also "business interfaces" for their respective stateless session beans, then control of the distributed transaction is achieved by declaring the calculateRevenueRecognitions, sendEmailMessage, and publishRevenueRecognitionCalculation methods to be transactional. The RecognitionService methods from the POJO example move unchanged to RecognitionServiceBeanImpl.

The important point about the example is that the *Service Layer* uses both operation scripting and domain object classes in coordinating the transactional response of the operation. The calculateRevenueRecognitions method scripts the application logic of the response required by the application's use cases, but it delegates to the domain object classes for domain logic. It also presents a couple of techniques for combating duplicated logic within operation scripts of a *Service Layer*. Responsibilities are factored into different objects (e.g., *Gateways (466)*) that can be reused via delegation. A *Layer Supertype (475)* provides convenient access to these other objects.

Some might argue that a more elegant implementation of the operation script would use the Observer pattern [Gang of Four], but Observer is difficult

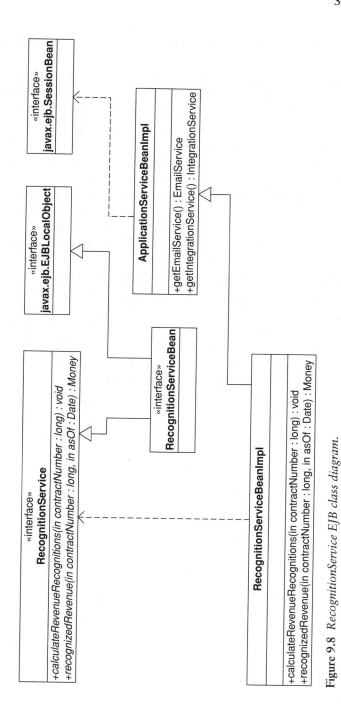

Figure 9.8 *RecognitionService EJB class diagram.*

to implement in a stateless, multithreaded *Service Layer*. In my opinion the open code of the operation script is clearer and simpler.

Some might also argue that the application logic responsibilities could be implemented in domain object methods, such as Contract.calculateRevenueRecognitions(), or even in the data source layer, thereby eliminating the need for a separate *Service Layer*. However, I find those allocations of responsibility undesirable for a number of reasons. First, domain object classes are less reusable across applications if they implement application-specific logic (and depend on application-specific *Gateways (466)*, and the like). They should model the parts of the problem domain that are of interest to the application, which doesn't mean all of the application's use case responsibilities. Second, encapsulating application logic in a "higher" layer dedicated to that purpose (which the data source layer isn't) facilitates changing the implementation of that layer—perhaps to use a workflow engine.

As an organization pattern for the logic layer of an enterprise application, *Service Layer* combines scripting and domain object classes, leveraging the best aspects of both. Several variations are possible in a *Service Layer* implementation—for example, domain facades or operation scripts, POJOs or session beans, or a combination of both. *Service Layer* can be designed for local invocation, remote invocation, or both. Most important, regardless of these variations, this pattern lays the foundation for encapsulated implementation of an application's business logic and consistent invocation of that logic by its various clients.

Chapter 10

Data Source Architectural Patterns

Table Data Gateway

An object that acts as a Gateway (466) to a database table.
One instance handles all the rows in the table.

Person Gateway
find (id) : RecordSet findWithLastName(String) : RecordSet update (id, lastname, firstname, numberOfDependents) insert (lastname, firstname, numberOfDependents) delete (id)

Mixing SQL in application logic can cause several problems. Many developers aren't comfortable with SQL, and many who are comfortable may not write it well. Database administrators need to be able to find SQL easily so they can figure out how to tune and evolve the database.

A *Table Data Gateway* holds all the SQL for accessing a single table or view: selects, inserts, updates, and deletes. Other code calls its methods for all interaction with the database.

How It Works

A *Table Data Gateway* has a simple interface, usually consisting of several find methods to get data from the database and update, insert, and delete methods. Each method maps the input parameters into a SQL call and executes the SQL against a database connection. The *Table Data Gateway* is usually stateless, as its role is to push data back and forth.

The trickiest thing about a *Table Data Gateway* is how it returns information from a query. Even a simple find-by-ID query will return multiple data items. In environments where you can return multiple items you can use that for a single row, but many languages give you only a single return value and many queries return multiple rows.

One alternative is to return some simple data structure, such as a map. A map works, but it forces data to be copied out of the record set that comes from the database into the map. I think that using maps to pass data around is bad form because it defeats compile time checking and isn't a very explicit interface, leading to bugs as people misspell what's in the map. A better alternative is to use a *Data Transfer Object (401)*. It's another object to create but one that may well be used elsewhere.

To save all this you can return the *Record Set (508)* that comes from the SQL query. This is conceptually messy, as ideally the in-memory object doesn't have to know anything about the SQL interface. It may also make it difficult to substitute the database for a file if you can't easily create record sets in your own code. Nevertheless, in many environments that use *Record Set (508)* widely, such as .NET, it's a very effective approach. A *Table Data Gateway* thus goes very well with *Table Module (125)*. If all of your updates are done through the *Table Data Gateway*, the returned data can be based on views rather than on the actual tables, which reduces the coupling between your code and the database.

If you're using a *Domain Model (116)*, you can have the *Table Data Gateway* return the appropriate domain object. The problem with this is that you then have bidirectional dependencies between the domain objects and the gateway. The two are closely connected, so that isn't necessarily a terrible thing, but it's something I'm always reluctant to do.

Most times when you use *Table Data Gateway*, you'll have one for each table in the database. For very simple cases, however, you can have a single *Table Data Gateway* that handles all methods for all tables. You can also have one for views or even for interesting queries that aren't kept in the database as views. Obviously, view-based *Table Data Gateways* often can't update and so won't have update behavior. However, if you can make updates to the underlying tables, then encapsulating the updates behind update operations on the *Table Data Gateway* is a very good technique.

When to Use It

As with *Row Data Gateway (152)* the decision regarding *Table Data Gateway* is first whether to use a *Gateway (466)* approach at all and then which one.

I find that *Table Data Gateway* is probably the simplest database interface pattern to use, as it maps so nicely onto a database table or record type. It also makes a natural point to encapsulate the precise access logic of the data source. I use it least with *Domain Model (116)* because I find that *Data Mapper (165)* gives a better isolation between the *Domain Model (116)* and the database.

Table Data Gateway works particularly well with *Table Module (125)*, where it produces a record set data structure for the *Table Module (125)* to work on. Indeed, I can't really imagine any other database-mapping approach for *Table Module (125)*.

Just like *Row Data Gateway (152)*, *Table Data Gateway* is very suitable for *Transaction Scripts (110)*. The choice between the two really boils down to how they deal with multiple rows of data. Many people like using a *Data Transfer Object (401)*, but that seems to me like more work than is worthwhile, unless the same *Data Transfer Object (401)* is used elsewhere. I prefer *Table Data Gateway* when the result set representation is convenient for the *Transaction Script (110)* to work with.

Interestingly, it often makes sense to have the *Data Mappers (165)* talk to the database via *Table Data Gateways*. Although this isn't useful when everything is handcoded, it can be very effective if you want to use metadata for the *Table Data Gateways* but prefer handcoding for the actual mapping to the domain objects.

One of the benefits of using a *Table Data Gateway* to encapsulate database access is that the same interface can work both for using SQL to manipulate the database and for using stored procedures. Indeed, stored procedures themselves are often organized as *Table Data Gateways*. That way the insert and update stored procedures encapsulate the actual table structure. The find procedures in this case can return views, which helps to hide the underlying table structure.

Further Reading

[Alur et al.] discusses the *Data Access Object* pattern, which is a *Table Data Gateway*. They show returning a collection of *Data Transfer Objects (401)* on the query methods. It's not clear whether they see this pattern as always being table based; the intent and discussion seems to imply either *Table Data Gateway* or *Row Data Gateway (152)*.

I've used a different name, partly because I see this pattern as a particular usage of the more general *Gateway (466)* concept and I want the pattern name to reflect that. Also, the term *Data Access Object* and its abbreviation *DAO* has its own particular meaning within the Microsoft world.

Example: Person Gateway (C#)

Table Data Gateway is the usual form of database access in the windows world, so it makes sense to illustrate one with C#. I have to stress, however, that this classic form of *Table Data Gateway* doesn't quite fit in the .NET environment since it doesn't take advantage of the ADO.NET data set; instead, it uses the data reader, which is a cursor-like interface to database records. The data reader is the right choice for manipulating larger amounts of information when you don't want to bring everything into memory in one go.

For the example I'm using a Person Gateway class that connects to a person table in a database. The Person Gateway contains the finder code, returning ADO.NET's data reader to access the returned data.

Data Source
Architectural
Patterns

class PersonGateway...

```
public IDataReader FindAll() {
    String sql = "select * from person";
    return new OleDbCommand(sql, DB.Connection).ExecuteReader();
}
public IDataReader FindWithLastName(String lastName) {
    String sql = "SELECT * FROM person WHERE lastname = ?";
    IDbCommand comm = new OleDbCommand(sql, DB.Connection);
    comm.Parameters.Add(new OleDbParameter("lastname", lastName));
    return comm.ExecuteReader();
}
public IDataReader FindWhere(String whereClause) {
    String sql = String.Format("select * from person where {0}", whereClause);
    return new OleDbCommand(sql, DB.Connection).ExecuteReader();
}
```

Almost always you'll want to pull back a bunch of rows with a reader. On a rare occasion you might want to get hold of an individual row of data with a method along these lines:

class PersonGateway...

```
public Object[] FindRow (long key) {
    String sql = "SELECT * FROM person WHERE id = ?";
    IDbCommand comm = new OleDbCommand(sql, DB.Connection);
    comm.Parameters.Add(new OleDbParameter("key",key));
    IDataReader reader = comm.ExecuteReader();
    reader.Read();
    Object [] result = new Object[reader.FieldCount];
    reader.GetValues(result);
    reader.Close();
    return result;
}
```

The update and insert methods receive the necessary data in arguments and invoke the appropriate SQL routines.

class PersonGateway...

```
public void Update (long key, String lastname, String firstname, long numberOfDependents){
    String sql = @"
        UPDATE person
            SET lastname = ?, firstname = ?, numberOfDependents = ?
            WHERE id = ?";
```

Table Data Gateway

```
    IDbCommand comm = new OleDbCommand(sql, DB.Connection);
    comm.Parameters.Add(new OleDbParameter ("last", lastname));
    comm.Parameters.Add(new OleDbParameter ("first", firstname));
    comm.Parameters.Add(new OleDbParameter ("numDep", numberOfDependents));
    comm.Parameters.Add(new OleDbParameter ("key", key));
    comm.ExecuteNonQuery();
}
```

```
class PersonGateway...
```

```
    public long Insert(String lastName, String firstName, long numberOfDependents) {
        String sql = "INSERT INTO person VALUES (?,?,?,?)";
        long key = GetNextID();
        IDbCommand comm = new OleDbCommand(sql, DB.Connection);
        comm.Parameters.Add(new OleDbParameter ("key", key));
        comm.Parameters.Add(new OleDbParameter ("last", lastName));
        comm.Parameters.Add(new OleDbParameter ("first", firstName));
        comm.Parameters.Add(new OleDbParameter ("numDep", numberOfDependents));
        comm.ExecuteNonQuery();
        return key;
    }
```

The deletion method just needs a key.

```
class PersonGateway...
```

```
    public void Delete (long key) {
        String sql = "DELETE FROM person WHERE id = ?";
        IDbCommand comm = new OleDbCommand(sql, DB.Connection);
        comm.Parameters.Add(new OleDbParameter ("key", key));
        comm.ExecuteNonQuery();
    }
```

Example: Using ADO.NET Data Sets (C#)

The generic *Table Data Gateway* works with pretty much any kind of platform since it's nothing but a wrapper for SQL statements. With .NET you use data sets more often, but *Table Data Gateway* is still useful although it comes in a different form.

A data set needs data adapters to load the data into it and update the data. In find it useful to define a holder for the data set and the adapters. A gateway then uses the holder to store them. Much of this behavior is generic and can be done in a superclass.

The holder indexes the data sets and adapters by the name of the table.

```
class DataSetHolder...
```

```
    public DataSet Data = new DataSet();
    private Hashtable DataAdapters = new Hashtable();
```

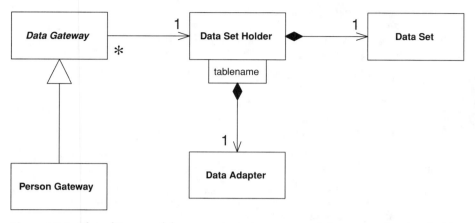

Figure 10.1 *Class diagram of data-set-oriented gateway and the supporting data holder.*

The gateway stores the holder and exposes the data set for its clients.

```
class DataGateway...

    public DataSetHolder Holder;
    public DataSet Data {
       get {return Holder.Data;}
    }
```

The gateway can act on an existing holder, or it can create a new one.

```
class DataGateway...

    protected DataGateway() {
       Holder = new DataSetHolder();
    }
    protected DataGateway(DataSetHolder holder) {
       this.Holder = holder;
    }
```

The find behavior can work a bit differently here. A data set is a container for table-oriented data and can hold data from several tables. For that reason it's better to load data into a data set.

```
class DataGateway...

    public void LoadAll() {
       String commandString = String.Format("select * from {0}", TableName);
       Holder.FillData(commandString, TableName);
    }
```

```
        public void LoadWhere(String whereClause) {
            String commandString =
                String.Format("select * from {0} where {1}", TableName,whereClause);
            Holder.FillData(commandString, TableName);
        }
        abstract public String TableName {get;}
```

class PersonGateway...

```
        public override String TableName {
            get {return "Person";}
        }
```

class DataSetHolder...

```
        public void FillData(String query, String tableName) {
            if (DataAdapters.Contains(tableName)) throw new MutlipleLoadException();
            OleDbDataAdapter da = new OleDbDataAdapter(query, DB.Connection);
            OleDbCommandBuilder builder = new OleDbCommandBuilder(da);
            da.Fill(Data, tableName);
            DataAdapters.Add(tableName, da);
        }
```

To update data you manipulate the data set directly in some client code.

```
        person.LoadAll();
        person[key]["lastname"] = "Odell";
        person.Holder.Update();
```

The gateway can have an indexer to make it easier to get to specific rows.

class DataGateway...

```
        public DataRow this[long key] {
            get {
                String filter = String.Format("id = {0}", key);
                return Table.Select(filter)[0];
            }
        }
        public override DataTable Table {
            get { return Data.Tables[TableName];}
        }
```

The update triggers update behavior on the holder.

class DataSetHolder...

```
        public void Update() {
            foreach (String table in DataAdapters.Keys)
                ((OleDbDataAdapter)DataAdapters[table]).Update(Data, table);
        }
        public DataTable this[String tableName] {
            get {return Data.Tables[tableName];}
        }
```

Insertion can be done much the same way: Get a data set, insert a new row in the data table, and fill in each column. However, an update method can do the insertion in one call.

class DataGateway...

```
public long Insert(String lastName, String firstname, int numberOfDependents) {
    long key = new PersonGatewayDS().GetNextID();
    DataRow newRow = Table.NewRow();
    newRow["id"] = key;
    newRow["lastName"] = lastName;
    newRow["firstName"] = firstname;
    newRow["numberOfDependents"] = numberOfDependents;
    Table.Rows.Add(newRow);
    return key;
}
```

**Data Source
Architectural
Patterns**

Row Data Gateway

An object that acts as a Gateway (466) to a single record in a data source. There is one instance per row.

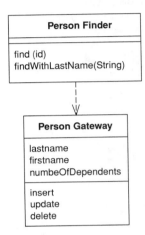

Embedding database access code in in-memory objects can leave you with a few disadvantages. For a start, if your in-memory objects have business logic of their own, adding the database manipulation code increases complexity. Testing is awkward too since, if your in-memory objects are tied to a database, tests are slower to run because of all the database access. You may have to access multiple databases with all those annoying little variations on their SQL.

A *Row Data Gateway* gives you objects that look exactly like the record in your record structure but can be accessed with the regular mechanisms of your programming language. All details of data source access are hidden behind this interface.

How It Works

A *Row Data Gateway* acts as an object that exactly mimics a single record, such as one database row. In it each column in the database becomes one field. The *Row Data Gateway* will usually do any type conversion from the data source types to the in-memory types, but this conversion is pretty simple. This pattern holds the data about a row so that a client can then access the *Row*

Data Gateway directly. The gateway acts as a good interface for each row of data. This approach works particularly well for *Transaction Scripts (110)*.

With a *Row Data Gateway* you're faced with the questions of where to put the find operations that generate this pattern. You can use static find methods, but they preclude polymorphism should you want to substitute different finder methods for different data sources. In this case it often makes sense to have separate finder objects so that each table in a relational database will have one finder class and one gateway class for the results (Figure 10.2).

It's often hard to tell the difference between a *Row Data Gateway* and an *Active Record (160)*. The crux of the matter is whether there's any domain logic present; if there is, you have an *Active Record (160)*. A *Row Data Gateway* should contain only database access logic and no domain logic.

As with any other form of tabular encapsulation, you can use a *Row Data Gateway* with a view or query as well as a table. Updates often turn out to be more complicated this way, as you have to update the underlying tables. Also, if you have two *Row Data Gateways* that operate on the same underlying tables, you may find that the second *Row Data Gateway* you update undoes the changes on the first. There's no general way to prevent this; developers just have to be aware of how virtual *Row Data Gateways* are formed. After all, the same thing can happen with updatable views. Of course, you can choose not to provide update operations.

Row Data Gateways tend to be somewhat tedious to write, but they're a very good candidate for code generation based on a *Metadata Mapping (306)*. This way all your database access code can be automatically built for you during your automated build process.

When to Use It

The choice of *Row Data Gateway* often takes two steps: first whether to use a gateway at all and second whether to use *Row Data Gateway* or *Table Data Gateway (144)*.

I use *Row Data Gateway* most often when I'm using a *Transaction Script (110)*. In this case it nicely factors out the database access code and allows it to be reused easily by different *Transaction Scripts (110)*.

I don't use a *Row Data Gateway* when I'm using a *Domain Model (116)*. If the mapping is simple, *Active Record (160)* does the same job without an additional layer of code. If the mapping is complex, *Data Mapper (165)* works better, as it's better at decoupling the data structure from the domain objects because the domain objects don't need to know the layout of the database. Of course, you can use the *Row Data Gateway* to shield the domain objects from

Row Data Gateway

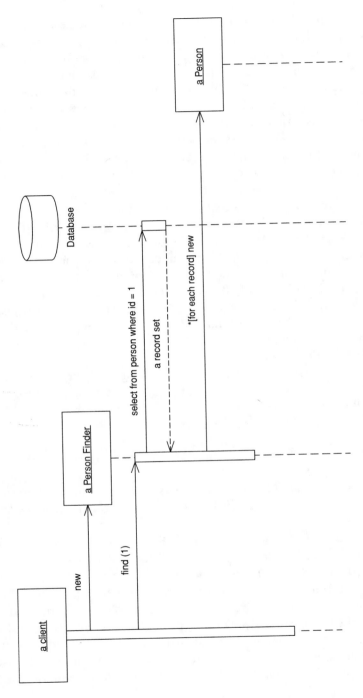

Figure 10.2 *Interactions for a find with a row-based* Row Data Gateway.

the database structure. That's a good thing if you're changing the database structure when using *Row Data Gateway* and you don't want to change the domain logic. However, doing this on a large scale leads you to three data representations: one in the business logic, one in the *Row Data Gateway*, and one in the database—and that's one too many. For that reason I usually have *Row Data Gateways* that mirror the database structure.

Interestingly, I've seen *Row Data Gateway* used very nicely with *Data Mapper (165)*. Although this seems like extra work, it can be effective iff the *Row Data Gateways* are automatically generated from metadata while the *Data Mappers (165)* are done by hand.

If you use *Transaction Script (110)* with *Row Data Gateway*, you may notice that you have business logic that's repeated across multiple scripts; logic that would make sense in the *Row Data Gateway*. Moving that logic will gradually turn your *Row Data Gateway* into an *Active Record (160)*, which is often good as it reduces duplication in the business logic.

Example: A Person Record (Java)

Here's an example for *Row Data Gateway*. It's a simple person table.

```
create table people (ID int primary key, lastname varchar,
                     firstname varchar, number_of_dependents int)
```

PersonGateway is a gateway for the table. It starts with data fields and accessors.

```
class PersonGateway...

  private String lastName;
  private String firstName;
  private int numberOfDependents;
  public String getLastName() {
    return lastName;
  }
  public void setLastName(String lastName) {
    this.lastName = lastName;
  }
  public String getFirstName() {
    return firstName;
  }
  public void setFirstName(String firstName) {
    this.firstName = firstName;
  }
  public int getNumberOfDependents() {
    return numberOfDependents;
  }
  public void setNumberOfDependents(int numberOfDependents) {
    this.numberOfDependents = numberOfDependents;
  }
```

The gateway class itself can handle updates and inserts.

class PersonGateway...

```
private static final String updateStatementString =
        "UPDATE people " +
        " set lastname = ?, firstname = ?, number_of_dependents = ? " +
        " where id = ?";
public void update() {
    PreparedStatement updateStatement = null;
    try {
        updateStatement = DB.prepare(updateStatementString);
        updateStatement.setString(1, lastName);
        updateStatement.setString(2, firstName);
        updateStatement.setInt(3, numberOfDependents);
        updateStatement.setInt(4, getID().intValue());
        updateStatement.execute();
    } catch (Exception e) {
        throw new ApplicationException(e);
    } finally {DB.cleanUp(updateStatement);
    }
}
private static final String insertStatementString =
        "INSERT INTO people VALUES (?, ?, ?, ?)";
public Long insert() {
    PreparedStatement insertStatement = null;
    try {
        insertStatement = DB.prepare(insertStatementString);
        setID(findNextDatabaseId());
        insertStatement.setInt(1, getID().intValue());
        insertStatement.setString(2, lastName);
        insertStatement.setString(3, firstName);
        insertStatement.setInt(4, numberOfDependents);
        insertStatement.execute();
        Registry.addPerson(this);
        return getID();
    } catch (SQLException e) {
        throw new ApplicationException(e);
    } finally { DB.cleanUp(insertStatement);
    }
}
```

To pull people out of the database, we have a separate PersonFinder. This works with the gateway to create new gateway objects.

class PersonFinder...

```
private final static String findStatementString =
        "SELECT id, lastname, firstname, number_of_dependents " +
        " from people " +
        " WHERE id = ?";
```

```
    public PersonGateway find(Long id) {
        PersonGateway result = (PersonGateway) Registry.getPerson(id);
        if (result != null) return result;
        PreparedStatement findStatement = null;
        ResultSet rs = null;
        try {
            findStatement = DB.prepare(findStatementString);
            findStatement.setLong(1, id.longValue());
            rs = findStatement.executeQuery();
            rs.next();
            result = PersonGateway.load(rs);
            return result;
        } catch (SQLException e) {
            throw new ApplicationException(e);
        } finally {DB.cleanUp(findStatement, rs);
        }
    }
    public PersonGateway find(long id) {
        return find(new Long(id));
    }
```

class PersonGateway...

```
    public static PersonGateway load(ResultSet rs) throws SQLException {
        Long id = new Long(rs.getLong(1));
        PersonGateway result = (PersonGateway) Registry.getPerson(id);
        if (result != null) return result;
        String lastNameArg = rs.getString(2);
        String firstNameArg = rs.getString(3);
        int numDependentsArg = rs.getInt(4);
        result = new PersonGateway(id, lastNameArg, firstNameArg, numDependentsArg);
        Registry.addPerson(result);
        return result;
    }
```

To find more than one person according to some criteria we can provide a suitable finder method.

class PersonFinder...

```
    private static final String findResponsibleStatement =
        "SELECT id, lastname, firstname, number_of_dependents " +
        "  from people " +
        "  WHERE number_of_dependents > 0";
    public List findResponsibles() {
        List result = new ArrayList();
        PreparedStatement stmt = null;
        ResultSet rs = null;
        try {
            stmt = DB.prepare(findResponsibleStatement);
            rs = stmt.executeQuery();
```

```
          while (rs.next()) {
              result.add(PersonGateway.load(rs));
          }
          return result;
      } catch (SQLException e) {
          throw new ApplicationException(e);
      } finally {DB.cleanUp(stmt, rs);
      }
  }
```

The finder uses a *Registry (480)* to hold *Identity Maps (195)*.

We can now use the gateways from a *Transaction Script (110)*

```
PersonFinder finder = new PersonFinder();
Iterator people = finder.findResponsibles().iterator();
StringBuffer result = new StringBuffer();
while (people.hasNext()) {
    PersonGateway each = (PersonGateway) people.next();
    result.append(each.getLastName());
    result.append("");
    result.append(each.getFirstName());
    result.append("");
    result.append(String.valueOf(each.getNumberOfDependents()));
    result.append("

}
return result.toString();
```

Example: A Data Holder for a Domain Object (Java)

I use *Row Data Gateway* mostly with *Transaction Script (110)*. If we want to use the *Row Data Gateway* from a *Domain Model (116)*, the domain objects need to get at the data from the gateway. Instead of copying the data to the domain object we can use the *Row Data Gateway* as a data holder for the domain object.

class Person...

```
  private PersonGateway data;
  public Person(PersonGateway data) {
      this.data = data;
  }
```

Accessors on the domain logic can then delegate to the gateway for the data.

class Person...

```
  public int getNumberOfDependents() {
      return data.getNumberOfDependents();
  }
```

The domain logic uses the getters to pull the data from the gateway.

class Person...

```
public Money getExemption() {
    Money baseExemption = Money.dollars(1500);
    Money dependentExemption = Money.dollars(750);
    return baseExemption.add(dependentExemption.multiply(this.getNumberOfDependents()));
}
```

Active Record

An object that wraps a row in a database table or view, encapsulates the database access, and adds domain logic on that data.

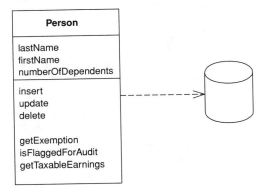

An object carries both data and behavior. Much of this data is persistent and needs to be stored in a database. *Active Record* uses the most obvious approach, putting data access logic in the domain object. This way all people know how to read and write their data to and from the database.

How It Works

The essence of an *Active Record* is a *Domain Model (116)* in which the classes match very closely the record structure of an underlying database. Each *Active Record* is responsible for saving and loading to the database and also for any domain logic that acts on the data. This may be all the domain logic in the application, or you may find that some domain logic is held in *Transaction Scripts (110)* with common and data-oriented code in the *Active Record*.

The data structure of the *Active Record* should exactly match that of the database: one field in the class for each column in the table. Type the fields the way the SQL interface gives you the data—don't do any conversion at this stage. You may consider *Foreign Key Mapping (236)*, but you may also leave the foreign keys as they are. You can use views or tables with *Active Record*, although updates through views are obviously harder. Views are particularly useful for reporting purposes.

The *Active Record* class typically has methods that do the following:

- Construct an instance of the *Active Record* from a SQL result set row

- Construct a new instance for later insertion into the table

- Static finder methods to wrap commonly used SQL queries and return *Active Record* objects

- Update the database and insert into it the data in the *Active Record*

- Get and set the fields

- Implement some pieces of business logic

Active Record

The getting and setting methods can do some other intelligent things, such as convert from SQL-oriented types to better in-memory types. Also, if you ask for a related table, the getting method can return the appropriate *Active Record*, even if you aren't using *Identity Field (216)* on the data structure (by doing a lookup).

In this pattern the classes are convenient, but they don't hide the fact that a relational database is present. As a result you usually see fewer of the other object-relational mapping patterns present when you're using *Active Record*.

Active Record is very similar to *Row Data Gateway (152)*. The principal difference is that a *Row Data Gateway (152)* contains only database access while an *Active Record* contains both data source and domain logic. Like most boundaries in software, the line between the two isn't terribly sharp, but it's useful.

Because of the close coupling between the *Active Record* and the database, I more often see static find methods in this pattern. However, there's no reason that you can't separate out the find methods into a separate class, as I discussed with *Row Data Gateway (152),* and that is better for testing.

As with the other tabular patterns, you can use *Active Record* with a view or query as well as a table.

When to Use It

Active Record is a good choice for domain logic that isn't too complex, such as creates, reads, updates, and deletes. Derivations and validations based on a single record work well in this structure.

In an initial design for a *Domain Model (116)* the main choice is between *Active Record* and *Data Mapper (165)*. *Active Record* has the primary advantage of simplicity. It's easy to build *Active Records*, and they are easy to understand. Their primary problem is that they work well only if the *Active Record* objects correspond directly to the database tables: an isomorphic schema. If your business logic is complex, you'll soon want to use your object's direct relationships, collections, inheritance, and so forth. These don't map easily onto *Active Record*, and adding them piecemeal gets very messy. That's what will lead you to use *Data Mapper (165)* instead.

Another argument against *Active Record* is the fact that it couples the object design to the database design. This makes it more difficult to refactor either design as a project goes forward.

Active Record is a good pattern to consider if you're using *Transaction Script (110)* and are beginning to feel the pain of code duplication and the difficulty in updating scripts and tables that *Transaction Script (110)* often brings. In this case you can gradually start creating *Active Records* and then slowly refactor behavior into them. It often helps to wrap the tables as a *Gateway (466)* first, and then start moving behavior so that the tables evolve to a *Active Record*.

Example: A Simple Person (Java)

This is a simple, even simplistic, example to show how the bones of *Active Record* work. We begin with a basic Person class.

class Person...

```
    private String lastName;
    private String firstName;
    private int numberOfDependents;
```

There's also an ID field in the superclass.

The database is set up with the same structure.

```
create table people (ID int primary key, lastname varchar,
                     firstname varchar, number_of_dependents int)
```

To load an object, the person class acts as the finder and also performs the load. It uses static methods on the person class.

class Person...

```
    private final static String findStatementString =
        "SELECT id, lastname, firstname, number_of_dependents" +
        "  FROM people" +
        "  WHERE id = ?";
    public static Person find(Long id) {
        Person result = (Person) Registry.getPerson(id);
        if (result != null) return result;
        PreparedStatement findStatement = null;
        ResultSet rs = null;
```

```
        try {
            findStatement = DB.prepare(findStatementString);
            findStatement.setLong(1, id.longValue());
            rs = findStatement.executeQuery();
            rs.next();
            result = load(rs);
            return result;
        } catch (SQLException e) {
            throw new ApplicationException(e);
        } finally {
            DB.cleanUp(findStatement, rs);
        }
    }
    public static Person find(long id) {
        return find(new Long(id));
    }
    public static Person load(ResultSet rs) throws SQLException {
        Long id = new Long(rs.getLong(1));
        Person result = (Person) Registry.getPerson(id);
        if (result != null) return result;
        String lastNameArg = rs.getString(2);
        String firstNameArg = rs.getString(3);
        int numDependentsArg = rs.getInt(4);
        result = new Person(id, lastNameArg, firstNameArg, numDependentsArg);
        Registry.addPerson(result);
        return result;
    }
```

Updating an object takes a simple instance method.

```
class Person...

    private final static String updateStatementString =
            "UPDATE people" +
            "  set lastname = ?, firstname = ?, number_of_dependents = ?" +
            "  where id = ?";
    public void update() {
        PreparedStatement updateStatement = null;
        try {
            updateStatement = DB.prepare(updateStatementString);
            updateStatement.setString(1, lastName);
            updateStatement.setString(2, firstName);
            updateStatement.setInt(3, numberOfDependents);
            updateStatement.setInt(4, getID().intValue());
            updateStatement.execute();
        } catch (Exception e) {
            throw new ApplicationException(e);
        } finally {
            DB.cleanUp(updateStatement);
        }
    }
```

Insertions are also mostly pretty simple.

```
class Person...
    private final static String insertStatementString =
        "INSERT INTO people VALUES (?, ?, ?, ?)";
    public Long insert() {
        PreparedStatement insertStatement = null;
        try {
            insertStatement = DB.prepare(insertStatementString);
            setID(findNextDatabaseId());
            insertStatement.setInt(1, getID().intValue());
            insertStatement.setString(2, lastName);
            insertStatement.setString(3, firstName);
            insertStatement.setInt(4, numberOfDependents);
            insertStatement.execute();
            Registry.addPerson(this);
            return getID();
        } catch (Exception e) {
            throw new ApplicationException(e);
        } finally {
            DB.cleanUp(insertStatement);
        }
    }
```

Active Record

Any business logic, such as calculating the exemption, sits directly in the Person class.

```
class Person...
    public Money getExemption() {
        Money baseExemption = Money.dollars(1500);
        Money dependentExemption = Money.dollars(750);
        return baseExemption.add(dependentExemption.multiply(this.getNumberOfDependents()));
    }
```

Data Mapper

*A layer of Mappers (473) that moves data between objects
and a database while keeping them independent of
each other and the mapper itself.*

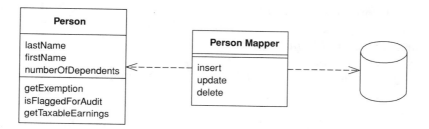

Objects and relational databases have different mechanisms for structuring
data. Many parts of an object, such as collections and inheritance, aren't
present in relational databases. When you build an object model with a lot of
business logic it's valuable to use these mechanisms to better organize the data
and the behavior that goes with it. Doing so leads to variant schemas; that is,
the object schema and the relational schema don't match up.

   You still need to transfer data between the two schemas, and this data transfer becomes a complexity in its own right. If the in-memory objects know
about the relational database structure, changes in one tend to ripple to the
other.

   The *Data Mapper* is a layer of software that separates the in-memory objects
from the database. Its responsibility is to transfer data between the two and
also to isolate them from each other. With *Data Mapper* the in-memory objects
needn't know even that there's a database present; they need no SQL interface
code, and certainly no knowledge of the database schema. (The database
schema is always ignorant of the objects that use it.) Since it's a form of *Mapper*
(473), *Data Mapper* itself is even unknown to the domain layer.

How It Works

The separation between domain and data source is the main function of a *Data
Mapper,* but there are plenty of details that have to be addressed to make this
happen. There's also a lot of variety in how mapping layers are built. Many of

the comments here are pretty broad, because I try to give a general overview of what you need to separate the cat from its skin.

We'll start with a very basic *Data Mapper* example. This is the simplest style of this layer that you can have and might not seem worth doing. With simple database mapping examples other patterns usually are simpler and thus better. If you are going to use *Data Mapper* at all you usually need more complicated cases. However, it's easier to explain the ideas if we start simple at a very basic level.

A simple case would have a Person and Person Mapper class. To load a person from the database, a client would call a find method on the mapper (Figure 10.3). The mapper uses an *Identity Map (195)* to see if the person is already loaded; if not, it loads it.

Updates are shown in Figure 10.4. A client asks the mapper to save a domain object. The mapper pulls the data out of the domain object and shuttles it to the database.

The whole layer of *Data Mapper* can be substituted, either for testing purposes or to allow a single domain layer to work with different databases.

A simple *Data Mapper* would just map a database table to an equivalent in-memory class on a field-to-field basis. Of course, things aren't usually simple. Mappers need a variety of strategies to handle classes that turn into multiple fields, classes that have multiple tables, classes with inheritance, and the joys of connecting together objects once they've been sorted out. The various object-relational mapping patterns in this book are all about that. It's usually easier to deploy these patterns with a *Data Mapper* than it is with the other organizing alternatives.

When it comes to inserts and updates, the database mapping layer needs to understand what objects have changed, which new ones have been created, and which ones have been destroyed. It also has to fit the whole workload into a transactional framework. The *Unit of Work (184)* pattern is a good way to organize this.

Figure 10.3 suggests that a single request to a find method results in a single SQL query. This isn't always true. Loading a typical order with multiple order lines may involve loading the order lines as well. The request from the client will usually lead to a graph of objects being loaded, with the mapper designer deciding exactly how much to pull back in one go. The point of this is to minimize database queries, so the finders typically need to know a fair bit about how clients use the objects in order to make the best choices for pulling data back.

This example leads to cases where you load multiple classes of domain objects from a single query. If you want to load orders and order lines, it will usually be faster to do a single query that joins the orders and order line tables. You then use the result set to load both the order and the order line instances (page 243).

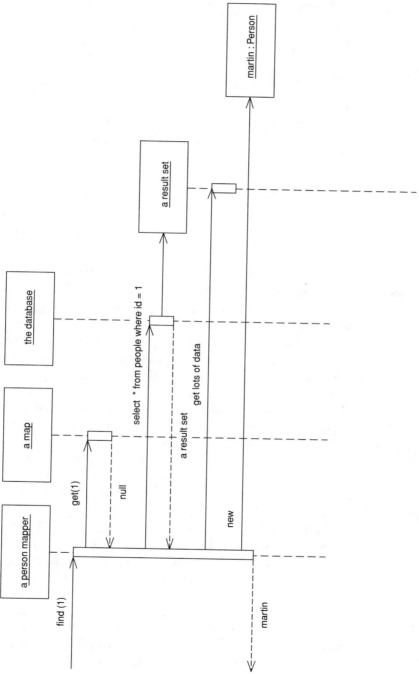

Figure 10.3 *Retrieving data from a database.*

Data Mapper

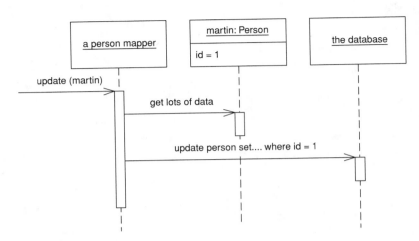

Figure 10.4 *Updating data.*

Since objects are very interconnected, you usually have to stop pulling the data back at some point. Otherwise, you're likely to pull back the entire database with a request. Again, mapping layers have techniques to deal with this while minimizing the impact on the in-memory objects, using *Lazy Load (200)*. Hence, the in-memory objects can't be entirely ignorant of the mapping layer. They may need to know about the finders and a few other mechanisms.

An application can have one *Data Mapper* or several. If you're hardcoding your mappers, it's best to use one for each domain class or root of a domain hierarchy. If you're using *Metadata Mapping (306)*, you can get away with a single mapper class. In the latter case the limiting problem is your find methods. With a large application it can be too much to have a single mapper with lots of find methods, so it makes sense to split these methods up by each domain class or head of the domain hierarchy. You get a lot of small finder classes, but it's easy for a developer to locate the finder she needs.

As with any database find behavior, the finders need to use an *Identity Map (195)* in order to maintain the identity of the objects read from the database. Either you can have a *Registry (480)* of *Identity Maps (195)*, or you can have each finder hold an *Identity Map (195)* (providing there is only one finder per class per session).

Handling Finders In order to work with an object, you have to load it from the database. Usually the presentation layer will initiate things by loading some initial objects. Then control moves into the domain layer, at which point the code will mainly move from object to object using associations between them. This will work effectively providing that the domain layer has all the objects it needs loaded into memory or that you use *Lazy Load (200)* to load in additional objects when needed.

On occasion you may need the domain objects to invoke find methods on the *Data Mapper*. However, I've found that with a good *Lazy Load (200)* you can completely avoid this. For simpler applications, though, may not be worth trying to manage everything with associations and *Lazy Load (200)*. Still, you don't want to add a dependency from your domain objects to your *Data Mapper*.

You can solve this dilemma by using *Separated Interface (476)*. Put any find methods needed by the domain code into an interface class that you can place in the domain package.

Mapping Data to Domain Fields Mappers need access to the fields in the domain objects. Often this can be a problem because you need public methods to support the mappers you don't want for domain logic. (I'm assuming that you won't commit the cardinal sin of making fields public.) There's no easy to answer to this. You could use a lower level of visibility by packaging the mappers closer to the domain objects, such as in the same package in Java, but this confuses the bigger dependency picture because you don't want other parts of the system that know the domain objects to know about the mappers. You can use reflection, which can often bypass the visibility rules of the language. It's slower, but the slower speed may end up as just a rounding error compared to the time taken by the SQL call. Or you can use public methods, but guard them with a status field so that they throw an exception if they're used outside the context of a database load. If so, name them in such a way that they're not mistaken for regular getters and setters.

Tied to this is the issue of when you create the object. In essence you have two options. One is to create the object with a **rich constructor** so that it's at least created with all its mandatory data. The other is to create an empty object and then populate it with the mandatory data. I usually prefer the former since it's nice to have a well-formed object from the start. This also means that, if you have an immutable field, you can enforce it by not providing any method to change its value.

The problem with a rich constructor is that you have to be aware of cyclic references. If you have two objects that reference each other, each time you try to load one it will try to load the other, which will in turn try to load the first one, and so on, until you run out of stack space. Avoiding this requires special case code, often using *Lazy Load (200)*. Writing this special case code is messy, so it's worth trying to do without it. You can do this by creating an **empty**

object. Use a no-arg constructor to create a blank object and insert that empty object immediately into the *Identity Map (195)*. That way, if you have a cycle, the *Identity Map (195)* will return an object to stop the recursive loading.

Using an empty object like this means you may need some setters for values that are truly immutable when the object is loaded. A combination of a naming convention and perhaps some status-checking guards can fix this. You can also use reflection for data loading.

Metadata-Based Mappings One of the decisions you need to make concerns storing the information about how fields in domain objects are mapped to columns in the database. The simplest, and often best, way to do this is with explicit code, which requires a mapper class for each domain object. The mapper does the mapping through assignments and has fields (usually constant strings) to store the SQL for database access. An alternative is to use *Metadata Mapping (306)*, which stores the metadata as data, either in a class or in a separate file. The great advantage of metadata is that all the variation in the mappers can be handled through data without the need for more source code, either by use of code generation or reflective programming.

When to Use It

The primary occasion for using *Data Mapper* is when you want the database schema and the object model to evolve independently. The most common case for this is with a *Domain Model (116)*. *Data Mapper's* primary benefit is that when working on the domain model you can ignore the database, both in design and in the build and testing process. The domain objects have no idea what the database structure is, because all the correspondence is done by the mappers.

This helps you in the code because you can understand and work with the domain objects without having to understand how they're stored in the database. You can modify the *Domain Model (116)* or the database without having to alter either. With complicated mappings, particularly those involving existing databases, this is very valuable.

The price, of course, is the extra layer that you don't get with *Active Record (160)*, so the test for using these patterns is the complexity of the business logic. If you have fairly simple business logic, you probably won't need a *Domain Model (116)* or a *Data Mapper*. More complicated logic leads you to *Domain Model (116)* and therefore to *Data Mapper*.

I wouldn't choose *Data Mapper* without *Domain Model (116)*, but can I use *Domain Model (116)* without *Data Mapper*? If the domain model is pretty simple, and the database is under the domain model developers' control, then it's reasonable for the domain objects to access the database directly with *Active Record (160)*. Effectively this puts the mapper behavior discussed here into the domain objects themselves. As things become more complicated, it's better to refactor the database behavior out into a separate layer.

Remember that you don't have to build a full-featured database-mapping layer. It's a complicated beast to build, and there are products available that do this for you. For most cases I recommend buying a database-mapping layer rather than building one yourself.

Example: A Simple Database Mapper (Java)

Here's an absurdly simple use of *Data Mapper* to give you a feel for the basic structure. Our example is a person with an isomorphic people table.

class Person...

```
private String lastName;
private String firstName;
private int numberOfDependents;
```

The database schema looks like this:

```
create table people (ID int primary key, lastname varchar,
                     firstname varchar, number_of_dependents int)
```

We'll use the simple case here, where the Person Mapper class also implements the finder and *Identity Map (195)*. However, I've added an abstract mapper *Layer Supertype (475)* to indicate where I can pull out some common behavior. Loading involves checking that the object isn't already in the *Identity Map (195)* and then pulling the data from the database.

The find behavior starts in the Person Mapper, which wraps calls to an abstract find method to find by ID.

class PersonMapper...

```
protected String findStatement() {
    return "SELECT " + COLUMNS +
       "  FROM people" +
       "  WHERE id = ?";
}
public static final String COLUMNS = " id, lastname, firstname, number_of_dependents ";
public Person find(Long id) {
    return (Person) abstractFind(id);
}
public Person find(long id) {
    return find(new Long(id));
}
```

```
class AbstractMapper...

   protected Map loadedMap = new HashMap();
   abstract protected String findStatement();
   protected DomainObject abstractFind(Long id) {
      DomainObject result = (DomainObject) loadedMap.get(id);
      if (result != null) return result;
      PreparedStatement findStatement = null;
      try {
         findStatement = DB.prepare(findStatement());
         findStatement.setLong(1, id.longValue());
         ResultSet rs = findStatement.executeQuery();
         rs.next();
         result = load(rs);
         return result;
      } catch (SQLException e) {
         throw new ApplicationException(e);
      } finally {
         DB.cleanUp(findStatement);
      }
   }
```

The find method calls the load method, which is split between the abstract
and person mappers. The abstract mapper checks the ID, pulling it from the
data and registering the new object in the *Identity Map (195)*.

```
class AbstractMapper...

   protected DomainObject load(ResultSet rs) throws SQLException {
      Long id = new Long(rs.getLong(1));
      if (loadedMap.containsKey(id)) return (DomainObject) loadedMap.get(id);
      DomainObject result = doLoad(id, rs);
      loadedMap.put(id, result);
      return result;
   }
   abstract protected DomainObject doLoad(Long id, ResultSet rs) throws SQLException;

class PersonMapper...

   protected DomainObject doLoad(Long id, ResultSet rs) throws SQLException {
      String lastNameArg = rs.getString(2);
      String firstNameArg = rs.getString(3);
      int numDependentsArg = rs.getInt(4);
      return new Person(id, lastNameArg, firstNameArg, numDependentsArg);
   }
```

Notice that the *Identity Map (195)* is checked twice, once by abstractFind and
once by load. There's a reason for this madness.

I need to check the map in the finder because, if the object is already there, I
can save myself a trip to the database—I always want to save myself that long
hike if I can. But I also need to check in the load because I may have queries

that I can't be sure of resolving in the *Identity Map (195)*. Say I want to find everyone whose last name matches some search pattern. I can't be sure that I have all such people already loaded, so I have to go to the database and run a query.

class PersonMapper...

```
    private static String findLastNameStatement =
        "SELECT " + COLUMNS +
        "  FROM people " +
        "  WHERE UPPER(lastname) like UPPER(?)" +
        "  ORDER BY lastname";
    public List findByLastName(String name) {
        PreparedStatement stmt = null;
        ResultSet rs = null;
        try {
            stmt = DB.prepare(findLastNameStatement);
            stmt.setString(1, name);
            rs = stmt.executeQuery();
            return loadAll(rs);
        } catch (SQLException e) {
            throw new ApplicationException(e);
        } finally {
            DB.cleanUp(stmt, rs);
        }
    }
```

class AbstractMapper...

```
    protected List loadAll(ResultSet rs) throws SQLException {
        List result = new ArrayList();
        while (rs.next())
            result.add(load(rs));
        return result;
    }
```

When I do this I may pull back some rows in the result set that correspond to people I've already loaded. I have to ensure that I don't make a duplicate, so I have to check the *Identity Map (195)* again.

Writing a find method this way in each subclass that needs it involves some basic, but repetitive, coding, which I can eliminate by providing a general method.

class AbstractMapper...

```
    public List findMany(StatementSource source) {
        PreparedStatement stmt = null;
        ResultSet rs = null;
        try {
```

```
        stmt = DB.prepare(source.sql());
        for (int i = 0; i < source.parameters().length; i++)
            stmt.setObject(i+1, source.parameters()[i]);
        rs = stmt.executeQuery();
        return loadAll(rs);
    } catch (SQLException e) {
        throw new ApplicationException(e);
    } finally {
        DB.cleanUp(stmt, rs);
    }
}
```

For this to work I need an interface that wraps both the SQL string and the loading of parameters into the prepared statement.

interface StatementSource...

```
    String sql();
    Object[] parameters();
```

I can then use this facility by providing a suitable implementation as an inner class.

class PersonMapper...

```
    public List findByLastName2(String pattern) {
        return findMany(new FindByLastName(pattern));
    }
    static class FindByLastName implements StatementSource {
        private String lastName;
        public FindByLastName(String lastName) {
            this.lastName = lastName;
        }
        public String sql() {
            return
                "SELECT " + COLUMNS +
                "  FROM people " +
                "  WHERE UPPER(lastname) like UPPER(?)" +
                "  ORDER BY lastname";
        }
        public Object[] parameters() {
            Object[] result = {lastName};
            return result;
        }
    }
```

This kind of work can be done in other places where there's repetitive statement invocation code. On the whole I've made the examples here more straight to make them easier to follow. If you find yourself writing a lot of repetitive straight-ahead code you should consider doing something similar.

With the update the JDBC code is specific to the subtype.

class PersonMapper...

```
private static final String updateStatementString =
    "UPDATE people " +
    "  SET lastname = ?, firstname = ?, number_of_dependents = ? " +
    "  WHERE id = ?";
public void update(Person subject) {
    PreparedStatement updateStatement = null;
    try {
        updateStatement = DB.prepare(updateStatementString);
        updateStatement.setString(1, subject.getLastName());
        updateStatement.setString(2, subject.getFirstName());
        updateStatement.setInt(3, subject.getNumberOfDependents());
        updateStatement.setInt(4, subject.getID().intValue());
        updateStatement.execute();
    } catch (Exception e) {
        throw new ApplicationException(e);
    } finally {
        DB.cleanUp(updateStatement);
    }
}
```

For the insert some code can be factored into the *Layer Supertype (475)*

class AbstractMapper...

```
public Long insert(DomainObject subject) {
    PreparedStatement insertStatement = null;
    try {
        insertStatement = DB.prepare(insertStatement());
        subject.setID(findNextDatabaseId());
        insertStatement.setInt(1, subject.getID().intValue());
        doInsert(subject, insertStatement);
        insertStatement.execute();
        loadedMap.put(subject.getID(), subject);
        return subject.getID();
    } catch (SQLException e) {
        throw new ApplicationException(e);
    } finally {
        DB.cleanUp(insertStatement);
    }
}
abstract protected String insertStatement();
abstract protected void doInsert(DomainObject subject, PreparedStatement insertStatement)
    throws SQLException;
```

class PersonMapper...

```
protected String insertStatement() {
    return "INSERT INTO people VALUES (?, ?, ?, ?)";
```

```
        }
    protected void doInsert(
            DomainObject abstractSubject,
            PreparedStatement stmt)
            throws SQLException
    {
        Person subject = (Person) abstractSubject;
        stmt.setString(2, subject.getLastName());
        stmt.setString(3, subject.getFirstName());
        stmt.setInt(4, subject.getNumberOfDependents());
    }
```

Example: Separating the Finders (Java)

To allow domain objects to invoke finder behavior I can use *Separated Interface (476)* to separate the finder interfaces from the mappers (Figure 10.5). I can put these finder interfaces in a separate package that's visible to the domain layer, or, as in this case, I can put them in the domain layer itself.

One of the most common finds is one that finds an object according to a particular surrogate ID. Much of this processing is quite generic, so it can be handled by a suitable *Layer Supertype (475)*. All it needs is a *Layer Supertype (475)* for domain objects that know about IDs.

The interface for finding lies in the finder interface. It's usually best not made generic because you need to know what the return type is.

```
interface ArtistFinder...

    Artist find(Long id);
    Artist find(long id);
```

The finder interface is best declared in the domain package with the finders held in a *Registry (480)*. In this case I've made the mapper class implement the finder interface.

```
class ArtistMapper implements ArtistFinder...

    public Artist find(Long id) {
        return (Artist) abstractFind(id);
    }
    public Artist find(long id) {
        return find(new Long(id));
    }
```

The bulk of the find method is done by the mapper's *Layer Supertype (475)*, which checks the *Identity Map (195)* to see if the object is already in memory. If

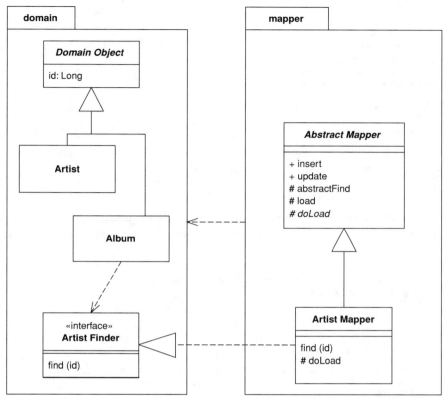

Figure 10.5 *Defining a finder interface in the domain package.*

not, it completes a prepared statement that's loaded in by the artist mapper and executes it.

```
class AbstractMapper...

    abstract protected String findStatement();
    protected Map loadedMap = new HashMap();
    protected DomainObject abstractFind(Long id) {
        DomainObject result = (DomainObject) loadedMap.get(id);
        if (result != null) return result;
        PreparedStatement stmt = null;
        ResultSet rs = null;
        try {
            stmt = DB.prepare(findStatement());
            stmt.setLong(1, id.longValue());
```

```
            rs = stmt.executeQuery();
            rs.next();
            result = load(rs);
            return result;
        } catch (SQLException e) {
            throw new ApplicationException(e);
        } finally {cleanUp(stmt, rs);
        }
    }
```

class ArtistMapper...

```
    protected String findStatement() {
        return "select " + COLUMN_LIST + " from artists art where ID = ?";
    }
    public static String COLUMN_LIST = "art.ID, art.name";
```

The find part of the behavior is about getting either the existing object or a new one. The load part is about putting the data from the database into a new object.

class AbstractMapper...

```
    protected DomainObject load(ResultSet rs) throws SQLException {
        Long id = new Long(rs.getLong("id"));
        if (loadedMap.containsKey(id)) return (DomainObject) loadedMap.get(id);
        DomainObject result = doLoad(id, rs);
        loadedMap.put(id, result);
        return result;
    }
    abstract protected DomainObject doLoad(Long id, ResultSet rs) throws SQLException;
```

class ArtistMapper...

```
    protected DomainObject doLoad(Long id, ResultSet rs) throws SQLException {
        String name = rs.getString("name");
        Artist result = new Artist(id, name);
        return result;
    }
```

Notice that the load method also checks the *Identity Map (195)*. Although redundant in this case, the load can be called by other finders that haven't already done this check. In this scheme all a subclass has to do is develop a doLoad method to load the actual data needed, and return a suitable prepared statement from the findStatement method.

You can also do a find based on a query. Say we have a database of tracks and albums and we want a finder that will find all the tracks on a specified album. Again the interface declares the finders.

interface TrackFinder...

```
    Track find(Long id);
    Track find(long id);
    List findForAlbum(Long albumID);
```

Since this is a specific find method for this class, it's implemented in a specific class, such as the track mapper class, rather than in a *Layer Supertype (475)*. As with any finder, there are two methods to the implementation. One sets up the prepared statement; the other wraps the call to the prepared statement and interprets the results.

```
class TrackMapper...

   public static final String findForAlbumStatement =
       "SELECT ID, seq, albumID, title " +
       "FROM tracks " +
       "WHERE albumID = ? ORDER BY seq";
   public List findForAlbum(Long albumID) {
       PreparedStatement stmt = null;
       ResultSet rs = null;
       try {
           stmt = DB.prepare(findForAlbumStatement);
           stmt.setLong(1, albumID.longValue());
           rs = stmt.executeQuery();
           List result = new ArrayList();
           while (rs.next())
               result.add(load(rs));
           return result;
       } catch (SQLException e) {
           throw new ApplicationException(e);
       } finally {cleanUp(stmt, rs);
       }
   }
```

The finder calls a load method for each row in the result set. This method has the responsibility of creating the in-memory object and loading it with the data. As in the previous example, some of this can be handled in a *Layer Supertype (475)*, including checking the *Identity Map (195)* to see if something is already loaded.

Example: Creating an Empty Object (Java)

There are two basic approaches for loading an object. One is to create a fully valid object with a constructor, which is what I've done in the examples above. This results in the following loading code:

```
class AbstractMapper...

   protected DomainObject load(ResultSet rs) throws SQLException {
       Long id = new Long(rs.getLong(1));
       if (loadedMap.containsKey(id)) return (DomainObject) loadedMap.get(id);
       DomainObject result = doLoad(id, rs);
       loadedMap.put(id, result);
       return result;
```

```
    }
    abstract protected DomainObject doLoad(Long id, ResultSet rs) throws SQLException;
```

class PersonMapper...

```
    protected DomainObject doLoad(Long id, ResultSet rs) throws SQLException {
        String lastNameArg = rs.getString(2);
        String firstNameArg = rs.getString(3);
        int numDependentsArg = rs.getInt(4);
        return new Person(id, lastNameArg, firstNameArg, numDependentsArg);
    }
```

The alternative is to create an empty object and load it with the setters later.

class AbstractMapper...

```
    protected DomainObjectEL load(ResultSet rs) throws SQLException {
        Long id = new Long(rs.getLong(1));
        if (loadedMap.containsKey(id)) return (DomainObjectEL) loadedMap.get(id);
        DomainObjectEL result = createDomainObject();
        result.setID(id);
        loadedMap.put(id, result);
        doLoad (result, rs);
        return result;
    }
    abstract protected DomainObjectEL createDomainObject();
    abstract protected void doLoad(DomainObjectEL obj, ResultSet rs) throws SQLException;
```

class PersonMapper...

```
    protected DomainObjectEL createDomainObject() {
        return new Person();
    }
    protected void doLoad(DomainObjectEL obj, ResultSet rs) throws SQLException {
        Person person = (Person) obj;
        person.dbLoadLastName(rs.getString(2));
        person.setFirstName(rs.getString(3));
        person.setNumberOfDependents(rs.getInt(4));
    }
```

Notice that I'm using a different kind of domain object *Layer Supertype (475)* here, because I want to control the use of the setters. Let's say that I want the last name of a person to be an immutable field. In this case I don't want to change the value of the field once it's loaded, so I add a status field to the domain object.

class DomainObjectEL...

```
    private int state = LOADING;
    private static final int LOADING = 0;
    private static final int ACTIVE = 1;
    public void beActive() {
        state = ACTIVE;
    }
```

I can then check the value of this during a load.

class Person...

```
public void dbLoadLastName(String lastName) {
    assertStateIsLoading();
    this.lastName = lastName;
}
```

class DomainObjectEL...

```
void assertStateIsLoading() {
    Assert.isTrue(state == LOADING);
}
```

What I don't like about this is that we now have a method in the interface that most clients of the Person class can't use. This is an argument for the mapper using reflection to set the field, which will completely bypass Java's protection mechanisms.

Is the status-based guard worth the trouble? I'm not entirely sure. On the one hand it will catch bugs caused by people calling update methods at the wrong time. On the other hand is the seriousness of the bugs worth the cost of the mechanism? At the moment I don't have a strong opinion either way.

Chapter 11

Object-Relational
Behavioral Patterns

Unit of Work

*Maintains a list of objects affected by a business transaction
and coordinates the writing out of changes and the
resolution of concurrency problems.*

Unit of Work
registerNew(object)
registerDirty (object)
registerClean(object)
registerDeleted(object)
commit()

When you're pulling data in and out of a database, it's important to keep track of what you've changed; otherwise, that data won't be written back into the database. Similarly you have to insert new objects you create and remove any objects you delete.

You can change the database with each change to your object model, but this can lead to lots of very small database calls, which ends up being very slow. Furthermore it requires you to have a transaction open for the whole interaction, which is impractical if you have a business transaction that spans multiple requests. The situation is even worse if you need to keep track of the objects you've read so you can avoid inconsistent reads.

A *Unit of Work* keeps track of everything you do during a business transaction that can affect the database. When you're done, it figures out everything that needs to be done to alter the database as a result of your work.

How It Works

The obvious things that cause you to deal with the database are changes: new object created and existing ones updated or deleted. *Unit of Work* is an object that keeps track of these things. As soon as you start doing something that may affect a database, you create a *Unit of Work* to keep track of the changes. Every time you create, change, or delete an object you tell the *Unit of Work*. You can also let it know about objects you've read so that it can check for inconsistent reads by verifying that none of the objects changed on the database during the business transaction.

The key thing about *Unit of Work* is that, when it comes time to commit, the *Unit of Work* decides what to do. It opens a transaction, does any concurrency checking (using *Pessimistic Offline Lock (426)* or *Optimistic Offline Lock (416)*), and writes changes out to the database. Application programmers never explicitly call methods for database updates. This way they don't have to keep track of what's changed or worry about how referential integrity affects the order in which they need to do things.

Of course for this to work the *Unit of Work* needs to know what objects it should keep track of. You can do this either by the caller doing it or by getting the object to tell the *Unit of Work*.

With **caller registration** (Figure 11.1), the user of an object has to remember to register the object with the *Unit of Work* for changes. Any objects that aren't registered won't be written out on commit. Although this allows forgetfulness

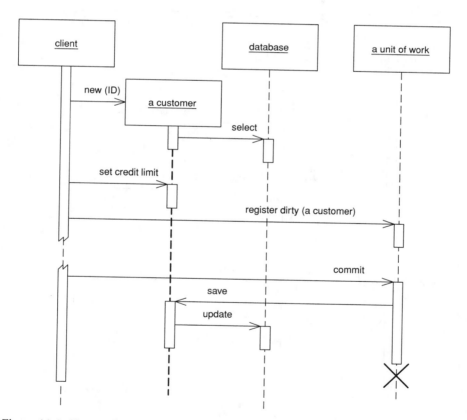

Figure 11.1 *Having the caller register a changed object.*

to cause trouble, it does give flexibility in allowing people to make in-memory changes that they don't want written out. Still, I would argue that it's going to cause far more confusion than would be worthwhile. It's better to make an explicit copy for that purpose.

With **object registration** (Figure 11.2), the onus is removed from the caller. The usual trick here is to place registration methods in object methods. Loading an object from the database registers the object as clean; the setting methods register the object as dirty. For this scheme to work the *Unit of Work* needs either to be passed to the object or to be in a well-known place. Passing the

Unit of Work

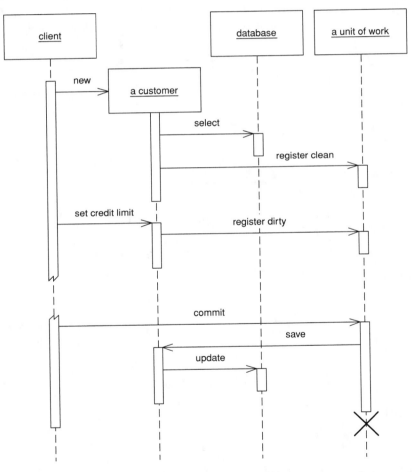

Figure 11.2 *Getting the receiver object to register itself.*

Unit of Work around is tedious but usually no problem to have it present in some kind of session object.

Even object registration leaves something to remember; that is, the developer of the object has to remember to add a registration call in the right places. The consistency becomes habitual, but is still an awkward bug when missed.

This is a natural place for code generation to generate appropriate calls, but that only works when you can clearly separate generated and nongenerated code. This problem turns out to be particularly suited to aspect-oriented programming. I've also come across post-processing of the object files to pull this off. In this example a post-processor examined all the Java .class files, looked for the appropriate methods and inserted registration calls into the byte code. Such finicking around feels dirty, but it separates the database code from the regular code. Aspect-oriented programming will do this more cleanly with source code, and as its tools become more commonplace I expect to see this strategy being used.

Another technique I've seen is **unit of work controller** (Figure 11.3), which the TOPLink product uses. Here the *Unit of Work* handles all reads from the database and registers clean objects whenever they're read. Rather than marking objects as dirty the *Unit of Work* takes a copy at read time and then compares the object at commit time. Although this adds overhead to the commit process, it allows a selective update of only those fields that were actually changed; it also avoids registration calls in the domain objects. A hybrid approach is to take copies only of changed objects. This requires registration, but it supports selective update and greatly reduces the overhead of the copy if there are many more reads than updates.

Object creation is often a special time to consider caller registration. It's not uncommon for people to create objects that are only supposed to be transient. A good example of this is in testing domain objects, where the tests run much faster without database writes. Caller registration can make this apparent. However, there are other solutions, such as providing a transient constructor that doesn't register with the *Unit of Work* or, better still, providing a *Special Case (496)Unit of Work* that does nothing with a commit.

Another area where a *Unit of Work* can be helpful is in update order when a database uses referential integrity. Most of the time you can avoid this issue by ensuring that the database only checks referential integrity when the transaction commits rather than with each SQL call. Most databases allow this, and if available there's no good reason not to do it. If not, the *Unit of Work* is the natural place to sort out the update order. In smaller systems this can be done with explicit code that contains details about which tables to write first based on the foreign key dependencies. In a larger application it's better to use metadata to

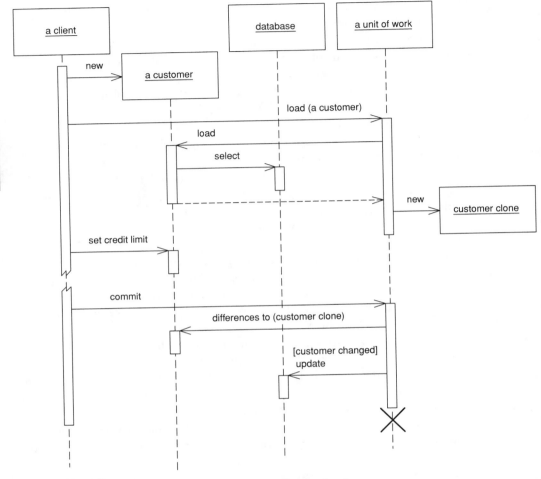

Figure 11.3 *Using the* Unit of Work *as the controller for database access.*

figure out which order to write to the database. How you do that is beyond the scope of this book, and it's a common reason to use a commercial tool. If you have to do it yourself, I'm told the key to the puzzle is a topological sort.

You can use a similar technique to minimize deadlocks. If every transaction uses the same sequence of tables to edit, you greatly reduce the risk of deadlocks. The *Unit of Work* is an ideal place to hold a fixed sequence of table writes so that you always touch the tables in the same order.

Objects need to be able to find their current *Unit of Work*. A good way to do this is with a thread-scoped *Registry (480)*. Another way is to pass the *Unit of*

Work to objects that need it, either in method calls or when you create an object. In either case make sure that more than one thread can't get access to a *Unit of Work*—there lies the way to madness.

Unit of Work makes an obvious point of handling batch updates. The idea behind a **batch update** is to send multiple SQL commands as a single unit so that they can be processed in a single remote call. This is particularly important when many updates, inserts, and deletes are sent in rapid succession. Different environments provide different levels of support for batch updates. JDBC has a facility that allows you to batch individual statements. If you don't have this feature, you can mimic it by building up a string that has multiple SQL statements and then submitting as one statement. [Nilsson] describes an example of this for Microsoft platforms. However, if you do this check to see if it interferes with statement precompilation.

Unit of Work works with any transactional resource, not just databases, so you can also use it to coordinate with message queues and transaction monitors.

.NET Implementation

In .NET the *Unit of Work* is done by the disconnected data set. This makes it a slightly different pattern from the classical variety. Most *Units of Work* I've come across register and track changes to objects. .NET reads data from the database into a data set, which is a series of objects arranged like database tables, rows, and columns. The data set is essentially an in-memory mirror image of the result of one or more SQL queries. Each data row has the concept of a version (current, original, proposed) and a state (unchanged, added, deleted, modified), which, together with the fact that the data set mimics the database structure, makes for straightforward writing of changes to the database.

When to Use It

The fundamental problem that *Unit of Work* deals with is keeping track of the various objects you've manipulated so that you know which ones you need to consider to synchronize your in-memory data with the database. If you're able to do all your work within a system transaction, the only objects you need to worry about are those you alter. Although *Unit of Work* is generally the best way of doing this, there are alternatives.

Perhaps the simplest alternative is to explicitly save any object whenever you alter it. The problem here is that you may get many more database calls than you want since, if you alter one object at three different points in your work, you get three calls rather than one call in its final state.

To avoid multiple database calls, you can leave all your updates to the end. To do this you need to keep track of all the objects that have changed. You can

Unit of Work

use variables in your code for this, but they soon become unmanageable once you have more than a few. Variables often work fine with a *Transaction Script (110)*, but they can be very difficult with a *Domain Model (116)*.

Rather than keep objects in variables you can give each object a dirty flag that you set when the object changes. Then you need to find all the dirty objects at the end of your transaction and write them out. The value of this technique hinges on how easy it is to find the dirty objects. If all of them are in a single hierarchy, then you can traverse the hierarchy and write out any that have been changed. However, a more general object network, such as a *Domain Model (116)*, is harder to traverse.

The great strength of *Unit of Work* is that it keeps all this information in one place. Once you have it working for you, you don't have to remember to do much in order to keep track of your changes. Also, *Unit of Work* is a firm platform for more complicated situations, such as handling business transactions that span several system transactions using *Optimistic Offline Lock (416)* and *Pessimistic Offline Lock (426)*.

Example: *Unit of Work* with Object Registration (Java)

by David Rice

Here's a *Unit of Work* that can track all changes for a given business transaction and then commit them to the database when instructed to do so. Our domain layer has a *Layer Supertype (475)*, DomainObject, with which the *Unit of Work* will interact. To store the change set we use three lists: new, dirty, and removed domain objects.

class UnitOfWork...

```
    private List newObjects = new ArrayList();
    private List dirtyObjects = new ArrayList();
    private List removedObjects = new ArrayList();
```

The registration methods maintain the state of these lists. They must perform basic assertions such as checking that an ID isn't null or that a dirty object isn't being registered as new.

class UnitOfWork...

```
    public void registerNew(DomainObject obj) {
        Assert.notNull("id not null", obj.getId());
        Assert.isTrue("object not dirty", !dirtyObjects.contains(obj));
        Assert.isTrue("object not removed", !removedObjects.contains(obj));
        Assert.isTrue("object not already registered new", !newObjects.contains(obj));
        newObjects.add(obj);
    }
```

```
public void registerDirty(DomainObject obj) {
    Assert.notNull("id not null", obj.getId());
    Assert.isTrue("object not removed", !removedObjects.contains(obj));
    if (!dirtyObjects.contains(obj) && !newObjects.contains(obj)) {
        dirtyObjects.add(obj);
    }
}
public void registerRemoved(DomainObject obj) {
    Assert.notNull("id not null", obj.getId());
    if (newObjects.remove(obj)) return;
    dirtyObjects.remove(obj);
    if (!removedObjects.contains(obj)) {
        removedObjects.add(obj);
    }
}
public void registerClean(DomainObject obj) {
    Assert.notNull("id not null", obj.getId());
}
```

Unit of Work

Notice that registerClean() doesn't do anything here. A common practice is to place an *Identity Map (195)* within a *Unit of Work*. An *Identity Map (195)* is necessary almost any time you store domain object state in memory because multiple copies of the same object would result in undefined behavior. Were an *Identity Map (195)* in place, registerClean() would put the registered object in it. Likewise registerNew() would put a new object in the map and registerRemoved() would remove a deleted object from the map. Without the *Identity Map (195)* you have the option of not including registerClean() in your *Unit of Work*. I've seen implementations of this method that remove changed objects from the dirty list, but partially rolling back changes is always tricky. Be careful when reversing any state in the change set.

commit() will locate the *Data Mapper (165)* for each object and invoke the appropriate mapping method. updateDirty() and deleteRemoved() aren't shown, but they would behave like insertNew(), which is as expected.

class UnitOfWork...

```
public void commit() {
    insertNew();
    updateDirty();
    deleteRemoved();
}
private void insertNew() {
    for (Iterator objects = newObjects.iterator(); objects.hasNext();) {
        DomainObject obj = (DomainObject) objects.next();
        MapperRegistry.getMapper(obj.getClass()).insert(obj);
    }
}
```

Not included in this *Unit of Work* is the tracking of any objects we've read and want to check for inconsistent read errors upon commit. This is addressed in *Optimistic Offline Lock (416)*.

Next we need to facilitate object registration. First each domain object needs to find the *Unit of Work* serving the current business transaction. Since that *Unit of Work* will be needed by the entire domain model, passing it around as a parameter is probably unreasonable. As each business transaction executes within a single thread we can associate the *Unit of Work* with the currently executing thread using the java.lang.ThreadLocal class. Keeping things simple, we'll add this functionality by using static methods on our *Unit of Work* class. If we already have some sort of session object associated with the business transaction execution thread we should place the current *Unit of Work* on that session object rather than add the management overhead of another thread mapping. Besides, the *Unit of Work* logically belongs to the session.

class UnitOfWork...

```
private static ThreadLocal current = new ThreadLocal();
public static void newCurrent() {
    setCurrent(new UnitOfWork());
}
public static void setCurrent(UnitOfWork uow) {
    current.set(uow);
}
public static UnitOfWork getCurrent() {
    return (UnitOfWork) current.get();
}
```

Now we can now give our abstract domain object the marking methods to register itself with the current *Unit of Work*.

class DomainObject...

```
protected void markNew() {
    UnitOfWork.getCurrent().registerNew(this);
}
protected void markClean() {
    UnitOfWork.getCurrent().registerClean(this);
}
protected void markDirty() {
    UnitOfWork.getCurrent().registerDirty(this);
}
protected void markRemoved() {
    UnitOfWork.getCurrent().registerRemoved(this);
}
```

Concrete domain objects need to remember to mark themselves new and dirty where appropriate.

class Album...

```
public static Album create(String name) {
   Album obj = new Album(IdGenerator.nextId(), name);
   obj.markNew();
   return obj;
}
public void setTitle(String title) {
   this.title = title;
   markDirty();
}
```

Not shown is that the registration of removed objects can be handled by a remove() method on the abstract domain object. Also, and if you've implemented registerClean() your *Data Mappers (165)* will need to register any newly loaded object as clean.

The final piece is to register and commit the *Unit of Work* where appropriate. This can be done either explicitly or implicitly. Here's what explicit *Unit of Work* management looks like:

class EditAlbumScript...

```
public static void updateTitle(Long albumId, String title) {
   UnitOfWork.newCurrent();
   Mapper mapper = MapperRegistry.getMapper(Album.class);
   Album album = (Album) mapper.find(albumId);
   album.setTitle(title);
   UnitOfWork.getCurrent().commit();
}
```

Beyond the simplest of applications, implicit *Unit of Work* management is more appropriate as it avoids repetitive, tedious coding. Here's a servlet *Layer Supertype (475)* that registers and commits the *Unit of Work* for its concrete subtypes. Subtypes will implement handleGet() rather than override doGet(). Any code executing within handleGet() will have a *Unit of Work* with which to work.

class UnitOfWorkServlet...

```
final protected void doGet(HttpServletRequest request, HttpServletResponse response)
      throws ServletException, IOException {
   try {
      UnitOfWork.newCurrent();
      handleGet(request, response);
      UnitOfWork.getCurrent().commit();
```

```
        } finally {
            UnitOfWork.setCurrent(null);
        }
    }
    abstract void handleGet(HttpServletRequest request, HttpServletResponse response)
        throws ServletException, IOException;
```

Unit of Work

The above servlet example is obviously a bit simplistic, in that it skips system transaction control. If you were using *Front Controller (344)*, you would be more likely to wrap *Unit of Work* management around your commands rather than doGet(). Similar wrapping can be done with just about any execution context.

Identity Map

Ensures that each object gets loaded only once by keeping every loaded object in a map. Looks up objects using the map when referring to them.

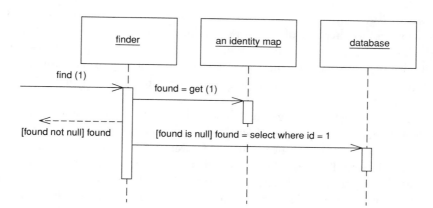

An old proverb says that a man with two watches never knows what time it is. If two watches are confusing, you can get in an even bigger mess with loading objects from a database. If you aren't careful you can load the data from the same database record into two different objects. Then, when you update them both you'll have an interesting time writing the changes out to the database correctly.

Related to this is an obvious performance problem. If you load the same data more than once you're incurring an expensive cost in remote calls. Thus, not loading the same data twice doesn't just help correctness, but can also speed up your application.

An *Identity Map* keeps a record of all objects that have been read from the database in a single business transaction. Whenever you want an object, you check the *Identity Map* first to see if you already have it.

How It Works

The basic idea behind the *Identity Map* is to have a series of maps containing objects that have been pulled from the database. In a simple case, with an isomorphic schema, you'll have one map per database table. When you load an object from the database, you first check the map. If there's an object in it that corresponds to the one you're loading, you return it. If not, you go to the database, putting the objects into the map for future reference as you load them.

There are a number of implementation choices to worry about. Also, since *Identity Maps* interact with concurrency management, so you should consider *Optimistic Offline Lock (416)* as well.

Identity Map

Choice of Keys The first thing to consider is the key for the map. The obvious choice is the primary key of the corresponding database table. This works well if the key is a single column and immutable. A surrogate primary key fits in very well with this approach because you can use it as the key in the map. The key will usually be a simple data type so the comparison behavior will work nicely.

Explicit or Generic You have to choose whether to make the *Identity Map* explicit or generic. An explicit *Identity Map* is accessed with distinct methods for each kind of object you need: such as findPerson(1). A generic map uses a single method for all kinds of objects, with perhaps a parameter to indicate which kind of object you need, such as find("Person", 1). The obvious advantage is that you can support a generic map with a generic and reusable object. It's easy to construct a reusable *Registry (480)* that work for all kinds of objects and doesn't need updating when you add a new map.

However, I prefer an explicit *Identity Map*. For a start this gives you compile-time checking in a strongly typed language. But more than that, it has all the other advantages of an explicit interface: it's easier to see what maps are available and what they're called. It does mean adding a method each time you add a new map, but that is a small overhead for the virtue of explicitness.

Your type of key affects the choice. You can only use a generic map if all your objects have the same type of key. This is a good argument for encapsulating different kinds of database key behind a single key object. (See *Identity Field (216)* for detail.)

How Many Here the decision varies between one map per class and one map for the whole session. A single map for the session works only if you have database-unique keys (see the discussion in *Identity Field (216)* for the trade-offs on that.) Once you have one *Identity Map*, the benefit is that you have only one place to go and no awkward decisions about inheritance.

If you have multiple maps, the obvious route is one map per class or per table, which works well if your database schema and object models are the same. If they look different, it's usually easier to base the maps on your objects rather than on your tables, as the objects shouldn't really know about the intricacies of the mapping.

Inheritance rears an ugly head here. If you have cars as a subtype of vehicle, do you have one map or separate maps? Keeping them separate can make polymorphic references much more awkward, since any lookup needs to know to look in all maps. As a result I prefer to use a single map for each inheritance tree, but that means that you should also make your keys unique across inheritance trees, which can be awkward if you use *Concrete Table Inheritance (293)*.

An advantage of a single map is that you don't have to add new ones when you add database tables. However, tying your maps to your *Data Mappers (165)* (see below) won't be any extra burden.

Where to Put Them *Identity Maps* need to be somewhere where they're easy to find. They're also tied to the process context you're working in. You need to ensure that each session gets it's own instance that's isolated from any other session's instance. Thus, you need to put the *Identity Map* on a session-specific object. If you're using *Unit of Work (184)* that's by far the best place for the *Identity Maps* since the *Unit of Work (184)* is the main place for keeping track of data coming in or out of the database. If you don't have a *Unit of Work (184)*, the best bet is a *Registry (480)* that's tied to the session.

As I've implied here, you usually see a single *Identity Map* for a session; otherwise, you need to provide transactional protection for your map, which is more work than any sane developer wants to do. However, there are a couple of exceptions. The biggest one is to use an object database as a transactional cache, even if you use a relational database for record data. While I haven't seen any independent performance studies, the possibilities suggest that it's worth taking a look at. Many people I respect are big fans of a transactional cache as a way to improve performance.

The other exception is for objects that are read-only in all cases. If an object can never be modified, there's no need to worry about it being shared across sessions. In performance-intensive systems it can be very beneficial to load in all read-only data once and have it available to the whole process. In this case you have your read-only *Identity Maps* held in a process context and your updatable *Identity Maps* in a session context. This also applies to objects that aren't completely read-only but are updated so rarely that you don't mind flushing the process-wide *Identity Map* and potentially bouncing the server when it happens.

Even if you're inclined to have only one *Identity Map* you can split it in two along read-only and updatable lines. You can avoid clients having to know which is which by providing an interface that checks both maps.

When to Use It

In general you use an *Identity Map* to manage any object brought from a database and modified. The key reason is that you don't want a situation where two in-memory objects correspond to a single database record—you might modify the two records inconsistently and thus confuse the database mapping.

Another value in *Identity Map* is that it acts as a cache for database reads, which means that you can avoid going to the database each time you need some data.

Identity Map

You may not need an *Identity Map* for immutable objects. If you can't change an object, then you don't have to worry about modification anomalies. Since *Value Objects (486)* are immutable, it follows that you don't need *Identity Map* for them. Still, *Identity Map* has advantages here, the most important of which is the performance advantages of the cache, another is that it helps to prevent the use of the wrong form of equality test, a problem prevalent in Java, where you can't override ==.

You don't need an *Identity Map* for a *Dependent Mapping (262)*. Since dependent objects have their persistence controlled by their parent, there's no need for a map to maintain identity. However, although you don't need a map, you may want to provide one if you need to access the object through a database key. In this case the map is merely an index, so it's arguable whether it really counts as a map at all.

Identity Map helps avoid update conflicts within a single session, but it doesn't do anything to handle conflicts that cross sessions. This is a complex problem that we discuss further in *Optimistic Offline Lock (416)* and *Pessimistic Offline Lock (426)*.

Example: Methods for an *Identity Map* (Java)

For each *Identity Map* we have a map field and accessors.

```
private Map people = new HashMap();
public static void addPerson(Person arg) {
    soleInstance.people.put(arg.getID(), arg);
}
public static Person getPerson(Long key) {
    return (Person) soleInstance.people.get(key);
}
public static Person getPerson(long key) {
    return getPerson(new Long(key));
}
```

One of the annoyances of Java is the fact that long isn't an object so you can't use it as an index for a map. This isn't as annoying as it could have been since we don't actually do any arithmetic on the index. The one place where it really hurts, though, is when you want to retrieve an object with a literal. You hardly ever need to do that in production code, but you often do in test code, so I've included a getting method that takes a long to make testing easier.

Identity Map

Lazy Load

*An object that doesn't contain all of the data you need
but knows how to get it.*

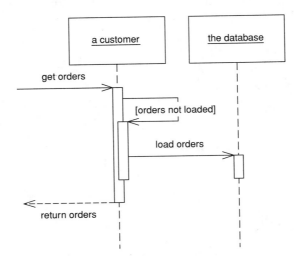

For loading data from a database into memory it's handy to design things so that as you load an object of interest you also load the objects that are related to it. This makes loading easier on the developer using the object, who otherwise has to load all the objects he needs explicitly.

However, if you take this to its logical conclusion, you reach the point where loading one object can have the effect of loading a huge number of related objects—something that hurts performance when only a few of the objects are actually needed.

A *Lazy Load* interrupts this loading process for the moment, leaving a marker in the object structure so that if the data is needed it can be loaded only when it is used. As many people know, if you're lazy about doing things you'll win when it turns out you don't need to do them at all.

How It Works

There are four main ways you can implement *Lazy Load*: lazy initialization, virtual proxy, value holder, and ghost.

Lazy initialization [Beck Patterns] is the simplest approach. The basic idea is that every access to the field checks first to see if it's null. If so, it calculates the value of the field before returning the field. To make this work you have to ensure that the field is self-encapsulated, meaning that all access to the field, even from within the class, is done through a getting method.

Using a null to signal a field that hasn't been loaded yet works well, unless null is a legal value field value. In this case you need something else to signal that the field hasn't been loaded, or you need to use a *Special Case (496)* for the null value.

Using lazy initialization is simple, but it does tend to force a dependency between the object and the database. For that reason it works best for *Active Record (160)*, *Table Data Gateway (144)*, and *Row Data Gateway (152)*. If you're using *Data Mapper (165)*, you'll need an additional layer of indirection, which you can obtain by using a **virtual proxy** [Gang of Four]. A virtual proxy is an object that looks like the object that should be in the field, but doesn't actually contain anything. Only when one of its methods is called does it load the correct object from the database.

The good thing about a virtual proxy is that it looks exactly like the object that's supposed to be there. The bad thing is that it isn't that object, so you can easily run into a nasty identity problem. Furthermore you can have more than one virtual proxy for the same real object. All of these proxies will have different object identities, yet they represent the same conceptual object. At the very least you have to override the equality method and remember to use it instead of an identity method. Without that, and discipline, you'll run into some very hard-to-track bugs.

In some environments another problem is that you end up having to create lots of virtual proxies, one for each class you're proxying. You can usually avoid this in dynamically typed languages, but in statically typed languages things often get messy. Even when the platform provides handy facilities, such as Java's proxies, other inconveniences can come up.

These problem don't hit you if you only use virtual proxies for collections classes, such as lists. Since collections are *Value Objects (486)*, their identity doesn't matter. Additionally you only have a few collection classes to write virtual collections for.

With domain classes you can get around these problems by using a **value holder**. This concept, which I first came across in Smalltalk, is an object that wraps some other object. To get the underlying object you ask the value holder for its value, but only on the first access does it pull the data from the database. The disadvantages of the value holder are that the class needs to know that it's present and that you lose the explicitness of strong typing. You can avoid identity problems by ensuring that the value holder is never passed out beyond its owning class.

A **ghost** is the real object in a partial state. When you load the object from the database it contains just its ID. Whenever you try to access a field it loads its full state. Think of a ghost as an object, where every field is lazy-initialized in one fell swoop, or as a virtual proxy, where the object is its own virtual proxy. Of course, there's no need to load all the data in one go; you may group it in groups that are commonly used together. If you use a ghost, you can put it immediately in its *Identity Map (195)*. This way you maintain identity and avoid all problems due to cyclic references when reading in data.

Lazy Load

A virtual proxy/ghost doesn't need to be completely devoid of data. If you have some data that's quick to get hold of and commonly used, it may make sense to load it when you load the proxy or ghost. (This is sometimes referred to as a "light object.")

Inheritance often poses a problem with *Lazy Load*. If you're going to use ghosts, you'll need to know what type of ghost to create, which you often can't tell without loading the thing properly. Virtual proxies can suffer from the same problem in statically typed languages.

Another danger with *Lazy Load* is that it can easily cause more database accesses than you need. A good example of this **ripple loading** is if you fill a collection with *Lazy Loads* and then look at them one at a time. This will cause you to go to the database once for each object instead of reading them all in at once. I've seen ripple loading cripple the performance of an application. One way to avoid it is never to have a collection of *Lazy Loads* but, rather make the collection itself a *Lazy Load* and, when you load it, load all the contents. The limitation of this tactic is when the collection is very large, such as all the IP addresses in the world. These aren't usually linked through associations in the object model, so that doesn't happen very often, but when it does you'll need a Value List Handler [Alur et al.].

Lazy Load is a good candidate for aspect-oriented programming. You can put *Lazy Load* behavior into a separate aspect, which allows you to change the lazy load strategy separately as well as freeing the domain developers from having to deal with lazy loading issues. I've also seen a project post-process Java bytecode to implement *Lazy Load* in a transparent way.

Often you'll run into situations where different use cases work best with different varieties of laziness. Some need one subset of the object graph; others need another subset. For maximum efficiency you want to load the right subgraph for the right use case.

The way to deal with this is to have separate database interaction objects for the different use cases. Thus, if you use *Data Mapper (165)*, you may have two order mapper objects: one that loads the line items immediately and one that loads them lazily. The application code chooses the appropriate mapper depending on the use case. A variation on this is to have the same basic loader object but defer to a strategy object to decide the loading pattern. This is a bit more sophisticated, but it can be a better way to factor behavior.

In theory you might want a range of different degrees of laziness, but in practice you really need only two: a complete load and enough of a load for identification purposes in a list. Adding more usually adds more complexity than is worthwhile.

When to Use It

Deciding when to use *Lazy Load* is all about deciding how much you want to pull back from the database as you load an object, and how many database calls that will require. It's usually pointless to use *Lazy Load* on a field that's stored in the same row as the rest of the object, because most of the time it doesn't cost any more to bring back extra data in a call, even if the data field is quite large—such as a *Serialized LOB (272)*. That means it's usually only worth considering *Lazy Load* if the field requires an extra database call to access.

In performance terms it's about deciding when you want to take the hit of bringing back the data. Often it's a good idea to bring everything you'll need in one call so you have it in place, particularly if it corresponds to a single interaction with a UI. The best time to use *Lazy Load* is when it involves an extra call and the data you're calling isn't used when the main object is used.

Adding *Lazy Load* does add a little complexity to the program, so my preference is not to use it unless I actively think I'll need it.

Example: Lazy Initialization (Java)

The essence of lazy initialization is code like this:

```
class Supplier...

    public List getProducts() {
        if (products == null) products = Product.findForSupplier(getID());
        return products;
    }
```

In this way the first access of the products field causes the data to be loaded from the database.

Example: Virtual Proxy (Java)

The key to the virtual proxy is providing a class that looks like the actual class you normally use but that actually holds a simple wrapper around the real class. Thus, a list of products for a supplier would be held with a regular list field.

class SupplierVL...

```
    private List products;
```

The most complicated thing about producing a list proxy like this is setting it up so that you can provide an underlying list that's created only when it's accessed. To do this we have to pass the code that's needed to create the list into the virtual list when it's instantiated. The best way to do this in Java is to define an interface for the loading behavior.

```
public interface VirtualListLoader {
    List load();
}
```

Then we can instantiate the virtual list with a loader that calls the appropriate mapper method.

class SupplierMapper...

```
    public static class ProductLoader implements VirtualListLoader {
        private Long id;
        public ProductLoader(Long id) {
            this.id = id;
        }
        public List load() {
            return ProductMapper.create().findForSupplier(id);
        }
    }
```

During the load method we assign the product loader to the list field.

class SupplierMapper...

```
    protected DomainObject doLoad(Long id, ResultSet rs) throws SQLException {
        String nameArg = rs.getString(2);
        SupplierVL result = new SupplierVL(id, nameArg);
        result.setProducts(new VirtualList(new ProductLoader(id)));
        return result;
    }
```

The virtual list's source list is self-encapsulated and evaluates the loader on first reference.

class VirtualList...

```
    private List source;
    private VirtualListLoader loader;
    public VirtualList(VirtualListLoader loader) {
        this.loader = loader;
```

Lazy Load

```
     }
     private List getSource() {
        if (source == null) source = loader.load();
        return source;
     }
```

The regular list methods to delegate are then implemented to the source list.

class VirtualList...

```
     public int size() {
        return getSource().size();
     }
     public boolean isEmpty() {
        return getSource().isEmpty();
     }
     // ... and so on for rest of list methods
```

This way the domain class knows nothing about how the mapper class does the *Lazy Load*. Indeed, the domain class isn't even aware that there is a *Lazy Load*.

Example: Using a Value Holder (Java)

A value holder can be used as a generic *Lazy Load*. In this case the domain type is aware that something is afoot, since the product field is typed as a value holder. This fact can be hidden from clients of the supplier by the getting method.

class SupplierVH...

```
     private ValueHolder products;
     public List getProducts() {
        return (List) products.getValue();
     }
```

The value holder itself does the *Lazy Load* behavior. It needs to be passed the necessary code to load its value when it's accessed. We can do this by defining a loader interface.

class ValueHolder...

```
     private Object value;
     private ValueLoader loader;
     public ValueHolder(ValueLoader loader) {
        this.loader = loader;
     }
     public Object getValue() {
        if (value == null) value = loader.load();
        return value;
     }
public interface ValueLoader {
   Object load();
}
```

A mapper can set up the value holder by creating an implementation of the loader and putting it into the supplier object.

class SupplierMapper...

```
protected DomainObject doLoad(Long id, ResultSet rs) throws SQLException {
    String nameArg = rs.getString(2);
    SupplierVH result = new SupplierVH(id, nameArg);
    result.setProducts(new ValueHolder(new ProductLoader(id)));
    return result;
}
public static class ProductLoader implements ValueLoader {
    private Long id;
    public ProductLoader(Long id) {
        this.id = id;
    }
    public Object load() {
        return ProductMapper.create().findForSupplier(id);
    }
}
```

Lazy Load

Example: Using Ghosts (C#)

Much of the logic for making objects ghosts can be built into *Layer Supertypes (475)*. As a consequence, if you use ghosts you tend to see them used everywhere. I'll begin our exploration of ghosts by looking at the domain object *Layer Supertype (475)*. Each domain object knows if it's a ghost or not.

class Domain Object...

```
    LoadStatus Status;
    public DomainObject (long key) {
        this.Key = key;
    }
    public Boolean IsGhost {
        get {return Status == LoadStatus.GHOST;}
    }
    public Boolean IsLoaded {
        get {return Status == LoadStatus.LOADED;}
    }
    public void MarkLoading() {
        Debug.Assert(IsGhost);
        Status = LoadStatus.LOADING;
    }
    public void MarkLoaded() {
        Debug.Assert(Status == LoadStatus.LOADING);
        Status = LoadStatus.LOADED;
    }
enum LoadStatus {GHOST, LOADING, LOADED};
```

Domain objects can be in three states: ghost, loading, and loaded. I like to wrap status information with read-only properties and explicit status change methods.

The most intrusive element of ghosts is that every accessor needs to be modified so that it will trigger a load if the object actually is a ghost.

class Employee...

```
    public String Name {
        get {
            Load();
            return _name;
        }
        set {
            Load();
            _name = value;
        }
    }
    String _name;
```

class Domain Object...

```
    protected void Load() {
        if (IsGhost)
            DataSource.Load(this);
    }
```

Such a need, which is annoying to remember, is an ideal target for aspect-oriented programming for post-processing the bytecode.

In order for the loading to work, the domain object needs to call the correct mapper. However, my visibility rules dictate that the domain code may not see the mapper code. To avoid the dependency, I need to use an interesting combination of *Registry (480)* and *Separated Interface (476)* (Figure 11.4). I define a *Registry (480)* for the domain for data source operations.

class DataSource...

```
    public static void Load (DomainObject obj) {
        instance.Load(obj);
    }
```

The instance of the data source is defined using an interface.

class DataSource...

```
  public interface IDataSource {
    void Load (DomainObject obj);
  }
```

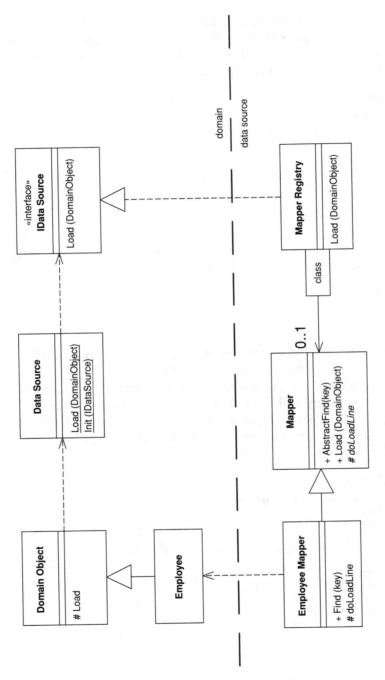

Figure 11.4 *Classes involved in loading a ghost.*

A registry of mappers, defined in the data source layer, implements the data source interface. In this case I've put the mappers in a dictionary indexed by domain type. The load method finds the correct mapper and tells it to load the appropriate domain object.

```
class MapperRegistry : IDataSource...

    public void Load (DomainObject obj) {
        Mapper(obj.GetType()).Load (obj);
    }
    public static Mapper Mapper(Type type) {
        return (Mapper) instance.mappers[type];
    }
    IDictionary mappers = new Hashtable();
```

The preceding code shows how the domain objects interact with the data source. The data source logic uses *Data Mappers (165)*. The update logic on the mappers is the same as in the case with no ghosts—the interesting behavior for this example lies in the finding and loading behavior.

Concrete mapper classes have their own find methods that use an abstract method and downcast the result.

```
class EmployeeMapper...

    public Employee Find (long key) {
        return (Employee) AbstractFind(key);
    }
```

```
class Mapper...

    public DomainObject AbstractFind (long key) {
        DomainObject result;
        result = (DomainObject) loadedMap[key];
        if (result == null) {
            result = CreateGhost(key);
            loadedMap.Add(key, result);
        }
        return result;
    }
    IDictionary loadedMap = new Hashtable();
    public abstract DomainObject CreateGhost(long key);
```

```
class EmployeeMapper...

    public override DomainObject CreateGhost(long key) {
        return new Employee(key);
    }
```

As you can see, the find method returns an object in its ghost state. The actual data does not come from the database until the load is triggered by accessing a property on the domain object.

Lazy Load

```
class Mapper...
    public void Load (DomainObject obj) {
        if (! obj.IsGhost) return;
        IDbCommand comm = new OleDbCommand(findStatement(), DB.connection);
        comm.Parameters.Add(new OleDbParameter("key",obj.Key));
        IDataReader reader = comm.ExecuteReader();
        reader.Read();
        LoadLine (reader, obj);
        reader.Close();
    }
    protected abstract String findStatement();
    public void LoadLine (IDataReader reader, DomainObject obj) {
        if (obj.IsGhost) {
            obj.MarkLoading();
            doLoadLine (reader, obj);
            obj.MarkLoaded();
        }
    }
    protected abstract void doLoadLine (IDataReader reader, DomainObject obj);
```

As is common with these examples, the *Layer Supertype (475)* handles all of the abstract behavior and then calls an abstract method for a particular subclass to play its part. For this example I've used a data reader, a cursor-based approach that's the more common for the various platforms at the moment. I'll leave it to you to extend this to a data set, which would actually be more suitable for most cases in .NET.

For this employee object, I'll show three kinds of property: a name that's a simple value, a department that's a reference to another object, and a list of timesheet records that shows the case of a collection. All are loaded together in the subclass's implementation of the hook method.

```
class EmployeeMapper...
    protected override void doLoadLine (IDataReader reader, DomainObject obj) {
        Employee employee = (Employee) obj;
        employee.Name = (String) reader["name"];
        DepartmentMapper depMapper =
            (DepartmentMapper) MapperRegistry.Mapper(typeof(Department));
        employee.Department = depMapper.Find((int) reader["departmentID"]);
        loadTimeRecords(employee);
    }
```

The name's value is loaded simply by reading the appropriate column from the data reader's current cursor. The department is read by using the find method on the department's mapper object. This will end up setting the property to a ghost of the department; the department's data will only be read when the department object itself is accessed.

The collection is the most complicated case. To avoid ripple loading, it's important to load all the time records in a single query. For this we need a special list implementation that acts as a ghost list. This list is just a thin wrapper around a real list object, to which all the real behavior is just delegated. The only thing the ghost does is ensure that any accesses to the real list triggers a load.

Lazy Load

class DomainList...

```
ILList data {
   get {
      Load();
      return _data;
   }
   set {_data = value;}
}
IList _data = new ArrayList();
public int Count {
   get {return data.Count;}
}
```

The domain list class is used by domain objects and is part of the domain layer. The actual loading needs access to SQL commands, so I use a delegate to define a loading function than can be supplied by the mapping layer.

class DomainList...

```
public void Load () {
   if (IsGhost) {
      MarkLoading();
      RunLoader(this);
      MarkLoaded();
   }
}
public delegate void Loader(DomainList list);
public Loader RunLoader;
```

Think of a delegate as a special variety of *Separated Interface (476)* for a single function. Indeed, declaring an interface with a single function in it is a reasonable alternative way of doing this.

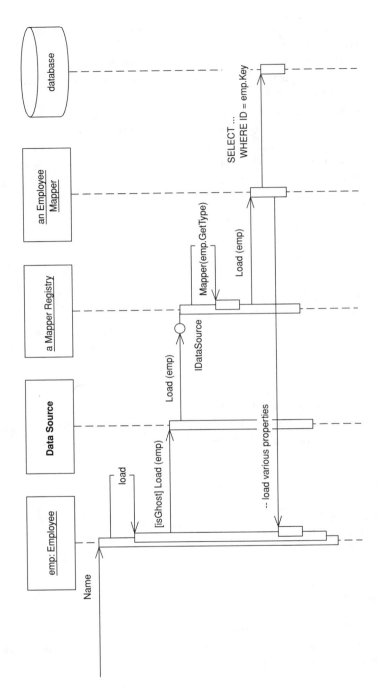

Figure 11.5 *The load sequence for a ghost.*

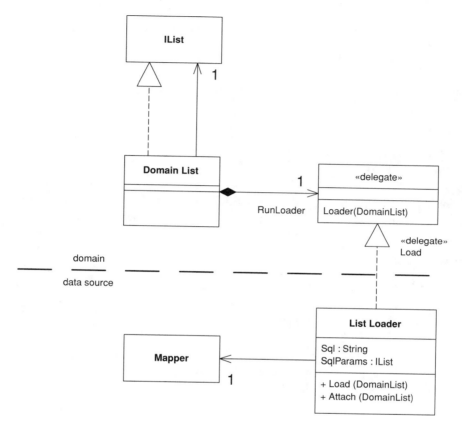

Figure 11.6 *Classes for a ghost list. As yet there's no accepted standard for showing delegates in UML models. This is my current approach.*

The loader itself has properties to specify the SQL for the load and mapper to use for mapping the time records. The employee's mapper sets up the loader when it loads the employee object.

```
class EmployeeMapper...

    void loadTimeRecords(Employee employee) {
        ListLoader loader = new ListLoader();
        loader.Sql = TimeRecordMapper.FIND_FOR_EMPLOYEE_SQL;
        loader.SqlParams.Add(employee.Key);
        loader.Mapper = MapperRegistry.Mapper(typeof(TimeRecord));
        loader.Attach((DomainList) employee.TimeRecords);
    }
```

```
class ListLoader...

    public String Sql;
    public IList SqlParams = new ArrayList();
    public Mapper Mapper;
```

Since the syntax for the delegate assignment is a bit complicated, I've given the loader an attach method.

```
class ListLoader...

    public void Attach (DomainList list) {
        list.RunLoader = new DomainList.Loader(Load);
    }
```

When the employee is loaded, the time records collection stays in a ghost state until one of the access methods fires to trigger the loader. At this point the loader executes the query to fill the list.

```
class ListLoader...

    public void Load (DomainList list) {
        list.IsLoaded = true;
        IDbCommand comm = new OleDbCommand(Sql, DB.connection);
        foreach (Object param in SqlParams)
            comm.Parameters.Add(new OleDbParameter(param.ToString(),param));
        IDataReader reader = comm.ExecuteReader();
        while (reader.Read()) {
            DomainObject obj = GhostForLine(reader);
            Mapper.LoadLine(reader, obj);
            list.Add (obj);
        }
        reader.Close();
    }
    private DomainObject GhostForLine(IDataReader reader) {
        return Mapper.AbstractFind((System.Int32)reader[Mapper.KeyColumnName]);
    }
```

Using ghost lists like this is important to reduce ripple loading. It doesn't completely eliminate it, as there are other cases where it appears. In this example, a more sophisticated mapping could load the department's data in a single query with the employee. However, always loading all the elements in a collection together helps eliminate the worst cases.

Chapter 12

Object-Relational Structural Patterns

Identity Field

Saves a database ID field in an object to maintain identity between
an in-memory object and a database row.

Person
id : long

Relational databases tell one row from another by using key—in particular, the primary key. However, in-memory objects don't need such a key, as the object system ensures the correct identity under the covers (or in C++'s case with raw memory locations). Reading data from a database is all very well, but in order to write data back you need to tie the database to the in-memory object system.

In essence, *Identity Field* is mind-numbingly simple. All you do is store the primary key of the relational database table in the object's fields.

How It Works

Although the basic notion of *Identity Field* is very simple, there are oodles of complicated issues that come up.

Choosing Your Key The first issue is what kind of key to choose in your database. Of course, this isn't always a choice, since you're often dealing with an existing database that already has its key structures in place. There's a lot of discussion and material on this in the database community. Still, mapping to objects does add some concerns to your decision.

The first concern is whether to use meaningful or meaningless keys. A **meaningful key** is something like the U.S. Social Security number for identifying a person. A **meaningless key** is essentially a random number the database dreams up that's never intended for human use. The danger with a meaningful key is that, while in theory they make good keys, in practice they don't. To work at all, keys need to be unique; to work well, they need to be immutable. While assigned numbers are supposed to be unique and immutable, human error often makes them neither. If you mistype my SSN for my wife's the resulting record is neither unique nor immutable (assuming you would like to fix the mistake.) The database should detect the uniqueness problem, but it can only do that after my record goes into the system, and of course that might not happen until after the mistake. As a result, meaningful keys should be distrusted. For small systems and/or very stable cases you may get away with it, but usually you should take a rare stand on the side of meaninglessness.

The next concern is simple versus compound keys. A **simple key** uses only one database field; a **compound key** uses more than one. The advantage of a compound key is that it's often easier to use when one table makes sense in the context of another. A good example is orders and line items, where a good key for the line item is a compound of the order number and a sequence number makes a good key for a line item. While compound keys often make sense, there is a lot to be said for the sheer uniformity of simple keys. If you use simple keys everywhere, you can use the same code for all key manipulation. Compound keys require special handling in concrete classes. (With code generation this isn't a problem). Compound keys also carry a bit of meaning, so be careful about the uniqueness and particularly the immutability rule with them.

Identity Field

You have to choose the type of the key. The most common operation you'll do with a key is equality checking, so you want a type with a fast equality operation. The other important operation is getting the next key. Hence a long integer type is often the best bet. Strings can also work, but equality checking may be slower and incrementing strings is a bit more painful. Your DBA's preferences may well decide the issue.

(Beware about using dates or times in keys. Not only are they meaningful, they also lead to problems with portability and consistency. Dates in particular are vulnerable to this because they are often stored to some fractional second precision, which can easily get out of sync and lead to identity problems.)

You can have keys that are unique to the table or unique database-wide. A **table-unique key** is unique across the table, which is what you need for a key in any case. A **database-unique key** is unique across every row in every table in the database. A table-unique key is usually fine, but a database-unique key is often easier to do and allows you to use a single *Identity Map (195)*. Modern values being what they are, it's pretty unlikely that you'll run out of numbers for new keys. If you really insist, you can reclaim keys from deleted objects with a simple database script that compacts the key space—although running this script will require that you take the application offline. However, if you use 64-bit keys (and you might as well) you're unlikely to need this.

Be wary of inheritance when you use table-unique keys. If you're using *Concrete Table Inheritance (293)* or *Class Table Inheritance (285)*, life is much easier with keys that are unique to the hierarchy rather than unique to each table. I still use the term "table-unique," even if it should strictly be something like "inheritance graph unique."

The size of your key may effect performance, particularly with indexes. This is dependent on your database system and/or how many rows you have, but it's worth doing a crude check before you get fixed into your decision.

Representing the *Identity Field* in an Object The simplest form of *Identity Field* is a field that matches the type of the key in the database. Thus, if you use a simple integral key, an integral field will work very nicely.

Compound keys are more problematic. The best bet with them is to make a key class. A generic key class can store a sequence of objects that act as the elements of the key. The key behavior for the key object (I have a quota of puns per book to fill) is equality. It's also useful to get parts of the key when you're mapping to the database.

If you use the same basic structure for all keys, you can do all of the key handling in a *Layer Supertype (475)*. You can put default behavior that will work for most cases in the *Layer Supertype (475)* and extend it for the exceptional cases in the particular subtypes.

You can have either a single key class, which takes a generic list of key objects, or key class for each domain class with explicit fields for each part of the key. I usually prefer to be explicit, but in this case I'm not sure it buys very much. You end up with lots of small classes that don't do anything interesting. The main benefit is that you can avoid errors caused by users putting the elements of the key in the wrong order, but that doesn't seem to be a big problem in practice.

If you're likely to import data between different database instances, you need to remember that you'll get key collisions unless you come up with some scheme to separate the keys between different databases. You can solve this with some kind of key migration on the imports, but this can easily get very messy.

Getting a New Key To create an object, you'll need a key. This sounds like a simple matter, but it can often be quite a problem. You have three basic choices: get the database to auto-generate, use a GUID, or generate your own.

The auto-generate route should be the easiest. Each time you insert data for the database, the database generates a unique primary key without you having to do anything. It sounds too good to be true, and sadly it often is. Not all databases do this the same way. Many that do, handle it in such a way that causes problems for object-relational mapping.

The most common auto-generation method is declaring one **auto-generated field**, which, whenever you insert a row, is incremented to a new value. The problem with this scheme is that you can't easily determine what value got gen-

Identity Field

erated as the key. If you want to insert an order and several line items, you need the key of the new order so you can put the value in the line item's foreign key. Also, you need this key before the transaction commits so you can save everything within the transaction. Sadly, databases usually don't give you this information, so you usually can't use this kind of auto-generation on any table in which you need to insert connected objects.

An alternative approach to auto-generation is a **database counter,** which Oracle uses with its sequence. An Oracle sequence works by sending a select statement that references a sequence; the database then returns an SQL record set consisting of the next sequence value. You can set a sequence to increment by any integer, which allows you to get multiple keys at once. The sequence query is automatically carried out in a separate transaction, so that accessing the sequence won't lock out other transactions inserting at the same time. A database counter like this is perfect for our needs, but it's nonstandard and not available in all databases.

A **GUID** (Globally Unique IDentifier) is a number generated on one machine that's guaranteed to be unique across all machines in space and time. Often platforms give you the API to generate a GUID. The algorithm is an interesting one involving ethernet card addresses, time of the day in nanoseconds, chip ID numbers, and probably the number of hairs on your left wrist. All that matters is that the resulting number is completely unique and thus a safe key. The only disadvantage to a GUID is that the resulting key string is big, and that can be an equally big problem. There are always times when someone needs to type in a key to a window or SQL expression, and long keys are hard both to type and to read. They may also lead to performance problems, particularly with indexes.

The last option is rolling your own. A simple staple for small systems is to use a **table scan** using the SQL max function to find the largest key in the table and then add one to use it. Sadly, this read-locks the entire table while you're doing it, which means that it works fine if inserts are rare, but your performance will be toasted if you have inserts running concurrently with updates on the same table. You also have to ensure you have complete isolation between transactions; otherwise, you can end up with multiple transactions getting the same ID value.

A better approach is to use a separate **key table.** This table is typically one with two columns: name and next available value. If you use database-unique keys, you'll have just one row in this table. If you use table-unique keys, you'll have one row for each table in the database. To use the key table, all you need to do is read that one row and note the number, the increment, the number and write it back to the row. You can grab many keys at a time by adding a suitable number when you update the key table. This cuts down on expensive database calls and reduces contention on the key table.

If you use a key table, it's a good idea to design it so that access to it is in a separate transaction from the one that updates the table you're inserting into. Say I'm inserting an order into the orders table. To do this I'll need to lock the orders row on the key table with a write lock (since I'm updating). That lock will last for the entire transaction that I'm in, locking out anyone else who wants a key. For table-unique keys, this means anyone inserting into the orders table; for database-unique keys it means anyone inserting anywhere.

Identity Field

By putting access to the key table in a separate transaction, you only lock the row for that, much shorter, transaction. The downside is that, if you roll back on your insert to the orders, the key you got from the key table is lost to everyone. Fortunately, numbers are cheap, so that's not a big issue. Using a separate transaction also allows you to get the ID as soon as you create the in-memory object, which is often some before you open the transaction to commit the business transaction.

Using a key table affects the choice of database-unique or table-unique keys. If you use a table-unique key, you have to add a row to the key table every time you add a table to the database. This is more effort, but it reduces contention on the row. If you keep your key table accesses in a different transaction, contention is not so much of a problem, especially if you get multiple keys in a single call. But if you can't arrange for the key table update to be in a separate transaction, you have a strong reason against database-unique keys.

It's good to separate the code for getting a new key into its own class, as that makes it easier to build a *Service Stub (504)* for testing purposes.

When to Use It

Use *Identity Field* when there's a mapping between objects in memory and rows in a database. This is usually when you use *Domain Model (116)* or *Row Data Gateway (152)*. You don't need this mapping if you're using *Transaction Script (110)*, *Table Module (125)*, or *Table Data Gateway (144)*.

For a small object with value semantics, such as a money or date range object that won't have its own table, it's better to use *Embedded Value (268)*. For a complex graph of objects that doesn't need to be queried within the relational database, *Serialized LOB (272)* is usually easier to write and gives faster performance.

One alternative to *Identity Field* is to extend *Identity Map (195)* to maintain the correspondence. This can be used for systems where you don't want to store an *Identity Field* in the in-memory object. *Identity Map (195)* needs to look up both ways: give me a key for an object or an object for a key. I don't see this very often because usually it's easier to store the key in the object.

Further Reading

[Marinescu] discusses several techniques for generating keys.

Example: Integral Key (C#)

The simplest form of *Identity Field* is a integral field in the database that maps to an integral field in an in-memory object.

class DomainObject...

```
public const long PLACEHOLDER_ID = -1;
public long Id = PLACEHOLDER_ID;
public Boolean isNew() {return Id == PLACEHOLDER_ID;}
```

Identity Field

An object that's been created in memory but not saved to the database will not have a value for its key. For a .NET value object this is a problem since .NET values cannot be null. Hence, the placeholder value.

The key becomes important in two places: finding and inserting. For finding you need to form a query using a key in a where clause. In .NET you can load many rows into a data set and then select a particular one with a find operation.

class CricketerMapper...

```
public Cricketer Find(long id) {
    return (Cricketer) AbstractFind(id);
}
```

class Mapper...

```
protected DomainObject AbstractFind(long id) {
    DataRow row = FindRow(id);
    return (row == null) ? null : Find(row);
}
protected DataRow FindRow(long id) {
    String filter = String.Format("id = {0}", id);
    DataRow[] results = table.Select(filter);
    return (results.Length == 0) ? null : results[0];
}
public DomainObject Find (DataRow row) {
    DomainObject result = CreateDomainObject();
    Load(result, row);
    return result;
}
abstract protected DomainObject CreateDomainObject();
```

Most of this behavior can live on the *Layer Supertype (475)*, but you'll often need to define the find on the concrete class just to encapsulate the downcast. Naturally, you can avoid this in a language that doesn't use compile-time typing.

With a simple integral *Identity Field* the insertion behavior can also be held at the *Layer Supertype (475)*.

class Mapper...

```
public virtual long Insert (DomainObject arg) {
    DataRow row = table.NewRow();
    arg.Id = GetNextID();
    row["id"] = arg.Id;
    Save (arg, row);
    table.Rows.Add(row);
    return arg.Id;
}
```

Identity Field

Essentially insertion involves creating the new row and using the next key for it. Once you have it you can save the in-memory object's data to this new row.

Example: Using a Key Table (Java)

by Matt Foemmel and Martin Fowler

If your database supports a database counter and you're not worried about being dependent on database-specific SQL, you should use the counter. Even if you're worried about being dependent on a database you should still consider it—as long as your key generation code is nicely encapsulated, you can always change it to a portable algorithm later. You could even have a strategy [Gang of Four] to use counters when you have them and roll your own when you don't.

For the moment let's assume that we have to do this the hard way. The first thing we need is a key table in the database.

```
CREATE TABLE keys (name varchar primary key, nextID int)
INSERT INTO keys VALUES ('orders', 1)
```

This table contains one row for each counter that's in the database. In this case we've initialized the key to 1. If you're preloading data in the database, you'll need to set the counter to a suitable number. If you want database-unique keys, you'll only need one row, if you want table-unique keys, you'll need one row per table.

You can wrap all of your key generation code into its own class. That way it's easier to use it more widely around one or more applications and it's easier to put key reservation into its own transaction.

We construct a key generator with its own database connection, together with information on how many keys to take from the database at one time.

class KeyGenerator...

```
private Connection conn;
private String keyName;
private long nextId;
private long maxId;
private int incrementBy;
public KeyGenerator(Connection conn, String keyName, int incrementBy) {
    this.conn = conn;
    this.keyName = keyName;
    this.incrementBy = incrementBy;
    nextId = maxId = 0;
    try {
        conn.setAutoCommit(false);
    } catch(SQLException exc) {
        throw new ApplicationException("Unable to turn off autocommit", exc);
    }
}
```

We need to ensure that no auto-commit is going on since we absolutely must have the select and update operating in one transaction.

When we ask for a new key, the generator looks to see if it has one cached rather than go to the database.

class KeyGenerator...

```
public synchronized Long nextKey() {
    if (nextId == maxId) {
        reserveIds();
    }
    return new Long(nextId++);
}
```

If the generator hasn't got one cached, it needs to go to the database.

class KeyGenerator...

```
private void reserveIds() {
    PreparedStatement stmt = null;
    ResultSet rs = null;
    long newNextId;
    try {
        stmt = conn.prepareStatement("SELECT nextID FROM keys WHERE name = ? FOR UPDATE");
        stmt.setString(1, keyName);
        rs = stmt.executeQuery();
        rs.next();
        newNextId = rs.getLong(1);
    }
```

```
      catch (SQLException exc) {
          throw new ApplicationException("Unable to generate ids", exc);
      }
      finally {
          DB.cleanUp(stmt, rs);
      }
      long newMaxId = newNextId + incrementBy;
      stmt = null;
      try {
          stmt = conn.prepareStatement("UPDATE keys SET nextID = ? WHERE name = ?");
          stmt.setLong(1, newMaxId);
          stmt.setString(2, keyName);
          stmt.executeUpdate();
          conn.commit();
          nextId = newNextId;
          maxId = newMaxId;
      }
      catch (SQLException exc) {
          throw new ApplicationException("Unable to generate ids", exc);
      }
      finally {
          DB.cleanUp(stmt);
      }
  }
```

In this case we use SELECT... FOR UPDATE to tell the database to hold a write lock on the key table. This is an Oracle-specific statement, so your mileage will vary if you're using something else. If you can't write-lock on the select, you run the risk of the transaction failing should another one get in there before you. In this case, however, you can pretty safely just rerun reserveIds until you get a pristine set of keys.

Example: Using a Compound Key (Java)

Using a simple integral key is a good, simple solution, but you often need other types or compound keys.

A Key Class As soon as you need something else it's worth putting together a key class. A key class needs to be able to store multiple elements of the key and to be able to tell if two keys are equal.

```
class Key...

   private Object[] fields;
   public boolean equals(Object obj) {
       if (!(obj instanceof Key)) return false;
       Key otherKey = (Key) obj;
       if (this.fields.length != otherKey.fields.length) return false;
```

```
        for (int i = 0; i < fields.length; i++)
            if (!this.fields[i].equals(otherKey.fields[i])) return false;
        return true;
    }
```

The most elemental way to create a key is with an array parameter.

class Key...

```
    public Key(Object[] fields) {
        checkKeyNotNull(fields);
        this.fields = fields;
    }
    private void checkKeyNotNull(Object[] fields) {
        if (fields == null) throw new IllegalArgumentException("Cannot have a null key");
        for (int i = 0; i < fields.length; i++)
            if (fields[i] == null)
                throw new IllegalArgumentException("Cannot have a null element of key");
    }
```

If you find you commonly create keys with certain elements, you can add convenience constructors. The exact ones will depend on what kinds of keys your application has.

class Key...

```
    public Key(long arg) {
        this.fields = new Object[1];
        this.fields[0] = new Long(arg);
    }
    public Key(Object field) {
        if (field == null) throw new IllegalArgumentException("Cannot have a null key");
        this.fields = new Object[1];
        this.fields[0] = field;
    }
    public Key(Object arg1, Object arg2) {
        this.fields = new Object[2];
        this.fields[0] = arg1;
        this.fields[1] = arg2;
        checkKeyNotNull(fields);
    }
```

Don't be afraid to add these convenience methods. After all, convenience is important to everyone using the keys.

Similarly you can add accessor functions to get parts of keys. The application will need to do this for the mappings.

class Key...

```
    public Object value(int i) {
        return fields[i];
    }
```

```
public Object value() {
   checkSingleKey();
   return fields[0];
}
private void checkSingleKey() {
   if (fields.length > 1)
      throw new IllegalStateException("Cannot take value on composite key");
}
public long longValue() {
   checkSingleKey();
   return longValue(0);
}
public long longValue(int i) {
   if (!(fields[i] instanceof Long))
      throw new IllegalStateException("Cannot take longValue on non long key");
   return ((Long) fields[i]).longValue();
}
```

Identity Field

In this example we'll map to an order and line item tables. The order table has a simple integral primary key, the line item table's primary key is a compound of the order's primary key and a sequence number.

```
CREATE TABLE orders (ID int primary key, customer varchar)
CREATE TABLE line_items (orderID int, seq int, amount int, product varchar,
                  primary key (orderID, seq))
```

The *Layer Supertype (475)* for domain objects needs to have a key field.

```
class DomainObjectWithKey...

   private Key key;
   protected DomainObjectWithKey(Key ID) {
      this.key = ID;
   }
   protected DomainObjectWithKey() {
   }
   public Key getKey() {
      return key;
   }
   public void setKey(Key key) {
      this.key = key;
   }
```

Reading As with other examples in this book I've split the behavior into find (which gets to the right row in the database) and load (which loads data from that row into the domain object). Both responsibilities are affected by the use of a key object.

The primary difference between these and the other examples in this book (which use simple integral keys) is that we have to factor out certain pieces of behavior that are overridden by classes that have more complex keys. For this example I'm assuming that most tables use simple integral keys. However, some use something else, so I've made the default case the simple integral and have embedded the behavior for it the mapper *Layer Supertype (475)*. The order class is one of those simple cases. Here's the code for the find behavior:

class OrderMapper...

```
    public Order find(Key key) {
        return (Order) abstractFind(key);
    }
    public Order find(Long id) {
        return find(new Key(id));
    }
    protected String findStatementString() {
        return "SELECT id, customer from orders WHERE id = ?";
    }
```

class AbstractMapper...

```
    abstract protected String findStatementString();
    protected Map loadedMap = new HashMap();
    public DomainObjectWithKey abstractFind(Key key) {
        DomainObjectWithKey result = (DomainObjectWithKey) loadedMap.get(key);
        if (result != null) return result;
        ResultSet rs = null;
        PreparedStatement findStatement = null;
        try {
            findStatement = DB.prepare(findStatementString());
            loadFindStatement(key, findStatement);
            rs = findStatement.executeQuery();
            rs.next();
            if (rs.isAfterLast()) return null;
            result = load(rs);
            return result;
        } catch (SQLException e) {
            throw new ApplicationException(e);
        } finally {
            DB.cleanUp(findStatement, rs);
        }
    }
    // hook method for keys that aren't simple integral
    protected void loadFindStatement(Key key, PreparedStatement finder) throws SQLException {
        finder.setLong(1, key.longValue());
    }
```

I've extracted out the building of the find statement, since that requires different parameters to be passed into the prepared statement. The line item is a compound key, so it needs to override that method.

```
class LineItemMapper...

    public LineItem find(long orderID, long seq) {
        Key key = new Key(new Long(orderID), new Long(seq));
        return (LineItem) abstractFind(key);
    }
    public LineItem find(Key key) {
        return (LineItem) abstractFind(key);
    }
    protected String findStatementString() {
        return
            "SELECT orderID, seq, amount, product " +
            "  FROM line_items " +
            "  WHERE (orderID = ?) AND (seq = ?)";
    }
    // hook methods overridden for the composite key
    protected void loadFindStatement(Key key, PreparedStatement finder) throws SQLException {
        finder.setLong(1, orderID(key));
        finder.setLong(2, sequenceNumber(key));
    }
    //helpers to extract appropriate values from line item's key
    private static long orderID(Key key) {
        return key.longValue(0);
    }
    private static long sequenceNumber(Key key) {
        return key.longValue(1);
    }
```

Identity Field

As well as defining the interface for the find methods and providing an SQL string for the find statement, the subclass needs to override the hook method to allow two parameters to go into the SQL statement. I've also written two helper methods to extract the parts of the key information. This makes for clearer code than I would get by just putting explicit accessors with numeric indices from the key. Such literal indices are a bad smell.

The load behavior shows a similar structure—default behavior in the *Layer Supertype (475)* for simple integral keys, overridden for the more complex cases. In this case the order's load behavior looks like this:

```
class AbstractMapper...

    protected DomainObjectWithKey load(ResultSet rs) throws SQLException {
        Key key = createKey(rs);
        if (loadedMap.containsKey(key)) return (DomainObjectWithKey) loadedMap.get(key);
        DomainObjectWithKey result = doLoad(key, rs);
        loadedMap.put(key, result);
        return result;
```

```
    }
    abstract protected DomainObjectWithKey doLoad(Key id, ResultSet rs) throws SQLException;
    // hook method for keys that aren't simple integral
    protected Key createKey(ResultSet rs) throws SQLException {
        return new Key(rs.getLong(1));
    }
```

class OrderMapper...

```
    protected DomainObjectWithKey doLoad(Key key, ResultSet rs) throws SQLException {
        String customer = rs.getString("customer");
        Order result = new Order(key, customer);
        MapperRegistry.lineItem().loadAllLineItemsFor(result);
        return result;
    }
```

The line item needs to override the hook to create a key based on two fields.

class LineItemMapper...

```
    protected DomainObjectWithKey doLoad(Key key, ResultSet rs) throws SQLException {
        Order theOrder = MapperRegistry.order().find(orderID(key));
        return doLoad(key, rs, theOrder);
    }
    protected DomainObjectWithKey doLoad(Key key, ResultSet rs, Order order)
            throws SQLException
    {
        LineItem result;
        int amount = rs.getInt("amount");
        String product = rs.getString("product");
        result = new LineItem(key, amount, product);
        order.addLineItem(result);//links to the order
        return result;
    }
    //overrides the default case
    protected Key createKey(ResultSet rs) throws SQLException {
        Key key = new Key(new Long(rs.getLong("orderID")), new Long(rs.getLong("seq")));
        return key;
    }
```

The line item also has a separate load method for use when loading all the lines for the order.

class LineItemMapper...

```
    public void loadAllLineItemsFor(Order arg) {
        PreparedStatement stmt = null;
        ResultSet rs = null;
        try {
            stmt = DB.prepare(findForOrderString);
            stmt.setLong(1, arg.getKey().longValue());
            rs = stmt.executeQuery();
            while (rs.next())
                load(rs, arg);
```

```
        } catch (SQLException e) {
            throw new ApplicationException(e);
        } finally { DB.cleanUp(stmt, rs);
        }
    }
    private final static String findForOrderString =
        "SELECT orderID, seq, amount, product " +
            "FROM line_items " +
            "WHERE orderID = ?";
    protected DomainObjectWithKey load(ResultSet rs, Order order) throws SQLException {
        Key key = createKey(rs);
        if (loadedMap.containsKey(key)) return (DomainObjectWithKey) loadedMap.get(key);
        DomainObjectWithKey result = doLoad(key, rs, order);
        loadedMap.put(key, result);
        return result;
    }
```

Identity Field

You need the special handling because the order object isn't put into the order's
Identity Map (195) until after it's created. Creating an empty object and inserting it directly into the *Identity Field* would avoid the need for this (page 169).

Insertion Like reading, inserting has a default action for a simple integral key
and the hooks to override this for more interesting keys. In the mapper supertype I've provided an operation to act as the interface, together with a template
method to do the work of the insertion.

class AbstractMapper...

```
    public Key insert(DomainObjectWithKey subject) {
        try {
            return performInsert(subject, findNextDatabaseKeyObject());
        } catch (SQLException e) {
            throw new ApplicationException(e);
        }
    }
    protected Key performInsert(DomainObjectWithKey subject, Key key) throws SQLException {
        subject.setKey(key);
        PreparedStatement stmt = DB.prepare(insertStatementString());
        insertKey(subject, stmt);
        insertData(subject, stmt);
        stmt.execute();
        loadedMap.put(subject.getKey(), subject);
        return subject.getKey();
    }
    abstract protected String insertStatementString();
```

class OrderMapper...

```
    protected String insertStatementString() {
        return "INSERT INTO orders VALUES(?,?)";
    }
```

The data from the object goes into the insert statement through two methods that separate the data of the key from the basic data of the object. I do this because I can provide a default implementation for the key that will work for any class, like order, that uses the default simple integral key.

class AbstractMapper...

```
protected void insertKey(DomainObjectWithKey subject, PreparedStatement stmt)
    throws SQLException
{
    stmt.setLong(1, subject.getKey().longValue());
}
```

The rest of the data for the insert statement is dependent on the particular subclass, so this behavior is abstract on the superclass.

Identity Field

class AbstractMapper...

```
abstract protected void insertData(DomainObjectWithKey subject, PreparedStatement stmt)
    throws SQLException;
```

class OrderMapper...

```
protected void insertData(DomainObjectWithKey abstractSubject, PreparedStatement stmt) {
    try {
        Order subject = (Order) abstractSubject;
        stmt.setString(2, subject.getCustomer());
    } catch (SQLException e) {
        throw new ApplicationException(e);
    }
}
```

The line item overrides both of these methods. It pulls two values out for key.

class LineItemMapper...

```
protected String insertStatementString() {
    return "INSERT INTO line_items VALUES (?, ?, ?, ?)";
}
protected void insertKey(DomainObjectWithKey subject, PreparedStatement stmt)
    throws SQLException
{
    stmt.setLong(1, orderID(subject.getKey()));
    stmt.setLong(2, sequenceNumber(subject.getKey()));
}
```

It also provides its own implementation of the insert statement for the rest of the data.

```
class LineItemMapper...

    protected void insertData(DomainObjectWithKey subject, PreparedStatement stmt)
            throws SQLException
    {
        LineItem item = (LineItem) subject;
        stmt.setInt(3, item.getAmount());
        stmt.setString(4, item.getProduct());
    }
```

Identity Field

Putting the data loading into the insert statement like this is only worthwhile if most classes use the same single field for the key. If there's more variation for the key handling, then having just one command to insert the information is probably easier.

Coming up with the next database key is also something that I can separate into a default and an overridden case. For the default case I can use the key table scheme that I talked about earlier. But for the line item we run into a problem. The line item's key uses the key of the order as part of its composite key. However, there's no reference from the line item class to the order class, so it's impossible to tell a line item to insert itself into the database without providing the correct order as well. This leads to the always messy approach of implementing the superclass method with an unsupported operation exception.

```
class LineItemMapper...

    public Key insert(DomainObjectWithKey subject) {
        throw new UnsupportedOperationException
            ("Must supply an order when inserting a line item");
    }
    public Key insert(LineItem item, Order order) {
        try {
            Key key = new Key(order.getKey().value(), getNextSequenceNumber(order));
            return performInsert(item, key);
        } catch (SQLException e) {
            throw new ApplicationException(e);
        }
    }
```

Of course, we can avoid this by having a back link from the line item to the order, effectively making the association between the two bidirectional. I've chosen not to do it here to illustrate what to do when you don't have that link.

By supplying the order, it's easy to get the order's part of the key. The next problem is to come up with a sequence number for the order line. To find that number, we need to find out what the next available sequence number is for an order, which we can do either with a max query in SQL or by looking at the line items on the order in memory. For this example I'll do the latter.

class LineItemMapper...

```
private Long getNextSequenceNumber(Order order) {
    loadAllLineItemsFor(order);
    Iterator it = order.getItems().iterator();
    LineItem candidate = (LineItem) it.next();
    while (it.hasNext()) {
        LineItem thisItem = (LineItem) it.next();
        if (thisItem.getKey() == null) continue;
        if (sequenceNumber(thisItem) > sequenceNumber(candidate)) candidate = thisItem;
    }
    return new Long(sequenceNumber(candidate) + 1);
}
private static long sequenceNumber(LineItem li) {
    return sequenceNumber(li.getKey());
}
//comparator doesn't work well here due to unsaved null keys
protected String keyTableRow() {
    throw new UnsupportedOperationException();
}
```

This algorithm would be much nicer if I used the Collections.max method, but since we may (and indeed will) have at least one null key, that method would fail.

Updates and Deletes After all of that, updates and deletes are mostly harmless. Again we have an abstract method for the assumed usual case and an override for the special cases.

Updates work like this:

class AbstractMapper...

```
public void update(DomainObjectWithKey subject) {
    PreparedStatement stmt = null;
    try {
        stmt = DB.prepare(updateStatementString());
        loadUpdateStatement(subject, stmt);
        stmt.execute();
    } catch (SQLException e) {
        throw new ApplicationException(e);
    } finally {
        DB.cleanUp(stmt);
    }
}
abstract protected String updateStatementString();
abstract protected void loadUpdateStatement(DomainObjectWithKey subject,
                    PreparedStatement stmt)
        throws SQLException;
```

class OrderMapper...

```
protected void loadUpdateStatement(DomainObjectWithKey subject, PreparedStatement stmt)
    throws SQLException
{
    Order order = (Order) subject;
    stmt.setString(1, order.getCustomer());
    stmt.setLong(2, order.getKey().longValue());
}
protected String updateStatementString() {
    return "UPDATE orders SET customer = ? WHERE id = ?";
}
```

class LineItemMapper...

```
protected String updateStatementString() {
    return
        "UPDATE line_items " +
        "  SET amount = ?, product = ? " +
        "  WHERE orderId = ? AND seq = ?";
}
protected void loadUpdateStatement(DomainObjectWithKey subject, PreparedStatement stmt)
    throws SQLException
{
    stmt.setLong(3, orderID(subject.getKey()));
    stmt.setLong(4, sequenceNumber(subject.getKey()));
    LineItem li = (LineItem) subject;
    stmt.setInt(1, li.getAmount());
    stmt.setString(2, li.getProduct());
}
```

Deletes work like this:

class AbstractMapper...

```
public void delete(DomainObjectWithKey subject) {
    PreparedStatement stmt = null;
    try {
        stmt = DB.prepare(deleteStatementString());
        loadDeleteStatement(subject, stmt);
        stmt.execute();
    } catch (SQLException e) {
        throw new ApplicationException(e);
    } finally {
        DB.cleanUp(stmt);
    }
}
abstract protected String deleteStatementString();
protected void loadDeleteStatement(DomainObjectWithKey subject, PreparedStatement stmt)
    throws SQLException
{
    stmt.setLong(1, subject.getKey().longValue());
}
```

class OrderMapper...

```java
protected String deleteStatementString() {
    return "DELETE FROM orders WHERE id = ?";
}
```

class LineItemMapper...

```java
protected String deleteStatementString() {
    return "DELETE FROM line_items WHERE orderid = ? AND seq = ?";
}
protected void loadDeleteStatement(DomainObjectWithKey subject, PreparedStatement stmt)
        throws SQLException
{
    stmt.setLong(1, orderID(subject.getKey()));
    stmt.setLong(2, sequenceNumber(subject.getKey()));
}
```

Foreign Key Mapping

Maps an association between objects to a foreign key reference between tables.

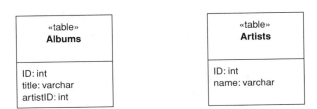

Objects can refer to each other directly by object references. Even the simplest object-oriented system will contain a bevy of objects connected to each other in all sorts of interesting ways. To save these objects to a database, it's vital to save these references. However, since the data in them is specific to the specific instance of the running program, you can't just save raw data values. Further complicating things is the fact that objects can easily hold collections of references to other objects. Such a structure violates the first normal form of relational databases.

A *Foreign Key Mapping* maps an object reference to a foreign key in the database.

How It Works

The obvious key to this problem is *Identity Field (216)*. Each object contains the database key from the appropriate database table. If two objects are linked together with an association, this association can be replaced by a foreign key in the database. Put simply, when you save an album to the database, you save the ID of the artist that the album is linked to in the album record, as in Figure 12.1.

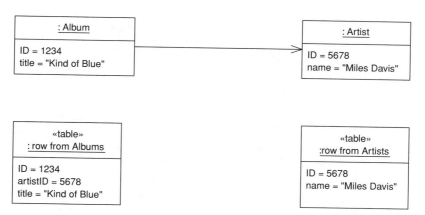

Figure 12.1 *Mapping a collection to a foreign key.*

That's the simple case. A more complicated case turns up when you have a collection of objects. You can't save a collection in the database, so you have to reverse the direction of the reference. Thus, if you have a collection of tracks in the album, you put the foreign key of the album in the track record, as in Figures 12.2 and 12.3. The complication occurs when you have an update. Updating implies that tracks can be added to and removed from the collection within an album. How can you tell what alterations to put in the database? Essentially you have three options: (1) delete and insert, (2) add a back pointer, and (3) diff the collection.

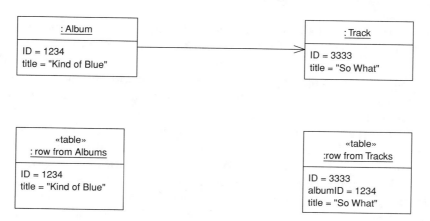

Figure 12.2 *Mapping a collection to a foreign key.*

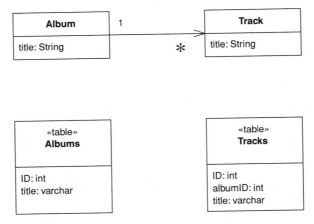

Figure 12.3 *Classes and tables for a multivalued reference.*

With delete and insert you delete all the tracks in the database that link to the album, and then insert all the ones currently on the album. At first glance this sounds pretty appalling, especially if you haven't changed any tracks. But the logic is easy to implement and as such it works pretty well compared to the alternatives. The drawback is that you can only do this if tracks are *Dependent Mappings (262)*, which means they must be owned by the album and can't be referred to outside it.

Adding a back pointer puts a link from the track back to the album, effectively making the association bidirectional. This changes the object model, but now you can handle the update using the simple technique for single-valued fields on the other side.

If neither of those appeals, you can do a diff. There are two possibilities here: diff with the current state of the database or diff with what you read the first time. Diffing with the database involves rereading the collection back from the database and then comparing the collection you read with the collection in the album. Anything in the database that isn't in the album was clearly removed; anything in the album that isn't on the disk is clearly a new item to be added. Then look at the logic of the application to decide what to do with each item.

Diffing with what you read in the first place means that you have to keep what you read. This is better as it avoids another database read. You may also need to diff with the database is you're using *Optimistic Offline Lock (416)*.

In the general case anything that's added to the collection needs to be checked first to see if it's a new object. You can do this by seeing if it has a key; if it doesn't, one needs to be added to the database. This step is made a lot easier with *Unit of Work (184)* because that way any new object will be automatically inserted first. In either case you then find the linked row in the database and update its foreign key to point to the current album.

For removal you have to know whether the track was moved to another album, has no album, or has been deleted altogether. If it's been moved to another album it should be updated when you update that other album. If it has no album, you need to null the foreign key. If the track was deleted, then it should be deleted when things get deleted. Handling deletes is much easier if the back link is mandatory, as it is here, where every track must be on an album. That way you don't have to worry about detecting items removed from the collection since they will be updated when you process the album they've been added to.

If the link is immutable, meaning that you can't change a track's album, then adding always means insertion and removing always means deletion. This makes things simpler still.

One thing to watch out for is cycles in your links. Say you need to load an order, which has a link to a customer (which you load). The customer has a set of payments (which you load), and each payment has orders that it's paying for, which might include the original order you're trying to load. Therefore, you load the order (now go back to the beginning of this paragraph.)

To avoid getting lost in cycles you have two choices that boil down to how you create your objects. Usually it's a good idea for a creation method to include data that will give you a fully formed object. If you do that, you'll need to place *Lazy Load (200)* at appropriate points to break the cycles. If you miss one, you'll get a stack overflow, but if you're testing is good enough you can manage that burden.

The other choice is to create empty objects and immediately put them in an *Identity Map (195)*. That way, when you cycle back around, the object is already loaded and you'll end the cycle. The objects you create aren't fully formed, but they should be by the end of the load procedure. This avoids having to make special case decisions about the use of *Lazy Load (200)* just to do a correct load.

When to Use It

A *Foreign Key Mapping* can be used for almost all associations between classes. The most common case where it isn't possible is with many-to-many associations. Foreign keys are single values, and first normal form means that you can't store multiple foreign keys in a single field. Instead you need to use *Association Table Mapping (248)*.

If you have a collection field with no back pointer, you should consider whether the many side should be a *Dependent Mapping (262)*. If so, it can simplify your handling of the collection.

If the related object is a *Value Object (486)* then you should use *Embedded Value (268)*.

Example: Single-Valued Reference (Java)

This is the simplest case, where an album has a single reference to an artist.

class Artist...

```
    private String name;
    public Artist(Long ID, String name) {
        super(ID);
        this.name = name;
    }
    public String getName() {
        return name;
    }
    public void setName(String name) {
        this.name = name;
    }
```

class Album...

```
    private String title;
    private Artist artist;
    public Album(Long ID, String title, Artist artist) {
        super(ID);
        this.title = title;
        this.artist = artist;
    }
    public String getTitle() {
        return title;
    }
    public void setTitle(String title) {
        this.title = title;
    }
    public Artist getArtist() {
        return artist;
    }
    public void setArtist(Artist artist) {
        this.artist = artist;
    }
```

Figure 12.4 shows how you can load an album. When an album mapper is told to load a particular album it queries the database and pulls back the result set for it. It then queries the result set for each foreign key field and finds that object. Now it can create the album with the appropriate found objects. If the

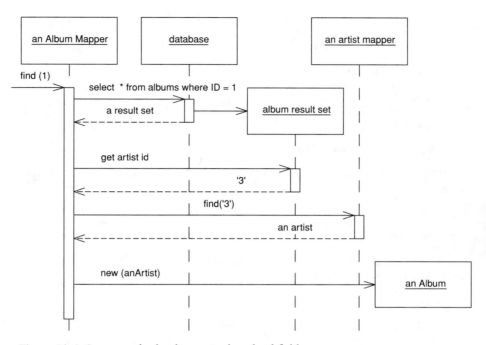

Figure 12.4 *Sequence for loading a single-valued field.*

artist object was already in memory it would be fetched from the cache; otherwise, it would be loaded from the database in the same way.

The find operation uses abstract behavior to manipulate an *Identity Map (195).*

```
class AlbumMapper...

    public Album find(Long id) {
        return (Album) abstractFind(id);
    }
    protected String findStatement() {
        return "SELECT ID, title, artistID FROM albums WHERE ID = ?";
    }

class AbstractMapper...

    abstract protected String findStatement();
    protected DomainObject abstractFind(Long id) {
        DomainObject result = (DomainObject) loadedMap.get(id);
        if (result != null) return result;
        PreparedStatement stmt = null;
        ResultSet rs = null;
        try {
```

```
            stmt = DB.prepare(findStatement());
            stmt.setLong(1, id.longValue());
            rs = stmt.executeQuery();
            rs.next();
            result = load(rs);
            return result;
        } catch (SQLException e) {
            throw new ApplicationException(e);
        } finally {cleanUp(stmt, rs);}
    }
    private Map loadedMap = new HashMap();
```

The find operation calls a load operation to actually load the data into the album.

**Foreign Key
Mapping**

```
class AbstractMapper...

    protected DomainObject load(ResultSet rs) throws SQLException {
        Long id = new Long(rs.getLong(1));
        if (loadedMap.containsKey(id)) return (DomainObject) loadedMap.get(id);
        DomainObject result = doLoad(id, rs);
        doRegister(id, result);
        return result;
    }
    protected void doRegister(Long id, DomainObject result) {
        Assert.isFalse(loadedMap.containsKey(id));
        loadedMap.put(id, result);
    }
    abstract protected DomainObject doLoad(Long id, ResultSet rs) throws SQLException;

class AlbumMapper...

    protected DomainObject doLoad(Long id, ResultSet rs) throws SQLException {
        String title = rs.getString(2);
        long artistID = rs.getLong(3);
        Artist artist = MapperRegistry.artist().find(artistID);
        Album result = new Album(id, title, artist);
        return result;
    }
```

To update an album the foreign key value is taken from the linked artist object.

```
class AbstractMapper...

    abstract public void update(DomainObject arg);

class AlbumMapper...

    public void update(DomainObject arg) {
        PreparedStatement statement = null;
        try {
```

```
        statement = DB.prepare(
            "UPDATE albums SET title = ?, artistID = ? WHERE id = ?");
        statement.setLong(3, arg.getID().longValue());
        Album album = (Album) arg;
        statement.setString(1, album.getTitle());
        statement.setLong(2, album.getArtist().getID().longValue());
        statement.execute();
    } catch (SQLException e) {
        throw new ApplicationException(e);
    } finally {
        cleanUp(statement);
    }
}
```

Example: Multitable Find (Java)

While it's conceptually clean to issue one query per table, it's often inefficient since SQL consists of remote calls and remote calls are slow. Therefore, it's often worth finding ways to gather information from multiple tables in a single query. I can modify the above example to use a single query to get both the album and the artist information with a single SQL call. The first alteration is that of the SQL for the find statement.

class AlbumMapper...

```
    public Album find(Long id) {
        return (Album) abstractFind(id);
    }
    protected String findStatement() {
        return "SELECT a.ID, a.title, a.artistID, r.name " +
            " from albums a, artists r " +
            " WHERE ID = ? and a.artistID = r.ID";
    }
```

I then use a different load method that loads both the album and the artist information together.

class AlbumMapper...

```
    protected DomainObject doLoad(Long id, ResultSet rs) throws SQLException {
        String title = rs.getString(2);
        long artistID = rs.getLong(3);
        ArtistMapper artistMapper = MapperRegistry.artist();
        Artist artist;
        if (artistMapper.isLoaded(artistID))
            artist = artistMapper.find(artistID);
        else
            artist = loadArtist(artistID, rs);
```

```
        Album result = new Album(id, title, artist);
        return result;
    }
    private Artist loadArtist(long id, ResultSet rs) throws SQLException {
        String name = rs.getString(4);
        Artist result = new Artist(new Long(id), name);
        MapperRegistry.artist().register(result.getID(), result);
        return result;
    }
```

There's tension surrounding where to put the method that maps the SQL result into the artist object. On the one hand it's better to put it in the artist's mapper since that's the class that usually loads the artist. On the other hand, the load method is closely coupled to the SQL and thus should stay with the SQL query. In this case I've voted for the latter.

Example: Collection of References (C#)

The case for a collection of references occurs when you have a field that constitutes a collection. Here I'll use an example of teams and players where we'll assume that we can't make player a *Dependent Mapping (262)* (Figure 12.5).

```
class Team...
        public String Name;
        public IList Players {
            get {return ArrayList.ReadOnly(playersData);}
            set {playersData = new ArrayList(value);}
        }
        public void AddPlayer(Player arg) {
            playersData.Add(arg);
        }
        private IList playersData = new ArrayList();
```

In the database this will be handled with the player record having a foreign key to the team (Figure 12.6).

```
class TeamMapper...
        public Team Find(long id) {
            return (Team) AbstractFind(id);
        }
```

Figure 12.5 *A team with multiple players.*

Figure 12.6 *Database structure for a team with multiple players.*

```
class AbstractMapper...

    protected DomainObject AbstractFind(long id) {
        Assert.True (id != DomainObject.PLACEHOLDER_ID);
        DataRow row = FindRow(id);
        return (row == null) ? null : Load(row);
    }
    protected DataRow FindRow(long id) {
        String filter = String.Format("id = {0}", id);
        DataRow[] results = table.Select(filter);
        return (results.Length == 0) ? null : results[0];
    }
    protected DataTable table {
        get {return dsh.Data.Tables[TableName];}
    }
    public DataSetHolder dsh;
    abstract protected String TableName {get;}

class TeamMapper...

    protected override String TableName {
        get {return "Teams";}
    }
```

Foreign Key Mapping

The data set holder is a class that holds onto the data set in use, together with the adapters needed to update it to the database.

```
class DataSetHolder...

    public DataSet Data = new DataSet();
    private Hashtable DataAdapters = new Hashtable();
```

For this example, we'll assume that it has already been populated by some appropriate queries.

The find method calls a load to actually load the data into the new object.

```
class AbstractMapper...

    protected DomainObject Load (DataRow row) {
        long id = (int) row ["id"];
        if (identityMap[id] != null) return (DomainObject) identityMap[id];
```

```
        else {
            DomainObject result = CreateDomainObject();
            result.Id = id;
            identityMap.Add(result.Id, result);
            doLoad(result,row);
            return result;
        }
    }
    abstract protected DomainObject CreateDomainObject();
    private IDictionary identityMap = new Hashtable();
    abstract protected void doLoad (DomainObject obj, DataRow row);
```

class TeamMapper...

```
    protected override void doLoad (DomainObject obj, DataRow row) {
        Team team = (Team) obj;
        team.Name = (String) row["name"];
        team.Players = MapperRegistry.Player.FindForTeam(team.Id);
    }
```

To bring in the players, I execute a specialized finder on the player mapper.

class PlayerMapper...

```
    public IList FindForTeam(long id) {
        String filter = String.Format("teamID = {0}", id);
        DataRow[] rows = table.Select(filter);
        IList result = new ArrayList();
        foreach (DataRow row in rows) {
            result.Add(Load (row));
        }
        return result;
    }
```

To update, the team saves its own data and delegates the player mapper to save the data into the player table.

class AbstractMapper...

```
    public virtual void Update (DomainObject arg) {
        Save (arg, FindRow(arg.Id));
    }
    abstract protected void Save (DomainObject arg, DataRow row);
```

class TeamMapper...

```
    protected override void Save (DomainObject obj, DataRow row){
        Team team = (Team) obj;
        row["name"] = team.Name;
        savePlayers(team);
    }
    private void savePlayers(Team team){
        foreach (Player p in team.Players) {
            MapperRegistry.Player.LinkTeam(p, team.Id);
        }
    }
```

```
class PlayerMapper...

    public void LinkTeam (Player player, long teamID) {
        DataRow row = FindRow(player.Id);
        row["teamID"] = teamID;
    }
```

The update code is made much simpler by the fact that the association from player to team is mandatory. If we move a player from one team to another, as long as we update both team, we don't have to do a complicated diff to sort the players out. I'll leave that case as an exercise for the reader.

Association Table Mapping

*Saves an association as a table with foreign keys to the tables
that are linked by the association.*

Objects can handle multivalued fields quite easily by using collections as field values. Relational databases don't have this feature and are constrained to single-valued fields only. When you're mapping a one-to-many association you can handle this using *Foreign Key Mapping (236)*, essentially using a foreign key for the single-valued end of the association. But a many-to-many association can't do this because there is no single-valued end to hold the foreign key.

The answer is the classic resolution that's been used by relational data people for decades: create an extra table to record the relationship. Then use *Association Table Mapping* to map the multivalued field to this link table.

How It Works

The basic idea behind *Association Table Mapping* is using a link table to store the association. This table has only the foreign key IDs for the two tables that are linked together, it has one row for each pair of associated objects.

The link table has no corresponding in-memory object. As a result it has no ID. Its primary key is the compound of the two primary keys of the tables that are associated.

In simple terms, to load data from the link table you perform two queries. Consider loading the skills for an employee. In this case, at least conceptually, you do queries in two stages. The first stage queries the skillsEmployees table to find all the rows that link to the employee you want. The second stage finds the skill object for the related ID for each row in the link table.

If all the information is already in memory, this scheme works fine. If it isn't, this scheme can be horribly expensive in queries, since you do a query for each skill that's in the link table. You can avoid this cost by joining the skills table to the link table, which allows you to get all the data in a single query, albeit at the cost of making the mapping a bit more complicated.

Updating the link data involves many of the issues in updating a many-valued field. Fortunately, the matter is made much easier since you can in many ways treat the link table like a *Dependent Mapping (262)*. No other table should refer to the link table, so you can freely create and destroy links as you need them.

Association Table Mapping

When to Use It

The canonical case for *Association Table Mapping* is a many-to-many association, since there are really no any alternatives for that situation.

Association Table Mapping can also be used for any other form of association. However, because it's more complex than *Foreign Key Mapping (236)* and involves an extra join, it's not usually the right choice. Even so, in a couple of cases *Association Table Mapping* is appropriate for a simpler association; both involve databases where you have less control over the schema. Sometimes you may need to link two existing tables, but you aren't able to add columns to those tables. In this case you can make a new table and use *Association Table Mapping*. Other times an existing schema uses an associative table, even when it isn't really necessary. In this case it's often easier to use *Association Table Mapping* than to simplify the database schema.

In a relational database design you may often have association tables that also carry information about the relationship. An example is a person/company associative table that also contains information about a person's employment with the company. In this case the person/company table really corresponds to a true domain object.

Example: Employees and Skills (C#)

Here's a simple example using the sketch's model. We have an employee class with a collection of skills, each of which can appear for more than one employee.

class Employee...

```
public IList Skills {
    get {return ArrayList.ReadOnly(skillsData);}
    set {skillsData = new ArrayList(value);}
}
public void AddSkill (Skill arg) {
    skillsData.Add(arg);
}
public void RemoveSkill (Skill arg) {
    skillsData.Remove(arg);
}
private IList skillsData = new ArrayList();
```

Association
Table
Mapping

To load an employee from the database, we need to pull in the skills using an employee mapper. Each employee mapper class has a find method that creates an employee object. All mappers are subclasses of the abstract mapper class that pulls together common services for the mappers.

class EmployeeMapper...

```
public Employee Find(long id) {
    return (Employee) AbstractFind(id);
}
```

class AbstractMapper...

```
protected DomainObject AbstractFind(long id) {
    Assert.True (id != DomainObject.PLACEHOLDER_ID);
    DataRow row = FindRow(id);
    return (row == null) ? null : Load(row);
}
protected DataRow FindRow(long id) {
    String filter = String.Format("id = {0}", id);
    DataRow[] results = table.Select(filter);
    return (results.Length == 0) ? null : results[0];
}
protected DataTable table {
    get {return dsh.Data.Tables[TableName];}
}
public DataSetHolder dsh;
abstract protected String TableName {get;}
```

```
class EmployeeMapper...

    protected override String TableName {
        get {return "Employees";}
    }
```

The data set holder is a simple object that contains an ADO.NET data set and the relevant adapters to save it to the database.

```
class DataSetHolder...

    public DataSet Data = new DataSet();
    private Hashtable DataAdapters = new Hashtable();
```

To make this example simple—indeed, simplistic—we'll assume that the data set has already been loaded with all the data we need.

The find method calls load methods to load data for the employee.

```
class AbstractMapper...

    protected DomainObject Load (DataRow row) {
        long id = (int) row ["id"];
        if (identityMap[id] != null) return (DomainObject) identityMap[id];
        else {
            DomainObject result = CreateDomainObject();
            result.Id = id;
            identityMap.Add(result.Id, result);
            doLoad(result,row);
            return result;
        }
    }
    abstract protected DomainObject CreateDomainObject();
    private IDictionary identityMap = new Hashtable();
    abstract protected void doLoad (DomainObject obj, DataRow row);
```

```
class EmployeeMapper...

    protected override void doLoad (DomainObject obj, DataRow row) {
        Employee emp = (Employee) obj;
        emp.Name = (String) row["name"];
        loadSkills(emp);
    }
```

Loading the skills is sufficiently awkward to demand a separate method to do the work.

```
class EmployeeMapper...

    private IList loadSkills (Employee emp) {
        DataRow[] rows = skillLinkRows(emp);
        IList result = new ArrayList();
```

```
        foreach (DataRow row in rows) {
            long skillID = (int)row["skillID"];
            emp.AddSkill(MapperRegistry.Skill.Find(skillID));
        }
        return result;
    }
    private DataRow[] skillLinkRows(Employee emp) {
        String filter = String.Format("employeeID = {0}", emp.Id);
        return skillLinkTable.Select(filter);
    }
    private DataTable skillLinkTable {
        get {return dsh.Data.Tables["skillEmployees"];}
    }
```

To handle changes in skills information we use an update method on the abstract mapper.

```
class AbstractMapper...

    public virtual void Update (DomainObject arg) {
        Save (arg, FindRow(arg.Id));
    }
    abstract protected void Save (DomainObject arg, DataRow row);
```

The update method calls a save method in the subclass.

```
class EmployeeMapper...

    protected override void Save (DomainObject obj, DataRow row) {
        Employee emp = (Employee) obj;
        row["name"] = emp.Name;
        saveSkills(emp);
    }
```

Again, I've made a separate method for saving the skills.

```
class EmployeeMapper...

    private void saveSkills(Employee emp) {
        deleteSkills(emp);
        foreach (Skill s in emp.Skills) {
            DataRow row = skillLinkTable.NewRow();
            row["employeeID"] = emp.Id;
            row["skillID"] = s.Id;
            skillLinkTable.Rows.Add(row);
        }
    }
    private void deleteSkills(Employee emp) {
        DataRow[] skillRows = skillLinkRows(emp);
        foreach (DataRow r in skillRows) r.Delete();
    }
```

The logic here does the simple thing of deleting all existing link table rows and creating new ones. This saves me having to figure out which ones have been added and deleted.

Example: Using Direct SQL (Java)

One of the nice things about ADO.NET is that it allows me to discuss the basics of an object-relational mapping without getting into the sticky details of minimizing queries. With other relational mapping schemes you're closer to the SQL and have to take much of that into account.

When you're going directly to the database it's important to minimize the queries. For my first version of this I'll pull back the employee and all her skills in two queries. This is easy to follow but not quite optimal, so bear with me.

Association
Table
Mapping

Here's the DDL for the tables:

```
create table employees (ID int primary key, firstname varchar, lastname varchar)
create table skills (ID int primary key, name varchar)
create table employeeSkills (employeeID int, skillID int, primary key (employeeID, skillID))
```

To load a single Employee I'll follow a similar approach to what I've done before. The employee mapper defines a simple wrapper for an abstract find method on the *Layer Supertype (475)*.

```
class EmployeeMapper...

    public Employee find(long key) {
        return find (new Long (key));
    }
    public Employee find (Long key) {
        return (Employee) abstractFind(key);
    }
    protected String findStatement() {
        return
            "SELECT " + COLUMN_LIST +
            "  FROM employees" +
            "  WHERE ID = ?";
    }
    public static final String COLUMN_LIST = " ID, lastname, firstname ";

class AbstractMapper...

    protected DomainObject abstractFind(Long id) {
        DomainObject result = (DomainObject) loadedMap.get(id);
        if (result != null) return result;
        PreparedStatement stmt = null;
        ResultSet rs = null;
```

```
    try {
        stmt = DB.prepare(findStatement());
        stmt.setLong(1, id.longValue());
        rs = stmt.executeQuery();
        rs.next();
        result = load(rs);
        return result;
    } catch (SQLException e) {
        throw new ApplicationException(e);
    } finally {DB.cleanUp(stmt, rs);
    }
}
abstract protected String findStatement();
protected Map loadedMap = new HashMap();
```

Association Table Mapping

The find methods then call load methods. An abstract load method handles the ID loading while the actual data for the employee is loaded on the employee's mapper.

class AbstractMapper...

```
protected DomainObject load(ResultSet rs) throws SQLException {
    Long id = new Long(rs.getLong(1));
    return load(id, rs);
}
public DomainObject load(Long id, ResultSet rs) throws SQLException {
    if (hasLoaded(id)) return (DomainObject) loadedMap.get(id);
    DomainObject result = doLoad(id, rs);
    loadedMap.put(id, result);
    return result;
}
abstract protected DomainObject doLoad(Long id, ResultSet rs) throws SQLException;
```

class EmployeeMapper...

```
protected DomainObject doLoad(Long id, ResultSet rs) throws SQLException {
    Employee result = new Employee(id);
    result.setFirstName(rs.getString("firstname"));
    result.setLastName(rs.getString("lastname"));
    result.setSkills(loadSkills(id));
    return result;
}
```

The employee needs to issue another query to load the skills, but it can easily load all the skills in a single query. To do this it calls the skill mapper to load in the data for a particular skill.

class EmployeeMapper...

```
protected List loadSkills(Long employeeID) {
    PreparedStatement stmt = null;
    ResultSet rs = null;
```

```
        try {
            List result = new ArrayList();
            stmt = DB.prepare(findSkillsStatement);
            stmt.setObject(1, employeeID);
            rs = stmt.executeQuery();
            while (rs.next()) {
                Long skillId = new Long (rs.getLong(1));
                result.add((Skill) MapperRegistry.skill().loadRow(skillId, rs));
            }
            return result;
        } catch (SQLException e) {
            throw new ApplicationException(e);
        } finally {DB.cleanUp(stmt, rs);
        }
    }
    private static final String findSkillsStatement =
        "SELECT skill.ID, " + SkillMapper.COLUMN_LIST +
        "  FROM skills skill, employeeSkills es " +
        "  WHERE es.employeeID = ? AND skill.ID = es.skillID";
```

class SkillMapper...

```
    public static final String COLUMN_LIST = " skill.name skillName ";
```

class AbstractMapper...

```
    protected DomainObject loadRow (Long id, ResultSet rs) throws SQLException {
        return load (id, rs);
    }
```

class SkillMapper...

```
    protected DomainObject doLoad(Long id, ResultSet rs) throws SQLException {
        Skill result = new Skill (id);
        result.setName(rs.getString("skillName"));
        return result;
    }
```

The abstract mapper can also help find employees.

class EmployeeMapper...

```
    public List findAll() {
        return findAll(findAllStatement);
    }
    private static final String findAllStatement =
        "SELECT " + COLUMN_LIST +
        "  FROM employees employee" +
        "  ORDER BY employee.lastname";
```

class AbstractMapper...

```
    protected List findAll(String sql) {
        PreparedStatement stmt = null;
        ResultSet rs = null;
```

```
try {
    List result = new ArrayList();
    stmt = DB.prepare(sql);
    rs = stmt.executeQuery();
    while (rs.next())
        result.add(load(rs));
    return result;
} catch (SQLException e) {
    throw new ApplicationException(e);
} finally {DB.cleanUp(stmt, rs);
}
}
```

Association Table Mapping

All of this works quite well and is pretty simple to follow. Still, there's a problem in the number of queries, and that is that each employee takes two SQL queries to load. Although we can load the basic employee data for many employees in a single query, we still need one query per employee to load the skills. Thus, loading a hundred employees takes 101 queries.

Example: Using a Single Query for Multiple Employees (Java)

It's possible to bring back many employees, with their skills, in a single query. This is a good example of multitable query optimization, which is certainly more awkward. For that reason do this when you need to, rather than every time. It's better to put more energy into speeding up your slow queries than into many queries that are less important.

The first case we'll look at is a simple one where we pull back all the skills for an employee in the same query that holds the basic data. To do this I'll use a more complex SQL statement that joins across all three tables.

```
class EmployeeMapper...

    protected String findStatement() {
        return
            "SELECT " + COLUMN_LIST +
            " FROM employees employee, skills skill, employeeSkills es" +
            " WHERE employee.ID = es.employeeID AND skill.ID = es.skillID AND employee.ID = ?";
    }
    public static final String COLUMN_LIST =
        " employee.ID, employee.lastname, employee.firstname, " +
        " es.skillID, es.employeeID, skill.ID skillID, " +
            SkillMapper.COLUMN_LIST;
```

The abstractFind and load methods on the superclass are the same as in the previous example, so I won't repeat them here. The employee mapper loads its data differently to take advantage of the multiple data rows.

```
class EmployeeMapper...

    protected DomainObject doLoad(Long id, ResultSet rs) throws SQLException {
        Employee result = (Employee) loadRow(id, rs);
        loadSkillData(result, rs);
        while (rs.next()){
            Assert.isTrue(rowIsForSameEmployee(id, rs));
            loadSkillData(result, rs);
        }
        return result;
    }
    protected DomainObject loadRow(Long id, ResultSet rs) throws SQLException {
        Employee result = new Employee(id);
        result.setFirstName(rs.getString("firstname"));
        result.setLastName(rs.getString("lastname"));
        return result;
    }
    private boolean rowIsForSameEmployee(Long id, ResultSet rs) throws SQLException {
        return id.equals(new Long(rs.getLong(1)));
    }
    private void loadSkillData(Employee person, ResultSet rs) throws SQLException {
        Long skillID = new Long(rs.getLong("skillID"));
        person.addSkill ((Skill)MapperRegistry.skill().loadRow(skillID, rs));
    }
```

In this case the load method for the employee mapper actually runs through the
rest of the result set to load in all the data.

All is simple when we're loading the data for a single employee. However,
the real benefit of this multitable query appears when we want to load lots of
employees. Getting the reading right can be tricky, particularly when we don't
want to force the result set to be grouped by employees. At this point it's handy
to introduce a helper class to go through the result set by focusing on the associative table itself, loading up the employees and skills as it goes along.

I'll begin with the SQL and the call to the special loader class.

```
class EmployeeMapper...

    public List findAll() {
        return findAll(findAllStatement);
    }
    private static final String findAllStatement =
            "SELECT " + COLUMN_LIST +
            "  FROM employees employee, skills skill, employeeSkills es" +
            "  WHERE employee.ID = es.employeeID AND skill.ID = es.skillID" +
            "  ORDER BY employee.lastname";
    protected List findAll(String sql) {
        AssociationTableLoader loader = new AssociationTableLoader(this, new SkillAdder());
        return loader.run(findAllStatement);
    }
```

```
class AssociationTableLoader...

    private AbstractMapper sourceMapper;
    private Adder targetAdder;
    public AssociationTableLoader(AbstractMapper primaryMapper, Adder targetAdder) {
        this.sourceMapper = primaryMapper;
        this.targetAdder = targetAdder;
    }
```

Don't worry about the skillAdder—that will become a bit clearer later. For the moment notice that we construct the loader with a reference to the mapper and then tell it to perform a load with a suitable query. This is the typical structure of a method object. A **method object** [Beck Patterns] is a way of turning a complicated method into an object on its own. The great advantage of this is that it allows you to put values in fields instead of passing them around in parameters. The usual way of using a method object is to create it, fire it up, and then let it die once its duty is done.

Association
Table
Mapping

The load behavior comes in three steps.

```
class AssociationTableLoader...

    protected List run(String sql) {
        loadData(sql);
        addAllNewObjectsToIdentityMap();
        return formResult();
    }
```

The loadData method forms the SQL call, executes it, and loops through the result set. Since this is a method object, I've put the result set in a field so I don't have to pass it around.

```
class AssociationTableLoader...

    private ResultSet rs = null;
    private void loadData(String sql) {
        PreparedStatement stmt = null;
        try {
            stmt = DB.prepare(sql);
            rs = stmt.executeQuery();
            while (rs.next())
                loadRow();
        } catch (SQLException e) {
            throw new ApplicationException(e);
        } finally {DB.cleanUp(stmt, rs);
        }
    }
```

The loadRow method loads the data from a single row in the result set. It's a bit complicated.

```
class AssociationTableLoader...

    private List resultIds = new ArrayList();
    private Map inProgress = new HashMap();
    private void loadRow() throws SQLException {
        Long ID = new Long(rs.getLong(1));
        if (!resultIds.contains(ID)) resultIds.add(ID);
        if (!sourceMapper.hasLoaded(ID)) {
            if (!inProgress.keySet().contains(ID))
                inProgress.put(ID, sourceMapper.loadRow(ID, rs));
            targetAdder.add((DomainObject) inProgress.get(ID), rs);
        }
    }
```

```
class AbstractMapper...

    boolean hasLoaded(Long id) {
        return loadedMap.containsKey(id);
    }
```

The loader preserves any order there is in the result set, so the output list of employees will be in the same order in which it first appeared. So I keep a list of IDs in the order I see them. Once I've got the ID I look to see if it's already fully loaded in the mapper—usually from a previous query. If it not I load what data I have and keep it in an in-progress list. I need such a list since several rows will combine to gather all the data from the employee and I may not hit those rows consecutively.

The trickiest part to this code is ensuring that I can add the skill I'm loading to the employees' list of skills, but still keep the loader generic so it doesn't depend on employees and skills. To achieve this I need to dig deep into my bag of tricks to find an inner interface—the Adder.

```
class AssociationTableLoader...

    public static interface Adder {
        void add(DomainObject host, ResultSet rs) throws SQLException ;
    }
```

The original caller has to supply an implementation for the interface to bind it to the particular needs of the employee and skill.

```
class EmployeeMapper...

    private static class SkillAdder implements AssociationTableLoader.Adder {
        public void add(DomainObject host, ResultSet rs) throws SQLException {
            Employee emp = (Employee) host;
            Long skillId = new Long (rs.getLong("skillId"));
            emp.addSkill((Skill) MapperRegistry.skill().loadRow(skillId, rs));
        }
    }
```

This is the kind of thing that comes more naturally to languages that have function pointers or closures, but at least the class and interface get the job done. (They don't have to be inner in this case, but it helps bring out their narrow scope.)

You may have noticed that I have a load and a loadRow method defined on the superclass and the implementation of the loadRow is to call load. I did this because there are times when you want to be sure that a load action will not move the result set forward. The load does whatever it needs to do to load an object, but loadRow guarantees to load data from a row without altering the position of the cursor. Most of the time these two are the same thing, but in the case of this employee mapper they're different.

Association Table Mapping

Now all the data is in from the result set. I have two collections: a list of all the employee IDs that were in the result set in the order of first appearance and a list of new objects that haven't yet made an appearance in the employee mapper's *Identity Map (195)*.

The next step is to put all the new objects into the *Identity Map (195)*.

class AssociationTableLoader...

```
    private void addAllNewObjectsToIdentityMap() {
        for (Iterator it = inProgress.values().iterator(); it.hasNext();)
            sourceMapper.putAsLoaded((DomainObject)it.next());
    }
```

class AbstractMapper...

```
    void putAsLoaded (DomainObject obj) {
        loadedMap.put (obj.getID(), obj);
    }
```

The final step is to assemble the result list by looking up the IDs from the mapper.

class AssociationTableLoader...

```
    private List formResult() {
        List result = new ArrayList();
        for (Iterator it = resultIds.iterator(); it.hasNext();) {
            Long id = (Long)it.next();
            result.add(sourceMapper.lookUp(id));
        }
        return result;
    }
```

class AbstractMapper...

```
    protected DomainObject lookUp (Long id) {
        return (DomainObject) loadedMap.get(id);
    }
```

Such code is more complex than the average loading code, but this kind of thing can help cut down the number of queries. Since it's complicated, this is something to be used sparingly when you have laggardly bits of database interaction. However, it's an example of how *Data Mapper (165)* can provide good queries without the domain layer being aware of the complexity involved.

Dependent Mapping

Has one class perform the database mapping for a child class.

Dependent
Mapping

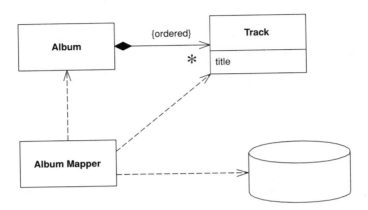

Some objects naturally appear in the context of other objects. Tracks on an album may be loaded or saved whenever the underlying album is loaded or saved. If they aren't referenced to by any other table in the database, you can simplify the mapping procedure by having the album mapper perform the mapping for the tracks as well—treating this mapping as a *dependent mapping*.

How It Works

The basic idea behind *Dependent Mapping* is that one class (the **dependent**) relies upon some other class (the **owner**) for its database persistence. Each dependent can have only one owner and must have one owner.

This manifests itself in terms of the classes that do the mapping. For *Active Record (160)* and *Row Data Gateway (152)*, the dependent class won't contain any database mapping code; its mapping code sits in the owner. With *Data Mapper (165)* there's no mapper for the dependent, the mapping code sits in the mapper for the owner. In a *Table Data Gateway (144)* there will typically be no dependent class at all, all the handling of the dependent is done in the owner.

In most cases every time you load an owner, you load the dependents too. If the dependents are expensive to load and infrequently used, you can use a *Lazy Load (200)* to avoid loading the dependents until you need them.

An important property of a dependent is that it doesn't have an *Identity Field (216)* and therefore isn't stored in a *Identity Map (195)*. It therefore cannot be loaded by a find method that looks up an ID. Indeed, there's no finder for a dependent since all finds are done with the owner.

A dependent may itself be the owner of another dependent. In this case the owner of the first dependent is also responsible for the persistence of the second dependent. You can have a whole hierarchy of dependents controlled by a single primary owner.

It's usually easier for the primary key on the database to be a composite key that includes the owner's primary key. No other table should have a foreign key into the dependent's table, unless that object has the same owner. As a result, no in-memory object other than the owner or its dependents should have a reference to a dependent. Strictly speaking, you can relax that rule providing that the reference isn't persisted to the database, but having a nonpersistent reference is itself a good source of confusion.

In a UML model, it's appropriate to use composition to show the relationship between an owner and its dependents.

Since the writing and saving of dependents is left to the owner, and there are no outside references, updates to the dependents can be handled through deletion and insertion. Thus, if you want to update the collection of dependents you can safely delete all rows that link to the owner and then reinsert all the dependents. This saves you from having to do an analysis of objects added or removed from the owner's collection.

Dependents are in many ways like *Value Objects (486)*, although they often don't need the full mechanics that you use in making something a *Value Object (486)* (such as overriding equals). The main difference is that there's nothing special about them from a purely in-memory point of view. The dependent nature of the objects is only really due to the database mapping behavior.

Using *Dependent Mapping* complicates tracking whether the owner has changed. Any change to a dependent needs to mark the owner as changed so that the owner will write the changes out to the database. You can simplify this considerably by making the dependent immutable, so that any change to it needs to be done by removing it and adding a new one. This can make the in-memory model harder to work with, but it does simplify the database mapping. While in theory the in-memory and database mapping should be independent when you're using *Data Mapper (165)*, in practice you have to make the occasional compromise.

When to Use It

You use *Dependent Mapping* when you have an object that's only referred to by one other object, which usually occurs when one object has a collection of dependents. *Dependent Mapping* is a good way of dealing with the awkward situation where the owner has a collection of references to its dependents but there's no back pointer. Providing that the many objects don't need their own identity, using *Dependent Mapping* makes it easier to manage their persistence.

For *Dependent Mapping* to work there are a number of preconditions.

- A dependent must have exactly one owner.

- There must be no references from any object other than the owner to the dependent.

Dependent Mapping

There is a school of OO design that uses the notion of entity objects and dependent objects when designing a *Domain Model (116)*. I tend to think of *Dependent Mapping* as a technique to simplify database mapping rather than as a fundamental OO design medium. In particular, I avoid large graphs of dependents. The problem with them is that it's impossible to refer to a dependent from outside the graph, which often leads to complex lookup schemes based around the root owner.

I don't recommend *Dependent Mapping* if you're using *Unit of Work (184)*. The delete and reinsert strategy doesn't help at all if you have a *Unit of Work (184)* keeping track of things. It can also lead to problems since the *Unit of Work (184)* isn't controlling the dependents. Mike Rettig told me about an application where a *Unit of Work (184)* would keep track of rows inserted for testing and then delete them all when done. Because it didn't track dependents, orphan rows appeared and caused failures in the test runs.

Example: Albums and Tracks (Java)

In this domain model (Figure 12.7) an album holds a collection of tracks. This uselessly simple application doesn't need anything else to refer to a track, so it's an obvious candidate for *Dependent Mapping*. (Indeed, anyone would think the example is deliberately constructed for the pattern.)

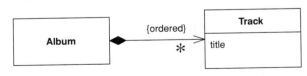

Figure 12.7 *An album with tracks that can be handled using* Dependent Mapping.

This track just has a title. I've defined it as an immutable class.

class Track...

```
private final String title;
public Track(String title) {
    this.title = title;
}
public String getTitle() {
    return title;
}
```

The tracks are held in the album class.

class Album...

```
private List tracks = new ArrayList();
public void addTrack(Track arg) {
    tracks.add(arg);
}
public void removeTrack(Track arg) {
    tracks.remove(arg);
};
public void removeTrack(int i) {
    tracks.remove(i);
}
public Track[] getTracks() {
    return (Track[]) tracks.toArray(new Track[tracks.size()]);
}
```

The album mapper class handles all the SQL for tracks and thus defines the SQL statements that access the tracks table.

class AlbumMapper...

```
protected String findStatement() {
    return
        "SELECT ID, a.title, t.title as trackTitle" +
        "  FROM albums a, tracks t" +
        "  WHERE a.ID = ? AND t.albumID = a.ID" +
        "  ORDER BY t.seq";
}
```

The tracks are loaded into the album whenever the album is loaded.

class AlbumMapper...

```
protected DomainObject doLoad(Long id, ResultSet rs) throws SQLException {
    String title = rs.getString(2);
    Album result = new Album(id, title);
    loadTracks(result, rs);
    return result;
```

```
    }
    public void loadTracks(Album arg, ResultSet rs) throws SQLException {
        arg.addTrack(newTrack(rs));
        while (rs.next()) {
            arg.addTrack(newTrack(rs));
        }
    }
    private Track newTrack(ResultSet rs) throws SQLException {
        String title = rs.getString(3);
        Track newTrack = new Track (title);
        return newTrack;
    }
```

Dependent Mapping

For clarity I've done the track load in a separate query. For performance, you might want to consider loading them in the same query along the lines of the example on page 243.

When the album is updated all the tracks are deleted and reinserted.

```
class AlbumMapper...

    public void update(DomainObject arg) {
        PreparedStatement updateStatement = null;
        try {
            updateStatement = DB.prepare("UPDATE albums SET title = ? WHERE id = ?");
            updateStatement.setLong(2, arg.getID().longValue());
            Album album = (Album) arg;
            updateStatement.setString(1, album.getTitle());
            updateStatement.execute();
            updateTracks(album);
        } catch (SQLException e) {
            throw new ApplicationException(e);
        } finally {DB.cleanUp(updateStatement);
        }
    }
    public void updateTracks(Album arg) throws SQLException {
        PreparedStatement deleteTracksStatement = null;
        try {
            deleteTracksStatement = DB.prepare("DELETE from tracks WHERE albumID = ?");
            deleteTracksStatement.setLong(1, arg.getID().longValue());
            deleteTracksStatement.execute();
            for (int i = 0; i < arg.getTracks().length; i++) {
                Track track = arg.getTracks()[i];
                insertTrack(track, i + 1, arg);
            }
        } finally {DB.cleanUp(deleteTracksStatement);
        }
    }
    public void insertTrack(Track track, int seq, Album album) throws SQLException {
        PreparedStatement insertTracksStatement = null;
```

```
    try {
      insertTracksStatement =
           DB.prepare("INSERT INTO tracks (seq, albumID, title) VALUES (?, ?, ?)");
      insertTracksStatement.setInt(1, seq);
      insertTracksStatement.setLong(2, album.getID().longValue());
      insertTracksStatement.setString(3, track.getTitle());
      insertTracksStatement.execute();
    } finally {DB.cleanUp(insertTracksStatement);
    }
}
```

Embedded Value

Maps an object into several fields of another object's table.

Employment
ID person: person period: DateRange salary: Money

«table» Employments
ID: int personID: int start: date end:date salaryAmount: decimal salaryCurrency: char

Many small objects make sense in an OO system that don't make sense as tables in a database. Examples include currency-aware money objects and date ranges. Although the default thinking is to save an object as a table, no sane person would want a table of money values.

An *Embedded Value* maps the values of an object to fields in the record of the object's owner. In the sketch we have an employment object with links to a date range object and a money object. In the resulting table the fields in those objects map to fields in the employment table rather than make new records themselves.

How It Works

This exercise is actually quite simple. When the owning object (employment) is loaded or saved, the dependent objects (date range and money) are loaded and saved at the same time. The dependent classes won't have their own persistence methods since all persistence is done by the owner. You can think of *Embedded Value* as a special case of *Dependent Mapping (262)*, where the value is a single dependent object.

When to Use It

This is one of those patterns where the doing of it is very straightforward, but knowing when to use it a little more complicated.

The simplest cases for *Embedded Value* are the clear, simple *Value Objects (486)* like money and date range. Since *Value Objects (486)* don't have identity, you can create and destroy them easily without worrying about such things as *Identity Maps (195)* to keep them all in sync. Indeed, all *Value Objects (486)* should be persisted as *Embedded Value*, since you would never want a table for them there.

The grey area is in whether it's worth storing reference objects, such as an order and a shipping object, using *Embedded Value*. The principal question here is whether the shipping data has any relevance outside the context of the order. One issue is the loading and saving. If you only load the shipping data into memory when you load the order, that's an argument for saving both in the same table. Another question is whether you'll want to access the shipping data separately though SQL. This can be important if you're reporting through SQL and don't have a separate database for reporting.

If you're mapping to an existing schema, you can use *Embedded Value* when a table contains data that you split into more than one object in memory. This may occur because you want a separate object to factor out some behavior in the object model, but it's all still one entity in the database. In this case you have to be careful that any change to the dependent marks the owner as dirty—which isn't an issue with *Value Objects (486)* that are replaced in the owner.

In most cases you'll only use *Embedded Value* on a reference object when the association between them is single valued at both ends (a one-to-one association). Occasionally you may use it if there are multiple candidate dependents and their number is small and fixed. Then you'll have numbered fields for each value. This is messy table design, and horrible to query in SQL, but it may have performance benefits. If this is the case, however, *Serialized LOB (272)* is usually the better choice.

Since so much of the logic for deciding when to use *Embedded Value* is the same as for *Serialized LOB (272)*, there's the obvious matter of choosing between the two. The great advantage of *Embedded Value* is that it allows SQL queries to be made against the values in the dependent object. Although using XML as the serialization, together with XML-based query add-ons to SQL, may alter that in the future, at the moment you really need *Embedded Value* if you want to use dependent values in a query. This may be important for separate reporting mechanisms on the database

Embedded Value can only be used for fairly simple dependents. A solitary dependent, or a few separated dependents, works well. *Serialized LOB (272)* works with more complex structures, including potentially large object subgraphs.

Further Reading

Embedded Value has been called a couple of different names in its history. TOPLink refers to it as *aggregate mapping*. Visual Age refers to it as *composer*.

Example: Simple Value Object (Java)

This is the classic example of a value object mapped with *Embedded Value*. We'll begin with a simple product offering class with the following fields.

class ProductOffering...

```
    private Product product;
    private Money baseCost;
    private Integer ID;
```

In these fields the ID is an *Identity Field (216)* and the product is a regular record mapping. We'll map the base cost using *Embedded Value*. We'll do the overall mapping with *Active Record (160)* to keep things simple.

Since we're using *Active Record (160)* we need save and load routines. These simple routines are in the product offering class because it's the owner. The money class has no persistence behavior at all. Here's the load method.

class ProductOffering...

```
    public static ProductOffering load(ResultSet rs) {
        try {
            Integer id = (Integer) rs.getObject("ID");
            BigDecimal baseCostAmount = rs.getBigDecimal("base_cost_amount");
            Currency baseCostCurrency = Registry.getCurrency(rs.getString("base_cost_currency"));
            Money baseCost = new Money(baseCostAmount, baseCostCurrency);
            Integer productID = (Integer) rs.getObject("product");
            Product product = Product.find((Integer) rs.getObject("product"));
            return new ProductOffering(id, product, baseCost);
        } catch (SQLException e) {
            throw new ApplicationException(e);
        }
    }
```

Here's the update behavior. Again it's a simple variation on the updates.

class ProductOffering...

```
    public void update() {
        PreparedStatement stmt = null;
        try {
            stmt = DB.prepare(updateStatementString);
            stmt.setBigDecimal(1, baseCost.amount());
            stmt.setString(2, baseCost.currency().code());
            stmt.setInt(3, ID.intValue());
```

Embedded Value

```
        stmt.execute();
    } catch (Exception e) {
        throw new ApplicationException(e);
    } finally {DB.cleanUp(stmt);}
}
private String updateStatementString =
    "UPDATE product_offerings" +
    "  SET base_cost_amount = ?, base_cost_currency = ? " +
    "  WHERE id = ?";
```

Embedded
Value

Serialized LOB

*Saves a graph of objects by serializing them into a single large object
(LOB), which it stores in a database field.*

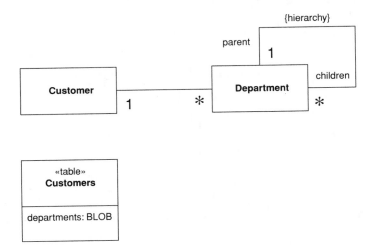

Serialized
LOB

Object models often contain complicated graphs of small objects. Much of the
information in these structures isn't in the objects but in the links between
them. Consider storing the organization hierarchy for all your customers. An
object model quite naturally shows the composition pattern to represent orga-
nizational hierarchies, and you can easily add methods that allow you to get
ancestors, siblings, descendents, and other common relationships.

Not so easy is putting all this into a relational schema. The basic schema is
simple—an organization table with a parent foreign key, however, its manipulation of the schema requires many joins, which are both slow and awkward.

Objects don't have to be persisted as table rows related to each other.
Another form of persistence is serialization, where a whole graph of objects is
written out as a single large object (LOB) in a table this *Serialized LOB* then
becomes a form of memento [Gang of Four].

How It Works

There are two ways you can do the serialization: as a binary (**BLOB**) or as textual characters (**CLOB**). The BLOB is often the simplest to create since many

platforms include the ability to automatically serialize an object graph. Saving the graph is a simple matter of applying the serialization in a buffer and saving that buffer in the relevant field.

The advantages of the BLOB are that it's simple to program (if your platform supports it) and that it uses the minimum of space. The disadvantages are that your database must support a binary data type for it and that you can't reconstruct the graph without the object, so the field is utterly impenetrable to casual viewing. The most serious problem, however, is versioning. If you change the department class, you may not be able to read all its previous serializations; since data can live in the database for a long time, this is no small thing.

The alternative is a CLOB. In this case you serialize the department graph into a text string that carries all the information you need. The text string can be read easily by a human viewing the row, which helps in casual browsing of the database. However the text approach will usually need more space, and you may need to create your own parser for the textual format you use. It's also likely to be slower than a binary serialization.

Many of the disadvantages of CLOBs can be overcome with XML. XML parsers are commonly available, so you don't have to write your own. Furthermore, XML is a widely supported standard so you can take advantage of tools as they become available to do further manipulations. The disadvantage that XML doesn't help with is the matter of space. Indeed, it makes the space issue much worse because its a very verbose format. One way to deal with that is to use a zipped XML format as your BLOB—you lose the direct human readability, but it's an option if space is a real issue.

When you use *Serialized LOB* beware of identity problems. Say you want to use *Serialized LOB* for the customer details on an order. For this don't put the customer LOB in the order table; otherwise, the customer data will be copied on every order, which makes updates a problem. (This is actually a good thing, however, if you want to store a snapshot of the customer data as it was at the placing of the order—it avoids temporal relationships.) If you want your customer data to be updated for each order in the classical relational sense, you need to put the LOB in a customer table so many orders can link to it. There's nothing wrong with a table that just has an ID and a single LOB field for its data.

In general, be careful of duplicating data when using this pattern. Often it's not a whole *Serialized LOB* that gets duplicated but part of one that overlaps with another one. The thing to do is to pay careful attention to the data that's stored in the *Serialized LOB* and be sure that it can't be reached from anywhere but a single object that acts as the owner of the *Serialized LOB*.

Serialized
LOB

When to Use It

Serialized LOB isn't considered as often as it might be. XML makes it much more attractive since it yields a easy-to-implement textual approach. Its main disadvantage is that you can't query the structure using SQL. SQL extensions appear to get at XML data within a field, but that's still not the same (or portable).

This pattern works best when you can chop out a piece of the object model and use it to represent the LOB. Think of a LOB as a way to take a bunch of objects that aren't likely to be queried from any SQL route outside the application. This graph can then be hooked into the SQL schema.

Serialized LOB works poorly when you have objects outside the LOB reference objects buried in it. To handle this you have to come up with some form of referencing scheme that can support references to objects inside a LOB—it's by no means impossible, but it's awkward, awkward enough usually not to be worth doing. Again XML, or rather XPath, reduces this awkwardness somewhat.

If you're using a separate database for reporting and all other SQL goes against that database, you can transform the LOB into a suitable table structure. The fact that a reporting database is usually denormalized means that structures suitable for *Serialized LOB* are often also suitable for a separate reporting database.

Example: Serializing a Department Hierarchy in XML (Java)

For this example we'll take the notion of customers and departments from the sketch and show how you might serialize all the departments into an XML CLOB. As I write this, Java's XML handling is somewhat primitive and volatile, so the code may look different when you get to it (I'm also using an early version of JDOM).

The object model of the sketch turns into the following class structures:

```
class Customer...

    private String name;
    private List departments = new ArrayList();
```

```
class Department...

    private String name;
    private List subsidiaries = new ArrayList();
```

The database for this has only one table.

```
create table customers (ID int primary key, name varchar, departments varchar)
```

We'll treat the customer as an *Active Record (160)* and illustrate writing the data with the insert behavior.

```
class Customer...

    public Long insert() {
        PreparedStatement insertStatement = null;
        try {
            insertStatement = DB.prepare(insertStatementString);
            setID(findNextDatabaseId());
            insertStatement.setInt(1, getID().intValue());
            insertStatement.setString(2, name);
            insertStatement.setString(3, XmlStringer.write(departmentsToXmlElement()));
            insertStatement.execute();
            Registry.addCustomer(this);
            return getID();
        } catch (SQLException e) {
            throw new ApplicationException(e);
        } finally {DB.cleanUp(insertStatement);
        }
    }
    public Element departmentsToXmlElement() {
        Element root = new Element("departmentList");
        Iterator i = departments.iterator();
        while (i.hasNext()) {
            Department dep = (Department) i.next();
            root.addContent(dep.toXmlElement());
        }
        return root;
    }

class Department...

    Element toXmlElement() {
        Element root = new Element("department");
        root.setAttribute("name", name);
        Iterator i = subsidiaries.iterator();
        while (i.hasNext()) {
            Department dep = (Department) i.next();
            root.addContent(dep.toXmlElement());
        }
        return root;
    }
```

The customer has a method for serializing its departments field into a single XML DOM. Each department has a method for serializing itself (and its subsidiaries recursively) into a DOM as well. The insert method then takes the DOM of the departments, converts it into a string (via a utility class) and puts it in the database. We aren't particularly concerned with the structure of the string. It's human readable, but we aren't going to look at it on a regular basis.

```xml
<?xml version="1.0" encoding="UTF-8"?>
<departmentList>
    <department name="US">
        <department name="New England">
            <department name="Boston" />
            <department name="Vermont" />
        </department>
        <department name="California" />
        <department name="Mid-West" />
    </department>
    <department name="Europe" />
</departmentList>
```

Serialized LOB

Reading back is a fairly simple reversal of this process.

```
class Customer...

    public static Customer load(ResultSet rs) throws SQLException {
        Long id = new Long(rs.getLong("id"));
        Customer result = (Customer) Registry.getCustomer(id);
        if (result != null) return result;
        String name = rs.getString("name");
        String departmentLob = rs.getString("departments");
        result = new Customer(name);
        result.readDepartments(XmlStringer.read(departmentLob));
        return result;
    }
    void readDepartments(Element source) {
        List result = new ArrayList();
        Iterator it = source.getChildren("department").iterator();
        while (it.hasNext())
            addDepartment(Department.readXml((Element) it.next()));
    }
```

```
class Department...

    static Department readXml(Element source) {
        String name = source.getAttributeValue("name");
        Department result = new Department(name);
        Iterator it = source.getChildren("department").iterator();
        while (it.hasNext())
            result.addSubsidiary(readXml((Element) it.next()));
        return result;
    }
```

The load code is obviously a mirror image of the insert code. The department knows how to create itself (and its subsidiaries) from an XML element, and the customer knows how to take an XML element and create the list of departments from it. The load method uses a utility class to turn the string from the database into a utility element.

An obvious danger here is that someone may try to edit the XML by hand in the database and mess up the XML, making it unreadable by the load routine. More sophisticated tools that would support adding a DTD or XML schema to a field as validation will obviously help with that.

Single Table Inheritance

*Represents an inheritance hierarchy of classes as a single table that
has columns for all the fields of the various classes.*

Single Table
Inheritance

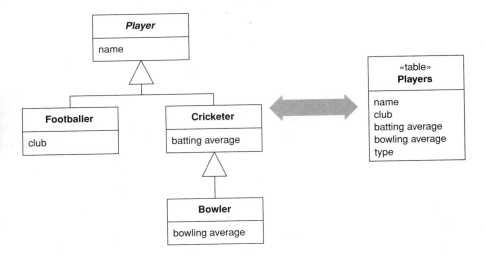

Relational databases don't support inheritance, so when mapping from objects
to databases we have to consider how to represent our nice inheritance structures in relational tables. When mapping to a relational database, we try to
minimize the joins that can quickly mount up when processing an inheritance
structure in multiple tables. *Single Table Inheritance* maps all fields of all classes
of an inheritance structure into a single table.

How It Works

In this inheritance mapping scheme we have one table that contains all the data
for all the classes in the inheritance hierarchy. Each class stores the data that's
relevant to it in one table row. Any columns in the database that aren't relevant
are left empty. The basic mapping behavior follows the general scheme of
Inheritance Mappers (302).

   When loading an object into memory you need to know which class to
instantiate. For this you have a field in the table that indicates which class
should be used. This can be the name of the class or a code field. A code field
needs to be interpreted by some code to map it to the relevant class. This code

needs to be extended when a class is added to the hierarchy. If you embed the class name in the table you can just use it directly to instantiate an instance. The class name, however, will take up more space and may be less easy to process by those using the database table structure directly. As well it may more closely couple the class structure to the database schema.

In loading data you read the code first to figure out which subclass to instantiate. On saving the data the code needs be written out by the superclass in the hierarchy.

When to Use It

Single Table Inheritance is one of the options for mapping the fields in an inheritance hierarchy to a relational database. The alternatives are *Class Table Inheritance (285)* and *Concrete Table Inheritance (293)*.

These are the strengths of *Single Table Inheritance:*

- There's only a single table to worry about on the database.

- There are no joins in retrieving data.

- Any refactoring that pushes fields up or down the hierarchy doesn't require you to change the database.

The weaknesses of *Single Table Inheritance* are

- Fields are sometimes relevant and sometimes not, which can be confusing to people using the tables directly.

- Columns used only by some subclasses lead to wasted space in the database. How much this is actually a problem depends on the specific data characteristics and how well the database compresses empty columns. Oracle, for example, is very efficient in trimming wasted space, particularly if you keep your optional columns to the right side of the database table. Each database has its own tricks for this.

- The single table may end up being too large, with many indexes and frequent locking, which may hurt performance. You can avoid this by having separate index tables that either list keys of rows that have a certain property or that copy a subset of fields relevant to an index.

- You only have a single namespace for fields, so you have to be sure that you don't use the same name for different fields. Compound names with the name of the class as a prefix or suffix help here.

Rremember that you don't need to use one form of inheritance mapping for your whole hierarchy. It's perfectly fine to map half a dozen similar classes in a

Single Table Inheritance

single table, as long as you use *Concrete Table Inheritance (293)* for any classes that have a lot of specific data.

Example: A Single Table for Players (C#)

Like the other inheritance examples, I've based this one on *Inheritance Mappers (302)*, using the classes in Figure 12.8. Each mapper needs to be linked to a data table in an ADO.NET data set. This link can be made generically in the mapper superclass. The gateway's data property is a data set that can be loaded by a query.

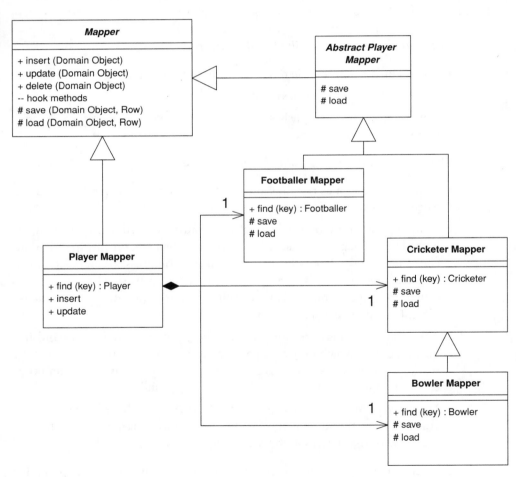

Figure 12.8 *The generic class diagram of* Inheritance Mappers (302).

```
class Mapper...

    protected DataTable table {
        get {return Gateway.Data.Tables[TableName];}
    }
    protected Gateway Gateway;
    abstract protected String TableName {get;}
```

Since there is only one table, this can be defined by the abstract player mapper.

```
class AbstractPlayerMapper...

    protected override String TableName {
        get {return "Players";}
    }
```

Each class needs a type code to help the mapper code figure out what kind of player it's dealing with. The type code is defined on the superclass and implemented in the subclasses.

```
class AbstractPlayerMapper...

    abstract public String TypeCode {get;}
```

```
class CricketerMapper...

    public const String TYPE_CODE = "C";
    public override String TypeCode {
        get {return TYPE_CODE;}
    }
```

The player mapper has fields for each of the three concrete mapper classes.

```
class PlayerMapper...

    private BowlerMapper bmapper;
    private CricketerMapper cmapper;
    private FootballerMapper fmapper;
    public PlayerMapper (Gateway gateway) : base (gateway) {
        bmapper = new BowlerMapper(Gateway);
        cmapper = new CricketerMapper(Gateway);
        fmapper = new FootballerMapper(Gateway);
    }
```

Loading an Object from the Database

Each concrete mapper class has a find method to get an object from the data.

```
class CricketerMapper...

    public Cricketer Find(long id) {
        return (Cricketer) AbstractFind(id);
    }
```

This calls generic behavior to find an object.

class Mapper...

```
protected DomainObject AbstractFind(long id) {
    DataRow row = FindRow(id);
    return (row == null) ? null : Find(row);
}
protected DataRow FindRow(long id) {
    String filter = String.Format("id = {0}", id);
    DataRow[] results = table.Select(filter);
    return (results.Length == 0) ? null : results[0];
}
public DomainObject Find (DataRow row) {
    DomainObject result = CreateDomainObject();
    Load(result, row);
    return result;
}
abstract protected DomainObject CreateDomainObject();
```

class CricketerMapper...

```
protected override DomainObject CreateDomainObject() {
    return new Cricketer();
}
```

I load the data into the new object with a series of load methods, one on each class in the hierarchy.

class CricketerMapper...

```
protected override void Load(DomainObject obj, DataRow row) {
    base.Load(obj,row);
    Cricketer cricketer = (Cricketer) obj;
    cricketer.battingAverage = (double)row["battingAverage"];
}
```

class AbstractPlayerMapper...

```
protected override void Load(DomainObject obj, DataRow row) {
    base.Load(obj, row);
    Player player = (Player) obj;
    player.name = (String)row["name"];
}
```

class Mapper...

```
protected virtual void Load(DomainObject obj, DataRow row) {
    obj.Id = (int) row ["id"];
}
```

Single Table Inheritance

I can also load a player through the player mapper. It needs to read the data and use the type code to determine which concrete mapper to use.

class PlayerMapper...

```
public Player Find (long key) {
    DataRow row = FindRow(key);
    if (row == null) return null;
    else {
        String typecode = (String) row["type"];
        switch (typecode){
            case BowlerMapper.TYPE_CODE:
                return (Player) bmapper.Find(row);
            case CricketerMapper.TYPE_CODE:
                return (Player) cmapper.Find(row);
            case FootballerMapper.TYPE_CODE:
                return (Player) fmapper.Find(row);
            default:
                throw new Exception("unknown type");
        }
    }
}
```

Single Table Inheritance

Updating an Object The basic operation for updating is the same for all objects, so I can define the operation on the mapper superclass.

class Mapper...

```
public virtual void Update (DomainObject arg) {
    Save (arg, FindRow(arg.Id));
}
```

The save method is similar to the load method—each class defines it to save the data it contains.

class CricketerMapper...

```
protected override void Save(DomainObject obj, DataRow row) {
    base.Save(obj, row);
    Cricketer cricketer = (Cricketer) obj;
    row["battingAverage"] = cricketer.battingAverage;
}
```

class AbstractPlayerMapper...

```
protected override void Save(DomainObject obj, DataRow row) {
    Player player = (Player) obj;
    row["name"] = player.name;
    row["type"] = TypeCode;
}
```

The player mapper forwards to the appropriate concrete mapper.

```
class PlayerMapper...

    public override void Update (DomainObject obj) {
        MapperFor(obj).Update(obj);
    }
    private Mapper MapperFor(DomainObject obj) {
        if (obj is Footballer)
            return fmapper;
        if (obj is Bowler)
            return bmapper;
        if (obj is Cricketer)
            return cmapper;
        throw new Exception("No mapper available");
    }
```

Single Table
Inheritance

Inserting an Object Insertions are similar to updates; the only real difference is that a new row needs to be made in the table before saving.

```
class Mapper...

    public virtual long Insert (DomainObject arg) {
        DataRow row = table.NewRow();
        arg.Id = GetNextID();
        row["id"] = arg.Id;
        Save (arg, row);
        table.Rows.Add(row);
        return arg.Id;
    }
```

```
class PlayerMapper...

    public override long Insert (DomainObject obj) {
        return MapperFor(obj).Insert(obj);
    }
```

Deleting an Object Deletes are pretty simple. They're defined at the abstract mapper level or in the player wrapper.

```
class Mapper...

    public virtual void Delete(DomainObject obj) {
        DataRow row = FindRow(obj.Id);
        row.Delete();
    }
```

```
class PlayerMapper...

    public override void Delete (DomainObject obj) {
        MapperFor(obj).Delete(obj);
    }
```

Class Table Inheritance

*Represents an inheritance hierarchy of classes
with one table for each class.*

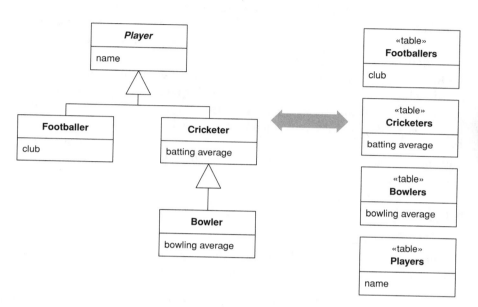

A very visible aspect of the object-relational mismatch is the fact that relational databases don't support inheritance. You want database structures that map clearly to the objects and allow links anywhere in the inheritance structure. *Class Table Inheritance* supports this by using one database table per class in the inheritance structure.

How It Works

The straightforward thing about *Class Table Inheritance* is that it has one table per class in the domain model. The fields in the domain class map directly to fields in the corresponding tables. As with the other inheritance mappings the fundamental approach of *Inheritance Mappers (302)* applies.

One issue is how to link the corresponding rows of the database tables. A possible solution is to use a common primary key value so that, say, the row of key 101 in the footballers table and the row of key 101 in the players table correspond to the same domain object. Since the superclass table has a row for each row in the other tables, the primary keys are going to be unique across the tables if you use this scheme. An alternative is to let each table have its own primary keys and use foreign keys into the superclass table to tie the rows together.

The biggest implementation issue with *Class Table Inheritance* is how to bring the data back from multiple tables in an efficient manner. Obviously, making a call for each table isn't good since you have multiple calls to the database. You can avoid this by doing a join across the various component tables; however, joins for more than three or four tables tend to be slow because of the way databases do their optimizations.

On top of this is the problem that in any given query you often don't know exactly which tables to join. If you're looking for a footballer, you know to use the footballer table, but if you're looking for a group of players, which tables do you use? To join effectively when some tables have no data, you'll need to do an outer join, which is nonstandard and often slow. The alternative is to read the root table first and then use a code to figure out what tables to read next, but this involves multiple queries.

Class Table
Inheritance

When to Use It

Class Table Inheritance, *Single Table Inheritance (278)* and *Concrete Table Inheritance (293)* are the three alternatives to consider for inheritance mapping.

The strengths of *Class Table Inheritance* are

- All columns are relevant for every row so tables are easier to understand and don't waste space.

- The relationship between the domain model and the database is very straightforward.

The weaknesses of *Class Table Inheritance* are

- You need to touch multiple tables to load an object, which means a join or multiple queries and sewing in memory.

- Any refactoring of fields up or down the hierarchy causes database changes.

- The supertype tables may become a bottleneck because they have to be accessed frequently.

- The high normalization may make it hard to understand for ad hoc queries.

You don't have to choose just one inheritance mapping pattern for one class hierarchy. You can use *Class Table Inheritance* for the classes at the top of the hierarchy and a bunch of *Concrete Table Inheritance (293)* for those lower down.

Further Reading

A number of IBM texts refer to this pattern as Root-Leaf Mapping [Brown et al.].

Example: Players and Their Kin (C#)

Here's an implementation for the sketch. Again I'll follow the familiar (if perhaps a little tedious) theme of players and the like, using *Inheritance Mappers (302)* (Figure 12.9).

Each class needs to define the table that holds its data and a type code for it.

```
class AbstractPlayerMapper...

    abstract public String TypeCode {get;}
    protected static String TABLENAME = "Players";
```

```
class FootballerMapper...

    public override String TypeCode {
        get {return "F";}
    }
    protected new static String TABLENAME = "Footballers";
```

Unlike the other inheritance examples, this one doesn't have a overridden table name because we have to have the table name for this class even when the instance is an instance of the subclass.

Loading an Object If you've been reading the other mappings, you know the first step is the find method on the concrete mappers.

```
class FootballerMapper...

    public Footballer Find(long id) {
        return (Footballer) AbstractFind (id, TABLENAME);
    }
```

The abstract find method looks for a row matching the key and, if successful, creates a domain object and calls the load method on it.

```
class Mapper...

    public DomainObject AbstractFind(long id, String tablename) {
        DataRow row = FindRow (id, tableFor(tablename));
        if (row == null) return null;
        else {
            DomainObject result = CreateDomainObject();
            result.Id = id;
```

Class Table Inheritance

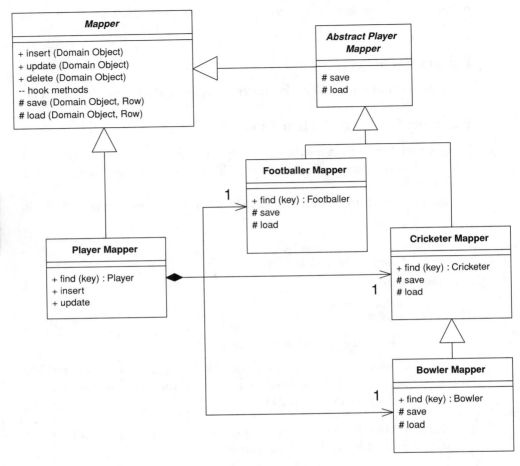

Figure 12.9 *The generic class diagram of* Inheritance Mappers (302).

```
            Load(result);
            return result;
        }
    }
    protected DataTable tableFor(String name) {
        return Gateway.Data.Tables[name];
    }
    protected DataRow FindRow(long id, DataTable table) {
        String filter = String.Format("id = {0}", id);
        DataRow[] results = table.Select(filter);
        return (results.Length == 0) ? null : results[0];
```

```
    }
    protected DataRow FindRow (long id, String tablename) {
        return FindRow(id, tableFor(tablename));
    }
    protected abstract DomainObject CreateDomainObject();
```

class FootballerMapper...

```
    protected override DomainObject CreateDomainObject(){
        return new Footballer();
    }
```

There's one load method for each class which loads the data defined by that class.

class FootballerMapper...

```
    protected override void Load(DomainObject obj) {
        base.Load(obj);
        DataRow row = FindRow (obj.Id, tableFor(TABLENAME));
        Footballer footballer = (Footballer) obj;
        footballer.club = (String)row["club"];
    }
```

class AbstractPlayerMapper...

```
    protected override void Load(DomainObject obj) {
        DataRow row = FindRow (obj.Id, tableFor(TABLENAME));
        Player player = (Player) obj;
        player.name = (String)row["name"];
    }
```

**Class Table
Inheritance**

As with the other sample code, but more noticeably in this case, I'm relying on the fact that the ADO.NET data set has brought the data from the database and cached it into memory. This allows me to make several accesses to the table-based data structure without a high performance cost. If you're going directly to the database, you'll need to reduce that load. For this example you might do this by creating a join across all the tables and manipulating it.

The player mapper determines which kind of player it has to find and then delegates the correct concrete mapper.

class PlayerMapper...

```
    public Player Find (long key) {
        DataRow row = FindRow(key, tableFor(TABLENAME));
        if (row == null) return null;
        else {
            String typecode = (String) row["type"];
            if (typecode == bmapper.TypeCode)
                return bmapper.Find(key);
            if (typecode == cmapper.TypeCode)
                return cmapper.Find(key);
```

```
        if (typecode == fmapper.TypeCode)
            return fmapper.Find(key);
        throw new Exception("unknown type");
    }
  }
  protected static String TABLENAME = "Players";
```

Updating an Object The update method appears on the mapper superclass

class Mapper...

```
    public virtual void Update (DomainObject arg) {
        Save (arg);
    }
```

Class Table Inheritance

It's implemented through a series of save methods, one for each class in the hierarchy.

class FootballerMapper...

```
    protected override void Save(DomainObject obj) {
        base.Save(obj);
        DataRow row = FindRow (obj.Id, tableFor(TABLENAME));
        Footballer footballer = (Footballer) obj;
        row["club"] = footballer.club;
    }
```

class AbstractPlayerMapper...

```
    protected override void Save(DomainObject obj) {
        DataRow row = FindRow (obj.Id, tableFor(TABLENAME));
        Player player = (Player) obj;
        row["name"] = player.name;
        row["type"] = TypeCode;
    }
```

The player mapper's update method overrides the general method to forward to the correct concrete mapper.

class PlayerMapper...

```
    public override void Update (DomainObject obj) {
        MapperFor(obj).Update(obj);
    }
    private Mapper MapperFor(DomainObject obj) {
        if (obj is Footballer)
          return fmapper;
        if (obj is Bowler)
          return bmapper;
        if (obj is Cricketer)
          return cmapper;
        throw new Exception("No mapper available");
    }
```

Inserting an Object The method for inserting an object is declared on the mapper superclass. It has two stages: creating new database rows and then using the save methods to update these blank rows with the necessary data.

class Mapper...

```
public virtual void Update (DomainObject arg) {
    Save (arg);
}
```

Each class inserts a row into its table.

class FootballerMapper...

```
protected override void AddRow (DomainObject obj) {
    base.AddRow(obj);
    InsertRow (obj, tableFor(TABLENAME));
}
```

class AbstractPlayerMapper...

```
protected override void AddRow (DomainObject obj) {
    InsertRow (obj, tableFor(TABLENAME));
}
```

class Mapper...

```
abstract protected void AddRow (DomainObject obj);
protected virtual void InsertRow (DomainObject arg, DataTable table) {
    DataRow row = table.NewRow();
    row["id"] = arg.Id;
    table.Rows.Add(row);
}
```

The player mapper delegates to the appropriate concrete mapper.

class PlayerMapper...

```
public override long Insert (DomainObject obj) {
    return MapperFor(obj).Insert(obj);
}
```

Deleting an Object To delete an object, each class deletes a row from the corresponding table in the database.

class FootballerMapper...

```
public override void Delete(DomainObject obj) {
    base.Delete(obj);
    DataRow row = FindRow(obj.Id, TABLENAME);
    row.Delete();
}
```

Class Table
Inheritance

```
class AbstractPlayerMapper...

    public override void Delete(DomainObject obj) {
        DataRow row = FindRow(obj.Id, tableFor(TABLENAME));
        row.Delete();
    }
```

```
class Mapper...

    public abstract void Delete(DomainObject obj);
```

The player mapper again wimps out of all the hard work and just delegates to the concrete mapper.

```
class PlayerMapper...

    override public void Delete(DomainObject obj) {
        MapperFor(obj).Delete(obj);
    }
```

Concrete Table Inheritance

*Represents an inheritance hierarchy of classes with
one table per concrete class in the hierarchy.*

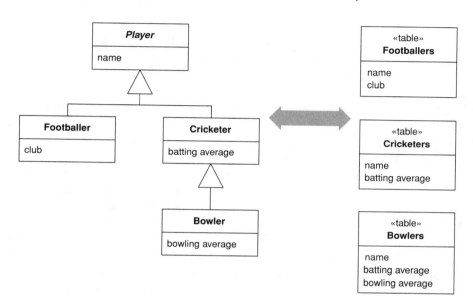

Concrete
Table
Inheritance

As any object purist will tell you, relational databases don't support inheritance—a fact that complicates object-relational mapping. Thinking of tables from an object instance point of view, a sensible route is to take each object in memory and map it to a single database row. This implies *Concrete Table Inheritance*, where there's a table for each concrete class in the inheritance hierarchy.

I'll confess to having had some difficulty naming this pattern. Most people think of it as leaf oriented since you usually have one table per leaf class in a hierarchy. Following that logic, I could call this pattern leaf table inheritance, and the term "leaf" is often used for this pattern. Strictly, however, a concrete class that isn't a leaf usually gets a table as well, so I decided to go with the more correct, if less intuitive term.

How It Works

Concrete Table Inheritance uses one database table for each concrete class in the hierarchy. Each table contains columns for the concrete class and all its ancestors, so any fields in a superclass are duplicated across the tables of the subclasses. As with all of these inheritance schemes the basic behavior uses *Inheritance Mappers (302)*.

You need to pay attention to the keys with this pattern. Punningly, the key thing is to ensure that keys are unique not just to a table but to all the tables from a hierarchy. A classic example of where you need this is if you have a collection of players and you're using *Identity Field (216)* with table-wide keys. If keys can be duplicated between the tables that map the concrete classes, you'll get multiple rows for a particular key value. Thus, you thus need a key allocation system that keeps track of key usage across tables; also, you can't rely on the database's primary key uniqueness mechanism.

This becomes particularly awkward if you're hooking up to databases used by other systems. In many of these cases you can't guarantee key uniqueness across tables. In this situation you either avoid using superclass fields or use a compound key that involves a table identifier.

You can get around some of this by not having fields that are typed to the superclass, but obviously that compromises the object model. As alternative is to have accessors for the supertype in the interface but to use several private fields for each concrete type in the implementation. The interface then combines values from the private fields. If the public interface is a single value, it picks whichever of the private values aren't null. If the public interface is a collection value, it replies with the union of values from the implementation fields.

For compound keys you can use a special key object as your ID field for *Identity Field (216)*. This key uses both the primary key of the table and the table name to determine uniqueness.

Related to this are problems with referential integrity in the database. Consider an object model like Figure 12.10. To implement referential integrity you need a link table that contains foreign key columns for the charity function and for the player. The problem is that there's no table for the player, so you can't put together a referential integrity constraint for the foreign key field that takes either footballers or cricketers. Your choice is to ignore referential integrity or use multiple link tables, one for each of the actual tables in the database. On top of this you have problems if you can't guarantee key uniqueness.

If you're searching for players with a select statement, you need to look at all tables to see which ones contain the appropriate value. This means using multiple queries or using an outer join, both of which are bad for performance. You don't suffer the performance hit when you know the class you need, but you do have to use the concrete class to improve performance.

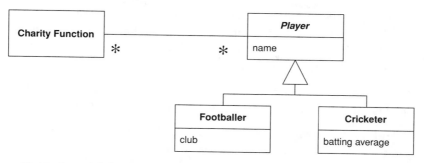

Figure 12.10 *A model that causes referential integrity problems for Concrete Table Inheritance.*

This pattern is often referred to as along the lines of **leaf table inheritance**. Some people prefer a variation where you have one table per leaf class instead of one table per concrete class. If you don't have any concrete superclasses in the hierarchy, this ends up as the same thing. Even if you do have concrete superclasses the difference is pretty minor.

When to Use It

When figuring out how to map inheritance, *Concrete Table Inheritance*, *Class Table Inheritance (285)*, and *Single Table Inheritance (278)* are the alternatives.
    The strengths of *Concrete Table Inheritance* are:

- Each table is self-contained and has no irrelevant fields. As a result it makes good sense when used by other applications that aren't using the objects.

- There are no joins to do when reading the data from the concrete mappers.

- Each table is accessed only when that class is accessed, which can spread the access load.

The weaknesses of *Concrete Table Inheritance* are:

- Primary keys can be difficult to handle.

- You can't enforce database relationships to abstract classes.

- If the fields on the domain classes are pushed up or down the hierarchy, you have to alter the table definitions. You don't have to do as much alteration as with *Class Table Inheritance (285)*, but you can't ignore this as you can with *Single Table Inheritance (278)*.

- If a superclass field changes, you need to change each table that has this field because the superclass fields are duplicated across the tables.

- A find on the superclass forces you to check all the tables, which leads to multiple database accesses (or a weird join).

Remember that the trio of inheritance patterns can coexist in a single hierarchy. So you might use *Concrete Table Inheritance* for one or two subclasses and *Single Table Inheritance (278)* for the rest.

Concrete
Table
Inheritance

Example: Concrete Players (C#)

Here I'll show you an implementation for the sketch. As with all inheritance examples in this chapter, I'm using the basic design of classes from *Inheritance Mappers (302)*, shown in Figure 12.11.

Each mapper is linked to the database table that's the source of the data. In ADO.NET a data set holds the data table.

class Mapper...

```
public Gateway Gateway;
private IDictionary identityMap = new Hashtable();
public Mapper (Gateway gateway) {
    this.Gateway = gateway;
}
private DataTable table {
    get {return Gateway.Data.Tables[TableName];}
}
abstract public String TableName {get;}
```

The gateway class holds the data set within its data property. The data can be loaded up by supplying suitable queries.

class Gateway...

```
public DataSet Data = new DataSet();
```

Each concrete mapper needs to define the name of the table that holds its data.

class CricketerMapper...

```
public override String TableName {
    get {return "Cricketers";}
}
```

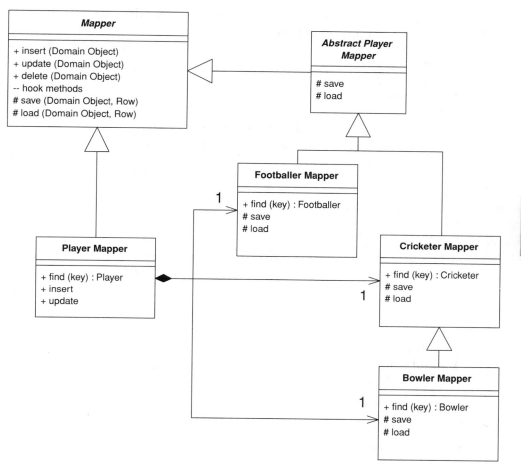

Figure 12.11 *The generic class diagram of* Inheritance Mappers (302).

The player mapper has fields for each concrete mapper.

```
class PlayerMapper...

    private BowlerMapper bmapper;
    private CricketerMapper cmapper;
    private FootballerMapper fmapper;
    public PlayerMapper (Gateway gateway) : base (gateway) {
        bmapper = new BowlerMapper(Gateway);
        cmapper = new CricketerMapper(Gateway);
        fmapper = new FootballerMapper(Gateway);
    }
```

Loading an Object from the Database Each concrete mapper class has a find method that returns an object given a key value.

class CricketerMapper...

```
public Cricketer Find(long id) {
    return (Cricketer) AbstractFind(id);
}
```

The abstract behavior on the superclass finds the right database row for the ID, creates a new domain object of the correct type, and uses the load method to load it up (I'll describe the load in a moment).

class Mapper...

```
public DomainObject AbstractFind(long id) {
    DataRow row = FindRow(id);
    if (row == null) return null;
    else {
        DomainObject result = CreateDomainObject();
        Load(result, row);
        return result;
    }
}
private DataRow FindRow(long id) {
    String filter = String.Format("id = {0}", id);
    DataRow[] results = table.Select(filter);
    if (results.Length == 0) return null;
    else return results[0];
}
protected abstract DomainObject CreateDomainObject();
```

class CricketerMapper...

```
protected override DomainObject CreateDomainObject(){
    return new Cricketer();
}
```

The actual loading of data from the database is done by the load method, or rather by several load methods: one each for the mapper class and for all its superclasses.

class CricketerMapper...

```
protected override void Load(DomainObject obj, DataRow row) {
    base.Load(obj,row);
    Cricketer cricketer = (Cricketer) obj;
    cricketer.battingAverage = (double)row["battingAverage"];
}
```

```
class AbstractPlayerMapper...

    protected override void Load(DomainObject obj, DataRow row) {
        base.Load(obj, row);
        Player player = (Player) obj;
        player.name = (String)row["name"];

class Mapper...

    protected virtual void Load(DomainObject obj, DataRow row) {
        obj.Id = (int) row ["id"];
    }
```

This is the logic for finding an object using a mapper for a concrete class. You can also use a mapper for the superclass: the player mapper, which it needs to find an object from whatever table it's living in. Since all the data is already in memory in the data set, I can do this like so:

Concrete Table Inheritance

```
class PlayerMapper...

    public Player Find (long key) {
        Player result;
        result = fmapper.Find(key);
        if (result != null) return result;
        result = bmapper.Find(key);
        if (result != null) return result;
        result = cmapper.Find(key);
        if (result != null) return result;
        return null;
    }
```

Remember, this is reasonable only because the data is already in memory. If you need to go to the database three times (or more for more subclasses) this will be slow. It may help to do a join across all the concrete tables, which will allow you to access the data in one database call. However, large joins are often slow in their own right, so you'll need to do some benchmarks with your own application to find out what works and what doesn't. Also, this will be an outer join, and as well as slowing the syntax it's nonportable and often cryptic.

Updating an Object The update method can be defined on the mapper superclass.

```
class Mapper...

    public virtual void Update (DomainObject arg) {
        Save (arg, FindRow(arg.Id));
    }
```

Similar to loading, we use a sequence of save methods for each mapper class.

class CricketerMapper...

```
protected override void Save(DomainObject obj, DataRow row) {
    base.Save(obj, row);
    Cricketer cricketer = (Cricketer) obj;
    row["battingAverage"] = cricketer.battingAverage;
}
```

class AbstractPlayerMapper...

```
protected override void Save(DomainObject obj, DataRow row) {
    Player player = (Player) obj;
    row["name"] = player.name;
}
```

Concrete
Table
Inheritance

The player mapper needs to find the correct concrete mapper to use and then delegate the update call.

class PlayerMapper...

```
public override void Update (DomainObject obj) {
    MapperFor(obj).Update(obj);
}
private Mapper MapperFor(DomainObject obj) {
    if (obj is Footballer)
        return fmapper;
    if (obj is Bowler)
        return bmapper;
    if (obj is Cricketer)
        return cmapper;
    throw new Exception("No mapper available");
}
```

Inserting an Object   Insertion is a variation on updating. The extra behavior is creating the new row, which can be done on the superclass.

class Mapper...

```
public virtual long Insert (DomainObject arg) {
    DataRow row = table.NewRow();
    arg.Id = GetNextID();
    row["id"] = arg.Id;
    Save (arg, row);
    table.Rows.Add(row);
    return arg.Id;
}
```

Again, the player class delegates to the appropriate mapper.

class PlayerMapper...

```
public override long Insert (DomainObject obj) {
    return MapperFor(obj).Insert(obj);
}
```

Deleting an Object Deletion is very straightforward. As before, we have a method defined on the superclass:

class Mapper...

```
public virtual void Delete(DomainObject obj) {
    DataRow row = FindRow(obj.Id);
    row.Delete();
}
```

and a delegating method on the player mapper.

class PlayerMapper...

```
public override void Delete (DomainObject obj) {
    MapperFor(obj).Delete(obj);
}
```

Inheritance Mappers

*A structure to organize database mappers
that handle inheritance hierarchies.*

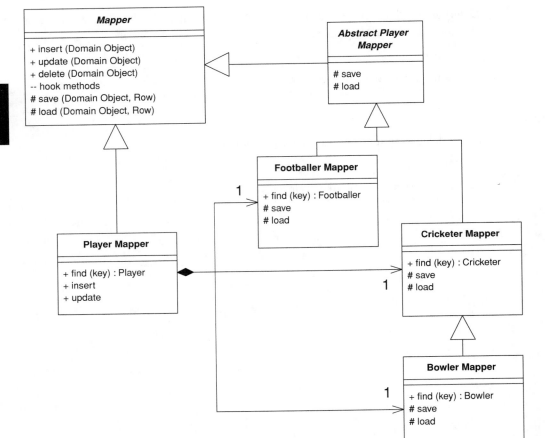

When you map from an object-oriented inheritance hierarchy in memory to a relational database you have to minimize the amount of code needed to save and load the data to the database. You also want to provide both abstract and concrete mapping behavior that allows you to save or load a superclass or a subclass.

Although the details of this behavior vary with your inheritance mapping scheme (*Single Table Inheritance (278)*, *Class Table Inheritance (285)*, and *Concrete Table Inheritance (293)*) the general structure works the same for all of them.

How It Works

You can organize the mappers with a hierarchy so that each domain class has a mapper that saves and loads the data for that domain class. This way you have one point where you can change the mapping. This approach works well for concrete mappers that know how to map the concrete objects in the hierarchy. There are times, however, where you also need mappers for the abstract classes. These can be implemented with mappers that are actually outside of the basic hierarchy but delegate to the appropriate concrete mappers.

Inheritance Mappers

To best explain how this works, I'll start with the concrete mappers. In the sketch the concrete mappers are the mappers for footballer, cricketer, and bowler. Their basic behavior includes the find, insert, update, and delete operations.

The find methods are declared on the concrete subclasses because they will return a concrete class. Thus, the find method on BowlerMapper should return a bowler, not an abstract class. Common OO languages can't let you change the declared return type of a method, so it's not possible to inherit the find operation and still declare a specific return type. You can, of course, return an abstract type, but that forces the user of the class to downcast—which is best to avoid. (A language with dynamic typing doesn't have this problem.)

The basic behavior of the find method is to find the appropriate row in the database, instantiate an object of the correct type (a decision that's made by the subclass), and then load the object with data from the database. The load method is implemented by each mapper in the hierarchy which loads the behavior for its corresponding domain object. This means that the bowler mapper's load method loads the data specific to the bowler class and calls the superclass method to load the data specific to the cricketer, which calls its superclass method, and so on.

The insert and update methods operate in a similar way using a save method. Here you can define the interface on the superclass—indeed, on a *Layer Supertype (475)*. The insert method creates a new row and then saves the data from the domain object using the save hook methods. The update method just saves the data, also using the save hook methods. These methods operate similarly to the load hook methods, with each class storing its specific data and calling the superclass save method.

This scheme makes it easy to write the appropriate mappers to save the information needed for a particular part of the hierarchy. The next step is to support loading and saving an abstract class—in this example, a player. While a first thought is to put appropriate methods on the superclass mapper, that actually gets awkward. While concrete mapper classes can just use the abstract mapper's insert and update methods, the player mapper's insert and update need to override these to call a concrete mapper instead. The result is one of those combinations of generalization and composition that twist your brain cells into a knot.

I prefer to separate the mappers into two classes. The abstract player mapper is responsible for loading and saving the specific player data to the database. This is an abstract class whose behavior is just used only by the concrete mapper objects. A separate player mapper class is used for the interface for operations at the player level. The player mapper provides a find method and overrides the insert and update methods. For all of these its responsibility is to figure out which concrete mapper should handle the task and delegate to it.

Although a broad scheme like this makes sense for each type of inheritance mapping, the details do vary. Therefore, it's not possible to show a code example for this case. You can find good examples in each of the inheritance mapping pattern sections: *Single Table Inheritance (278)*, *Class Table Inheritance (285)*, and *Concrete Table Inheritance (293)*.

When to Use It

This general scheme makes sense for any inheritance-based database mapping. The alternatives involve such things as duplicating superclass mapping code among the concrete mappers and folding the player's interface into the abstract player mapper class. The former is a heinous crime, and the latter is possible but leads to a player mapper class that's messy and confusing. On the whole, then, its hard to think of a good alternative to this pattern.

Chapter 13

Object-Relational Metadata Mapping Patterns

Metadata Mapping

Holds details of object-relational mapping in metadata.

Much of the code that deals with object-relational mapping describes how fields in the database correspond to fields in in-memory objects. The resulting code tends to be tedious and repetitive to write. A *Metadata Mapping* allows developers to define the mappings in a simple tabular form, which can then be processed by generic code to carry out the details of reading, inserting, and updating the data.

Metadata Mapping

How It Works

The biggest decision in using *Metadata Mapping* is how the information in the metadata manifests itself in terms of running code. There are two main routes to take: code generation and reflective programming.

With **code generation** you write a program whose input is the metadata and whose output is the source code of classes that do the mapping. These classes look as though they're hand-written, but they're entirely generated during the build process, usually just prior to compilation. The resulting mapper classes are deployed with the server code.

If you use code generation, you should make sure that it's fully integrated into your build process with whatever build scripts you're using. The generated classes should never be edited by hand and thus shouldn't need to be held in source code control.

A **reflective program** may ask an object for a method named setName, and then run an invoke method on the setName method passing in the appropriate argument. By treating methods (and fields) as data the reflective program can read in field and method names from a metadata file and use them to carry out the mapping. I usually counsel against reflection, partly because it's slow but mainly because it often causes code that's hard to debug. Even so, reflection is actually quite appropriate for database mapping. Since you're reading in the names of fields and methods from a file, you're taking full advantage of reflection's flexibility.

Code generation is a less dynamic approach since any changes to the mapping require recompiling and redeploying at least that part of the software. With a reflective approach, you can just change the mapping data file and the existing classes will use the new metadata. You can even do this during runtime, rereading the metadata when you get a particular kind of interrupt. As it turns out, mapping changes should be pretty rare, since they imply database or code changes. Modern environments also make it easy to redeploy part of an application.

Reflective programming often suffers in speed, although the problem here depends very much on the actual environment you're using—in some a reflective call can be an order of magnitude slower. Remember, though, that the reflection is being done in the context of an SQL call, so its slower speed may not make that much difference considering the slow speed of the remote call. As with any performance issue, you need to measure within your environment to find out how much of a factor this is.

Both approaches can be a little awkward to debug. The comparison between them depends very much on how used to generated and reflective code developers are. Generated code is more explicit so you can see what's going on in the debugger; as a result I usually prefer generation to reflection, and I think it's usually easier for less sophisticated developers (which I guess makes me unsophisticated).

On most occasions you keep the metadata in a separate file format. These days XML is a popular choice as it provides hierarchic structuring while freeing you from writing your own parsers and other tools. A loading step takes this metadata and turns it into programming language structure, which then drive either the code generation output or the reflective mapping.

In simpler cases you can skip the external file format and create the metadata representation directly in source code. This saves you from having to parse, but it makes editing the metadata somewhat harder.

Another alternative is to hold the mapping information in the database itself, which keeps it together with the data. If the database schema changes, the mapping information is right there.

When you're deciding which way to hold the metadata information, you can mostly neglect the performance of access and parsing. If you use code generation, access and parsing take place only during the build and not during execution. If you use reflective programming, you'll typically access and parse during execution but only once during system startup; then you can keep the in-memory representation.

How complex to make your metadata is one of your biggest decisions. When you're faced with a general relational mapping problem, there are a lot of different factors to keep in metadata, but many projects can manage with much less than a fully general scheme and so their metadata can be much simpler. On the whole it's worth evolving your design as your needs grow, as it isn't hard to add new capabilities to metadata-driven software.

One of the challenges of metadata is that although a simple metadata scheme often works well 90 percent of the time, there are often special cases that make life much more tricky. To handle these minority cases you often have to add a lot of complexity to metadata. A useful alternative is to override the generic code with subclasses where the special code is handwritten. Such special-case subclasses would be subclasses of either the generated code or the reflective routines. Since these special cases are . . . well . . . special, it isn't easy to describe in general terms how you arrange things to support the overriding. My advice is to handle them on a case-by-case basis. As you need the overriding, alter the generated/reflective code to isolate a single method that should be overridden and then override it in your special case.

Metadata Mapping

When to Use It

Metadata Mapping can greatly reduce the amount of work needed to handle database mapping. However, some setup work is required to prepare the *Metadata Mapping* framework. Also, while it's often easy to handle most cases with *Metadata Mapping*, you can find exceptions that really tangle the metadata.

It's no surprise that the commercial object-relational mapping tools use *Metadata Mapping*—when selling a product producing a sophisticated *Metadata Mapping* is always worth the effort.

If you're building your own system, you should evaluate the trade-offs yourself. Compare adding new mappings using handwritten code with using *Metadata Mapping*. If you use reflection, look into its consequences for performance; sometimes it causes slowdowns, but sometimes it doesn't. Your own measurements will reveal whether this is an issue for you.

The extra work of hand-coding can be greatly reduced by creating a good *Layer Supertype (475)* that handles all the common behavior. That way you should only have a few hook routines to add in for each mapping. Usually *Metadata Mapping* can further reduce the number.

Metadata Mapping can interfere with refactoring, particularly if you're using automated tools. If you change the name of a private field, it can break an application unexpectedly. Even automated refactoring tools won't be able to find the field name hidden in a XML data file of a map. Using code generation is a little easier, since search mechanisms can find the usage. Still, any automated update will get lost when you regenerate the code. A tool can warn you of a problem, but it's up to you to change the metadata yourself. If you use reflection, you won't even get the warning.

On the other hand, *Metadata Mapping* can make refactoring the database easier, since the metadata represents a statement of the interface of your database schema. Thus, alterations to the database can be contained by changes in the *Metadata Mapping*.

Example: Using Metadata and Reflection (Java)

Most examples in this book use explicit code because it's the easiest to understand. However, it does lead to pretty tedious programming, and tedious programming is a sign that something is wrong. You can remove a lot of tedious programming by using metadata.

Holding the Metadata The first question to ask about metadata is how it's going to be kept. Here I'm keeping it in two classes. The data map corresponds to the mapping of one class to one table. This is a simple mapping, but it will do for illustration.

```
class DataMap...

    private Class domainClass;
    private String tableName;
    private List columnMaps = new ArrayList();
```

The data map contains a collection of column maps that map columns in the table to fields.

```
class ColumnMap...

    private String columnName;
    private String fieldName;
    private Field field;
    private DataMap dataMap;
```

This isn't a terribly sophisticated mapping. I'm just using the default Java type mappings, which means there's no type conversion between fields and columns. I'm also forcing a one-to-one relationship between tables and classes.

These structures hold the mappings. The next question is how they're populated. For this example I'm going to populate them with Java code in specific mapper classes. That may seem a little odd, but it buys most of the benefit of metadata—avoiding repetitive code.

class PersonMapper...

```
protected void loadDataMap(){
    dataMap = new DataMap (Person.class, "people");
    dataMap.addColumn ("lastname", "varchar", "lastName");
    dataMap.addColumn ("firstname", "varchar", "firstName");
    dataMap.addColumn ("number_of_dependents", "int", "numberOfDependents");
}
```

During construction of the column mapper, I build the link to the field. Strictly speaking, this is an optimization so you may not have to calculate the fields. However, doing so reduces the subsequent accesses by an order of magnitude on my little laptop.

class ColumnMap...

```
public ColumnMap(String columnName, String fieldName, DataMap dataMap) {
    this.columnName = columnName;
    this.fieldName = fieldName;
    this.dataMap = dataMap;
    initField();
}
private void initField() {
    try {
        field = dataMap.getDomainClass().getDeclaredField(getFieldName());
        field.setAccessible(true);
    } catch (Exception e) {
        throw new ApplicationException ("unable to set up field: " + fieldName, e);
    }
}
```

It's not much of a challenge to see how I can write a routine to load the map from an XML file or from a metadata database. Paltry that challenge may be, but I'll decline it and leave it to you.

Now that the mappings are defined, I can make use of them. The strength of the metadata approach is that all of the code that actually manipulates things is in a superclass, so I don't have to write the mapping code that I wrote in the explicit cases.

Find by ID I'll begin with the find by ID method.

class Mapper...

```
public Object findObject (Long key) {
    if (uow.isLoaded(key)) return uow.getObject(key);
    String sql = "SELECT" + dataMap.columnList() + " FROM " + dataMap.getTableName() + " WHERE
        ID = ?";
    PreparedStatement stmt = null;
```

Metadata Mapping

```
        ResultSet rs = null;
        DomainObject result = null;
        try {
            stmt = DB.prepare(sql);
            stmt.setLong(1, key.longValue());
            rs = stmt.executeQuery();
            rs.next();
            result = load(rs);
        } catch (Exception e) {throw new ApplicationException (e);
        } finally {DB.cleanUp(stmt, rs);
        }
      return result;
    }
    private UnitOfWork uow;
    protected DataMap dataMap;

class DataMap...

    public String columnList() {
        StringBuffer result = new StringBuffer(" ID");
        for (Iterator it = columnMaps.iterator(); it.hasNext();) {
            result.append(",");
            ColumnMap columnMap = (ColumnMap)it.next();
            result.append(columnMap.getColumnName());
        }
        return result.toString();
    }
    public String getTableName() {
        return tableName;
    }
```

The select is built more dynamically than the other examples, but it's still worth preparing in a way that allows the database session to cache it properly. If it's an issue, the column list can be calculated during construction and cached, since there's no call for updating the columns during the life of the data map. For this example I'm using a *Unit of Work (184)* to handle the database session.

As is common with the examples in this book I've separated the load from the find, so that we can use the same load method from other find methods.

class Mapper...

```
    public DomainObject load(ResultSet rs)
          throwsInstantiationException, IllegalAccessException, SQLException
    {
        Long key = new Long(rs.getLong("ID"));
        if (uow.isLoaded(key)) return uow.getObject(key);
        DomainObject result = (DomainObject) dataMap.getDomainClass().newInstance();
        result.setID(key);
        uow.registerClean(result);
        loadFields(rs, result);
        return result;
    }
```

```
private void loadFields(ResultSet rs, DomainObject result) throws SQLException {
    for (Iterator it = dataMap.getColumns(); it.hasNext();) {
        ColumnMap columnMap = (ColumnMap)it.next();
        Object columnValue = rs.getObject(columnMap.getColumnName());
        columnMap.setField(result, columnValue);
    }
}
```

class ColumnMap...

```
public void setField(Object result, Object columnValue) {
    try {
        field.set(result, columnValue);
    } catch (Exception e) { throw new ApplicationException ("Error in setting " + fieldName, e);
    }
}
```

This is a classic reflected program. We go through each of the column maps and use them to load the field in the domain object. I separated the loadFields method to show how we might extend this for more complicated cases. If we have a class and a table where the simple assumptions of the metadata don't hold, I can just override loadFields in a subclass mapper to put in arbitrarily complex code. This is a common technique with metadata—providing a hook to override for more wacky cases. It's usually a lot easier to override the wacky cases with subclasses than it is to build metadata sophisticated enough to hold a few rare special cases.

Of course, if we have a subclass, we might as well use it to avoid downcasting.

class PersonMapper...

```
public Person find(Long key) {
    return (Person) findObject(key);
}
```

Writing to the Database For updates I have a single update routine.

class Mapper...

```
public void update (DomainObject obj) {
    String sql = "UPDATE " + dataMap.getTableName() + dataMap.updateList() + " WHERE ID = ?";
    PreparedStatement stmt = null;
    try {
        stmt = DB.prepare(sql);
        int argCount = 1;
        for (Iterator it = dataMap.getColumns(); it.hasNext();) {
            ColumnMap col = (ColumnMap) it.next();
            stmt.setObject(argCount++, col.getValue(obj));
        }
        stmt.setLong(argCount, obj.getID().longValue());
        stmt.executeUpdate();
```

```
        } catch (SQLException e) {throw new ApplicationException (e);
        } finally {DB.cleanUp(stmt);
        }
    }

class DataMap...

    public String updateList() {
        StringBuffer result = new StringBuffer(" SET ");
        for (Iterator it = columnMaps.iterator(); it.hasNext();) {
            ColumnMap columnMap = (ColumnMap)it.next();
            result.append(columnMap.getColumnName());
            result.append("=?,");
        }
        result.setLength(result.length() - 1);
        return result.toString();
    }
    public Iterator getColumns() {
        return Collections.unmodifiableCollection(columnMaps).iterator();
    }

class ColumnMap...

    public Object getValue (Object subject) {
        try {
            return field.get(subject);
        } catch (Exception e) {
            throw new ApplicationException (e);
        }
    }
```

Inserts use a similar scheme.

```
class Mapper...

    public Long insert (DomainObject obj) {
        String sql = "INSERT INTO " + dataMap.getTableName() + " VALUES (?" + dataMap.insertList()
                + ")";
        PreparedStatement stmt = null;
        try {
            stmt = DB.prepare(sql);
            stmt.setObject(1, obj.getID());
            int argCount = 2;
            for (Iterator it = dataMap.getColumns(); it.hasNext();) {
                ColumnMap col = (ColumnMap) it.next();
                stmt.setObject(argCount++, col.getValue(obj));
            }
            stmt.executeUpdate();
        } catch (SQLException e) {throw new ApplicationException (e);
        } finally {DB.cleanUp(stmt);
        }
        return obj.getID();
    }
```

Metadata Mapping

```
class DataMap...

    public String insertList() {
        StringBuffer result = new StringBuffer();
        for (int i = 0; i < columnMaps.size(); i++) {
            result.append(",");
            result.append("?");
        }
        return result.toString();
    }
```

Multi-Object Finds There are a couple of routes you can take to get multiple objects with a query. If you want a generic query capability on the generic mapper, you can have a query that takes a SQL where clause as an argument.

```
class Mapper...

    public Set findObjectsWhere (String whereClause) {
        String sql = "SELECT" + dataMap.columnList() + " FROM " + dataMap.getTableName() + " WHERE "
            + whereClause;
        PreparedStatement stmt = null;
        ResultSet rs = null;
        Set result = new HashSet();
        try {
            stmt = DB.prepare(sql);
            rs = stmt.executeQuery();
            result = loadAll(rs);
        } catch (Exception e) {
            throw new ApplicationException (e);
        } finally {DB.cleanUp(stmt, rs);
        }
      return result;
    }
    public Set loadAll(ResultSet rs) throws SQLException, InstantiationException,
        IllegalAccessException {
        Set result = new HashSet();
        while (rs.next()) {
            DomainObject newObj = (DomainObject) dataMap.getDomainClass().newInstance();
            newObj = load (rs);
            result.add(newObj);
        }
        return result;
    }
```

An alternative is to provide special case finders on the mapper subtypes.

```
class PersonMapper...

    public Set findLastNamesLike (String pattern) {
        String sql =
            "SELECT" + dataMap.columnList() +
            " FROM " + dataMap.getTableName() +
            " WHERE UPPER(lastName) like UPPER(?)";
```

```
       PreparedStatement stmt = null;
       ResultSet rs = null;
       try {
          stmt = DB.prepare(sql);
          stmt.setString(1, pattern);
          rs = stmt.executeQuery();
          return loadAll(rs);
       } catch (Exception e) {throw new ApplicationException (e);
       } finally {DB.cleanUp(stmt, rs);
       }
    }
```

A further alternative for general selects is a *Query Object (316)*.

On the whole, the great advantage of the metadata approach is that I can now add new tables and classes to my data mapping and all I have to do is to provide a loadMap method and any specialized finders that I may fancy.

Metadata Mapping

Query Object

An object that represents a database query.

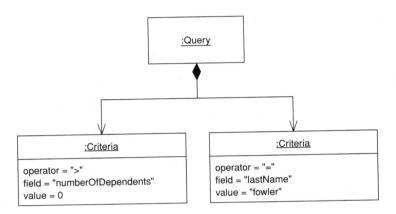

SQL can be an involved language, and many developers aren't particularly familiar with it. Furthermore, you need to know what the database schema looks like to form queries. You can avoid this by creating specialized finder methods that hide the SQL inside parameterized methods, but that makes it difficult to form more ad hoc queries. It also leads to duplication in the SQL statements should the database schema change.

A *Query Object* is an interpreter [Gang of Four], that is, a structure of objects that can form itself into a SQL query. You can create this query by referring to classes and fields rather than tables and columns. In this way those who write the queries can do so independently of the database schema and changes to the schema can be localized in a single place.

How It Works

A *Query Object* is an application of the Interpreter pattern geared to represent a SQL query. Its primary roles are to allow a client to form queries of various kinds and to turn those object structures into the appropriate SQL string.

In order to represent any query, you need a flexible *Query Object*. Often, however, applications can make do with a lot less than the full power of SQL, in which case your *Query Object* can be simpler. It won't be able to represent anything, but it can satisfy your particular needs. Moreover, it's usually no more work to enhance it when you need more capability than it is to create a fully capable *Query Object* right from the beginning. As a result you should create a minimally functional *Query Object* for your current needs and evolve it as those needs grow.

A common feature of *Query Object* is that it can represent queries in the language of the in-memory objects rather than the database schema. That means that, instead of using table and column names, you can use object and field names. While this isn't important if your objects and database have the same structure, it can be very useful if you get variations between the two. In order to perform this change of view, the *Query Object* needs to know how the database structure maps to the object structure, a capability that really needs *Metadata Mapping (306)*.

For multiple databases you can design your *Query Object* so that it produces different SQL depending on which database the query is running against. At it's simplest level it can take into account the annoying differences in SQL syntax that keep cropping up; at a more ambitious level it can use different mappings to cope with the same classes being stored in different database schemas.

Query Object

A particularly sophisticated use of *Query Object* is to eliminate redundant queries against a database. If you see that you've run the same query earlier in a session, you can use it to select objects from the *Identity Map (195)* and avoid a trip to the database. A more sophisticated approach can detect whether one query is a particular case of an earlier query, such as a query that is the same as an earlier one but with an additional clause linked with an AND.

Exactly how to achieve these more sophisticated features is beyond the scope of this book, but they're the kind of features that O/R mapping tools may provide.

A variation on the *Query Object* is to allow a query to be specified by an example domain object. Thus, you might have a person object whose last name is set to Fowler but all of those other attributes are set to null. You can treat it as a query by example that's processed like the Interpreter-style *Query Object*. That returns all people in the database whose last name is Fowler, and it's very simple and convenient to use. However, it breaks down for complex queries.

When to Use It

Query Objects are a pretty sophisticated pattern to put together, so most projects don't use them if they have a handbuilt data source layer. You only really need them when you're using *Domain Model (116)* and *Data Mapper (165)*; you also really need *Metadata Mapping (306)* to make serious use of them.

Even then *Query Objects* aren't always necessary, as many developers are comfortable with SQL. You can hide many of the details of the database schema behind specific finder methods.

The advantages of *Query Object* come with more sophisticated needs: keeping database schemas encapsulated, supporting multiple databases, supporting multiple schemas, and optimizing to avoid multiple queries. Some projects with a particularly sophisticated data source team might want to build these capabilities themselves, but most people who use *Query Object* do so with a commercial tool. My inclination is that you're almost always better off buying a tool.

All that said, you may find that a limited *Query Object* fulfills your needs without being difficult to build on a project that doesn't justify a fully featured version. The trick is to pare down the functionality to no more than you actually use.

Query Object

Further Reading

You can find an example of *Query Object* in [Alpert et al.] in the discussion of interpreters. *Query Object* is also closely linked to the Specification pattern in [Evans and Fowler] and [Evans].

Example: A Simple *Query Object* (Java)

This is a simple example of a *Query Object*—rather less than would be useful for most situations but enough to give you an idea of what a *Query Object* is about. It can query a single table based on set of criteria "AND'ed" together (in slightly more technical language, it can handle a conjunction of elementary predicates).

The *Query Object* is set up using the language of domain objects rather than that of the table structure. Thus, a query knows the class that it's for and a collection of criteria that correspond to the clauses of a where clause.

class QueryObject...

```
private Class klass;
private List criteria = new ArrayList();
```

A simple criterion is one that takes a field and a value and an SQL operator to compare them.

class Criteria...

```
private String sqlOperator;
protected String field;
protected Object value;
```

To make it easier to create the right criteria, I can provide an appropriate creation method.

class Criteria...

```
    public static Criteria greaterThan(String fieldName, int value) {
        return Criteria.greaterThan(fieldName, new Integer(value));
    }
    public static Criteria greaterThan(String fieldName, Object value) {
        return new Criteria(" > ", fieldName, value);
    }
    private Criteria(String sql, String field, Object value) {
        this.sqlOperator = sql;
        this.field = field;
        this.value = value;
    }
```

This allows me to find everyone with dependents by forming a query such as

class Criteria...

```
        QueryObject query = new QueryObject(Person.class);
        query.addCriteria(Criteria.greaterThan("numberOfDependents", 0));
```

Query Object

Thus, if I have a person object such as this:

class Person...

```
    private String lastName;
    private String firstName;
    private int numberOfDependents;
```

I can ask for all people with dependents by creating a query for person and adding a criterion.

```
        QueryObject query = new QueryObject(Person.class);
        query.addCriteria(Criteria.greaterThan("numberOfDependents", 0));
```

That's enough to describe the query. Now the query needs to execute by turning itself into a SQL select. In this case I assume that my mapper class supports a method that finds objects based on a string that's a where clause.

class QueryObject...

```
    public Set execute(UnitOfWork uow) {
        this.uow = uow;
        return uow.getMapper(klass).findObjectsWhere(generateWhereClause());
    }
```

class Mapper...

```
    public Set findObjectsWhere (String whereClause) {
        String sql = "SELECT" + dataMap.columnList() + " FROM " + dataMap.getTableName() + " WHERE "
            + whereClause;
```

```
        PreparedStatement stmt = null;
        ResultSet rs = null;
        Set result = new HashSet();
        try {
            stmt = DB.prepare(sql);
            rs = stmt.executeQuery();
            result = loadAll(rs);
        } catch (Exception e) {
            throw new ApplicationException (e);
        } finally {DB.cleanUp(stmt, rs);
        }
    return result;
}
```

Here I'm using a *Unit of Work (184)* that holds mappers indexed by the class and a mapper that uses *Metadata Mapping (306)*. The code is the same as that in the example in *Metadata Mapping (306)* to save repeating the code in this section.

To generate the where clause, the query iterates through the criteria and has each one print itself out, tying them together with ANDs.

class QueryObject...

```
    private String generateWhereClause() {
        StringBuffer result = new StringBuffer();
        for (Iterator it = criteria.iterator(); it.hasNext();) {
            Criteria c = (Criteria)it.next();
            if (result.length() != 0)
                result.append(" AND ");
            result.append(c.generateSql(uow.getMapper(klass).getDataMap()));
        }
        return result.toString();
    }
```

class Criteria...

```
    public String generateSql(DataMap dataMap) {
        return dataMap.getColumnForField(field) + sqlOperator + value;
    }
```

class DataMap...

```
    public String getColumnForField (String fieldName) {
        for (Iterator it = getColumns(); it.hasNext();) {
            ColumnMap columnMap = (ColumnMap)it.next();
            if (columnMap.getFieldName().equals(fieldName))
                return columnMap.getColumnName();
        }
        throw new ApplicationException ("Unable to find column for " + fieldName);
    }
```

As well as criteria with simple SQL operators, we can create more complex criteria classes that do a little more. Consider a case-insensitive pattern match query, like one that finds all people whose last names start with F. We can form a query object for all people with such dependents.

```
QueryObject query = new QueryObject(Person.class);
query.addCriteria(Criteria.greaterThan("numberOfDependents", 0));
query.addCriteria(Criteria.matches("lastName", "f%"));
```

This uses a different criteria class that forms a more complex clause in the where statement.

class Criteria...

```
public static Criteria matches(String fieldName, String pattern){
  return new MatchCriteria(fieldName, pattern);
}
```

class MatchCriteria extends Criteria...

```
public String generateSql(DataMap dataMap) {
  return "UPPER(" + dataMap.getColumnForField(field) + ") LIKE UPPER('" + value + "')";
}
```

Repository

by Edward Hieatt and Rob Mee

Mediates between the domain and data mapping layers using a collection-like interface for accessing domain objects.

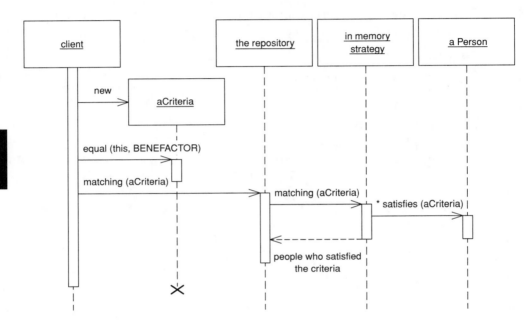

Repository

A system with a complex domain model often benefits from a layer, such as the one provided by *Data Mapper (165)*, that isolates domain objects from details of the database access code. In such systems it can be worthwhile to build another layer of abstraction over the mapping layer where query construction code is concentrated. This becomes more important when there are a large number of domain classes or heavy querying. In these cases particularly, adding this layer helps minimize duplicate query logic.

A *Repository* mediates between the domain and data mapping layers, acting like an in-memory domain object collection. Client objects construct query specifications declaratively and submit them to *Repository* for satisfaction. Objects can be added to and removed from the *Repository*, as they can from a simple collection of objects, and the mapping code encapsulated by the *Reposi-*

tory will carry out the appropriate operations behind the scenes. Conceptually, a *Repository* encapsulates the set of objects persisted in a data store and the operations performed over them, providing a more object-oriented view of the persistence layer. *Repository* also supports the objective of achieving a clean separation and one-way dependency between the domain and data mapping layers.

How It Works

Repository is a sophisticated pattern that makes use of a fair number of the other patterns described in this book. In fact, it looks like a small piece of an object-oriented database and in that way it's similar to *Query Object (316)*, which development teams may be more likely to encounter in an object-relational mapping tool than to build themselves. However, if a team has taken the leap and built *Query Object (316)*, it isn't a huge step to add a *Repository* capability. When used in conjunction with *Query Object (316)*, *Repository* adds a large measure of usability to the object-relational mapping layer without a lot of effort.

Repository

In spite of all the machinery behind the scenes, *Repository* presents a simple interface. Clients create a criteria object specifying the characteristics of the objects they want returned from a query. For example, to find person objects by name we first create a criteria object, setting each individual criterion like so: `criteria.equals(Person.LAST_NAME, "Fowler")`, and `criteria.like(Person.FIRST_NAME, "M")`. Then we invoke `repository.matching(criteria)` to return a list of domain objects representing people with the last name Fowler and a first name starting with M. Various convenience methods similar to matching (criteria) can be defined on an abstract repository; for example, when only one match is expected `soleMatch(criteria)` might return the found object rather than a collection. Other common methods include `byObjectId(id)`, which can be trivially implemented using `soleMatch`.

To code that uses a *Repository*, it appears as a simple in-memory collection of domain objects. The fact that the domain objects themselves typically aren't stored directly in the *Repository* is not exposed to the client code. Of course, code that uses *Repository* should be aware that this apparent collection of objects might very well map to a product table with hundreds of thousands of records. Invoking `all()` on a catalog system's `ProductRepository` might not be such a good idea.

Repository replaces specialized finder methods on *Data Mapper (165)* classes with a specification-based approach to object selection [Evans and Fowler]. Compare this with the direct use of *Query Object (316)*, in which client code may construct a criteria object (a simple example of the specification pattern), add() that directly to the *Query Object (316)*, and execute the query. With a *Repository*, client code constructs the criteria and then passes them to the *Repository*, asking it to select those of its objects that match. From the client code's perspective, there's no notion of query "execution"; rather there's the selection of appropriate objects through the "satisfaction" of the query's specification. This may seem an academic distinction, but it illustrates the declarative flavor of object interaction with *Repository*, which is a large part of its conceptual power.

Under the covers, *Repository* combines *Metadata Mapping (329)* with a *Query Object (316)* to automatically generate SQL code from the criteria. Whether the criteria know how to add themselves to a query, the *Query Object (316)* knows how to incorporate criteria objects, or the *Metadata Mapping (306)* itself controls the interaction is an implementation detail.

The object source for the *Repository* may not be a relational database at all, which is fine as *Repository* lends itself quite readily to the replacement of the data-mapping component via specialized strategy objects. For this reason it can be especially useful in systems with multiple database schemas or sources for domain objects, as well as during testing when use of exclusively in-memory objects is desirable for speed.

Repository can be a good mechanism for improving readability and clarity in code that uses querying extensively. For example, a browser-based system featuring a lot of query pages needs a clean mechanism to process HttpRequest objects into query results. The handler code for the request can usually convert the HttpRequest into a criteria object without much fuss, if not automatically; submitting the criteria to the appropriate *Repository* should require only an additional line or two of code.

When to Use It

In a large system with many domain object types and many possible queries, *Repository* reduces the amount of code needed to deal with all the querying that goes on. *Repository* promotes the Specification pattern (in the form of the criteria object in the examples here), which encapsulates the query to be performed in a pure object-oriented way. Therefore, all the code for setting up a *query object* in specific cases can be removed. Clients need never think in SQL and can write code purely in terms of objects.

However, situations with multiple data sources are where we really see *Repository* coming into its own. Suppose, for example, that we're sometimes interested in using a simple in-memory data store, commonly when we wants to run a suite of unit tests entirely in memory for better performance. With no database access, many lengthy test suites run significantly faster. Creating fixture for unit tests can also be more straightforward if all we have to do is construct some domain objects and throw them in a collection rather than having to save them to the database in setup and delete them at teardown.

It's also conceivable, when the application is running normally, that certain types of domain objects should always be stored in memory. One such example is immutable domain objects (those that can't be changed by the user), which once in memory, should remain there and never be queried for again. As we'll see later in this chapter, a simple extension to the *Repository* pattern allows different querying strategies to be employed depending on the situation.

Another example where *Repository* might be useful is when a data feed is used as a source of domain objects—say, an XML stream over the Internet, perhaps using SOAP, might be available as a source. An XMLFeedRepositoryStrategy might be implemented that reads from the feed and creates domain objects from the XML.

Further Reading

The specification pattern hasn't made it into a really good reference source yet. The best published description so far is [Evans and Fowler]. A better description is currently in the works in [Evans].

Example: Finding a Person's Dependents (Java)

From the client object's perspective, using a *Repository* is simple. To retrieve its dependents from the database a person object creates a criteria object representing the search criteria to be matched and sends it to the appropriate *Repository*.

```java
public class Person {
    public List dependents() {
        Repository repository = Registry.personRepository();
        Criteria criteria = new Criteria();
        criteria.equal(Person.BENEFACTOR, this);
        return repository.matching(criteria);
    }
}
```

Common queries can be accommodated with specialized subclasses of *Repository*. In the previous example we might make a PersonRepository subclass of *Repository* and move the creation of the search criteria into the *Repository* itself.

```
public class PersonRepository extends Repository {
    public List dependentsOf(aPerson) {
        Criteria criteria = new Criteria();
        criteria.equal(Person.BENEFACTOR, aPerson);
        return matching(criteria);
    }
}
```

The person object then calls the dependents() method directly on its *Repository*.

```
public class Person {
    public List dependents() {
        return Registry.personRepository().dependentsOf(this);
    }
}
```

Example: Swapping *Repository* Strategies (Java)

Because *Repository*'s interface shields the domain layer from awareness of the data source, we can refactor the implementation of the querying code inside the *Repository* without changing any calls from clients. Indeed, the domain code needn't care about the source or destination of domain objects. In the case of the in-memory store, we want to change the matching() method to select from a collection of domain objects the ones satisfy the criteria. However, we're not interested in permanently changing the data store used but rather in being able to switch between data stores at will. From this comes the need to change the implementation of the matching() method to delegate to a strategy object that does the querying. The power of this, of course, is that we can have multiple strategies and we can set the strategy as desired. In our case, it's appropriate to have two: RelationalStrategy, which queries the database, and InMemoryStrategy, which queries the in-memory collection of domain objects. Each strategy implements the RepositoryStrategy interface, which exposes the matching() method, so we get the following implementation of the *Repository* class:

```
abstract class Repository {
    private RepositoryStrategy strategy;
    protected List matching(aCriteria) {
        return strategy.matching(aCriteria);
    }
}
```

A RelationalStrategy implements matching() by creating a *Query Object* from the criteria and then querying the database using it. We can set it up with the appropriate fields and values as defined by the criteria, assuming here that the *Query Object* knows how to populate itself from criteria:

```
public class RelationalStrategy implements RepositoryStrategy {
    protected List matching(Criteria criteria) {
        Query query = new Query(myDomainObjectClass())
        query.addCriteria(criteria);
        return query.execute(unitOfWork());
    }
}
```

An InMemoryStrategy implements matching() by iterating over a collection of domain objects and asking the criteria at each domain object if it's satisfied by it. The criteria can implement the satisfaction code using reflection to interrogate the domain objects for the values of specific fields. The code to do the selection looks like this:

```
public class InMemoryStrategy implements RepositoryStrategy {
    private Set domainObjects;
    protected List matching(Criteria criteria) {
        List results = new ArrayList();
        Iterator it = domainObjects.iterator();
        while (it.hasNext()) {
            DomainObject each = (DomainObject) it.next();
            if (criteria.isSatisfiedBy(each))
                results.add(each);
        }
        return results;
    }
}
```

Chapter 14

Web Presentation Patterns

Model View Controller

Splits user interface interaction into three distinct roles.

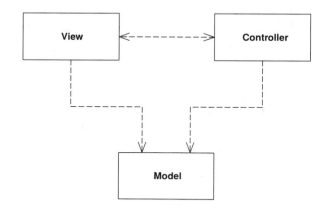

Model View Controller (MVC) is one of the most quoted (and most misquoted) patterns around. It started as a framework developed by Trygve Reenskaug for the Smalltalk platform in the late 1970s. Since then it has played an influential role in most UI frameworks and in the thinking about UI design.

How It Works

MVC considers three roles. The model is an object that represents some information about the domain. It's a nonvisual object containing all the data and behavior other than that used for the UI. In its most pure OO form the model is an object within a *Domain Model (116)*. You might also think of a *Transaction Script (110)* as the model providing that it contains no UI machinery. Such a definition stretches the notion of model, but fits the role breakdown of MVC.

The view represents the display of the model in the UI. Thus, if our model is a customer object our view might be a frame full of UI widgets or an HTML page rendered with information from the model. The view is only about display of information; any changes to the information are handled by the third member of the MVC trinity: the controller. The controller takes user input, manipulates the model, and causes the view to update appropriately. In this way UI is a combination of the view and the controller.

As I think about MVC I see two principal separations: separating the presentation from the model and separating the controller from the view.

Of these the **separation of presentation from model** is one of the most fundamental heuristics of good software design. This separation is important for several reasons.

• Fundamentally presentation and model are about different concerns. When you're developing a view you're thinking about the mechanisms of UI and how to lay out a good user interface. When you're working with a model you are thinking about business policies, perhaps database interactions. Certainly you will use different very different libraries when working with one or the other. Often people prefer one area to another and they specialize in one side of the line.

• Depending on context, users want to see the same basic model information in different ways. Separating presentation and view allows you to develop multiple presentations—indeed, entirely different interfaces—and yet use the same model code. Most noticeably this could be providing the same model with a rich client, a Web browser, a remote API, and a command-line interface. Even within a single Web interface you might have different customer pages at different points in an application.

Model View Controller

• Nonvisual objects are usually easier to test than visual ones. Separating presentation and model allows you to test all the domain logic easily without resorting to things like awkward GUI scripting tools.

A key point in this separation is the direction of the dependencies: the presentation depends on the model but the model doesn't depend on the presentation. People programming in the model should be entirely unaware of what presentation is being used, which both simplifies their task and makes it easier to add new presentations later on. It also means that presentation changes can be made freely without altering the model.

This principle introduces a common issue. With a rich-client interface of multiple windows it's likely that there will be several presentations of a model on a screen at once. If a user makes a change to the model from one presentation, the others need to change as well. To do this without creating a dependency you usually need an implementation of the Observer pattern [Gang of Four], such as event propagation or a listener. The presentation acts as the observer of the model: whenever the model changes it sends out an event and the presentations refresh the information.

The second division, the **separation of view and controller**, is less important. Indeed, the irony is that almost every version of Smalltalk didn't actually make a view/controller separation. The classic example of why you'd want to separate them is to support editable and noneditable behavior, which you can do with one view and two controllers for the two cases, where the controllers are strategies [Gang of Four] for the view. In practice most systems have only one controller per view, however, so this separation is usually not done. It has come back into vogue with Web interfaces where it becomes useful for separating the controller and view again.

The fact that most GUI frameworks combine view and controller has led to many misquotations of MVC. The model and the view are obvious, but where's the controller? The common idea is that it sits between the model and the view, as in the *Application Controller (379)*—it doesn't help that the word "controller" is used in both contexts. Whatever the merits of a *Application Controller (379)*, it's a very different beast from an MVC controller.

For the purposes of this set of patterns these principles are really all you need to know. If you want to dig deeper into MVC the best available reference is [POSA].

When to Use It

As I said, the value of MVC lies in its two separations. Of these the separation of presentation and model is one of the most important design principles in software, and the only time you shouldn't follow it is in very simple systems where the model has no real behavior in it anyway. As soon as you get some nonvisual logic you should apply the separation. Unfortunately, a lot of UI frameworks make it difficult, and those that don't are often taught without a separation.

The separation of view and controller is less important, so I'd only recommend doing it when it is really helpful. For rich-client systems, that ends up being hardly ever, although it's common in Web front ends where the controller is separated out. Most of the patterns on Web design here are based on that principle.

Page Controller

*An object that handles a request for a specific
page or action on a Web site.*

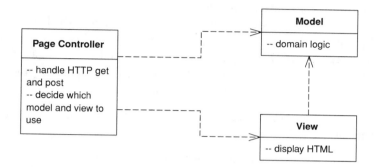

Most people's basic Web experience is with static HTML pages. When you request static HTML you pass to the Web server the name and path for a HTML document stored on it. The key notion is that each page on the Web site is a separate document on the server. With dynamic pages things can get much more interesting since there's a much more complex relationship between path names and the file that responds. However, the approach of one path leading to one file that handles the request is a simple model to understand.

As a result, *Page Controller* has one input controller for each logical page of the Web site. That controller may be the page itself, as it often is in server page environments, or it may be a separate object that corresponds to that page.

How It Works

The basic idea behind a *Page Controller* is to have one module on the Web server act as the controller for each page on the Web site. In practice, it doesn't work out to exactly one module per page, since you may hit a link sometimes and get a different page depending on dynamic information. More strictly, the controllers tie in to each *action,* which may be clicking a link or a button.

The *Page Controller* can be structured either as a script (CGI script, servlet, etc.) or as a server page (ASP, PHP, JSP, etc.). Using a server page usually combines the *Page Controller* and a *Template View (350)* in the same file. This works well for the *Template View (350)* but less well for the *Page Controller* because it's more awkward to properly structure the module. If the page is a simple display, this isn't a problem. However, if there's logic involved in either pulling data out of the request or deciding which actual view to display, then you can end up with awkward scriptlet code in the server page.

One way of dealing with scriptlet code is to use a helper object. In this case the first thing the server page does is call the helper object to handle all the logic. The helper may return control to the original server page, or it may forward to a different server page to act as the view, in which case the server page is the request handler but most of the controller logic lies in the helper.

Another approach is to make a script the handler and controller. The Web server passes control to the script; the script carries out the controller's responsibilities and finally forwards to an appropriate view to display any results.

The basic responsibilities of a *Page Controller* are:

- Decode the URL and extract any form data to figure out all the data for the action.

- Create and invoke any model objects to process the data. All relevant data from the HTML request should be passed to the model so that the model objects don't need any connection to the HTML request.

- Determine which view should display the result page and forward the model information to it.

The *Page Controller* needn't be a single class but can invoke helper objects. This is particularly useful if several handlers have to do similar tasks. A helper class can then be a good spot to put any code that would otherwise be duplicated.

There's no reason that you can't have some URLs handled by server pages and some by scripts. Any URLs that have little or no controller logic are best handled with a server page, since that provides a simple mechanism that's easy to understand and modify. Any URLs with more complicated logic go to a script. I've come across teams who want to handle everything the same way: all server page or everything is a script. Any advantages of consistency in such an application are usually offset by the problems of either scriptlet-laden server pages or lots of simple pass-through scripts.

When to Use It

The main decision point is whether to use *Page Controller* or *Front Controller (344)*. Of the two, *Page Controller* is the most familiar to work with and leads to a natural structuring mechanism where particular actions are handled by particular server pages or script classes. Your trade-off is thus the greater complexity of *Front Controller (344)* against the various advantages of *Front Con-*

troller, most of which make a difference in Web sites that have more navigational complexity.

Page Controller works particularly well in a site where most of the controller logic is pretty simple. In this case most URLs can be handled with a server page and the more complicated cases with helpers. When your controller logic is simple, *Front Controller (344)* adds a lot of overhead.

It's not uncommon to have a site where some requests are dealt with by *Page Controllers* and others are dealt with by *Front Controllers (344)*, particularly when a team is refactoring from one to another. Actually, the two patterns mix without too much trouble.

Example: Simple Display with a Servlet Controller and a JSP View (Java)

A simple example of an *Page Controller* displays some information about something. Here we'll show it displaying some information about a recording artist. The URL runs along the lines of `http://www.thingy.com/recordingApp/artist?name=danielaMercury`.

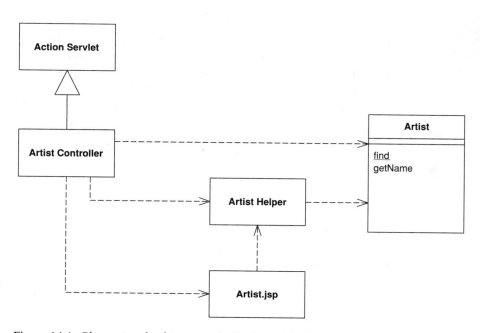

Figure 14.1 *Classes involved in a simple display with a* Page Controller *servlet and a JSP view.*

The Web server needs to be configured to recognize **/artist** as a call to Artist-Controller. In Tomcat you do this with the following code in the web.xml file:

```
<servlet>
    <servlet-name>artist</servlet-name>
    <servlet-class>actionController.ArtistController</servlet-class>
</servlet>
<servlet-mapping>
    <servlet-name>artist</servlet-name>
    <url-pattern>/artist</url-pattern>
</servlet-mapping>
```

The artist controller needs to implement a method to handle the request.

```
class ArtistController...

    public void doGet(HttpServletRequest request, HttpServletResponse response)
        throws IOException, ServletException {
        Artist artist = Artist.findNamed(request.getParameter("name"));
        if (artist == null)
            forward("/MissingArtistError.jsp", request, response);
        else {
            request.setAttribute("helper", new ArtistHelper(artist));
            forward("/artist.jsp", request, response);
        }
    }
```

Page Controller

Although this is a very simple case, it covers the salient points. First the controller needs to create the necessary model objects to do their thing, here just finding the correct model object to display. Second it puts the right information in the HTTP request so that the JSP can display it properly. In this case it creates a helper and puts it into the request. Finally it forwards to the *Template View (350)* to handle the display. Forwarding is a common behavior, so it sits naturally on a superclass for all *Page Controllers*.

```
class ActionServlet...

    protected void forward(String target,
                    HttpServletRequest request,
                    HttpServletResponse response)
        throws IOException, ServletException
    {
        RequestDispatcher dispatcher = getServletContext().getRequestDispatcher(target);
        dispatcher.forward(request, response);
    }
```

The main point of coupling between the *Template View (350)* and the *Page Controller* is the parameter names in the request to pass on any objects that the JSP needs.

The controller logic here is really very simple, but as it gets more complex we can continue to use the servlet as a controller. We can have a similar behavior for albums, with the twist that classical albums both have a different model object and are rendered with a different JSP. To do this behavior we can again use a controller class.

```
class AlbumController...

  public void doGet(HttpServletRequest request, HttpServletResponse response)
      throws IOException, ServletException
  {
    Album album = Album.find(request.getParameter("id"));
    if (album == null) {
      forward("/missingAlbumError.jsp", request, response);
      return;
    }
    request.setAttribute("helper", album);
    if (album instanceof ClassicalAlbum)
      forward("/classicalAlbum.jsp", request, response);
    else
      forward("/album.jsp", request, response);
  }
```

Notice that in this case I'm using the model objects as helpers rather than creating a separate helper class. This is worth doing if a helper class is just a dumb forwarder to the model class. If you do it, though, make sure that the model class doesn't contain any servlet-dependent code. Any servlet-dependent code should be in a separate helper class.

Example: Using a JSP as a Handler (Java)

Using a servlet as a controller is one route to take, but the most common route is to make the server page itself the controller. The problem with this approach is that it results in scriptlet code at the beginning of the server page and, as you may have gathered, I think that scriptlet code has the same relationship to well-designed software that professional wrestling has to sport.

Despite this you can make a server page as the request handler while delegating control to the helper to actually carry out the controller function. This preserves the simple property of having your URLs denoted by server pages. I'll do this for the album display, using the URL of the form http://localhost:8080/isa/ album.jsp?id=zero. Most albums are displayed directly with the album JSP, but classical recordings require a different display, a classical album JSP.

This controller behavior appears in a helper class to the JSP. The helper is set up in the album JSP itself.

album.jsp...

```
<jsp:useBean id="helper" class="actionController.AlbumConHelper"/>
<%helper.init(request, response);%>
```

The call to init sets the helper up to carry out the controller behavior.

class AlbumConHelper extends HelperController...

```
public void init(HttpServletRequest request, HttpServletResponse response) {
    super.init(request, response);
    if (getAlbum() == null) forward("missingAlbumError.jsp", request, response);
    if (getAlbum() instanceof ClassicalAlbum) {
        request.setAttribute("helper", getAlbum());
        forward("/classicalAlbum.jsp", request, response);
    }
}
```

Common helper behavior naturally sits on a helper superclass.

class HelperController...

```
public void init(HttpServletRequest request, HttpServletResponse response) {
    this.request = request;
    this.response = response;
}
protected void forward(String target,
                       HttpServletRequest request,
                       HttpServletResponse response)
{
    try {
        RequestDispatcher dispatcher = request.getRequestDispatcher(target);
        if (dispatcher == null) response.sendError(response.SC_NO_CONTENT);
        else dispatcher.forward(request, response);
    } catch (IOException e) {
        throw new ApplicationException(e);
    } catch (ServletException e) {
        throw new ApplicationException(e);
    }
}
```

Page Controller

The key difference between the controller behavior here and that when using a servlet is that the handler JSP is also the default view and, unless the controller forwards to a different JSP, control reverts to the original handler. This is an advantage when you have pages where the JSP directly acts as the view most of the time and so there's no forwarding to be done. The initialization of the helper acts to kick off any model behavior and set things up for the view later on. It's a simple model to follow, since people generally associate a Web page with the server page that acts as its view. Often this also fits naturally with Web server configuration.

The call to initialize the handler is a little clumsy. In a JSP environment this awkwardness can be much better handled with a custom tag. Such a tag can automatically create an appropriate object, put it in the request, and initialize it. With that all you need is a simple tag in the JSP page.

```
<helper:init name = "actionController.AlbumConHelper"/>
```

The custom tag's implementation then does the work.

```
class HelperInitTag extends HelperTag...

    private String helperClassName;
    public void setName(String helperClassName) {
        this.helperClassName = helperClassName;
    }
    public int doStartTag() throws JspException {
        HelperController helper = null;
        try {
            helper = (HelperController) Class.forName(helperClassName).newInstance();
        } catch (Exception e) {
            throw new ApplicationException("Unable to instantiate " + helperClassName, e);
        }
        initHelper(helper);
        pageContext.setAttribute(HELPER, helper);
        return SKIP_BODY;
    }
    private void initHelper(HelperController helper) {
        HttpServletRequest request = (HttpServletRequest) pageContext.getRequest();
        HttpServletResponse response = (HttpServletResponse) pageContext.getResponse();
        helper.init(request, response);
    }

class HelperTag...

    public static final String HELPER = "helper";
```

If I'm going to use custom tags like this, I might as well make them for property access too.

```
class HelperGetTag extends HelperTag...

    private String propertyName;
    public void setProperty(String propertyName) {
        this.propertyName = propertyName;
    }
    public int doStartTag() throws JspException {
        try {
            pageContext.getOut().print(getProperty(propertyName));
```

```
    } catch (IOException e) {
        throw new JspException("unable to print to writer");
    }
    return SKIP_BODY;
}
```

```
class HelperTag...
```

```
    protected Object getProperty(String property) throws JspException {
        Object helper = getHelper();
        try {
            final Method getter = helper.getClass().getMethod(gettingMethod(property), null);
            return getter.invoke(helper, null);
        } catch (Exception e) {
            throw new JspException
                ("Unable to invoke " + gettingMethod(property) + " - " + e.getMessage());
        }
    }
    private Object getHelper() throws JspException {
        Object helper = pageContext.getAttribute(HELPER);
        if (helper == null) throw new JspException("Helper not found.");
        return helper;
    }
    private String gettingMethod(String property) {
        String methodName = "get" + property.substring(0, 1).toUpperCase() +
            property.substring(1);
        return methodName;
    }
}
```

**Page
Controller**

(You may think it's better to use the Java Beans mechanism than to just invoke a getter using reflection. If so, you're probably right . . . and also probably intelligent enough to figure out how to change the method to do that.)

With the getting tag defined, I can use it to pull information out of the helper. The tag is shorter and eliminates any chance of my mizpelling "helper."

```
<B><helper:get property = "title"/></B>
```

Example: Page Handler with a Code Behind (C#)

The Web system in .NET is designed to work with the *Page Controller* and *Template View (350)* patterns, although you can certainly decide to handle Web events with a different approach. In this next example, I'll use the preferred style of .NET, building the presentation layer on top of a domain using *Table Module (125)* and using data sets as the main carrier of information between layers.

This time we'll have a page that displays runs scored and the run rate for one innings of a cricket match. As I know I'll have many readers who are afflicted with no material experience of this art form, let me summarize by saying that the runs scored are the score of the batsman and the run rate is how many runs he scores divided by the number of balls he faces. The runs scored and balls faced are in the database; the run rate needs to be calculated by the application—a tiny but pedagogically useful piece of domain logic.

The handler in this design is an ASP.NET Web page, captured in a .aspx file. As with other server page constructs, this file allows you to embed programming logic directly into the page as scriptlets. Since you know I'd rather drink bad beer than write scriptlets, you know there's little chance that I'd do that. My savior in this case is ASP.NET's **code behind** mechanism that allows you to associate a regular file and class with the aspx page, signaled in the header of the aspx page.

```
<%@ Page language="c#" Codebehind="bat.aspx.cs" AutoEventWireup="false" trace="False"
    Inherits="batsmen.BattingPage" %>
```

The page is set up as a subclass of the code behind class, and as such can use all its protected properties and methods. The page object is the handler of the request, and the code behind can define the handling by defining a Page_Load method. If most pages follow a common flow, I can define a *Layer Supertype (475)* that has a template method [Gang of Four] for this.

class CricketPage...

```
    protected void Page_Load(object sender, System.EventArgs e) {
        db = new OleDbConnection(DB.ConnectionString);
        if (hasMissingParameters())
            errorTransfer (missingParameterMessage);
        DataSet ds = getData();
        if (hasNoData (ds))
            errorTransfer ("No data matches your request");
        applyDomainLogic (ds);
        DataBind();
        prepareUI(ds);
    }
```

Page Controller

The template method breaks down the request handling into a number of common steps. This way we can define a single common flow for handling Web requests, while allowing each *Page Controller* to supply implementations for the specific steps. If you do this, once you've written a few *Page Controllers*, you'll know what common flow to use for the template method. If any page needs to do something completely different, it can always override the page load method.

The first task is to do validation on the parameters coming into the page. In a more realistic example this might entail initial sanity checking of various form values, but in this case we're just decoding a URL of the form http://localhost/batsmen/bat.aspx?team=England&innings=2&match=905. The only validation in this example is that the various parameters required for the database query are present. As usual I've been overly simplistic in the error handling until somebody writes a good set of patterns on validation—so here the particular page defines a set of mandatory parameters and the *Layer Supertype (475)* has the logic for checking them.

```
class CricketPage...

    abstract protected String[] mandatoryParameters();
    private Boolean hasMissingParameters() {
        foreach (String param in mandatoryParameters())
            if (Request.Params[param] == null) return true;
        return false;
    }
    private String missingParameterMessage {
        get {
            String result = "<P>This page is missing mandatory parameters:</P>";
            result += "<UL>";
            foreach (String param in mandatoryParameters())
                if (Request.Params[param] == null)
                    result += String.Format("<LI>{0}</LI>", param);
            result += "</UL>";
            return result;
        }
    }
    protected void errorTransfer (String message) {
        Context.Items.Add("errorMessage", message);
        Context.Server.Transfer("Error.aspx");
    }
```

Page
Controller

```
class BattingPage...

    override protected String[] mandatoryParameters() {
        String[] result = {"team", "innings", "match"};
        return result;
    }
```

The next stage is to pull the data out of the database and put it in an ADO.NET disconnected data set object. Here this is a single query to the batting table.

```
class CricketPage...

    abstract protected DataSet getData();
    protected Boolean hasNoData(DataSet ds) {
        foreach (DataTable table in ds.Tables)
            if (table.Rows.Count != 0) return false;
        return true;
    }
```

```
class BattingPage...
```

```
override protected DataSet getData() {
    OleDbCommand command = new OleDbCommand(SQL, db);
    command.Parameters.Add(new OleDbParameter("team", team));
    command.Parameters.Add(new OleDbParameter("innings", innings));
    command.Parameters.Add(new OleDbParameter("match", match));
    OleDbDataAdapter da = new OleDbDataAdapter(command);
    DataSet result = new DataSet();
    da.Fill(result, Batting.TABLE_NAME);
    return result;
}
private const String SQL =
    @"SELECT * from batting
        WHERE team = ? AND innings = ? AND matchID = ?
        ORDER BY battingOrder";
```

Now the domain logic gets its turn to play, organized as a *Table Module (125)*. The controller passes the retrieved data set to the *Table Module (125)* for processing.

class CricketPage...

```
    protected virtual void applyDomainLogic (DataSet ds) {}
```

class BattingPage...

```
    override protected void applyDomainLogic (DataSet dataSet) {
        batting = new Batting(dataSet);
        batting.CalculateRates();
    }
```

Page Controller

At this point the controller part of the page handler is done. By this I mean, in classic *Model View Controller (330)* terms, that the controller should now hand over to the view to do display. In this design the BattingPage acts as both the controller and the view and the last call to prepareUI is part of the view behavior. I can now say farewell to this example in this pattern. However, I suspect you'll find this to lack a certain dramatic closure, so you can find the example continued later (page 350).

Front Controller

A controller that handles all requests for a Web site.

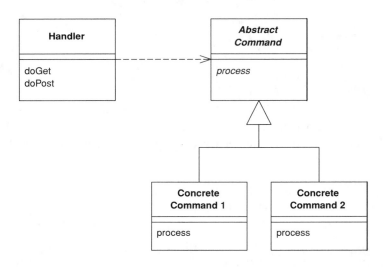

In a complex Web site there are many similar things you need to do when handling a request. These things include security, internationalization, and providing particular views for certain users. If the input controller behavior is scattered across multiple objects, much of this behavior can end up duplicated. Also, it's difficult to change behavior at runtime.

The *Front Controller* consolidates all request handling by channeling requests through a single handler object. This object can carry out common behavior, which can be modified at runtime with decorators. The handler then dispatches to command objects for behavior particular to a request.

How It Works

A *Front Controller* handles all calls for a Web site, and is usually structured in two parts: a Web handler and a command hierarchy. The Web handler is the object that actually receives post or get requests from the Web server. It pulls just enough information from the URL and the request to decide what kind of action to initiate and then delegates to a command to carry out the action (see Figure 14.2).

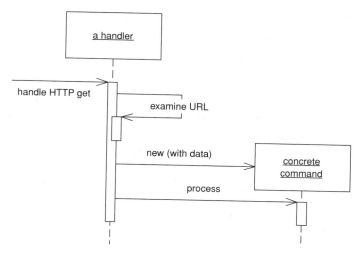

Figure 14.2 *How the* Front Controller *works.*

The Web handler is almost always implemented as a class rather than as a server page, as it doesn't produce any response. The commands are also classes rather than server pages and in fact don't need any knowledge of the Web environment, although they're often passed the HTTP information. The Web handler itself is usually a fairly simple program that does nothing other than decide which command to run.

The Web handler can decide which command to run either statically or dynamically. The static version involves parsing the URL and using conditional logic; the dynamic version usually involves taking a standard piece of the URL and using dynamic instantiation to create a command class.

The static case has the advantage of explicit logic, compile time error checking on the dispatch, and lots of flexibility in the look of your URLs. The dynamic case allows you to add new commands without changing the Web handler.

With dynamic invocation you can put the name of the command class into the URL or you can use a properties file that binds URLs to command class names. The properties file is another file to edit, but it does make it easier to change your class names without a lot of searching through your Web pages.

A particularly useful pattern to use in conjunction with *Front Controller* is *Intercepting Filter*, described in [Alur et al.]. This is essentially a decorator that wraps the handler of the front controller allowing you to build a *filter chain* (or

Front Controller

pipeline of filters) to handle issues such as authentication, logging, and locale identification. Using filters allows you to dynamically set up the filters to use at configuration time.

Rob Mee showed me an interesting variation of *Front Controller* using a two stage Web handler separated into a degenerate Web handler and a dispatcher. The degenerate Web handler pulls the basic data out of the http parameters and hands it to the dispatcher in such a way that the dispatcher is completely independent of the Web server framework. This makes testing easier because test code can drive the dispatcher directly without having to run in a Web server.

Remember that both the handler and the commands are part of the controller. As a result the commands can (and should) choose which view to use for the response. The only responsibility of the handler is in choosing which command to execute. Once that's done, it plays no further part in that request.

When to Use It

The *Front Controller* is a more complicated design than its obvious counterpart, *Page Controller (333)*. It therefore needs a few advantages to be worth the effort.

Only one *Front Controller* has to be configured into the Web server; the Web handler does the rest of the dispatching. This simplifies the configuration of the Web server, which is an advantage if the Web server is awkward to configure. With dynamic commands you can add new commands without changing anything. They also ease porting since you only have to register the handler in a Web-server-specific way.

Because you create new command objects with each request, you don't have to worry about making the command classes thread-safe. In this way you avoid the headaches of multi-threaded programming; however, you do have to make sure that you don't share any other objects, such as the model objects.

A commonly stated advantage of a *Front Controller* is that it allows you to factor out code that's otherwise duplicated in *Page Controller (333)*. To be fair, however, you can also do much of this with a superclass *Page Controller (333)*.

There's just one controller, so you can easily enhance its behavior at runtime with decorators [Gang of Four]. You can have decorators for authentication, character encoding, internationalization, and so forth, and add them using a configuration file or even while the server is running. ([Alur et al.] describe this approach in detail under the name *Intercepting Filter*.)

Further Reading

[Alur et al.] give a detailed description of how to implement *Front Controller* in Java. They also describe *Intercepting Filter,* which goes very well with *Front Controller.*

A number of Java Web frameworks use this pattern. An excellent example appears in [Struts].

Example: Simple Display (Java)

Here's a simple case of using *Front Controller* for the original and innovative task of displaying information about a recording artist. We'll use dynamic commands with a URL of the form `http://localhost:8080/isa/music?name=barelyWorks&command=Artist`. The command parameter tells the Web handler which command to use.

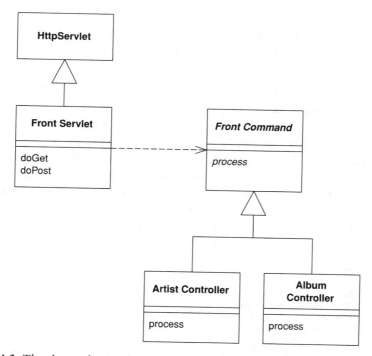

Front Controller

Figure 14.3 *The classes that implement* Front Controller.

We'll begin with the handler, which I've implemented as a servlet.

```
class FrontServlet...

    public void doGet(HttpServletRequest request, HttpServletResponse response)
            throws IOException, ServletException {
      FrontCommand command = getCommand(request);
      command.init(getServletContext(), request, response);
      command.process();
    }
    private FrontCommand getCommand(HttpServletRequest request) {
        try {
            return (FrontCommand) getCommandClass(request).newInstance();
        } catch (Exception e) {
            throw new ApplicationException(e);
        }
    }
    private Class getCommandClass(HttpServletRequest request) {
        Class result;
        final String commandClassName =
            "frontController." + (String) request.getParameter("command") + "Command";
        try {
            result = Class.forName(commandClassName);
        } catch (ClassNotFoundException e) {
            result = UnknownCommand.class;
        }
        return result;
    }
```

**Front
Controller**

The logic is straightforward. The handler tries to instantiate a class named by concatenating the command name and "Command." Once it has the new command it initializes it with the necessary information from the HTTP server. I've passed in what I need for this simple example. You may well need more, such as the HTTP session. If you can't find a command, I've used the *Special Case (496)* pattern and returned an unknown command. As is often the case, *Special Case (496)* allows you to avoid a lot of extra error checking.

Commands share a fair bit of data and behavior. They all need to be initialized with information from the Web server.

```
class FrontCommand...

    protected ServletContext context;
    protected HttpServletRequest request;
    protected HttpServletResponse response;
    public void init(ServletContext context,
                HttpServletRequest request,
                HttpServletResponse response)
```

```
    {
        this.context = context;
        this.request = request;
        this.response = response;
    }
```

They can also provide common behavior, such as a forward method, and define an abstract process command for the actual commands to override.

class FrontCommand...

```
    abstract public void process()throws ServletException, IOException ;
    protected void forward(String target) throws ServletException, IOException
    {
        RequestDispatcher dispatcher = context.getRequestDispatcher(target);
        dispatcher.forward(request, response);
    }
```

The command object is very simple, at least in this case. It just implements the process method, which involves invoking the appropriate behavior on the model objects, putting the information needed for the view into the request, and forwarding to a *Template View (350)*.

class ArtistCommand...

```
    public void process() throws ServletException, IOException {
        Artist artist = Artist.findNamed(request.getParameter("name"));
        request.setAttribute("helper", new ArtistHelper(artist));
        forward("/artist.jsp");
    }
```

Front Controller

The unknown command just brings up a boring error page.

class UnknownCommand...

```
    public void process() throws ServletException, IOException {
        forward("/unknown.jsp");
    }
```

Template View

Renders information into HTML by embedding markers in an HTML page.

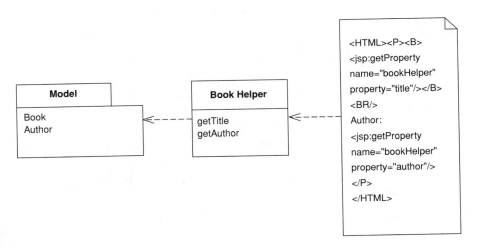

Template View

Writing a program that spits out HTML is often more difficult than you might imagine. Although programming languages are better at creating text than they used to be (some of us remember character handling in Fortran and standard Pascal), creating and concatenating string constructs is still painful. If there isn't much to do, it isn't too bad, but a whole HTML page is a lot of text manipulation.

With static HTML pages—those that don't change from request to request—you can use nice WYSIWG editors. Even those of us who like raw text editors find it easier to just type in the text and tags rather than fiddle with string concatenation in a programming language.

Of course the issue is with dynamic Web pages—those that take the results of something like database queries and embed them into the HTML. The page looks different with each result, and as a result regular HTML editors aren't up to the job.

The best way to work is to compose the dynamic Web page as you do a static page but put in markers that can be resolved into calls to gather dynamic information. Since the static part of the page acts as a template for the particular response, I call this a *Template View*.

How It Works

The basic idea of *Template View* is to embed markers into a static HTML page when it's written. When the page is used to service a request, the markers are replaced by the results of some computation, such as a database query. This way the page can be laid out in the usual manner, often with WYSIWYG editors, often by people who aren't programmers. The markers then communicate with real programs to put in the results.

A lot of tools use *Template View*. As a result this pattern isn't about how to build one yourself, but about how to use one effectively and what the alternative is.

Embedding the Markers There are a number of ways markers can be placed in the HTML. One is to use HTML-like tags. This works well with WYSIWYG editors because they realize that anything between the angled brackets (<>) is special and so either ignore it or treat it differently. If the tags follow the rules for well-formed XML you can also use XML tools on the resulting document (providing your HTML is XHMTL, of course).

Another way to do this is to use special text markers in the body text. WYSIWYG editors treat that as regular text, still ignoring it but probably doing annoying things to it like spell checking. The advantage is that the syntax can be easier than the clunky syntax of HTML/XML.

Many environments provide the set of tags you use but more and more platforms now give you the ability to define your own tags and markers so you can design them to fit in with your particular needs.

One of the most popular forms of *Template View* is a **server page** such as ASP, JSP, or PHP. These actually go a step further than the basic form of a *Template View* in that they allow you to embed arbitrary programming logic, referred to as **scriptlets**, into the page. In my view, however, this feature is actually a big problem and you're better off limiting yourself to basic *Template View* behavior when you use server page technology.

The most obvious disadvantage of putting a lot of scriptlets into a page is that it eliminates the possibility of nonprogrammers editing the page. This is particularly important when you're using graphic designers for the page design. However, the biggest problems of embedding scriptlets into the page come from the fact that a page is poor module for a program. Even with an object-oriented language the page construct loses you most of the structural features that make it possible to do a modular design either in OO or in procedural style.

Even worse, putting a lot of scriptlets into the page makes it too easy to mingle the different layers of an enterprise application. When domain logic starts turning up on server pages it becomes far too difficult to structure it well and far too easy to duplicate it across different server pages. All in all, the worst code I've seen in the last few years has been server page code.

Helper Object The key to avoiding scriptlets is to provide a regular object as a **helper** to each page. This helper has all the real programming logic. The page only has calls into it, which simplifies the page and makes it a more pure *Template View*. The resulting simplicity allows nonprogrammers to edit the page and programmers to concentrate on the helper. Depending on the actual tool you're using, you can often reduce all the templates in a page to HTML/XML tags, which keeps the page more consistent and more amenable to tool support.

This sounds like a simple and commendable principle, but as ever quite a few dirty issues make things more complicated. The simplest markers are those that get some information from the rest of the system and put in the correct place on the page. They are easily translated into calls to the helper that result in text, (or something that's trivially turned into text), and the engine places the text on the page.

Template
View

Conditional Display A more knotty issue is conditional page behavior. The simplest case is the situation where something is displayed only if a condition is true. That might be some kind of conditional tag along the lines of `<IF condition = "$pricedrop > 0.1"> ...show some stuff </IF>`. The trouble with this is that when you start having conditional tags like this, you start going down the path of turning the templates into a programming language in and of themselves. This leads you into all the same problems you face when you embed scriptlets in the page. If you need a full programming language, you might as well use scriptlets, but you know what I think of that idea!

As a result, I see purely conditional tags as a bad smell, something you should try to avoid. You can't always avoid them, but you should try to come up with something more focused than a general purpose `<IF>` tag.

If you're displaying some text conditionally, one option is to move the condition into the helper. The page will then always insert the result of the call into helper. It's just that if the condition isn't true the helper will send back an empty string, but this way the helper holds all the logic. This approach works best if there's no markup for the returned text or it's enough to return empty markup that gets ignored by the browser.

This doesn't work if, say, you want to highlight good-selling items in a list by putting their names in bold. In such a situation you always need the names displayed but sometimes you want the special markup. One way to get it is to have the helper generate the markup. This keeps all the logic out of the page, at the cost of moving the choice of highlighting mechanism away from the page designer and giving it to the programming code.

In order to keep the choice of HTML in the hands of the page design, you need some form of conditional tag. However it's important to look beyond a simple <IF>. A good route to go is a focused tag, so rather than a tag that looks like this:

```
<IF expression = "isHighSelling()"><B></IF>
<property name = "price"/>
<IF expression = "isHighSelling()"></B></IF>
```

you have one like

```
<highlight condition = "isHighSelling" style = "bold">
   <property name = "price"/>
</highlight>
```

In either case it's important that the condition be done based on a single Boolean property of the helper. Putting any more complex expression into the page is actually putting the logic into the page itself.

Another example would be putting information on a page that depends on the locale on which the system is running. Consider some text that should only be shown in the United States or Canada, which, rather than

```
<IF expression = "locale = 'US' || 'CA'"> ...special text </IF>
```

Would be something like

```
<locale includes = "US, CA"> ...special text </locale>
```

Iteration Iterating over a collection presents similar issues. If you want a table where each line corresponds to a line item on an order, you need a construct that allows easy display of information for each line. Here it's hard to avoid a general iteration over a collection tag, but it usually works simply enough to fit in quite well.

Of course the kinds of tag you have to work with are often limited by the environment you're in. Some environments give you a fixed set of templates, in which case you may be more limited than you would like in following these kinds of guidelines. In other environments, however, you may have more choice in the tags to use; many of them even allow you to define your own tag libraries.

When to Process The name *Template View* brings out the fact that the primary function of this pattern is to play the view in *Model View Controller (330)*. For many systems the *Template View* should only play the view. In simpler systems it may be reasonable for it to play the controller, and possibly even the model, although I would strive to separate model processing as much as possible. Where *Template View* is taking on responsibilities beyond the view, it's important to ensure that these responsibilities are handled by the helper, not by the page. Controller and model responsibilities involve program logic, which program logic everywhere, should sit in the helper.

Any template system needs extra processing by the Web server. This can either be done by compiling the page after it's created, compiling the page or on its first request, or by interpreting the page on each request. Obviously the latter isn't a good idea if the interpretation takes a while to do.

One thing to watch with *Template View* is exceptions. If an exception works its way up to the Web container, you may find yourself with a half-handled page that provides some decidedly odd output to the calling browser instead of a redirect. You need to look into how your Web server handles exceptions; if it does something strange, catch all exceptions yourself in the helper class (yet another reason to disdain scriptlets.)

Using Scripts Although server pages are one of the most common forms of *Template View* these days, you can write scripts in a *Template View* style. I've seen a fair bit of Perl done this way. Most noticeably demonstrated by perl's CGI.pm, the trick is to avoid concatenating strings by having function calls that output the appropriate tags to the response. This way you can write the script in your programming language and avoid the mess of interspersing print strings with programming logic.

When to Use It

For implementing the view in *Model View Controller (330)* the main choice is between *Template View* and *Transform View (361)*. The strength of *Template View* is that it allows you to compose the content of the page by looking at the page structure. This seems to be easier for most people to do and to learn. In particular it nicely supports the idea of a graphic designer laying out a page with a programmer working on the helper.

Template View has two significant weaknesses. First, the common implementations make it too easy to put complicated logic in the page, thus making it hard to maintain, particularly by nonprogrammers. You need good discipline to keep the page simple and display oriented, putting logic in the helper. The second weakness is that *Template View* is harder to test than *Transform View (361)*. Most implementations of *Template View* are designed to work within a Web server and are very difficult or impossible to test otherwise. *Transform*

View (361) implementations are much easier to hook into a testing harness and test without a running Web server.

In thinking about a view you also need to consider *Two Step View (365)*. Depending on your template scheme you may be able to implement this pattern using specialized tags. However, you may find it easier to implement it based on a *Transform View (361)*. If you're going to need *Two Step View (365)* you need to take that into account in your choice.

Example: Using a JSP as a View with a Separate Controller (Java)

When using a JSP as a view only, it's always be invoked from a controller rather than directly from the servlet container. Thus, it's important to pass to the JSP any information it will need to figure out what to display. A good way to do this is to have the controller create a helper object and pass it to the JSP using the HTTP request. We'll show this with the simple display example from *Page Controller (333)*. The Web-handling method for the servlet looks like this:

class ArtistController...

```
    public void doGet(HttpServletRequest request, HttpServletResponse response)
        throws IOException, ServletException {
      Artist artist = Artist.findNamed(request.getParameter("name"));
      if (artist == null)
        forward("/MissingArtistError.jsp", request, response);
      else {
         request.setAttribute("helper", new ArtistHelper(artist));
         forward("/artist.jsp", request, response);
      }
    }
```

As far as the *Template View* is concerned the important behavior is creating the helper and placing it in the request. The server page can now reach the helper with the useBean tag.

```
<jsp:useBean id="helper" type="actionController.ArtistHelper" scope="request"/>
```

With the helper in place we can use it to access the information we need to display. The model information the helper needs was passed to it when it was created.

class ArtistHelper...

```
  private Artist artist;
  public ArtistHelper(Artist artist) {
    this.artist = artist;
  }
```

Template
View

We can use the helper to get appropriate information from the model. In the simplest case we provide a method to get some simple data, such as the artist's name.

class ArtistHelper...

```
public String getName() {
    return artist.getName();
}
```

Then we access this information by a Java expression.

```
<B> <%=helper.getName()%></B>
```

or a property

```
<B><jsp:getProperty name="helper" property="name"/></B>
```

The choice between properties or expressions depends on who is editing the JSP. Programmers find expressions easy to read and more compact, but HTML editors may not be able to handle them. Nonprogrammers will probably prefer tags, since they fits in the general form of HTML and leave less room for confusing errors.

Template View

Using a helper is one way to remove awkward scriptlet code. If you want to show a list of albums for an artist, you need to run a loop, which you can do with a scriptlet in the server page.

```
<UL>
<%
    for (Iterator it = helper.getAlbums().iterator(); it.hasNext();) {
        Album album = (Album) it.next();%>
    <LI><%=album.getTitle()%></LI>
<% } %>
</UL>
```

Frankly, this mix of Java and HTML is really horrible to read. An alternative is to move the for loop to the helper.

class ArtistHelper...

```
public String getAlbumList() {
    StringBuffer result = new StringBuffer();
    result.append("<UL>");
    for (Iterator it = getAlbums().iterator(); it.hasNext();) {
        Album album = (Album) it.next();
        result.append("<LI>");
        result.append(album.getTitle());
        result.append("</LI>");
    }
```

```
    result.append("</UL>");
    return result.toString();
  }
  public List getAlbums() {
    return artist.getAlbums();
  }
```

I find this easier to follow because the amount of HTML is quite small. It also allows you to use a property to get the list. Many people don't like putting HTML code in helpers. While I prefer not to, given the choice between this and scriptlets I'd choose HTML in helpers any day or night.

The best route to go is a specialized tag for iteration.

```
<UL><tag:forEach host = "helper" collection = "albums" id = "each">
  <LI><jsp:getProperty name="each" property="title"/></LI>
</tag:forEach></UL>
```

This is a much nicer alternative as it keeps scriptlets out of the JSP and HTML out of the helper.

Example: ASP.NET Server Page (C#)

This example continues the one I started in *Page Controller (333)* (page 340). To remind you, it shows the scores made by batsmen in a single innings of a cricket match. For those who think that cricket is a small noisy insect, I'll pass over the long rhapsodies about the world's most immortal sport and boil it all down to the fact that the page displays three essential pieces of information:

- An ID number to reference the match

- Which team's scores are shown and which innings the scores are for

- A table showing each batsman's name, score, and run rate (the number of balls he faced divided by the runs he scored)

If you don't understand what these statistics mean, don't worry about it. Cricket is full of statistics—perhaps its greatest contribution to humanity is providing odd statistics for eccentric papers.

The *Page Controller (333)* discussion covered how a Web request is handled. To sum up, the object that acts as both the controller and the view is the aspx ASP.NET page. To keep the controller code out of a scriptlet, you define a separate code behind class.

```
<%@ Page language="c#" Codebehind="bat.aspx.cs" AutoEventWireup="false" trace="False"
    Inherits="batsmen.BattingPage" %>
```

Template
View

The page can access the methods and properties of the code behind class directly. Furthermore, the code behind can define a Page_Load method to handle the request. In this case I've defined the Page_Load as a template method [Gang of Four] on a *Layer Supertype (475)*.

class CricketPage...

```
protected void Page_Load(object sender, System.EventArgs e) {
    db = new OleDbConnection(DB.ConnectionString);
    if (hasMissingParameters())
        errorTransfer (missingParameterMessage);
    DataSet ds = getData();
    if (hasNoData (ds))
        errorTransfer ("No data matches your request");
    applyDomainLogic (ds);
    DataBind();
    prepareUI(ds);
}
```

For the purposes of *Template View* I can ignore all but the last couple of lines of the page load. The call to DataBind allows various page variables to be properly bound to their underlying data sources. That will do for the simpler cases, but for more complicated cases the last line calls a method in the particular page's code behind to prepare any objects for its use.

The match ID number, team, and innings are single values for the page, all of which came into the page as parameters in the HTTP request. I can provide these values by using properties on the code behind class.

class BattingPage...

```
protected String team {
    get {return Request.Params["team"];}
}
protected String match {
    get {return Request.Params["match"];}
}
protected String innings {
    get {return Request.Params["innings"];}
}
protected String ordinalInnings{
    get {return (innings == "1") ? "1st" : "2nd";}
}
```

With the properties defined, I can use them in the text of the page.

```
<P>
    Match id:
    <asp:label id="matchLabel" Text="<%# match %>" runat="server" font-bold="True">
    </asp:label> 
</P>
<P>
```

```
<asp:label id=teamLabel Text="<%# team %>" runat="server" font-bold="True">
</asp:label> 
<asp:Label id=inningsLabel Text="<%# ordinalInnings %>" runat="server">
</asp:Label> innings</P>
<P>
```

The table is a little more complicated, but actually works easily in practice because of the graphical design facilities in Visual Studio. Visual Studio provides a data grid control that can be bound to a single table from a data set. I can do this binding in the prepareUI method that's called by the Page_Load method.

class BattingPage...

```
override protected void prepareUI(DataSet ds) {
    DataGrid1.DataSource = ds;
    DataGrid1.DataBind();
}
```

The batting class is a *Table Module (125)* that provides domain logic for the batting table in the database. Its data property is the data from that table enriched by domain logic from *Table Module (125)*. Here the enrichment is the run rate, which is calculated rather than stored in the database.

With the ASP.NET data grid you can select which table columns you wish to display in the Web page, together with information about the table's appearance. In this case we can select name, runs, and rate columns.

Template View

```
<asp:DataGrid id="DataGrid1" runat="server" Width="480px" Height="171px"
        BorderColor="#336666" BorderStyle="Double" BorderWidth="3px" BackColor="White"
        CellPadding="4" GridLines="Horizontal" AutoGenerateColumns="False">
    <SelectedItemStyle Font-Bold="True" ForeColor="White" BackColor="#339966"></
        SelectedItemStyle>
    <ItemStyle ForeColor="#333333" BackColor="White"></ItemStyle>
    <HeaderStyle Font-Bold="True" ForeColor="White" BackColor="#336666"></HeaderStyle>
    <FooterStyle ForeColor="#333333" BackColor="White"></FooterStyle>
    <Columns>
        <asp:BoundColumn DataField="name" HeaderText="Batsman">
            <HeaderStyle Width="70px"></HeaderStyle>
        </asp:BoundColumn>
        <asp:BoundColumn DataField="runs" HeaderText="Runs">
            <HeaderStyle Width="30px"></HeaderStyle>
        </asp:BoundColumn>
        <asp:BoundColumn DataField="rateString" HeaderText="Rate">
            <HeaderStyle Width="30px"></HeaderStyle>
        </asp:BoundColumn>
    </Columns>
    <PagerStyle HorizontalAlign="Center" ForeColor="White" BackColor="#336666"
        Mode="NumericPages"></PagerStyle>
</asp:DataGrid></P>
```

The HTML for this data grid looks intimidating, but in Visual Studio you don't manipulate it directly but through property sheets in the development environment, as you do for much of the rest of the page.

This ability to have Web form controls on the Web page that understand the ADO.NET abstractions of data sets and data tables is the strength, and limitation, of this scheme. The strength is that you transfer information through data sets, thanks to the kind of tools that Visual Studio provides. The limitation is that it only works seamlessly when you use patterns such as *Table Module (125)*. If you have very complex domain logic, then a *Domain Model (116)* becomes helpful; to take advantage of the tools, the *Domain Model (116)* needs to create its own data set.

**Template
View**

Transform View

A view that processes domain data element by element and transforms it into HTML.

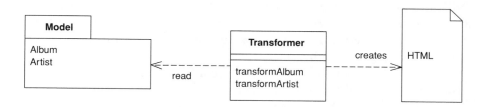

When you issue requests for data to the domain and data source layers, you get back all the data you need to satisfy them, but without the formatting you need to make a proper Web page. The role of the view in *Model View Controller (330)* is to render this data into a Web page. Using *Transform View* means thinking of this as a transformation where you have the model's data as input and its HTML as output.

How It Works

The basic notion of *Transform View* is writing a program that looks at domain-oriented data and converts it to HTML. The program walks the structure of the domain data and, as it recognizes each form of domain data, it writes out the particular piece of HTML for it. If you think about this in an imperative way, you might have a method called renderCustomer that takes a customer object and renders it into HTML. If the customer contains a lot of orders, this method loops over the orders calling renderOrder.

The key difference between *Transform View* and *Template View (350)* is the way in which the view is organized. A *Template View (350)* is organized around the output. A *Transform View* is organized around separate transforms for each kind of input element. The transform is controlled by something like a simple loop that looks at each input element, finds the appropriate transform for that element, and then calls the transform on it. A typical *Transform View*'s rules can be arranged in any order without affecting the resulting output.

You can write a *Transform View* in any language; at the moment, however, the dominant choice is XSLT. The interesting thing about this is that XSLT is a functional programming language, similar to Lisp, Haskell, and other languages that never quite made it into the IS mainstream. As such it has a different kind of structure to it. For example, rather than explicitly calling routines, XSLT recognizes elements in the domain data and then invokes the appropriate rendering transformations.

To carry out an XSLT transform we need to begin with some XML data. The simplest way this can happen is if the natural return type of the domain logic is either XML or something automatically transformable to it—for example, a .NET. Failing that, we need to produce the XML ourselves, perhaps by populating a *Data Transfer Object (401)* that can serialize itself into XML. That way the data can be assembled using a convenient API. In simpler cases a *Transaction Script (110)* can return XML directly.

The XML that's fed into the transform don't have to be a string, unless a string form is needed to cross a communication line. It's usually quicker and easier to produce a DOM and hand that to the transform.

Once we have the XML we pass it to an XSLT engine, which is becoming increasingly available commercially. The logic for the transform is captured in an XSLT style sheet, which we also pass to the transformer. The transformer then applies the stylesheet to the input XML to yield the output HTML, which we can write directly to the HTTP response.

Transform
View

When to Use It

The choice between a *Transform View* and a *Template View (350)* mostly comes down to which environment the team working on the view software prefers. The presence of tools is a key factor here. There are more and more HTML editors that you can use to write *Template Views (350)*. Tools for XSLT are, at least so far, much less sophisticated. Also, XSLT can be an awkward language to master because of its functional programming style coupled with its awkward XML syntax.

One of the strengths of XSLT is its portability to almost any Web platform. You can use the same XSLT to transform XML created from J2EE or .NET, which can help in putting a common HTML view on data from different sources.

XSLT is also often easier if you're building a view on an XML document. Other environments usually require you to transform such a document into an object or to indulge in walking the XML DOM, which can be complicated. XSLT fits naturally in an XML world.

Transform View avoids two of the biggest problems with *Template View (350)*. It's easier to keep the transform focused only on rendering HTML, thus avoiding having too much other logic in the view. It's also easy to run the *Transform View* and capture the output for testing. This makes it easier to test the view and you don't need a Web server to run the tests.

Transform View transforms directly from domain-oriented XML into HTML. If you need to change the overall appearance of a Web site, this can force you to change multiple transform programs. Using common transforms, such as with XSLT includes, helps reduce this problem. Indeed it's much easier to call common transformations using *Transform View* than it is using *Template View (350)*. If you need to make global changes easily or support multiple appearances for the same data, you might consider *Two Step View (365)*, which uses a two-stage process.

Example: Simple Transform (Java)

Setting up a simple transform involves preparing Java code for invoking the right style sheet to form the response. It also involves preparing the style sheet to format the response. Most of the response to a page is pretty generic, so it makes sense to use *Front Controller (344)*. I'll describe only the command here, and you should look at *Front Controller (344)* to see how the command object fits in with the rest of the request-response handling.

All the command object does is invoke the methods on the model to obtain an XML input document, and then pass that XML document through the XML processor.

Transform
View

```
class AlbumCommand...

    public void process() {
        try {
            Album album = Album.findNamed(request.getParameter("name"));
            Assert.notNull(album);
            PrintWriter out = response.getWriter();
            XsltProcessor processor = new SingleStepXsltProcessor("album.xsl");
            out.print(processor.getTransformation(album.toXmlDocument()));
        } catch (Exception e) {
            throw new ApplicationException(e);
        }
    }
}
```

The XML document may look something like this:

```
<album>
    <title>Stormcock</title>
    <artist>Roy Harper</artist>
    <trackList>
        <track><title>Hors d'Oeuvres</title><time>8:37</time></track>
        <track><title>The Same Old Rock</title><time>12:24</time></track>
        <track><title>One Man Rock and Roll Band</title><time>7:23</time></track>
        <track><title>Me and My Woman</title><time>13:01</time></track>
    </trackList>
</album>
```

The translation of the XML document is done by an XSLT program. Each template matches a particular part of the XML and produces the appropriate HTML output for the page. In this case I've kept the formatting to a excessively simple level to show just the essentials. The following template clauses match the basic elements of the XML file.

```
<xsl:template match="album">
    <HTML><BODY bgcolor="white">
    <xsl:apply-templates/>
    </BODY></HTML>
</xsl:template>
<xsl:template match="album/title">
    <h1><xsl:apply-templates/></h1>
</xsl:template>
<xsl:template match="artist">
        <P><B>Artist: </B><xsl:apply-templates/></P>
</xsl:template>
```

These template matches handle the table, which here has alternating rows highlighted in different colors. This is a good example of something that isn't possible with cascading style sheets but is reasonable with XML.

Transform View

```
<xsl:template match="trackList">
    <table><xsl:apply-templates/></table>
</xsl:template>
<xsl:template match="track">
    <xsl:variable name="bgcolor">
        <xsl:choose>
            <xsl:when test="(position() mod 2) = 1">linen</xsl:when>
            <xsl:otherwise>white</xsl:otherwise>
        </xsl:choose>
    </xsl:variable>
    <tr bgcolor="{$bgcolor}"><xsl:apply-templates/></tr>
</xsl:template>
<xsl:template match="track/title">
    <td><xsl:apply-templates/></td>
</xsl:template>
<xsl:template match="track/time">
    <td><xsl:apply-templates/></td>
</xsl:template>
```

Two Step View

Turns domain data into HTML in two steps: first by forming some kind of logical page, then rendering the logical page into HTML.

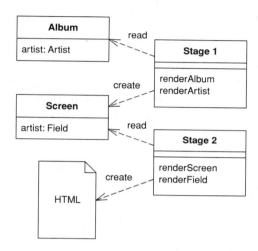

If you have a Web application with many pages, you often want a consistent look and organization to the site. If every page looks different, you end up with a site that users find confusing. You may also want to make global changes to the appearance of the site easily, but common approaches using *Template View (350)* or *Transform View (361)* make this difficult because presentation decisions are often duplicated across multiple pages or transform modules. A global change can force you to change several files.

Two Step View deals with this problem by splitting the transformation into two stages. The first transforms the model data into a logical presentation without any specific formatting; the second converts that logical presentation with the actual formatting needed. This way you can make a global change by altering the second stage, or you can support multiple output looks and feels with one second stage each.

How It Works

The key to this pattern is in making the transformation to HTML a two-stage process. The first stage assembles the information in a logical screen structure that is suggestive of the display elements yet contains no HTML. The second stage takes that presentation-oriented structure and renders it into HTML

This intermediate form is a kind of logical screen. Its elements might include things like fields, headers, footers, tables, choices, and the like. As such it's certainly presentation-oriented and certainly forces the screens to follow a definite style. You can think of the presentation-oriented model as one that defines the various widgets you can have and the data they contain but doesn't specify the HTML appearance.

This presentation-oriented structure is assembled by specific code written for each screen. The first stage's responsibility is to access a domain-oriented model, either a database, an actual domain model, or a domain-oriented *Data Transfer Object (401)*; to extract the relevant information for that screen; and then to put that information into the presentation-oriented structure.

The second stage turns this presentation-oriented structure into HTML. It knows about each element in the presentation-oriented structure and how to show it as HTML. Thus, a system with many screens can be rendered as HTML by a single second stage so that all the HTML formatting decisions are made in one place. Of course, the constraint is that the resulting screen must be derivable from the presentation-oriented structure.

Two Step
View

There are several ways to build a *Two Step View*. Perhaps the easiest is with two-step XSLT. Single-step XSLT follows the approach in *Transform View (361)*, in which each page has a single XSLT style sheet that transforms the domain-oriented XML into HTML. In the two-step approach there are two XSLT style sheets. The first-stage style sheet transforms the domain-oriented XML into presentation-oriented XML, the second-stage style sheet renders that XML into HTML.

Another way is to use classes. Here you define the presentation-oriented structure as a set of classes: with a table class, a row class, and so forth. The first stage takes domain information and instantiates these classes into a structure that models a logical screen. The second stage renders the classes into HTML, either by getting each presentation-oriented class to generate HTML for itself or by having a separate HTML renderer class to do the job.

Both approaches are based on *Transform View (361)*. You can also use a *Template View (350)* based approach, in which you pick templates based on the idea of a logical screen—for example:

```
<field label = "Name" value = "getName" />
```

The template system then converts these logical tags into HTML. In such a scheme the page definition includes no HTML but only these logical screen tags. As a result it will probably be an XML document, which of course means that you lose the ability to use WYSIWYG HTML editors.

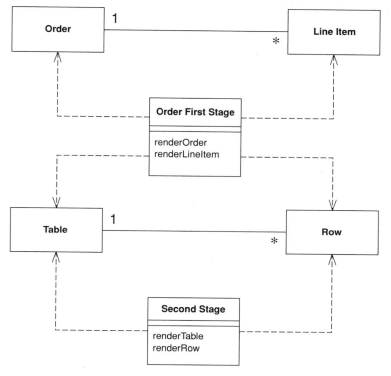

Figure 14.4 *Sample classes for two-step rendering.*

Two Step
View

When to Use It

Two Step View's key value comes from the separation of first and second stages, allowing you to make global changes more easily. It helps to think of two situations: multiappearance Web applications and single-appearance Web applications. Multiappearance apps are the rarer breed but a growing one. In them the same basic functionality is provided through multiple organizations and each organization has its own distinct look. A current example of this is airline travel sites, where as you look at them you can tell from the page layout and design that they're all variations on one base site. I suspect many airlines want that same functionality but with a distinctly individual appearance.

Single-appearance apps are more common. Only one organization fronts them, and they want a consistent look throughout the site. This makes them the easiest case to consider first.

With a single-stage view (either *Template View (350)* or *Transform View (361)*, you build one view module per Web page (see Figure 14.6). With a *Two*

Two Step View

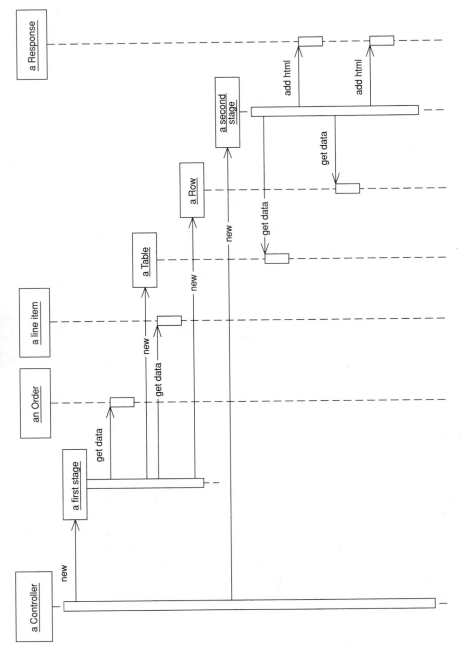

Figure 14.5 *Sequence diagram for two-step rendering.*

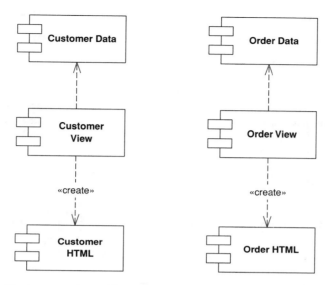

Figure 14.6 *Single-stage view with one appearance.*

Step View you have two stages: one first-stage module per page and one second-stage module for the entire application (Figure 14.7). Your pay-off in using *Two Step View* is that any change to the appearance of the site in the second stage is much easier to make, since one second-stage change affects the site as a whole.

With a multiappearance app this advantage is compounded because you have a single-stage view for each combination of screen and appearance (Figure 14.8). Thus, ten screens and three appearances require thirty single stage view modules. Using *Two Step View*, however (see Figure 14.9), you can get away with ten first stages and three second stages. The more screens and appearances you have, the bigger the saving.

Nevertheless, your ability to pull this off is entirely dependent on how well you can make the presentation-oriented structure to really serve the needs of the appearance. A design-heavy site, where each page is supposed to look different, won't work well with *Two Step View* because it's hard to find enough commonality between the screens to get a simple enough presentation-oriented structure. Essentially the site design is constrained by the presentation-oriented structure, and for many sites that's too much of a limitation.

Another drawback of *Two Step View* is the tools required to use it. There are a lot of tools for designers with no programming skills to lay out HTML pages

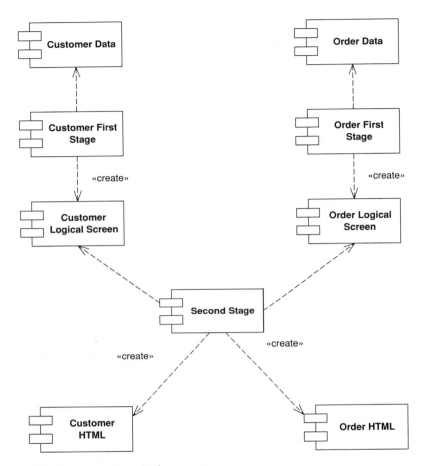

Figure 14.7 *Two-stage view with one appearance.*

using *Template View (350)*, but *Two Step View* forces programmers to write the renderer and controller objects. Thus programmers have to be involved in any design change.

It's also true that *Two Step View*, with its multiple layers, presents a harder programming model to learn, although once you're used to it it's not that difficult, and may help reduce repetitive boilerplate code.

A variation on the theme of multiple appearances is providing different second stages for different devices, so you can have one second stage for a browser and another for a PDA. The usual limitation here is that both appearances must

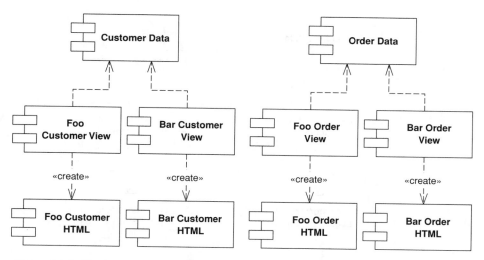

Figure 14.8 *Single-stage view with two appearances.*

follow the same logical screen, and for very different devices this may be too much to ask.

Example: Two Stage XSLT (XSLT)

This approach to a *Two Step View* uses a two-stage XLST transformation. The first stage transforms domain-specific XML into logical screen XML; the second transforms the logical screen XML into HTML.

The initial domain oriented XML looks like this:

```
<album>
    <title>Zero Hour</title>
    <artist>Astor Piazzola</artist>
    <trackList>
        <track><title>Tanguedia III</title><time>4:39</time></track>
        <track><title>Milonga del Angel</title><time>6:30</time></track>
        <track><title>Concierto Para Quinteto</title><time>9:00</time></track>
        <track><title>Milonga Loca</title><time>3:05</time></track>
        <track><title>Michelangelo '70</title><time>2:50</time></track>
        <track><title>Contrabajisimo</title><time>10:18</time></track>
        <track><title>Mumuki</title><time>9:32</time></track>
    </trackList>
</album>
```

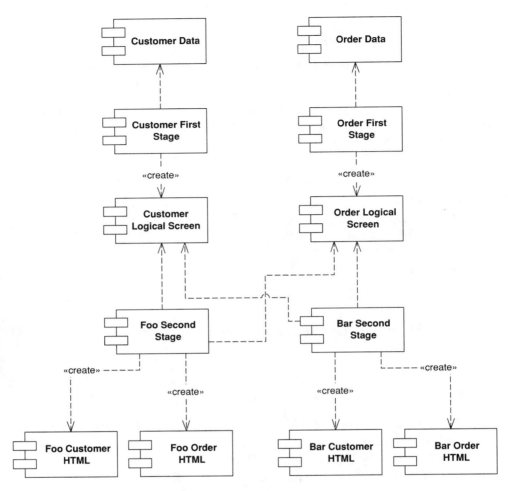

Figure 14.9 *Two-stage view with two appearances.*

The first stage XSLT processor transforms it into this screen-oriented XML:

```
<screen>
    <title>Zero Hour</title>
    <field label="Artist">Astor Piazzola</field>
    <table>
        <row><cell>Tanguedia III</cell><cell>4:39</cell></row>
        <row><cell>Milonga del Angel</cell><cell>6:30</cell></row>
        <row><cell>Concierto Para Quinteto</cell><cell>9:00</cell></row>
        <row><cell>Milonga Loca</cell><cell>3:05</cell></row>
```

```
      <row><cell>Michelangelo '70</cell><cell>2:50</cell></row>
      <row><cell>Contrabajisimo</cell><cell>10:18</cell></row>
      <row><cell>Mumuki</cell><cell>9:32</cell></row>
    </table>
  </screen>
```

To do this we need the following XSLT program:

```
<xsl:template match="album">
  <screen><xsl:apply-templates/></screen>
</xsl:template>
<xsl:template match="album/title">
  <title><xsl:apply-templates/></title>
</xsl:template>
<xsl:template match="artist">
  <field label="Artist"><xsl:apply-templates/></field>
</xsl:template>
<xsl:template match="trackList">
  <table><xsl:apply-templates/></table>
</xsl:template>
<xsl:template match="track">
  <row><xsl:apply-templates/></row>
</xsl:template>
<xsl:template match="track/title">
  <cell><xsl:apply-templates/></cell>
</xsl:template>
<xsl:template match="track/time">
  <cell><xsl:apply-templates/></cell>
</xsl:template>
```

The screen-oriented XML is very plain. To turn it into HTML we use a second-stage XSLT program.

```
<xsl:template match="screen">
  <HTML><BODY bgcolor="white">
  <xsl:apply-templates/>
  </BODY></HTML>
</xsl:template>
<xsl:template match="title">
  <h1><xsl:apply-templates/></h1>
</xsl:template><xsl:template match="field">
  <P><B><xsl:value-of select = "@label"/>: </B><xsl:apply-templates/></P>
</xsl:template>
<xsl:template match="table">
  <table><xsl:apply-templates/></table>
</xsl:template>
<xsl:template match="table/row">
  <xsl:variable name="bgcolor">
    <xsl:choose>
      <xsl:when test="(position() mod 2) = 1">linen</xsl:when>
      <xsl:otherwise>white</xsl:otherwise>
    </xsl:choose>
```

```
    </xsl:variable>
    <tr bgcolor="{$bgcolor}"><xsl:apply-templates/></tr>
</xsl:template>
<xsl:template match="table/row/cell">
    <td><xsl:apply-templates/></td>
</xsl:template>
```

In assembling the two stages, I used *Front Controller (344)* to help separate the code that does the work.

```
class AlbumCommand...

    public void process() {
        try {
            Album album = Album.findNamed(request.getParameter("name"));
            album = Album.findNamed("1234");
            Assert.notNull(album);
            PrintWriter out = response.getWriter();
            XsltProcessor processor = new TwoStepXsltProcessor("album2.xsl", "second.xsl");
            out.print(processor.getTransformation(album.toXmlDocument()));
        } catch (Exception e) {
            throw new ApplicationException(e);
        }
    }
```

Two Step View

It's useful to compare this to the single-stage approach in *Transform View (361)*. If you want to change the colors of the alternating rows, *Transform View (361)* requires editing every XSLT program, but with *Two Step View* only the single second-stage XSLT program needs to be changed. It might be possible to use callable templates to do something similar, but this needs a fair bit of XSLT gymnastics to pull off. The down side of *Two Step View* is that the final HTML is very much constrained by the screen-oriented XML.

Example: JSP and Custom Tags (Java)

Although the XSLT route is conceptually the easiest way to think about implementing *Two Step View*, plenty of other ways exist. For this example I'll use JSPs and custom tags. Although they're both more awkward and less powerful than XSLT, they do show how the pattern can manifest itself in different ways. I'm being a bit cheeky with this example, for I haven't seen this done in the field. But I feel a somewhat speculative example will give you an idea of what might be possible.

The key rule of *Two Step View* is that choosing what to display and choosing the HTML that displays it are totally separate. For this example my first stage is handled by a JSP page and its helper; my second stage, by a set of custom tags. The interesting part of the first stage is the JSP page.

```
<%@ taglib uri="2step.tld" prefix = "2step" %>
<%@ page session="false"%>
<jsp:useBean id="helper" class="actionController.AlbumConHelper"/>
<%helper.init(request, response);%>
<2step:screen>
<2step:title><jsp:getProperty name = "helper" property = "title"/></2step:title>
<2step:field label = "Artist"><jsp:getProperty name = "helper" property = "artist"/></2step:field>
<2step:table host = "helper" collection = "trackList" columns = "title, time"/>
</2step:screen>
```

I'm using *Page Controller (333)* for the JSP page with a helper object you can flick over to *Page Controller (333)* to read more about that. The important thing here is to look at the tags that are part of the 2step namespace. They are the ones I'm using to invoke the second stage. Also notice that there is no HTML on the JSP page; the only tags present are either second-stage tags or bean manipulation tags to get values out of the helper.

Each second-stage tag has an implementation to pump out the necessary HTML for that logical screen element. The simplest of these is the title.

```
class TitleTag...

   public int doStartTag() throws JspException {
      try {
         pageContext.getOut().print("<H1>");
      } catch (IOException e) {
         throw new JspException("unable to print start");
      }
      return EVAL_BODY_INCLUDE;
   }
   public int doEndTag() throws JspException {
      try {
         pageContext.getOut().print("</H1>");
      } catch (IOException e) {
         throw new JspException("unable to print end");
      }
      return EVAL_PAGE;
   }
```

For those that haven't indulged, a custom tag works by implementing hook methods called at the beginning and the end of the tagged text. This tag simply wraps its body content with an <H1> tag. A more complex tag, such as the field, can take an attribute. The attribute is tied into the tag class using a setting method.

class FieldTag...

```
private String label;
public void setLabel(String label) {
    this.label = label;
}
```

Once the value is set, you can use it in the output.

class FieldTag...

```
public int doStartTag() throws JspException {
    try {
        pageContext.getOut().print("<P>" + label + ": <B>");
    } catch (IOException e) {
        throw new JspException("unable to print start");
    }
    return EVAL_BODY_INCLUDE;
}
public int doEndTag() throws JspException {
    try {
        pageContext.getOut().print("</B></P>");
    } catch (IOException e) {
        throw new JspException("how are checked exceptions helping me here?");
    }
    return EVAL_PAGE;
}
```

Two Step View

The Table is the most sophisticated of the tags. As well as allowing the JSP writer to choose which columns to put in the table, it highlights alternate rows. The tag implementation acts as the second stage, so the highlighting is done there so that a system-wide change can be made globally.

The Table tag takes attributes for the name of the collection property, the object on which the collection property sits, and a comma-separated list of column names.

class TableTag...

```
private String collectionName;
private String hostName;
private String columns;
public void setCollection(String collectionName) {
    this.collectionName = collectionName;
}
public void setHost(String hostName) {
    this.hostName = hostName;
```

```
    }
    public void setColumns(String columns) {
       this.columns = columns;
    }
```

I made a helper method to get a property out of an object. There's a good argument for using the various classes that support Java beans, rather than just invoking a "getsomething" method, but this will do for the example.

class TableTag...

```
    private Object getProperty(Object obj, String property) throws JspException {
       try {
          String methodName = "get" + property.substring(0, 1).toUpperCase() +
             property.substring(1);
          Object result = obj.getClass().getMethod(methodName, null).invoke(obj, null);
          return result;
       } catch (Exception e) {
          throw new JspException("Unable to get property " + property + " from " + obj);
       }
    }
```

This tag doesn't have a body. When it's called it pulls the named collection out of the request property and iterates through the collection to generate the rows of the table.

Two Step
View

class TableTag...

```
    public int doStartTag() throws JspException {
       try {
          JspWriter out = pageContext.getOut();
          out.print("<table>");
          Collection coll = (Collection) getPropertyFromAttribute(hostName, collectionName);
          Iterator rows = coll.iterator();
          int rowNumber = 0;
          while (rows.hasNext()) {
             out.print("<tr");
             if ((rowNumber++ % 2) == 0) out.print(" bgcolor = " + HIGHLIGHT_COLOR);
             out.print(">");
             printCells(rows.next());
             out.print("</tr>");
          }
          out.print("</table>");
       } catch (IOException e) {
          throw new JspException("unable to print out");
       }
       return SKIP_BODY;
    }
    private Object getPropertyFromAttribute(String attribute, String property)
          throws JspException
```

```
  {
     Object hostObject = pageContext.findAttribute(attribute);
     if (hostObject == null)
        throw new JspException("Attribute " + attribute + " not found.");
     return getProperty(hostObject, property);
  }
  public static final String HIGHLIGHT_COLOR = "'linen'";
```

During the iteration it sets every other row to the linen background to highlight them.

To print the cells for each row, I use the column names as property values on the objects in the collection.

```
class TableTag...
    private void printCells(Object obj) throws IOException, JspException {
        JspWriter out = pageContext.getOut();
        for (int i = 0; i < getColumnList().length; i++) {
            out.print("<td>");
            out.print(getProperty(obj, getColumnList()[i]));
            out.print("</td>");
        }
    }
    private String[] getColumnList() {
        StringTokenizer tk = new StringTokenizer(columns, ", ");
        String[] result = new String[tk.countTokens()];
        for (int i = 0; tk.hasMoreTokens(); i++)
            result[i] = tk.nextToken();
        return result;
    }
```

Two Step View

Compared to the XSLT implementation, this solution is rather less constraining on the uniformity of the site's layout. An author of one page wanting to slip some individual HTML into it will find that easier to do. Of course, while this allows tweaking of design-intensive pages, it's also open to inappropriate use by people who are unfamiliar with how things work. Sometimes constraints help prevent mistakes. That's a trade-off a team has to decide for themselves.

Application Controller

*A centralized point for handling screen navigation
and the flow of an application.*

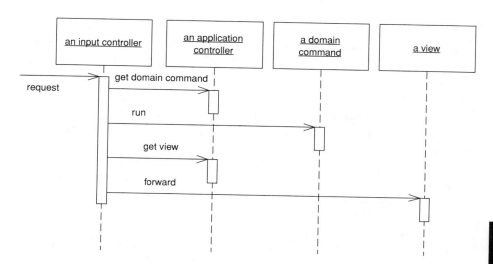

Some applications contain a significant amount of logic about the screens to use at different points, which may involve invoking certain screens at certain times in an application. This is the wizard style of interaction, where the user is led through a series of screens in a certain order. In other cases we may see screens that are only brought in under certain conditions, or choices between different screens that depend on earlier input.

To some degree the various *Model View Controller (330)* input controllers can make some of these decisions, but as an application gets more complex this can lead to duplicated code as several controllers for different screens need to know what to do in a certain situation.

You can remove this duplication by placing all the flow logic in an *Application Controller.* Input controllers then ask the *Application Controller* for the appropriate commands for execution against a model and the correct view to use depending on the application context.

How It Works

An *Application Controller* has two main responsibilities: deciding which domain logic to run and deciding the view with which display the response. To do this it typically holds two structured collections of class references, one for domain commands to execute against in the domain layer and one of views (Figure 14.10).

For both the domain commands and the view, the *application controller* needs a way to store something it can invoke. A Command [Gang of Four] is a good choice, since it allows it to easily get hold of and run a block of code. Languages that can manipulate functions can hold references to them. Another option is to hold a string that can be used to invoke a method by reflection.

The domain commands can be command objects that are part of the *Application Controller* layer, or they can be references to a *Transaction Script (110)* or domain object methods in the domain layer.

If you're using server pages as your views, you can use the server page name. If you're using a class, a command or a string for a reflective call makes sense. You might also use an XSLT transform, to which the *Application Controller* can hold a string as a reference.

One decision you'll need to make is how much to separate the *Application Controller* from the rest of the presentation. At the first level this decision manifests itself in whether the *Application Controller* has dependencies to the UI machinery. Perhaps it directly accesses the HTTP session data, forwards to a server page, or invokes methods on a rich-client class.

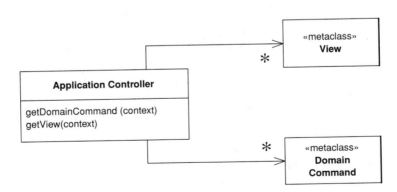

Figure 14.10 *An application controller has two collections of references to classes, one for domain logic and one for view.*

Although I've seen direct *Application Controllers*, my preference is for the *Application Controller* to have no links to the UI machinery. For a start this makes it possible to test the *Application Controller* independently of the UI, which is a major benefit. It's also important to do this if you're going to use the same *Application Controller* with multiple presentations. For these reasons many people like to think of the *Application Controller* as an intermediate layer between the presentation and the domain.

An application can have multiple *Application Controllers* to handle each of its different parts. This allows you to split up complex logic into several classes. In this case I usually see the work divided up into broad areas of the user interface and build separate *Application Controllers* for each area. On a simpler application I might need only a single *Application Controller*.

If you have multiple presentations, such as a Web front end, a rich client, and a PDA, you may be able to use the same *Application Controller* for each presentation, but don't be too eager. Often different UIs need a different screen flow to achieve a really usable user interface. However, reusing a single *Application Controller* may reduce the development effort, and that decreased effort may be worth the cost of a more awkward UI.

A common way of thinking about a UI is as a state machine, where certain events trigger different responses depending on the state of certain key objects in the application. In this case the *Application Controller* is particularly amenable to using metadata to represent the state machine's control flow. The metadata can either be set up by programming language calls (the simplest way) or it can be stored in a separate configuration file.

You may find domain logic particular to one request placed in an *Application Controller (379)*. As you might suspect, I come down pretty hard against that notion. However, the boundary between domain and application logic does get very murky. Say I'm handling insurance applications and I need to show a separate screen of questions only if the applicant is a smoker. Is this application logic or domain logic? If I have only a few such cases I can probably put that kind of logic in the *Application Controller (379)*, but if it occurs in lots of places I need to design the *Domain Model (116)* in such a way to drive this.

Application Controller

When to Use It

If the flow and navigation of your application are simple enough so that anyone can visit any screen in pretty much any order, there's little value in a *Application Controller*. The strength of an *Application Controller* comes from definite rules about the order in which pages should be visited and different views depending on the state of objects.

A good signal to use an *Application Controller* is if you find yourself having to make similar changes in lots of different places when your application's flow changes.

Further Reading

Most of the ideas that underlie the writing of this pattern came from [Knight and Dai]. Although their ideas aren't exactly new, I found their explanations remarkably clear and compelling.

Example: State Model *Application Controller* (Java)

State models are a common way of thinking about user interfaces. They're particularly appropriate when you need to react differently to events depending on the state of some object. In this example I have a simple state model for a couple of commands on an asset (Figure 14.11). ThoughtWork's leasing experts would faint at the virulent oversimplification of this model, but it will do as an example of a state-based *Application Controller*.

As far as the code is concerned our rules are these:

- When we receive a return command and we're in the On lease state, we display a page to capture information about the return of the asset.

- A return event in the in Inventory state is an error, so we show an illegal action page.

- When we receive a damage command we show different pages depending on whether the asset is in the Inventory or the On lease state.

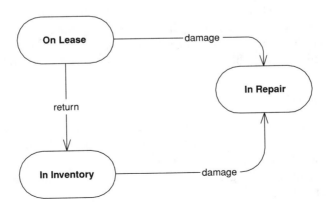

Figure 14.11 *A simple state diagram for an asset.*

The input controller is a *Front Controller (344)*. It services the request like this:

```
class FrontServlet...

    public void service(HttpServletRequest request, HttpServletResponse response)
            throws IOException, ServletException
    {
        ApplicationController appController = getApplicationController(request);
        String commandString = (String) request.getParameter("command");
        DomainCommand comm =
            appController.getDomainCommand(commandString, getParameterMap(request));
        comm.run(getParameterMap(request));
        String viewPage =
            "/" + appController.getView(commandString, getParameterMap(request)) + ".jsp";
        forward(viewPage, request, response);
    }
```

The flow of the service method is pretty straightforward: We find the right application controller for a given request, ask the application controller for the domain command, execute the domain command, ask the application controller for a view, and, finally, forward to the view.

In this scheme I'm assuming a number of *Application Controllers*, all of which implement the same interface.

```
interface ApplicationController...

    DomainCommand getDomainCommand (String commandString, Map params);
    String getView (String commandString, Map params);
```

For our commands the appropriate *Application Controller* is an asset application controller. It uses a response class to hold the domain commands and view references. For the domain command I use a reference to a class; for the view I use a string, which the front controller will turn into a URL for a JSP.

```
class Response...

    private Class domainCommand;
    private String viewUrl;
    public Response(Class domainCommand, String viewUrl) {
        this.domainCommand = domainCommand;
        this.viewUrl = viewUrl;
    }
    public DomainCommand getDomainCommand() {
        try {
            return (DomainCommand) domainCommand.newInstance();
        } catch (Exception e) {throw new ApplicationException (e);
        }
    }
    public String getViewUrl() {
        return viewUrl;
    }
```

The application controller holds on to the responses using a map of maps indexed by the command string and an asset status (Figure 14.12).

```
class AssetApplicationController...
    private Response getResponse(String commandString, AssetStatus state) {
        return (Response) getResponseMap(commandString).get(state);
    }
    private Map getResponseMap (String key) {
        return (Map) events.get(key);
    }
    private Map events = new HashMap();
```

When asked for a domain command, the controller looks at the request to figure out the asset ID, goes to the domain to determine the status of that asset,

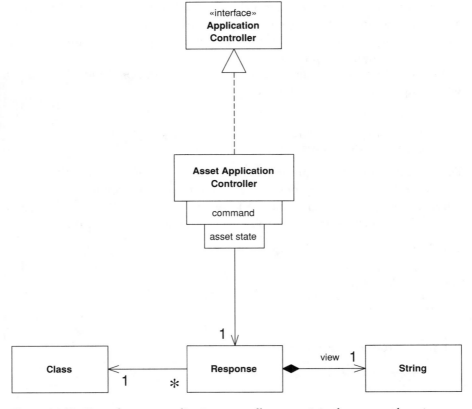

Figure 14.12 *How the asset application controller stores its references to domain commands and views*

looks up the appropriate domain command class, instantiates that class, and returns the new object.

```
class AssetApplicationController...

    public DomainCommand getDomainCommand (String commandString, Map params) {
        Response reponse = getResponse(commandString, getAssetStatus(params));
        return reponse.getDomainCommand();
    }
    private AssetStatus getAssetStatus(Map params) {
        String id = getParam("assetID", params);
        Asset asset = Asset.find(id);
        return asset.getStatus();
    }
    private String getParam(String key, Map params) {
        return ((String[]) params.get(key))[0];
    }
```

All the domain commands follow a simple interface that allows the front controller to run them.

```
interface DomainCommand...

    abstract public void run(Map params);
```

Once the domain command has done what it needs to do, the *Application Controller* comes into play again when it's asked for the view.

```
class AssetApplicationController...

    public String getView (String commandString, Map params) {
        return getResponse(commandString, getAssetStatus(params)).getViewUrl();
    }
```

In this case the *Application Controller* doesn't return the full URL to the JSP. It returns a string that the front controller turns into an URL. I do this to avoid duplicating the URL paths in the responses. It also makes it easy to add further indirection later should I need it.

The *Application Controller* can be loaded for use with code.

```
class AssetApplicationController...

    public void addResponse(String event, Object state, Class domainCommand, String view) {
        Response newResponse = new Response (domainCommand, view);
        if ( ! events.containsKey(event))
            events.put(event, new HashMap());
        getResponseMap(event).put(state, newResponse);
    }
    private static void loadApplicationController(AssetApplicationController appController) {
        appController = AssetApplicationController.getDefault();
```

```
appController.addResponse("return", AssetStatus.ON_LEASE,
                          GatherReturnDetailsCommand.class, "return");
appController.addResponse("return", AssetStatus.IN_INVENTORY,
                          NullAssetCommand.class, "illegalAction");
appController.addResponse("damage", AssetStatus.ON_LEASE,
                          InventoryDamageCommand.class, "leaseDamage");
appController.addResponse("damage", AssetStatus.IN_INVENTORY,
                          LeaseDamageCommand.class, "inventoryDamage");
}
```

Doing this from a file instead isn't rocket science, but even so I'll leave it to you.

**Application
Controller**

Chapter 15

Distribution Patterns

Remote Facade

Provides a coarse-grained facade on fine-grained
objects to improve efficiency over a network.

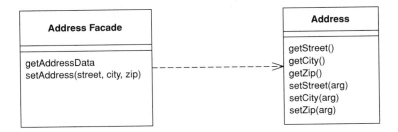

In an object-oriented model, you do best with small objects that have small methods. This gives you lots of opportunity for control and substitution of behavior, and to use good intention revealing naming to make an application easier to understand. One of the consequences of such fine-grained behavior is that there's usually a great deal of interaction between objects, and that interaction usually requires lots of method invocations.

Within a single address space fine-grained interaction works well, but this happy state does not exist when you make calls between processes. Remote calls are much more expensive because there's a lot more to do: Data may have to be marshaled, security may need to be checked, packets may need to be routed through switches. If the two processes are running on machines on opposite sides of the globe, the speed of light may be a factor. The brutal truth is that any inter-process call is orders of magnitude more expensive than an in-process call—even if both processes are on the same machine. Such a performance effect cannot be ignored, even for believers in lazy optimization.

As a result any object that's intended to be used as a remote objects needs a coarse-grained interface that minimizes the number of calls needed to get something done. Not only does this affect your method calls, it also affects your objects. Rather than ask for an order and its order lines individually, you need to access and update the order and order lines in a single call. This affects your entire object structure. You give up the clear intention and fine-grained control you get with small objects and small methods. Programming becomes more difficult and your productivity slows.

A *Remote Facade* is a coarse-grained facade [Gang of Four] over a web of fine-grained objects. None of the fine-grained objects have a remote interface,

Remote
Facade

and the *Remote Facade* contains no domain logic. All the *Remote Facade* does is translate coarse-grained methods onto the underlying fine-grained objects.

How It Works

Remote Facade tackles the distribution problem which the standard OO approach of separating distinct responsibilities into different objects; and as a result it has become the standard pattern for this problem. I recognize that fine-grained objects are the right answer for complex logic, so I ensure that any complex logic is placed in fine-grained objects that are designed to collaborate within a single process. To allow efficient remote access to them, I make a separate facade object that acts as a remote interface. As the name implies, the facade is merely a thin skin that switches from a coarse-grained to a fine-grained interface.

In a simple case, like an address object, a *Remote Facade* replaces all the getting and setting methods of the regular address object with one getter and one setter, often referred to as **bulk accessors**. When a client calls a bulk setter, the address facade reads the data from the setting method and calls the individual accessors on the real address object (see Figure 15.1) and does nothing more. This way all the logic of validation and computation stays on the address object where it can be factored cleanly and can be used by other fine-grained objects.

In a more complex case a single *Remote Facade* may act as a remote gateway for many fine-grained objects. For example, an order facade may be used to get

Remote
Facade

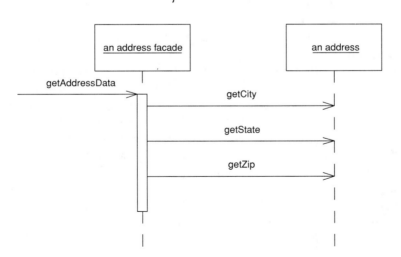

Figure 15.1 *One call to a facade causes several calls from the facade to the domain object*

and update information for an order, all its order lines, and maybe some customer data as well.

In transferring information in bulk like this, you need it to be in a form that can easily move over the wire. If your fine-grained classes are present on both sides of the connection and they're serializable, you can transfer them directly by making a copy. In this case a getAddressData method creates a copy of the original address object. The setAddressData receives an address object and uses it to update the actual address object's data. (This assumes that the original address object needs to preserve its identity and thus can't be simply replaced with the new address.)

Often you can't do this, however. You may not want to duplicate your domain classes on multiple processes, or it may be difficult to serialize a segment of a domain model due to its complicated relationship structure. The client may not want the whole model but just a simplified subset of it. In these cases it makes sense to use a *Data Transfer Object (401)* as the basis of the transfer.

In the sketch I've shown a *Remote Facade* that corresponds to a single domain object. This isn't uncommon and it's easy to understand, but it isn't the most usual case. A single *Remote Facade* would have a number of methods, each designed to pass on information from several objects. Thus, getAddressData and setAddressData would be methods defined on a class like CustomerService, which would also have methods along the lines of getPurchasingHistory and updateCreditData.

Granularity is one of the most tricky issues with *Remote Facade*. Some people like to make fairly small *Remote Facades*, such as one per use case. I prefer a coarser grained structure with much fewer *Remote Facades*. For even a moderate-sized application I might have just one and even for a large application I may have only half a dozen. This means that each *Remote Facade* has a lot of methods, but since these methods are small I don't see this as a problem.

You design a *Remote Facade* based on the needs of a particular client's usage—most commonly the need to view and update information through a user interface. In this case you might have a single *Remote Facade* for a family of screens, for each of which one bulk accessor method loads and saves the data. Pressing buttons on a screen, say to change an order's status, invokes command methods on the facade. Quite often you'll have different methods on the *Remote Facade* that do pretty much the same thing on the underlying objects. This is common and reasonable. The facade is designed to make life simpler for external users, not for the internal system, so if the client process thinks of it as a different command, it is a different command, even if it all goes to the same internal command.

Remote Facade can be stateful or stateless. A stateless *Remote Facade* can be pooled, which can improve resource usage and efficiency, especially in a B2C situation. However, if the interaction involves state across a session, then it needs to store session state somewhere using *Client Session State (456)* or *Database Session State (462)*, or an implementation of *Server Session State (458)*. As stateful a *Remote Facade* can hold on to its own state, which makes for an easy implementation of *Server Session State (458)*, but this may lead to performance issues when you have thousands of simultaneous users.

As well as providing a coarse-grained interface, several other responsibilities can be added to a *Remote Facade*. For example, its methods are a natural point at which to apply security. An access control list can say which users can invoke calls on which methods. The *Remote Facade* methods also are a natural point at which to apply transactional control. A *Remote Facade* method can start a transaction, do all the internal work, and then commit the transaction at the end. Each call makes a good transaction because you don't want a transaction open when return goes back to the client, since transactions aren't built to be efficient for such long running cases.

One of the biggest mistakes I see in a *Remote Facade* is putting domain logic in it. Repeat after me three times; "*Remote Facade* has no domain logic." Any facade should be a thin skin that has only minimal responsibilities. If you need domain logic for workflow or coordination either put it in your fine-grained objects or create a separate nonremotable *Transaction Script (110)* to contain it. You should be able to run the entire application locally without using the *Remote Facades* or having to duplicate any code.

Remote Facade and Session Facade Over the last couple of years the Session Facade [Alur et al.] pattern has been appearing in the J2EE community. In my earlier drafts I considered *Remote Facade* to be the same pattern as Session Facade and used the Session Facade name. In practice, however, there's a crucial difference. *Remote Facade* is all about having a thin remote skin—hence my diatribe against domain logic in it. In contrast, most descriptions of Session Facade involve putting logic in it, usually of a workflow kind. A large part of this is due to the common approach of using J2EE session beans to wrap entity beans. Any coordination of entity beans has to be done by another object since they can't be re-entrant.

As a result, I see a Session Facade as putting several *Transaction Scripts (110)* in a remote interface. That's a reasonable approach, but it isn't the same thing as a *Remote Facade*. Indeed, I would argue that, since the Session Facade contains domain logic, it shouldn't be called a facade at all!

Service Layer A concept familiar to facades is a *Service Layer (133)*. The main difference is that a service layer doesn't have to be remote and thus doesn't need to have only fine-grained methods. In simplifying the *Domain Model (116)*, you often end up with coarser-grained methods, but that's for clarity, not for network efficiency. Furthermore, there's no need for a service layer to use *Data Transfer Objects (401)*. Usually it can happily return real domain objects to the client.

If a *Domain Model (116)* is going to be used both within a process and remotely, you can have a *Service Layer (133)* and layer a separate *Remote Facade* on top of it. If the process is only used remotely, it's probably easier to fold the *Service Layer (133)* into the *Remote Facade*, providing the *Service Layer (133)* has no application logic. If there's any application logic in it, then I would make the *Remote Facade* a separate object.

When to Use It

Use *Remote Facade* whenever you need remote access to a fine-grained object model. You gain the advantages of a coarse-grained interface while still keeping the advantage of fine-grained objects, giving you the best of both worlds.

The most common use of this pattern is between a presentation and a *Domain Model (116)*, where the two may run on different processes. You'll get this between a swing UI and server domain model or with a servlet and a server object model if the application and Web servers are different processes.

Most often you run into this with different processes on different machines, but it turns out that the cost of an inter-process call on the same box is sufficiently large that you need a coarse-grained interface for any inter-process communication regardless of where the processes live.

If all your access is within a single process, you don't need this kind of conversion. Thus, I wouldn't use this pattern to communicate between a client *Domain Model (116)* and its presentation or between a CGI script and *Domain Model (116)* running in one Web server. You don't see *Remote Facade* used with a *Transaction Script (110)* as a rule, since a *Transaction Script (110)* is inherently coarser grained.

Remote Facades imply a synchronous—that is, a remote procedure call—style of distribution. Often you can greatly improve the responsiveness of an application by going with asynchronous, message-based remote communication. Indeed, an asynchronous approach has many compelling advantages. Sadly, discussion of asynchronous patterns is outside the scope of this book.

Example: Using a Java Session Bean as a *Remote Facade* (Java)

If you're working with the Enterprise Java platform, a good choice for a distributed facade is a session bean because its a remote object and may be stateful or stateless. In this example I'll run a bunch of POJOs (plain old Java objects) inside an EJB container and access them remotely through a session bean that's designed as a *Remote Facade*. Session beans aren't particularly complicated, so everything should make sense even if you haven't done any work with them before.

I feel the need for a couple of side notes here. First, I've been surprised by how many people seem to believe that you can't run plain objects inside an EJB container in Java. I hear the question, "Are the domain objects entity beans?" The answer is, they can be but they don't have to be. Simple Java objects work just fine, as in this example.

My second side note is just to point out that this isn't the only way to use session beans. They can also be used to host *Transaction Scripts (110)*.

In this example I'll look at remote interfaces for accessing information about music albums. The *Domain Model (116)* consists of fine-grained objects that represent an artist, and album, and tracks. Surrounding this are several other packages that provide the data sources for the application (see Figure 15.2).

In the figure, the dto package contains *Data Transfer Objects (401)* that help move data over the wire to the client. They have simple accessor behavior and also the ability to serialize themselves in binary or XML textual formats. In the

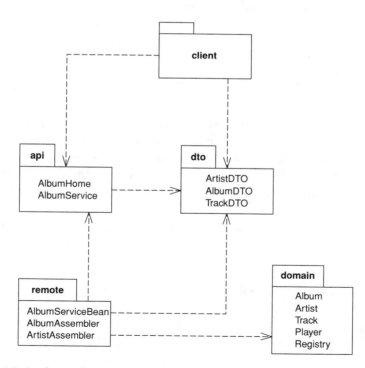

Figure 15.2 *Packages the remote interfaces.*

Remote
Facade

remote package are assembler objects that move data between the domain objects and the *Data Transfer Objects (401)*. If you're interested in how this works see the *Data Transfer Object (401)* discussion.

To explain the facade I'll assume that I can move data into and out of *Data Transfer Objects (401)* and concentrate on the remote interfaces. A single logical Java session bean has three actual classes. Two of them make up the remote API (and in fact are Java interfaces); the other is the class that implements the API. The two interfaces are the AlbumService itself and the home object, AlbumHome. The home object is used by the naming service to get access to the distributed facade, but that's an EJB detail that I'll skip over here. Our interest is in the *Remote Facade* itself; AlbumService. Its interface is declared in the API package to be used by the client and is just a list of methods.

class AlbumService...

```
String play(String id) throws RemoteException;
String getAlbumXml(String id) throws RemoteException;
AlbumDTO getAlbum(String id) throws RemoteException;
void createAlbum(String id, String xml) throws RemoteException;
void createAlbum(String id, AlbumDTO dto) throws RemoteException;
void updateAlbum(String id, String xml) throws RemoteException;
void updateAlbum(String id, AlbumDTO dto) throws RemoteException;
void addArtistNamed(String id, String name) throws RemoteException;
void addArtist(String id, String xml) throws RemoteException;
void addArtist(String id, ArtistDTO dto) throws RemoteException;
ArtistDTO getArtist(String id) throws RemoteException;
```

Remote Facade

Notice that even in this short example I see methods for two different classes in the *Domain Model (116)*: artist and album. I also see minor variations on the same method. Methods have variants that use either the *Data Transfer Object (401)* or an XML string to move data into the remote service. This allows the client to choose which form to use depending on the nature of the client and of the connection. As you can see, for even a small application this can lead to many methods on AlbumService.

Fortunately, the methods themselves are very simple. Here are the ones for manipulating albums:

class AlbumServiceBean...

```
public AlbumDTO getAlbum(String id) throws RemoteException {
    return new AlbumAssembler().writeDTO(Registry.findAlbum(id));
}
public String getAlbumXml(String id) throws RemoteException {
    AlbumDTO dto = new AlbumAssembler().writeDTO(Registry.findAlbum(id));
    return dto.toXmlString();
}
public void createAlbum(String id, AlbumDTO dto) throws RemoteException {
    new AlbumAssembler().createAlbum(id, dto);
```

```
    }
    public void createAlbum(String id, String xml) throws RemoteException {
        AlbumDTO dto = AlbumDTO.readXmlString(xml);
        new AlbumAssembler().createAlbum(id, dto);
    }
    public void updateAlbum(String id, AlbumDTO dto) throws RemoteException {
        new AlbumAssembler().updateAlbum(id, dto);
    }
    public void updateAlbum(String id, String xml) throws RemoteException {
        AlbumDTO dto = AlbumDTO.readXmlString(xml);
        new AlbumAssembler().updateAlbum(id, dto);
    }
```

As you can see, each method really does nothing more than delegate to another object, so it's only a line or two in length. This snippet illustrates nicely what a distributed facade should look like: a long list of very short methods with very little logic in them. The facade then is nothing more than a packaging mechanism, which is as it should be.

We'll just finish with a few words on testing. It's very useful to be able to do as much testing as possible in a single process. In this case I can write tests for the session bean implementation directly: these can be run without deploying to the EJB container.

```
class XmlTester...

    private AlbumDTO kob;
    private AlbumDTO newkob;
    private AlbumServiceBean facade = new AlbumServiceBean();
    protected void setUp() throws Exception {
        facade.initializeForTesting();
        kob = facade.getAlbum("kob");
        Writer buffer = new StringWriter();
        kob.toXmlString(buffer);
        newkob = AlbumDTO.readXmlString(new StringReader(buffer.toString()));
    }
    public void testArtist() {
        assertEquals(kob.getArtist(), newkob.getArtist());
    }
```

That was one of the JUnit tests to be run in memory. It showed how I can create an instance of the session bean outside the container and run tests on it, allowing a faster testing turnaround.

Example: Web Service (C#)

I was talking over this book with Mike Hendrickson, my editor at Addison-Wesley. Ever alert to the latest buzzwords, he asked me if I had anything about Web services in it. I'm actually loathe to rush to every fashion—after

Remote Facade

all, given the languid pace of book publishing any "latest fashion" that I write about will seem quaint by the time you read about it. Still, it's a good example of how core patterns so often keep their value even with the latest technological flip-flops.

At its heart a Web service is nothing more than an interface for remote usage (with a slow string-parsing step thrown in for good measure). As such the basic advice of *Remote Facade* holds: Build your functionality in a fine-grained manner and then layer a *Remote Facade* over the fine-grained model in order to handle Web services.

For the example, I'll use the same basic problem I described previously, but concentrate just on the request for information about a single album. Figure 15.3 shows the various classes that take part. They fall into the familiar groups: album service, the *Remote Facade*; two *Data Transfer Objects (401)*; three objects in a *Domain Model (116)*; and an assembler to pull data from the *Domain Model (116)* into the *Data Transfer Objects (401)*.

The *Domain Model (116)* is absurdly simple; indeed, for this kind of problem you're better off using a *Table Data Gateway (144)* to create the *Data Transfer Objects (401)* directly. However, that would rather spoil the example of a *Remote Facade* layered over a domain model.

Remote Facade

class Album...

```
    public String Title;
    public Artist Artist;
    public IList Tracks {
        get {return ArrayList.ReadOnly(tracksData);}
    }
    public void AddTrack (Track arg) {
        tracksData.Add(arg);
    }
    public void RemoveTrack (Track arg) {
        tracksData.Remove(arg);
    }
    private IList tracksData = new ArrayList();
```

class Artist...

```
    public String Name;
```

class Track...

```
    public String Title;
    public IList Performers {
        get {return ArrayList.ReadOnly(performersData);}
    }
    public void AddPerformer (Artist arg) {
        performersData.Add(arg);
    }
```

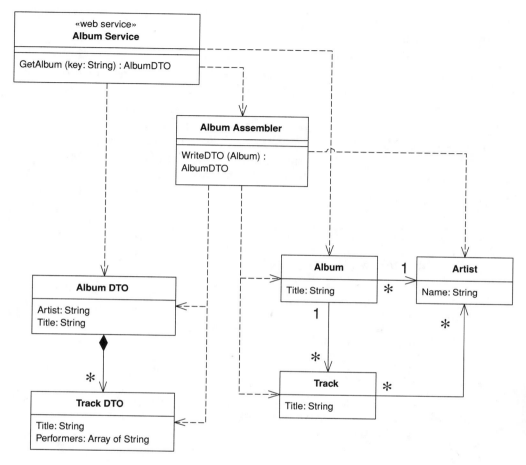

Figure 15.3 *Classes for the album Web service.*

```
public void RemovePerformer (Artist arg) {
    performersData.Remove(arg);
}
private IList performersData = new ArrayList();
```

I use *Data Transfer Objects (401)* for passing the data over the wire. These are just data holders that flatten the structure for the purposes of the Web service.

```
class AlbumDTO...

    public String Title;
    public String Artist;
    public TrackDTO[] Tracks;
```

Remote
Facade

`class TrackDTO...`

```
    public String Title;
    public String[] Performers;
```

Since this is .NET, I don't need to write any code to serialize and restore into XML. The .NET framework comes with the appropriate serializer class to do the job.

This is a Web service, so I also need to declare the structure of the *Data Transfer Objects (401)* in WSDL. The Visual Studio tools will generate the WSDL for me, and I'm a lazy kind of guy, so I'll let it do that. Here's the XML Schema definition that corresponds to the *Data Transfer Objects (401)*:

```
<s:complexType name="AlbumDTO">
  <s:sequence>
    <s:element minOccurs="1" maxOccurs="1" name="Title" nillable="true" type="s:string" />
    <s:element minOccurs="1" maxOccurs="1" name="Artist" nillable="true" type="s:string" />
    <s:element minOccurs="1" maxOccurs="1" name="Tracks"
          nillable="true" type="s0:ArrayOfTrackDTO" />
  </s:sequence>
</s:complexType>
<s:complexType name="ArrayOfTrackDTO">
  <s:sequence>
    <s:element minOccurs="0" maxOccurs="unbounded" name="TrackDTO"
          nillable="true" type="s0:TrackDTO" />
  </s:sequence>
</s:complexType>
<s:complexType name="TrackDTO">
  <s:sequence>
    <s:element minOccurs="1" maxOccurs="1" name="Title" nillable="true" type="s:string" />
    <s:element minOccurs="1" maxOccurs="1" name="Performers"
          nillable="true" type="s0:ArrayOfString" />
  </s:sequence>
</s:complexType>
<s:complexType name="ArrayOfString">
  <s:sequence>
    <s:element minOccurs="0" maxOccurs="unbounded" name="string"
          nillable="true" type="s:string" />
  </s:sequence>
</s:complexType>
```

Being XML, it's a particularly verbose data structure definition, but it does the job.

To get the data from the *Domain Model (116)* to the *Data Transfer Object (401)* I need an assembler.

`class AlbumAssembler...`

```
    public AlbumDTO WriteDTO (Album subject) {
        AlbumDTO result = new AlbumDTO();
        result.Artist = subject.Artist.Name;
```

```
        result.Title = subject.Title;
        ArrayList trackList = new ArrayList();
        foreach (Track t in subject.Tracks)
           trackList.Add (WriteTrack(t));
        result.Tracks = (TrackDTO[]) trackList.ToArray(typeof(TrackDTO));
        return result;
    }
    public TrackDTO WriteTrack (Track subject) {
        TrackDTO result = new TrackDTO();
        result.Title = subject.Title;
        result.Performers = new String[subject.Performers.Count];
        ArrayList performerList = new ArrayList();
        foreach (Artist a in subject.Performers)
           performerList.Add (a.Name);
        result.Performers = (String[]) performerList.ToArray(typeof (String));
        return result;
    }
```

The last piece we need is the service definition itself. This comes first from the C# class.

class AlbumService...

```
    [ WebMethod ]
    public AlbumDTO GetAlbum(String key) {
        Album result = new AlbumFinder()[key];
        if (result == null)
            throw new SoapException ("unable to find album with key: " +
                        key, SoapException.ClientFaultCode);
        else return new AlbumAssembler().WriteDTO(result);
    }
```

Remote Facade

Of course, this isn't the real interface definition—that comes from the WSDL file. Here are the relevant bits:

```
<portType name="AlbumServiceSoap">
   <operation name="GetAlbum">
     <input message="s0:GetAlbumSoapIn" />
     <output message="s0:GetAlbumSoapOut" />
    </operation>
</portType>
<message name="GetAlbumSoapIn">
   <part name="parameters" element="s0:GetAlbum" />
</message>
<message name="GetAlbumSoapOut">
   <part name="parameters" element="s0:GetAlbumResponse" />
</message>
<s:element name="GetAlbum">
   <s:complexType>
     <s:sequence>
       <s:element minOccurs="1" maxOccurs="1" name="key" nillable="true" type="s:string" />
     </s:sequence>
   </s:complexType>
```

```
</s:element>
<s:element name="GetAlbumResponse">
  <s:complexType>
    <s:sequence>
      <s:element minOccurs="1" maxOccurs="1" name="GetAlbumResult"
            nillable="true" type="s0:AlbumDTO" />
    </s:sequence>
  </s:complexType>
</s:element>
```

As expected, WSDL is rather more garrulous than your average politician, but unlike so many of them, it does get the job done. I can now invoke the service by sending a SOAP message of the form

```
<?xml version="1.0" encoding="utf-8"?>
<soap:Envelope xmlns:xsi="http://www.w3.org/2001/XMLSchema-instance"
        xmlns:xsd="http://www.w3.org/2001/XMLSchema"
        xmlns:soap="http://schemas.xmlsoap.org/soap/envelope/">
  <soap:Body>
    <GetAlbum xmlns="http://martinfowler.com">
      <key>aKeyString</key>
    </GetAlbum>
  </soap:Body>
</soap:Envelope>
```

The important thing to remember about this example isn't the cool gyrations with SOAP and .NET but the fundamental layering approach. Design an application without distribution, then layer the distribution ability on top of it with *Remote Facades* and *Data Transfer Objects (401)*.

Remote Facade

Data Transfer Object

*An object that carries data between processes in order
to reduce the number of method calls.*

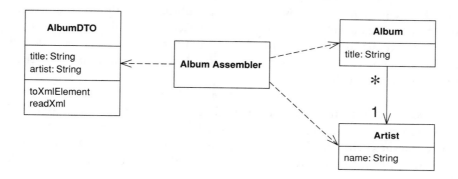

When you're working with a remote interface, such as *Remote Facade (388)*, each call to it is expensive. As a result you need to reduce the number of calls, and that means that you need to transfer more data with each call. One way to do this is to use lots of parameters. However, this is often awkward to program—indeed, it's often impossible with languages such as Java that return only a single value.

The solution is to create a *Data Transfer Object* that can hold all the data for the call. It needs to be serializable to go across the connection. Usually an assembler is used on the server side to transfer data between the DTO and any domain objects.

Many people in the Sun community use the term "Value Object" for this pattern. I use it to mean something else. See the discussion on page 487.

**Data Transfer
Object**

How It Works

In many ways, a *Data Transfer Object* is one of those objects our mothers told us never to write. It's often little more than a bunch of fields and the getters and setters for them. The value of this usually hateful beast is that it allows you to move several pieces of information over a network in a single call—a trick that's essential for distributed systems.

Whenever a remote object needs some data, it asks for a suitable *Data Transfer Object*. The *Data Transfer Object* will usually carries much more data than what the remote object requested, but it should carry all the data the remote object will need for a while. Due to the latency costs of remote calls, its better to err on the side of sending too much data than have to make multiple calls.

A single *Data Transfer Object* usually contains more than just a single server object. It aggregates data from all the server objects that the remote object is likely to want data from. Thus, if a remote object requests data about an order object, the returned *Data Transfer Object* will contain data from the order, the customer, the line items, the products on the line items, the delivery information—all sorts of stuff.

You can't usually transfer objects from a *Domain Model (116)*. This is because the objects are usually connected in a complex web that's difficult, if not impossible, to serialize. Also you usually don't want the domain object classes on the client, which is tantamount to copying the whole *Domain Model (116)* there. Instead you have to transfer a simplified form of the data from the domain objects.

The fields in a *Data Transfer Object* are fairly simple, being primitives, simple classes like strings and dates, or other *Data Transfer Objects*. Any structure between data transfer objects should be a simple graph structure—normally a hierarchy—as opposed to the more complicated graph structures that you see in a *Domain Model (116)*. Keep these simple attributes because they have to be serializable and they need to be understood by both sides of the wire. As a result the *Data Transfer Object* classes and any classes they reference must be present on both sides.

Data Transfer Object

It makes sense to design the *Data Transfer Object* around the needs of a particular client. That's why you often see them corresponding to Web pages or GUI screens. You may also see multiple *Data Transfer Objects* for an order, depending on the particular screen. Of course, if different presentations require similar data, then it makes sense to use a single *Data Transfer Object* to handle them all.

A related question to consider is using a single *Data Transfer Object* for a whole interaction versus different ones for each request. Different *Data Transfer Objects* make it easier to see what data is transferred in each call, but leads to a lot of *Data Transfer Objects*. One is less work to write, but makes it harder to see how each call transfers information. I'm inclined to use just one if there's a lot of commonality over the data, but I don't hesitate to use different *Data Transfer Objects* if a particular request suggests it. It's one of those things you can't make a blanket rule about, so I might use one *Data Transfer Object* for most of the interaction and use different ones for a couple of requests and responses.

A similar question is whether to have a single *Data Transfer Object* for both request and response or separate ones for each. Again, there's no blanket rule. If the data in each case is pretty similar, use one. If they're very different, I use two.

Some people like to make *Data Transfer Objects* immutable. In this scheme you receive one *Data Transfer Object* from the client and create and send back a different one, even if it's the same class. Other people alter the request *Data Transfer Object*. I don't have any strong opinions either way, but on the whole I prefer a mutable *Data Transfer Object* because it's easier to put the data in gradually, even if you make a new object for the response. Some arguments in favor of immutable *Data Transfer Object* have to do with the naming confusion with *Value Object (486)*.

A common form for *Data Transfer Object* is that of a *Record Set (508)*, that is, a set of tabular records—exactly what you get back from a SQL query. Indeed, a *Record Set (508)* is the *Data Transfer Object* for a SQL database. Architectures often use it throughout the design. A domain model can generate a *Record Set (508)* of data to transfer to a client, which the client treats as if it was coming directly from SQL. This is useful if the client has tools that bind to *Record Set (508)* structures. The *Record Set (508)* can be entirely created by the domain logic, but more likely it's generated from a SQL query and modified by the domain logic before it's passed on to the presentation. This style lends itself to *Table Module (125)*.

Another form of *Data Transfer Object* is as a generic collection data structure. I've seen arrays used for this, but I discourage that because the array indices obscure the code. The best collection is a dictionary because you can use meaningful strings as keys. The problem is that you lose the advantage of an explicit interface and strong typing. A dictionary can be worth using for ad hoc cases when you don't have a generator at hand, as it's easier to manipulate one than to write an explicit object by hand. However, with a generator I think you're better off with an explicit interface, especially when you consider that it is being used as communication protocol between different components.

Serializing the *Data Transfer Object* Other than simple getters and setters, the *Data Transfer Object* is also usually responsible for serializing itself into some format that will go over the wire. Which format depends on what's on either side of the connection, what can run over the connection itself, and how easy the serialization is. A number of platforms provide built in serialization for simple objects. For example, Java has a built-in binary serialization and .NET has built-in binary and XML serializations. If there's a built-in serialization, it usually works right out of the box because *Data Transfer Objects* are simple structures that don't deal with the complexities you run into with objects in a domain model. As a result I always use the automatic mechanism if I can.

If you don't have an automatic mechanism, you can usually create one yourself. I've seen several code generators that take a simple record descriptions and generate appropriate classes to hold the data, provide accessors, and read and write the data serializations. The important thing is to make the generator only as complicated as you actually need it to be, and don't try to put in features you only think you'll need. It can be a good idea to write the first classes by hand and then use them to help you write the generator.

You can also use reflective programming to handle the serialization. That way you only have to write the serialization and deserialization routines once and put them in a superclass. There may be a performance cost to this; you'll have to measure it to find out if the cost is significant.

You have to choose a mechanism that both ends of the connection will work with. If you control both ends, you pick the easiest one; if you don't, you may be able to provide a connector at the end you don't own. Then you can use a simple *Data Transfer Object* on both sides of the connection and use the connector to adapt to the foreign component.

One of the most common issues you face with Data Transfer Object is whether to use a text or a binary serialization form. Text serializations are easy to read to learn what's being communicated. XML is popular because you can easily get tools to create and parse XML documents. The big disadvantages with text are that it needs more bandwidth to send the same data (something particularly true of XML) and there's often a performance penalty, which can be quite significant.

An important factor for serialization is the synchronization of the *Data Transfer Object* on each side of the wire. In theory, whenever the server changes the definition of the *Data Transfer Object,* the client updates as well but in practice this may not happen. Accessing a server with an out-of-date client always leads to problems, but the serialization mechanism can make the problems more or less painful. With a pure binary serialization of a *Data Transfer Object* the result will be that its communication is entirely lost, since any change to its structure usually causes an error on deserialization. Even an innocuous change, such as adding an optional field, will have this effect. As a result direct binary serialization can introduce a lot of fragility into the communication lines.

Data Transfer Object

Other serialization schemes can avoid this. One is XML serialization, which can usually be written in a way that makes the classes more tolerant of changes. Another is a more tolerant binary approach, such as serializing the data using a dictionary. Although I don't like using a dictionary as the *Data Transfer Object*, it can be a useful way of doing a binary serialization of the data, since that introduces some tolerance into the synchronization.

Assembling a *Data Transfer Object* from Domain Objects   A *Data Transfer Object* doesn't know about how to connect with domain objects. This is because it should be deployed on both sides of the connection. For that reason I don't want the *Data Transfer Object* to be dependent on the domain object. Nor do I want the domain objects to be dependent of the *Data Transfer Object* since the *Data Transfer Object* structure will change when I alter interface formats. As a general rule, I want to keep the domain model independent of the external interfaces.

As a result I like to make a separate assembler object responsible for creating a *Data Transfer Object* from the domain model and updating the model from it (Figure 15.4). The assembler is an example of a *Mapper (473)* in that it maps between the *Data Transfer Object* and the domain objects.

I may also have multiple assemblers share the same *Data Transfer Object*. A common case for this is different update semantics in different scenarios using

Data Transfer Object

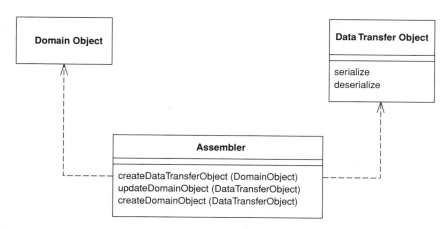

Figure 15.4 *An assembler object can keep the domain model and the data transfer objects independent of each other.*

the same data. Another reason to separate the assembler is that the *Data Transfer Object* can easily be generated automatically from a simple data description. Generating the assembler is more difficult and indeed often impossible.

When to Use It

Use a *Data Transfer Object* whenever you need to transfer multiple items of data between two processes in a single method call.

There are some alternatives to *Data Transfer Object*, although I'm not a fan of them. One is to not use an object at all but simply to use a setting method with many arguments or a getting method with several pass-by reference arguments. The problem is that many languages, such as Java, allow only one object as a return value, so, although this can be used for updates, it can't be used for retrieving information without playing games with callbacks.

Another alternative is to use a some form of string representation directly, without an object acting as the interface to it. Here the problem is that everything else is coupled to the string representation. It's good to hide the precise representation behind an explicit interface; that way, if you want to change the string or replace it with a binary structure, you don't have to change anything else.

In particular, it's worth creating a *Data Transfer Object* when you want to communicate between components using XML. The XML DOM is a pain in the neck to manipulate, and it's much better to use a *Data Transfer Object* that encapsulates it, especially since the *Data Transfer Object* is so easy to generate.

Another common purpose for a *Data Transfer Object* is to act as a common source of data for various components in different layers. Each component makes some changes to the *Data Transfer Object* and then passes it on to the next layer. The use of *Record Set (508)* in COM and .NET is a good example of this, where each layer knows how to manipulate record set based data, whether it comes directly from a SQL database or has been modified by other layers. .NET expands on this by providing a built-in mechanism to serialize record sets into XML.

Although this book focuses on synchronous systems, there's an interesting asynchronous use for *Data Transfer Object*. This is where you want to use an interface both synchronously and asynchronously. Return a *Data Transfer Object* as usual for the synchronous case; for the asynchronous case create a *Lazy Load (200)* of the *Data Transfer Object* and return that. Connect the *Lazy Load (200)* to wherever the results from the asynchronous call should appear. The user of the *Data Transfer Object* will block only when it tries to access the results of the call.

Data Transfer Object

Further Reading

[Alur et al.] discuss this pattern under the name *Value Object*, which I said earlier is equivalent to my *Data Transfer Object*; my *Value Object (486)* is a different pattern entirely. This is a name collision; many people have used "Value Object" in the sense that I use it. As far as I can tell, its use to mean what I call *Data Transfer Object* occurs only within the J2EE community. As a result, I've followed the more general usage.

The Value Object Assembler [Alur et al.] is a discussion of the assembler. I chose not to make it a separate pattern, although I use the "assembler" name rather than a name based on *Mapper (473)*.

[Marinescu] discusses *Data Transfer Object* and several implementation variants. [Riehle et al.] discuss flexible ways to serialize, including switching between different forms of serialization.

Example: Transferring Information About Albums (Java)

For this example I'll use the domain model in Figure 15.5. The data I want to transfer is the data about these linked objects, and the structure for the data transfer objects is the one in Figure 15.6.

The data transfer objects simplify this structure a good bit. The relevant data from the artist class is collapsed into the album DTO, and the performers for a track are represented as an array of strings. This is typical of the collapsing of

Data Transfer Object

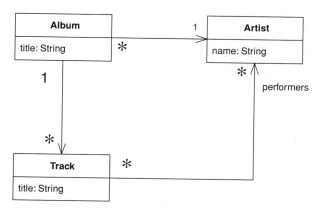

Figure 15.5 *A class diagram of artists and albums.*

Figure 15.6 *A class diagram of data transfer objects.*

structure you see for a data transfer object. There are two data transfer objects present, one for the album and one for each track. In this case I don't need one for the artist, as all the data is present on one of the other two. I only have the track as a transfer object because there are several tracks in the album and each one can contain more than one data item.

Here's the code to write a *Data Transfer Object* from the domain model. The assembler is called by whatever object is handling the remote interface, such as a *Remote Facade (388)*.

```
class AlbumAssembler...

    public AlbumDTO writeDTO(Album subject) {
        AlbumDTO result = new AlbumDTO();
        result.setTitle(subject.getTitle());
        result.setArtist(subject.getArtist().getName());
        writeTracks(result, subject);
        return result;
    }
    private void writeTracks(AlbumDTO result, Album subject) {
        List newTracks = new ArrayList();
        Iterator it = subject.getTracks().iterator();
        while (it.hasNext()) {
            TrackDTO newDTO = new TrackDTO();
            Track thisTrack = (Track) it.next();
            newDTO.setTitle(thisTrack.getTitle());
            writePerformers(newDTO, thisTrack);
            newTracks.add(newDTO);
        }
        result.setTracks((TrackDTO[]) newTracks.toArray(new TrackDTO[0]));
    }
    private void writePerformers(TrackDTO dto, Track subject) {
        List result = new ArrayList();
        Iterator it = subject.getPerformers().iterator();
        while (it.hasNext()) {
            Artist each = (Artist) it.next();
            result.add(each.getName());
        }
        dto.setPerformers((String[]) result.toArray(new String[0]));
    }
```

Data Transfer Object

Updating the model from the *Data Transfer Object* is usually more involved. For this example there's a difference between creating a new album and updating an existing one. Here's the creation code:

```
class AlbumAssembler...

    public void createAlbum(String id, AlbumDTO source) {
        Artist artist = Registry.findArtistNamed(source.getArtist());
        if (artist == null)
            throw new RuntimeException("No artist named " + source.getArtist());
        Album album = new Album(source.getTitle(), artist);
        createTracks(source.getTracks(), album);
        Registry.addAlbum(id, album);
    }
    private void createTracks(TrackDTO[] tracks, Album album) {
        for (int i = 0; i < tracks.length; i++) {
            Track newTrack = new Track(tracks[i].getTitle());
            album.addTrack(newTrack);
            createPerformers(newTrack, tracks[i].getPerformers());
        }
    }
    private void createPerformers(Track newTrack, String[] performerArray) {
        for (int i = 0; i < performerArray.length; i++) {
            Artist performer = Registry.findArtistNamed(performerArray[i]);
            if (performer == null)
                throw new RuntimeException("No artist named " + performerArray[i]);
            newTrack.addPerformer(performer);
        }
    }
```

Reading the DTO involves quite a few decisions. Noticeable here is how to deal with the artist names as they come in. My requirements are that artists should already be in a *Registry (480)* when I create the album, so if I can't find an artist this is an error. A different create method might decide to create artists when they're mentioned in the *Data Transfer Object*.

For this example I have a different method for updating an existing album.

```
class AlbumAssembler...

    public void updateAlbum(String id, AlbumDTO source) {
        Album current = Registry.findAlbum(id);
        if (current == null)
            throw new RuntimeException("Album does not exist: " + source.getTitle());
        if (source.getTitle() != current.getTitle()) current.setTitle(source.getTitle());
        if (source.getArtist() != current.getArtist().getName()) {
            Artist artist = Registry.findArtistNamed(source.getArtist());
            if (artist == null)
                throw new RuntimeException("No artist named " + source.getArtist());
            current.setArtist(artist);
        }
        updateTracks(source, current);
```

Data Transfer Object

```
    }
    private void updateTracks(AlbumDTO source, Album current) {
        for (int i = 0; i < source.getTracks().length; i++) {
            current.getTrack(i).setTitle(source.getTrackDTO(i).getTitle());
            current.getTrack(i).clearPerformers();
            createPerformers(current.getTrack(i), source.getTrackDTO(i).getPerformers());
        }
    }
```

As for updates you can decide to either update the existing domain object or destroy it and replace it with a new one. The question here is whether you have other objects referring to the object you want to update. In this code I'm updating the album since I have other objects referring to it and its tracks. However, for the title and performers of a track I just replace the objects that are there.

Another question concerns an artist changing. Is this changing the name of the existing artist or changing the artist the album is linked to? Again, these questions have to be settled on a case-by-use case basis, and I'm handling it by linking to a new artist.

In this example I've used native binary serialization, which means I have to be careful that the *Data Transfer Object* classes on both sides of the wire are kept in sync. If I make a change to the data structure of the server *Data Transfer Object* and don't change the client, I'll get errors in the transfer. I can make the transfer more tolerant by using a map as my serialization.

Data Transfer Object

```
class TrackDTO...

    public Map writeMap() {
        Map result = new HashMap();
        result.put("title", title);
        result.put("performers", performers);
        return result;
    }
    public static TrackDTO readMap(Map arg) {
        TrackDTO result = new TrackDTO();
        result.title = (String) arg.get("title");
        result.performers = (String[]) arg.get("performers");
        return result;
    }
```

Now, if I add a field to the server and use the old client, although the new field won't be picked up by the client, the rest of the data will transfer correctly.

Of course, writing the serialization and deserialization routines like this is tedious. I can avoid much of this tedium by using a reflective routine such as this on the *Layer Supertype (475)*:

```
class DataTransferObject...

  public Map writeMapReflect() {
     Map result = null;
     try {
        Field[] fields = this.getClass().getDeclaredFields();
        result = new HashMap();
        for (int i = 0; i < fields.length; i++)
            result.put(fields[i].getName(), fields[i].get(this));
     } catch (Exception e) {throw new ApplicationException (e);
     }
     return result;
  }
  public static TrackDTO readMapReflect(Map arg) {
     TrackDTO result = new TrackDTO();
     try {
        Field[] fields = result.getClass().getDeclaredFields();
        for (int i = 0; i < fields.length; i++)
            fields[i].set(result, arg.get(fields[i].getName()));
     } catch (Exception e) {throw new ApplicationException (e);
     }
     return result;
  }
```

Such a routine will handle most cases pretty well (although you'll have to add extra code to handle primitives).

Data Transfer Object

Example: Serializing Using XML (Java)

As I write this, Java's XML handling is very much in flux and APIs, still volatile, are generally getting better. By the time you read it this section may be out of date or completely irrelevant, but the basic concept of converting to XML is pretty much the same.

First I get the data structure for the *Data Transfer Object*; then I need to decide how to serialize it. In Java you get free binary serialization simply by using a marker interface. This works completely automatically for a *Data Transfer Object* so it's my first choice. However, text-based serialization is often necessary. For this example then, I'll use XML.

For this example, I'm using JDOM since that makes working with XML much easier than using the W3C standard interfaces. I write methods to read and write an XML element to represent that class each *Data Transfer Object* class.

class AlbumDTO...

```
Element toXmlElement() {
    Element root = new Element("album");
    root.setAttribute("title", title);
    root.setAttribute("artist", artist);
    for (int i = 0; i < tracks.length; i++)
        root.addContent(tracks[i].toXmlElement());
    return root;
}
static AlbumDTO readXml(Element source) {
    AlbumDTO result = new AlbumDTO();
    result.setTitle(source.getAttributeValue("title"));
    result.setArtist(source.getAttributeValue("artist"));
    List trackList = new ArrayList();
    Iterator it = source.getChildren("track").iterator();
    while (it.hasNext())
        trackList.add(TrackDTO.readXml((Element) it.next()));
    result.setTracks((TrackDTO[]) trackList.toArray(new TrackDTO[0]));
    return result;
}
```

class TrackDTO...

**Data Transfer
Object**

```
Element toXmlElement() {
    Element result = new Element("track");
    result.setAttribute("title", title);
    for (int i = 0; i < performers.length; i++) {
        Element performerElement = new Element("performer");
        performerElement.setAttribute("name", performers[i]);
        result.addContent(performerElement);
    }
    return result;
}
static TrackDTO readXml(Element arg) {
    TrackDTO result = new TrackDTO();
    result.setTitle(arg.getAttributeValue("title"));
    Iterator it = arg.getChildren("performer").iterator();
    List buffer = new ArrayList();
    while (it.hasNext()) {
        Element eachElement = (Element) it.next();
        buffer.add(eachElement.getAttributeValue("name"));
    }
    result.setPerformers((String[]) buffer.toArray(new String[0]));
    return result;
}
```

Of course, these methods only create the elements in the XML DOM. To perform the serialization I need to read and write text. Since the track is transferred only in the context of the album, I just need to write this album code.

class AlbumDTO...

```java
    public void toXmlString(Writer output) {
        Element root = toXmlElement();
        Document doc = new Document(root);
        XMLOutputter writer = new XMLOutputter();
        try {
            writer.output(doc, output);
        } catch (IOException e) {
            e.printStackTrace();
        }
    }
    public static AlbumDTO readXmlString(Reader input) {
        try {
            SAXBuilder builder = new SAXBuilder();
            Document doc = builder.build(input);
            Element root = doc.getRootElement();
            AlbumDTO result = readXml(root);
            return result;
        } catch (Exception e) {
            e.printStackTrace();
            throw new RuntimeException();
        }
    }
```

Although it isn't rocket science, I'll be glad when JAXB makes this kind of stuff unnecessary.

Data Transfer Object

Chapter 16

Offline Concurrency Patterns

Optimistic Offline Lock

by David Rice

*Prevents conflicts between concurrent business transactions
by detecting a conflict and rolling back the transaction.*

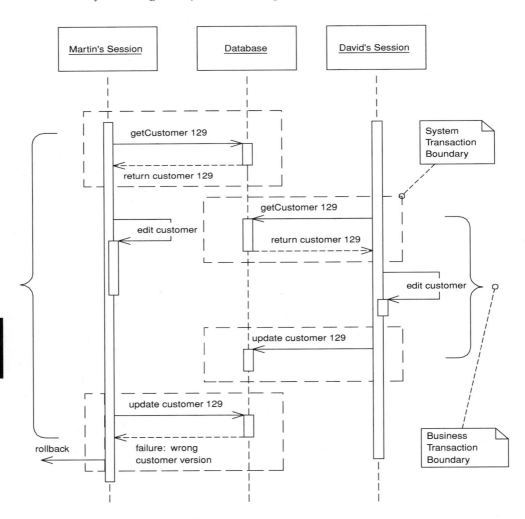

**Optimistic
Offline Lock**

Often a business transaction executes across a series of system transactions. Once outside the confines of a single system transaction, we can't depend on our database manager alone to ensure that the business transaction will leave the record data in a consistent state. Data integrity is at risk once two sessions begin to work on the same records and lost updates are quite possible. Also, with one session editing data that another is reading an inconsistent read becomes likely.

Optimistic Offline Lock solves this problem by validating that the changes about to be committed by one session don't conflict with the changes of another session. A successful pre-commit validation is, in a sense, obtaining a lock indicating it's okay to go ahead with the changes to the record data. So long as the validation and the updates occur within a single system transaction the business transaction will display consistency.

Whereas *Pessimistic Offline Lock (426)* assumes that the chance of session conflict is high and therefore limits the system's concurrency, *Optimistic Offline Lock* assumes that the chance of conflict is low. The expectation that session conflict isn't likely allows multiple users to work with the same data at the same time.

How It Works

An *Optimistic Offline Lock* is obtained by validating that, in the time since a session loaded a record, another session hasn't altered it. It can be acquired at any time but is valid only during the system transaction in which it is obtained. Thus, in order that a business transaction not corrupt record data it must acquire an *Optimistic Offline Lock* for each member of its change set during the system transaction in which it applies changes to the database.

The most common implementation is to associate a version number with each record in your system. When a record is loaded that number is maintained by the session along with all other session state. Getting the *Optimistic Offline Lock* is a matter of comparing the version stored in your session data to the current version in the record data. Once the verification succeeds, all changes, including an increment of the version, can be committed. The version increment is what prevents inconsistent record data, as a session with an old version can't acquire the lock.

With an RDBMS data store the verification is a matter of adding the version number to the criteria of any SQL statements used to update or delete a record. A single SQL statement can both acquire the lock and update the record data. The final step is for the business transaction to inspect the row count returned

Optimistic Offline Lock

by the SQL execution. A row count of 1 indicates success; 0 indicates that the record has been changed or deleted. With a row count of 0 the business transaction must rollback the system transaction to prevent any changes from entering the record data. At this point the business transaction must either abort or attempt to resolve the conflict and retry.

In addition to a version number for each record, storing information as to who last modified a record and when can be quite useful when managing concurrency conflicts. When informing a user of a failed update due to a concurrency violation a proper application will tell when the record was altered and by whom. It's a bad idea to use the modification timestamp rather than a version count for your optimistic checks because system clocks are simply too unreliable, especially if you're coordinating across multiple servers.

In an alternative implementation the where clause in the update includes every field in the row. The advantage here is that you can use the where clause without using some form of version field, which can be handy if you can't add a version field by altering the database tables. The problem is that this complicates the UPDATE statement with a potentially large where clause, which may also be a performance impact depending on how clever the database is about using the primary key index.

Optimistic Offline Lock

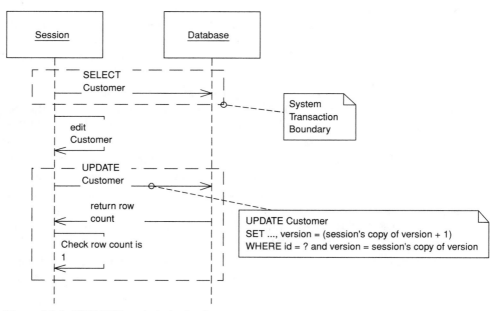

Figure 16.1 *UPDATE optimistic check.*

Often implementing *Optimistic Offline Lock* is left at including the version in UPDATE and DELETE statements, but this fails to address the problem of an inconsistent read. Think of a billing system that creates charges and calculates appropriate sales tax. A session creates the charge and then looks up the customer's address to calculate the tax on it, but during the charge generation session a separate customer maintenance session edits the customer's address. As tax rates depend on location, the rate calculated by the charge generation session might be invalid, but since the charge generation session didn't make any changes to the address the conflict won't be detected.

There's no reason why *Optimistic Offline Lock* can't be used to detect an inconsistent read. In the example above the charge generation session needs to recognize that its correctness depends on the value of the customer's address. It therefore should perform a version check on the address as well, perhaps by adding the address to the change set or maintaining a separate list of items to be version-checked. The latter requires a bit more work to set up, but results in code that more clearly states its intent. If you're checking for a consistent read simply by rereading the version rather than an artificial update, be especially aware of your system transaction isolation level. The version reread will only work with repeatable read or stronger isolation. Anything weaker requires an increment of the version.

A version check might be overkill for certain inconsistent read problems. Often a transaction depends only on the presence of a record or maybe the value of only one of its fields. In such a case you might improve your system's liveliness by checking conditions rather than the version, as fewer concurrent updates will result in the failure of competing business transactions. The better you understand your concurrency issues, the better you can manage them in your code.

The *Coarse-Grained Lock (438)* can help with certain inconsistent read conundrums by treating a group of objects as a single lockable item. Another option is to simply execute all of the steps of the problematic business transaction within a long-running transaction. The ease of implementation might prove worth the resource hit of using a few long transactions here and there.

Optimistic Offline Lock

Detection of an inconsistent read gets a bit difficult when your transaction is dependent on the results of a dynamic query rather than the reading of specific records. It's possible for you to save the initial results and compare them to the results of the same query at commit time as a means of obtaining an *Optimistic Offline Lock*.

As with all locking schemes, *Optimistic Offline Lock* by itself doesn't provide adequate solutions to some of the trickier concurrency and temporal issues in a business application. I can't stress enough that in a business application concurrency management is as much a domain issue as it is a technical one. Is the customer address scenario above really a conflict? It might be okay that I calculated the sales tax with an older version of the customer, but which version should I actually be using? This is a business issue. Or consider a collection. What if two sessions simultaneously add items to a collection? The typical *Optimistic Offline Lock* scheme won't prevent this even though it might very well be a violation of business rules.

There's one system using *Optimistic Offline Locks* that we all should be familiar with: source code management (SCM). When an SCM system detects a conflict between programmers it usually can figure out the correct merge and retry the commit. A quality merge strategy makes *Optimistic Offline Lock* very powerful not only because the system's concurrency is quite high but because users rarely have to redo any work. Of course, the big difference between an SCM system and an enterprise business application is that the SCM must implement only one type of merge while the business system might implement hundreds. Some might be of such complexity that they're not worth the cost of coding. Others might be of such value to the business that the merge should be coded by all means. Despite rarely being done, the merging of business objects is possible. In fact, merging business data is a pattern unto its own. I'll leave it at that rather than butcher the topic, but do understand the power that merging adds to *Optimistic Offline Lock*.

Optimistic Offline Lock only lets us know during the last system transaction if a business transaction will commit. But it's occasionally useful to know earlier if a conflict has occurred. For this you can provide a checkCurrent method that checks if anyone else has updated the data. It can't guarantee that you won't get a conflict, but it may be worthwhile to stop a complicated process if you can tell in advance that it won't commit. Use this checkCurrent at any time that failing early may be useful, but remember that it never guarantees that you won't fail at commit time.

Optimistic Offline Lock

When to Use It

Optimistic concurrency management is appropriate when the chance of conflict between any two business transactions is low. If conflicts are likely it's not user friendly to announce one only when the user has finished his work and is ready to commit. Eventually he'll assume the failure of business transactions and stop using the system. *Pessimistic Offline Lock (426)* is more appropriate when the chance of conflict is high or the expense of a conflict is unacceptable.

As optimistic locking is much easier to implement and not prone to the same defects and runtime errors as a *Pessimistic Offline Lock (426)*, consider using it as the default approach to business transaction conflict management in any system you build. The pessimistic version works well as a complement to its optimistic counterpart, so rather than asking when to use an optimistic approach to conflict avoidance, ask when the optimistic approach alone isn't good enough. The correct approach to concurrency management will maximize concurrent access to data while minimizing conflicts.

Example: Domain Layer with *Data Mappers (165)* (Java)

The shortest example of *Optimistic Offline Lock* would involve only a database table with a version column and UPDATE and DELETE statements that use that version as part of their update criteria. Of course, you'll be building more sophisticated applications so I present an implementation using a *Domain Model (116)* and *Data Mappers (165)*. This will reveal more of the issues that commonly arise when implementing *Optimistic Offline Lock*.

One of the first things to do is to make sure that your domain *Layer Supertype (475)* is capable of storing any information required to implement *Optimistic Offline Lock*—namely, modification and version data.

```
class DomainObject...

    private Timestamp modified;
    private String modifiedBy;
    private int version;
```

Our data is stored in a relational database, so each table must also store version and modification data. Here's the schema for a customer table as well as the standard CRUD SQL necessary to support the *Optimistic Offline Lock*:

```
table customer...

    create table customer(id bigint primary key, name varchar, createdby varchar,
        created datetime, modifiedby varchar, modified datetime, version int)

SQL customer CRUD...

    INSERT INTO customer VALUES (?, ?, ?, ?, ?, ?, ?)
    SELECT * FROM customer WHERE id = ?
    UPDATE customer SET name = ?, modifiedBy = ?, modified = ?, version = ?
        WHERE id = ? and version = ?
    DELETE FROM customer WHERE id = ? and version = ?
```

Once you have more than a few tables and domain objects, you'll want to introduce a *Layer Supertype (475)* for your *Data Mappers (165)* that handles the tedious, repetitive segments of O/R mapping. This not only saves a lot of work when writing *Data Mappers (165)* but also allows the use of an *Implicit Lock (449)* to prevent a developer from subverting a locking strategy by forgetting to code a bit of locking mechanics.

The first piece to move into your abstract mapper is SQL construction. This requires that you provide mappers with a bit of metadata about your tables. An alternative to having your mapper build SQL at runtime is to code-generate it. However, I'll leave the construction of SQL statements as an exercise for the reader. In the abstract mapper below you'll see that I've made a number of assumptions about the column names and positions for our modification data. This becomes less feasible with legacy data. The abstract mapper will likely require a bit of column metadata to be supplied by each concrete mapper.

Once the abstract mapper has SQL statements it can manage the CRUD operations. Here's how a find executes:

```
class AbstractMapper...

    public AbstractMapper(String table, String[] columns) {
        this.table = table;
        this.columns = columns;
        buildStatements();
    }
    public DomainObject find(Long id) {
        DomainObject obj = AppSessionManager.getSession().getIdentityMap().get(id);
        if (obj == null) {
            Connection conn = null;
            PreparedStatement stmt = null;
            ResultSet rs = null;
            try {
                conn = ConnectionManager.INSTANCE.getConnection();
                stmt = conn.prepareStatement(loadSQL);
                stmt.setLong(1, id.longValue());
                rs = stmt.executeQuery();
                if (rs.next()) {
                    obj = load(id, rs);
                    String modifiedBy = rs.getString(columns.length + 2);
                    Timestamp modified = rs.getTimestamp(columns.length + 3);
                    int version = rs.getInt(columns.length + 4);
                    obj.setSystemFields(modified, modifiedBy, version);
                    AppSessionManager.getSession().getIdentityMap().put(obj);
                } else {
                    throw new SystemException(table + " " + id + " does not exist");
                }
            } catch (SQLException sqlEx) {
                throw new SystemException("unexpected error finding " + table + " " + id);
            } finally {
                cleanupDBResources(rs, conn, stmt);
            }
        }
        return obj;
    }
    protected abstract DomainObject load(Long id, ResultSet rs) throws SQLException;
```

Optimistic
Offline Lock

There are a few items of note here. First, the mapper checks an *Identity Map (195)* to make sure that the object isn't loaded already. Not using an *Identity Map (195)* could result in different versions of an object being loaded at different times in a business transaction, leading to undefined behavior in your application as well as make a mess of any version checks. Once a result set is obtained the mapper defers to an abstract load method that each concrete mapper must implement to extract its fields and return an activated object. The mapper calls setSystemFields() to set the version and modification data on the abstract domain object. While a constructor might seem the more appropriate means of passing this data, doing so would push part of the version storage responsibility down to each concrete mapper and domain object and thus weaken the *Implicit Lock (449)*.

Here's what a concrete load() method looks like:

```
class CustomerMapper extends AbstractMapper...

    protected DomainObject load(Long id, ResultSet rs) throws SQLException {
        String name = rs.getString(2);
        return Customer.activate(id, name, addresses);
    }
```

The abstract mapper will similarly manage execution of update and delete operations. The job here is to check that the database operation returns a row count of 1. If no rows have been updated, the optimistic lock can't be obtained and the mapper must then throw a concurrency exception. Here is the delete operation:

```
class class AbstractMapper...

    public void delete(DomainObject object) {
        AppSessionManager.getSession().getIdentityMap().remove(object.getId());
        Connection conn = null;
        PreparedStatement stmt = null;
        try {
            conn = ConnectionManager.INSTANCE.getConnection();
            stmt = conn.prepareStatement(deleteSQL);
            stmt.setLong(1, object.getId().longValue());
            int rowCount = stmt.executeUpdate();
            if (rowCount == 0) {
                throwConcurrencyException(object);
            }
        } catch (SQLException e) {
            throw new SystemException("unexpected error deleting");
        } finally {
            cleanupDBResources(conn, stmt);
        }
    }
```

**Optimistic
Offline Lock**

```
protected void throwConcurrencyException(DomainObject object) throws SQLException {
    Connection conn = null;
    PreparedStatement stmt = null;
    ResultSet rs = null;
    try {
        conn = ConnectionManager.INSTANCE.getConnection();
        stmt = conn.prepareStatement(checkVersionSQL);
        stmt.setInt(1, (int) object.getId().longValue());
        rs = stmt.executeQuery();
        if (rs.next()) {
            int version = rs.getInt(1);
            String modifiedBy = rs.getString(2);
            Timestamp modified = rs.getTimestamp(3);
            if (version > object.getVersion()) {
                String when = DateFormat.getDateTimeInstance().format(modified);
                throw new ConcurrencyException(table + " " + object.getId() +
                    " modified by " + modifiedBy + " at " + when);
            } else {
                throw new SystemException("unexpected error checking timestamp");
            }
        } else {
            throw new ConcurrencyException(table + " " + object.getId() +
                " has been deleted");
        }
    } finally {
        cleanupDBResources(rs, conn, stmt);
    }
}
```

The SQL used to check the version in a concurrency exception also needs to be known by the abstract mapper. Your mapper should construct it when it constructs the CRUD SQL. It will look something like this:

checkVersionSQL...

```
SELECT version, modifiedBy, modified FROM customer WHERE id = ?
```

This code doesn't give much of a feel for the various pieces executing across multiple system transactions within a single business transaction. The most important thing to remember is that acquisition of *Optimistic Offline Locks* must occur within the same system transaction that holds the commit of your changes in order to maintain record data consistency. With the check bundled into UPDATE and DELETE statements this won't be a problem.

Take a look at the use of a version object in the *Coarse-Grained Lock (438)* sample code. While *Coarse-Grained Lock (438)* can solve some inconsistent read problems, a simple nonshared version object can help detect inconsistent reads because it's a convenient place to add optimistic check behavior such as increment() or checkVersionIsLatest(). Here's a *Unit of Work (184)* where we add

Optimistic
Offline Lock

consistent read checks to our commit process via the more drastic measure of incrementing the version because we don't know the isolation level:

class UnitOfWork...

```
private List reads = new ArrayList();
public void registerRead(DomainObject object) {
    reads.add(object);
}
public void commit() {
    try {
        checkConsistentReads();
        insertNew();
        deleteRemoved();
        updateDirty();
    } catch (ConcurrencyException e) {
        rollbackSystemTransaction();
        throw e;
    }
}
public void checkConsistentReads() {
    for (Iterator iterator = reads.iterator(); iterator.hasNext();) {
        DomainObject dependent = (DomainObject) iterator.next();
        dependent.getVersion().increment();
    }
}
```

Notice that the *Unit of Work (184)* rolls back the system transaction when it detects a concurrency violation. Most likely you would decide to roll back for any exception during the commit. Do not forget this step! As an alternative to version objects, you can add version checks to your mapper interface.

Optimistic
Offline Lock

Pessimistic Offline Lock

by David Rice

Prevents conflicts between concurrent business transactions by allowing only one business transaction at a time to access data.

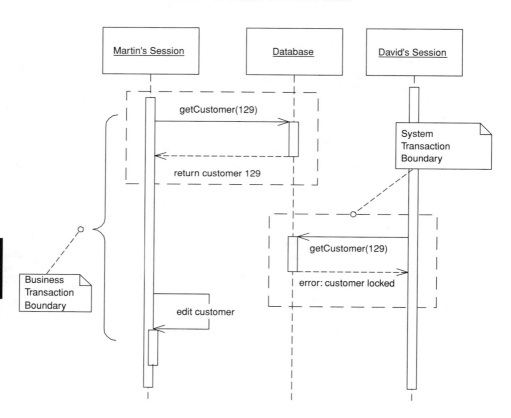

Since offline concurrency involves manipulating data for a business transaction that spans multiple requests, the simplest approach would seem to be having a system transaction open for the whole business transaction. Sadly, however, this doesn't always work well because transaction systems aren't geared to work with long transactions. For that reason you have to use multiple system transactions, at which point you're left to your own devices to manage concurrent access to your data.

The first approach to try is *Optimistic Offline Lock (416)*. However, that pattern has its problems. If several people access the same data within a business transaction, one of them will commit easily but the others will conflict and fail. Since the conflict is only detected at the end of the business transaction, the victims will do all the transaction work only to find at the last minute that the whole thing will fail and their time will have been wasted. If this happens a lot on lengthy business transactions the system will soon become very unpopular.

Pessimistic Offline Lock prevents conflicts by avoiding them altogether. It forces a business transaction to acquire a lock on a piece of data before it starts to use it, so that, most of the time, once you begin a business transaction you can be pretty sure you'll complete it without being bounced by concurrency control.

How It Works

You implement *Pessimistic Offline Lock* in three phases: determining what type of locks you need, building a lock manager, and defining procedures for a business transaction to use locks. Additionally, if you're using *Pessimistic Offline Lock* as a complement to *Optimistic Offline Lock (416)* you need to determine which record types to lock.

As for lock types, the first option is an **exclusive write lock**, which require only that a business transaction acquire a lock in order to edit session data. This avoids conflict by not allowing two business transactions to make changes to the same record simultaneously. What this locking scheme ignores is the reading of data, so if it's not critical that a view session have the most recent data this strategy will suffice.

If it becomes critical that a business transaction must always have the most recent data, regardless of its intention to edit, use the **exclusive read lock**. This requires that a business transaction acquire a lock simply to load the record. Clearly such a strategy has the potential to severely restrict a system's concurrency. For most enterprise systems the exclusive write lock will afford much more concurrent record access than this lock will.

A third strategy combines the two lock types to provide the restrictive locking of the exclusive read lock as well as the increased concurrency of the exclusive write lock. Called the **read/write lock**, it's a bit more complicated than the first two. The relationship of the read and write locks is the key to getting the best of both worlds:

- Read and write locks are mutually exclusive. A record can't be write-locked if any other business transaction owns a read lock on it; it can't be read-locked if any other business transaction owns a write lock on it.

- Concurrent read locks are acceptable. The existence of a single read lock prevents any business transaction from editing the record, so there's no harm in allowing any number of sessions as readers once one has been allowed to read.

Allowing multiple read locks is what increases system concurrency. The downside of this scheme is that it's a bit nasty to implement and presents more of a challenge for domain experts to wrap their heads around when they're modeling the system.

In choosing the correct lock type think about maximizing system concurrency, meeting business needs, and minimizing code complexity. Also keep in mind that the locking strategy must be understood by domain modelers and analysts. Locking is not just a technical problem; the wrong lock type, simply locking every record, or locking the wrong types of records can result an ineffective *Pessimistic Offline Lock* strategy. An ineffective *Pessimistic Offline Lock* strategy is one that doesn't prevent conflict at the onset of the business transaction or that degrades the concurrency of your multi-user system such that it seems more like single-user system. The wrong locking strategy can't be saved by a proper technical implementation. In fact, it's not a bad idea to include *Pessimistic Offline Lock* in your domain model.

Once you've decided upon your lock type, define your lock manager. The lock manager's job is to grant or deny any request by a business transaction to acquire or release a lock. To do its job it needs to know what's being locked as well as the intended owner of the lock—the business transaction. It's quite possible that your concept of a business transaction isn't some *thing* that can be uniquely identified, which makes it a bit difficult to pass a business transaction to the lock manager. In this case consider your concept of a session, as you're more likely to have a session object at your disposal. The terms "session" and "business transaction" are fairly interchangeable. As long as business transactions execute serially within a session the session will be fine as a *Pessimistic Offline Lock* owner. The code example should shed some light on this idea.

The lock manager shouldn't consist of much more than a table that maps locks to owners. A simple one might wrap an in-memory hash table, or it might be a database table. Whatever, you must have one and only one lock table, so if

**Pessimistic
Offline Lock**

it's in memory be sure to use a singleton [Gang of Four]. If your application server is clustered, an in-memory lock table won't work unless it's pinned to a single server instance. The database-based lock manager is probably more appropriate once you're in a clustered application server environment.

The lock, whether implemented as an object or as SQL against a database table, should remain private to the lock manager. Business transactions should interact only with the lock manager, never with a lock object.

Now it's time to define the protocol according to which a business transaction must use the lock manager. This protocol has to include what to lock and when, when to release a lock, and how to act when a lock can't be acquired.

What to lock depends upon when to lock, so let's look at when first. Generally, the business transaction should acquire a lock before loading the data, as there's not much point in acquiring a lock without a guarantee that you'll have the latest version of the locked item. Since we're acquiring locks within a system transaction, however, there are circumstances where the order of the lock and load won't matter. Depending on your lock type, if you're using serializable or repeatable read transactions, the order in which you load objects and acquire locks might not matter. An option is to perform an optimistic check on an item after you acquire the *Pessimistic Offline Lock*. You should be very sure that you have the latest version of an object after you've locked it, which usually translates to acquiring the lock before loading the data.

Now, what are we locking? It seems that we're locking objects or records or just about anything, but what we usually lock is actually the ID, or primary key, that we use to find those objects. This allows us to obtain the lock before we load them. Locking the object works fine so long as it doesn't force you to break the rule about an object's being current after you acquire its lock.

Pessimistic Offline Lock

The simplest rule for releasing locks is to do it when the business transaction completes. Releasing a lock prior to completion might be allowable, depending on your lock type and your intention to use that object again within the transaction. Still, unless you have a very specific reason to release early, such as a particularly nasty system liveliness issue, stick to doing it upon completion of the business transaction.

The easiest course of action for a business transaction that can't acquire a lock is to abort. The user should find this acceptable since *Pessimistic Offline Lock* should result in failure rather early in the transaction. The developer and designer can certainly help the situation by not waiting until late in the transaction to acquire a particularly contentious lock. If at all possible acquire all of your locks before the user begins work.

For any given item that you intend to lock, access to the lock table must by serialized. With an in-memory lock table it's easiest to serialize access to the entire lock manager with whatever constructs your programming language provides. If you need concurrency greater than this affords, be aware you are entering complex territory.

If the lock table is stored in a database the first rule, of course, is to interact with it within a system transaction. Take full advantage of the serialization capabilities that a database provides. With the exclusive read and exclusive write locks serialization is a simple matter of having the database enforce a uniqueness constraint on the column storing the lockable item's ID. Storing read/write locks in a database makes things a bit more difficult since the logic requires reads of the lock table in addition to inserts and so it becomes imperative to avoid inconsistent reads. A system transaction with an isolation level of serializable provides ultimate safety as it guarantees no inconsistent reads. Using serializable transactions throughout our system might get us into performance trouble, but a separate serializable system transaction for lock acquisition and a less strict isolation level for other work might ease this problem. Another option is to investigate whether a stored procedure might help with lock management. Concurrency management can be tough, so don't be afraid to defer to your database at key moments.

The serial nature of lock management screams performance bottleneck. A big consideration here is lock granularity, as the fewer locks required the less of a bottleneck you'll have. A *Coarse-Grained Lock (438)* can address lock table contention.

Pessimistic
Offline Lock

With a system transaction pessimistic locking scheme, such as "SELECT FOR UPDATE..." or entity EJBs, deadlock is a distinct possibility because these locking mechanisms will wait until a lock becomes available. Think of deadlock this way. Two users need resources A and B. If one gets the lock on A and the other gets the lock on B, both transactions might sit and wait forever for the other lock. Given that we're spanning multiple system transactions, waiting for a lock doesn't make much sense, especially since a business transaction might take 20 minutes. Nobody wants to wait for those locks. And this is good because coding for a wait involves timeouts and quickly gets complicated. Simply have your lock manager throw an exception as soon as a lock is unavailable. This removes the burden of coping with deadlock.

A final requirement is managing lock timeouts for lost sessions. If a client machine crashes in the middle of a transaction that lost transaction is unable to complete and release any owned locks. This is a big deal for a Web application where sessions are regularly abandoned by users. Ideally you'll have a timeout mechanism managed by your application server rather than make your application handle timeouts. Web application servers provide an HTTP session for this. Timeouts can be implemented by registering a utility object that releases all locks when the HTTP session becomes invalid. Another option is to associate a time-stamp with each lock and consider invalid any lock older than a certain age.

When to Use It

Pessimistic Offline Lock is appropriate when the chance of conflict between concurrent sessions is high. A user should never have to throw away work. Locking is also appropriate when the cost of a conflict is too high regardless of its likelihood. Locking every entity in a system will almost surely create tremendous data contention problems, so remember that *Pessimistic Offline Lock* is very complementary to *Optimistic Offline Lock (416)* and only use *Pessimistic Offline Lock* where it's truly required.

If you have to use *Pessimistic Offline Lock,* you should also consider a long transaction. Long transactions are never a good thing, but in some situations they may be no more damaging than *Pessimistic Offline Lock* and much easier to program. Do some load testing before you choose.

Don't use these techniques if your business transactions fit within a single system transaction. Many system transaction pessimistic locking techniques ship with the application and database servers you're already using, among them the "SELECT FOR UPDATE" SQL statement for database locking and the entity EJB for application server locking. Why worry about timeouts, lock visibility, and such, when there's no need to? Understanding these locking types can certainly add a lot of value to your implementation of *Pessimistic Offline Lock.* Understand, though, that the inverse isn't true! What you read here won't prepare you to write a database manager or transaction monitor. All the offline locking techniques presented in this book depend on your system having a real transaction monitor of its own.

**Pessimistic
Offline Lock**

Example: Simple Lock Manager (Java)

In this example we'll first build a lock manager for exclusive read locks—remember that you need these locks to read or edit an object. Then we'll demonstrate how the lock manager might be used for a business transaction that spans multiple system transactions.

The first step is to define our lock manager interface.

```
interface ExclusiveReadLockManager...

    public static final ExclusiveReadLockManager INSTANCE =
        (ExclusiveReadLockManager) Plugins.getPlugin(ExclusiveReadLockManager.class);
    public void acquireLock(Long lockable, String owner) throws ConcurrencyException;
    public void releaseLock(Long lockable, String owner);
    public void relaseAllLocks(String owner);
```

Notice that we're identifying lockable with a long and owner with a string. Lockable is a long because each table in our database uses a long primary key that's unique across the entire system and so serves as a nice lockable ID (which must be unique across all types handled by the lock table). The owner ID is a string because the example will be a Web application, and the HTTP session ID makes a good lock owner within it.

We'll write a lock manager that interacts directly with a lock table in our database rather than with a lock object. Note that this is our own table called lock, like any other application table, and not part of the database's internal locking mechanism. Acquiring a lock is a matter of successfully inserting a row into the lock table. Releasing it is a matter of deleting that row. Here's the schema for the lock table and part of the lock manager implementation:

table lock...

```
create table lock(lockableid bigint primary key, ownerid bigint)
```

class ExclusiveReadLockManagerDBImpl implements ExclusiveLockManager...

```
private static final String INSERT_SQL =
    "insert into lock values(?, ?)";
private static final String DELETE_SINGLE_SQL =
    "delete from lock where lockableid = ? and ownerid = ?";
private static final String DELETE_ALL_SQL =
    "delete from lock where ownerid = ?";
private static final String CHECK_SQL =
    "select lockableid from lock where lockableid = ? and ownerid = ?";
public void acquireLock(Long lockable, String owner) throws ConcurrencyException {
    if (!hasLock(lockable, owner)) {
        Connection conn = null;
        PreparedStatement pstmt = null;
        try {
            conn = ConnectionManager.INSTANCE.getConnection();
            pstmt = conn.prepareStatement(INSERT_SQL);
            pstmt.setLong(1, lockable.longValue());
            pstmt.setString(2, owner);
            pstmt.executeUpdate();
        } catch (SQLException sqlEx) {
            throw new ConcurrencyException("unable to lock " + lockable);
        } finally {
            closeDBResources(conn, pstmt);
        }
    }
}
public void releaseLock(Long lockable, String owner) {
    Connection conn = null;
    PreparedStatement pstmt = null;
    try {
        conn = ConnectionManager.INSTANCE.getConnection();
        pstmt = conn.prepareStatement(DELETE_SINGLE_SQL);
```

Pessimistic Offline Lock

```
            pstmt.setLong(1, lockable.longValue());
            pstmt.setString(2, owner);
            pstmt.executeUpdate();
        } catch (SQLException sqlEx) {
            throw new SystemException("unexpected error releasing lock on " + lockable);
        } finally {
            closeDBResources(conn, pstmt);
        }
    }
```

Not shown in the lock manager are the public releaseAllLocks() and the private hasLock() methods. releaseAllLocks() does exactly as its name implies and releases all locks for an owner. hasLock() queries the database to check if an owner already owns a lock. It's not uncommon for session code to attempt to acquire a lock it already owns. This means that acquireLock() must first check that the owner doesn't already have the lock before attempting to insert the lock row. As the lock table is usually a point of resource contention, these repetitive reads can degrade application performance. It may be necessary for you to cache owned locks at the session level for the ownership checks. Be careful doing this.

Now let's put together a simple Web application to maintain customer records. First we'll set up a bit of infrastructure to facilitate business transaction processing. Some concept of a user session will be required by the layers beneath the Web tier, so we won't be able to rely solely on the HTTP session. Let's refer to this new session as the application session to distinguish it from the HTTP session. Application sessions will store their ID, a user name, and an *Identity Map (195)* to cache objects loaded or created during the business transaction. They'll be associated with the currently executing thread in order that they be found.

Pessimistic Offline Lock

```
class AppSession...

    private String user;
    private String id;
    private IdentityMap imap;
    public AppSession(String user, String id, IdentityMap imap) {
        this.user = user;
        this.imap = imap;
        this.id = id;
    }
```

```
class AppSessionManager...

    private static ThreadLocal current = new ThreadLocal();
    public static AppSession getSession() {
        return (AppSession) current.get();
    }
    public static void setSession(AppSession session) {
        current.set(session);
    }
```

We're going to use a *Front Controller (344)* to handle requests, so we'll need to define a command. The first thing each command must do is indicate its intention to either start a new business transaction or continue one that already exists. This is a matter of setting up a new application session or finding the current one. Here we have an abstract command that provides convenience methods for establishing business transaction context.

```
interface Command...

    public void init(HttpServletRequest req, HttpServletResponse rsp);
    public void process() throws Exception;

abstract class BusinessTransactionCommand implements Command...

    public void init(HttpServletRequest req, HttpServletResponse rsp) {
        this.req = req;
        this.rsp = rsp;
    }
    protected void startNewBusinessTransaction() {
        HttpSession httpSession = getReq().getSession(true);
        AppSession appSession = (AppSession) httpSession.getAttribute(APP_SESSION);
        if (appSession != null) {
            ExclusiveReadLockManager.INSTANCE.relaseAllLocks(appSession.getId());
        }
        appSession = new AppSession(getReq().getRemoteUser(),
                    httpSession.getId(), new IdentityMap());
        AppSessionManager.setSession(appSession);
        httpSession.setAttribute(APP_SESSION, appSession);
        httpSession.setAttribute(LOCK_REMOVER,
                    new LockRemover(appSession.getId()));
    }
    protected void continueBusinessTransaction() {
        HttpSession httpSession = getReq().getSession();
        AppSession appSession = (AppSession) httpSession.getAttribute(APP_SESSION);
        AppSessionManager.setSession(appSession);
    }
    protected HttpServletRequest getReq() {
        return req;
    }
    protected HttpServletResponse getRsp() {
        return rsp;
    }
```

Notice that when we establish a new application session we remove locks for any existing one. We also add a listener to the HTTP session's binding events that will remove any locks owned by an application session when the corresponding HTTP session expires.

```
class LockRemover implements HttpSessionBindingListener...

    private String sessionId;
    public LockRemover(String sessionId) {
        this.sessionId = sessionId;
    }
    public void valueUnbound(HttpSessionBindingEvent event) {
        try {
            beginSystemTransaction();
            ExclusiveReadLockManager.INSTANCE.relaseAllLocks(this.sessionId);
            commitSystemTransaction();
        } catch (Exception e) {
            handleSeriousError(e);
        }
    }
```

Our commands contain both standard business logic and lock management, and each command must execute within the bounds of a single system transaction. To ensure this we can decorate [Gang of Four] it with a transactional command object. Be sure that all locking and standard domain business for a single request occur within a single system transaction. The methods that define system transaction boundaries depend on your deployment context. It's mandatory to roll back the system transaction when a concurrency exception, and any other exception in this case, is detected, as that will prevent any changes from entering the permanent record data when a conflict occurs.

```
class TransactionalComamnd implements Command...

    public TransactionalCommand(Command impl) {
        this.impl = impl;
    }
    public void process() throws Exception {
        beginSystemTransaction();
        try {
            impl.process();
            commitSystemTransaction();
        } catch (Exception e) {
            rollbackSystemTransaction();
            throw e;
        }
    }
```

Pessimistic Offline Lock

Now it's a matter of writing the controller servlet and concrete commands. The controller servlet has the responsibility of wrapping each command with transaction control. The concrete commands are required to establish business transaction context, execute domain logic, and acquire and release locks where appropriate.

```
class ControllerServlet extends HttpServlet...

    protected void doGet(HttpServletRequest req, HttpServletResponse rsp)
                    throws ServletException, IOException {
        try {
            String cmdName = req.getParameter("command");
            Command cmd = getCommand(cmdName);
            cmd.init(req, rsp);
            cmd.process();
        } catch (Exception e) {
            writeException(e, rsp.getWriter());
        }
    }
    private Command getCommand(String name) {
        try {
            String className = (String) commands.get(name);
            Command cmd = (Command) Class.forName(className).newInstance();
            return new TransactionalCommand(cmd);
        } catch (Exception e) {
            e.printStackTrace();
            throw new SystemException("unable to create command object for " + name);
        }
    }
```

```
class EditCustomerCommand implements Command...

    public void process() throws Exception {
        startNewBusinessTransaction();
        Long customerId = new Long(getReq().getParameter("customer_id"));
        ExclusiveReadLockManager.INSTANCE.acquireLock(
                customerId, AppSessionManager.getSession().getId());
        Mapper customerMapper = MapperRegistry.INSTANCE.getMapper(Customer.class);
        Customer customer = (Customer) customerMapper.find(customerId);
        getReq().getSession().setAttribute("customer", customer);
        forward("/editCustomer.jsp");
    }
```

```
class SaveCustomerCommand implements Command...

    public void process() throws Exception {
        continueBusinessTransaction();
        Customer customer = (Customer) getReq().getSession().getAttribute("customer");
        String name = getReq().getParameter("customerName");
        customer.setName(name);
        Mapper customerMapper = MapperRegistry.INSTANCE.getMapper(Customer.class);
        customerMapper.update(customer);
        ExclusiveReadLockManager.INSTANCE.releaseLock(customer.getId(),
                            AppSessionManager.getSession().getId());
        forward("/customerSaved.jsp");
    }
```

Pessimistic Offline Lock

The commands just shown will prevent any two sessions from working with the same customer at the same time. Any other command in the application that works with a customer object must be sure either to acquire the lock or to work only with a customer locked by a previous command in the same business transaction. Given that we have a hasLock() check in the lock manager we could simply acquire the lock in every command. This might be bad for performance, but it would certainly guarantee that we have a lock. *Implicit Lock (449)* discusses other foolproof approaches to locking mechanics.

The amount of framework code might seem a bit out of proportion to the amount of domain code. Indeed, *Pessimistic Offline Lock* requires at a minimum choreographing an application session, a business transaction, a lock manager, and a system transaction, which is clearly a challenge. This example serves more as an inspiration than as an architecture template, as it lacks robustness in many areas.

**Pessimistic
Offline Lock**

Coarse-Grained Lock

by David Rice and Matt Foemmel

Locks a set of related objects with a single lock.

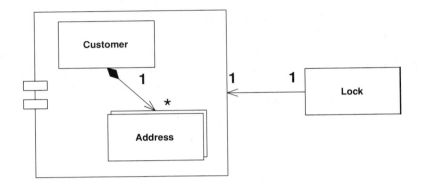

Objects can often be edited as a group. Perhaps you have a customer and its set of addresses. If so, when using the application it makes sense to lock all of these items if you want to lock any one of them. Having a separate lock for individual objects presents a number of challenges. First, anyone manipulating them has to write code that can find them all in order to lock them. This is easy enough for a customer and its addresses, but it gets tricky as you get more locking groups. And what if the groups get complicated? Where is this behavior when your framework is managing lock acquisition? If your locking strategy requires that an object be loaded in order to be locked, such as with *Optimistic Offline Lock (416)*, locking a large group affects performance. And with *Pessimistic Offline Lock (426)* a large lock set is a management headache and increases lock table contention.

A *Coarse-Grained Lock* is a single lock that covers many objects. It not only simplifies the locking action itself but also frees you from having to load all the members of a group in order to lock them.

How It Works

The first step in implementing *Coarse-Grained Lock* is to create a single point of contention for locking a group of objects. This makes only one lock necessary for locking the entire set. Then you provide the shortest path possible to finding that single lock point in order to minimize the group members that must be identified and possibly loaded into memory in the process of obtaining that lock.

With *Optimistic Offline Lock (416)*, having each item in a group share a version (see Figure 16.2) creates the single point of contention, which means sharing the *same* version, not an *equal* version. Incrementing this version will lock the entire group with a **shared lock**. Set up your model to point every member of the group at the shared version and you have certainly minimized the path to the point of contention.

A shared *Pessimistic Offline Lock (426)* requires that each member of the group share some sort of lockable token, on which it must then be acquired. As *Pessimistic Offline Lock (426)* is often used as a complement to *Optimistic Offline Lock (416)*, a shared version object makes an excellent candidate for the lockable token role (Figure 16.3).

Eric Evans and David Siegel [Evans] define an **aggregate** as a cluster of associated objects that we treat as a unit for data changes. Each aggregate has a **root** that provides the only access point to members of the set and a **boundary** that defines what's included in the set. The aggregate's characteristics call for a *Coarse-Grained Lock,* since working with any of its members requires locking all of them. Locking an aggregate yields an alternative to a shared lock that I call a **root lock** (see Figure 16.4). By definition locking the root locks all members of the aggregate. The root lock gives us a single point of contention.

Using a root lock as a *Coarse-Grained Lock* makes it necessary to implement navigation to the root in your object graph. This allows a locking mechanism, when asked to lock any object in the aggregate, to navigate to the root and lock

Coarse-Grained Lock

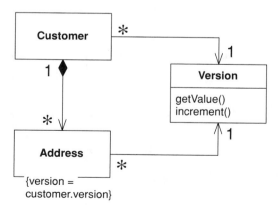

Figure 16.2 *Sharing a version.*

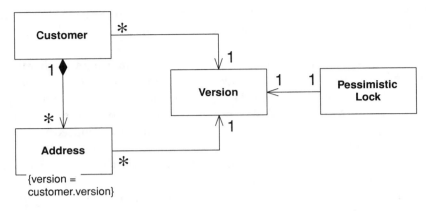

Figure 16.3 *Locking a shared version.*

it instead. This navigation can be accomplished in a couple of ways. You can maintain a direct navigation to the root for each object in the aggregate, or you can use a sequence of intermediate relationships. For example, in a hierarchy the obvious root is the top level parent, to which you can link the descendents directly. Alternatively, you can give each node a link to its immediate parent and navigate that structure to reach the root. In a large graph the latter strategy might cause performance problems as each parent must be loaded in order to determine whether it has a parent of its own. Be sure to use a *Lazy Load (200)* when loading the objects that make up the path to your root. This not only pre-

Coarse-Grained Lock

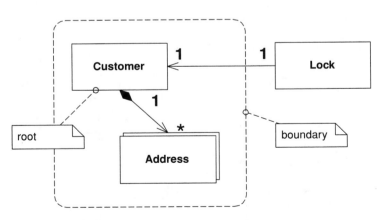

Figure 16.4 *Locking the root.*

vents objects from being loaded before they're needed but prevents an infinite mapping loop when you map a bidirectional relationship. Be wary of the fact that *Lazy Loads (200)* for a single aggregate can occur across multiple system transactions and so you may end up with an aggregate built from inconsistent parts. Of course, that's not good.

Note that a shared lock also works for aggregate locking as locking any object in the aggregate will simultaneously lock the root.

The shared lock and root lock implementations of *Coarse-Grained Lock* both have their trade-offs. When using a relational database the shared lock carries the burden that almost all of your selects will require a join to the version table. But loading objects while navigating to the root can be a performance hit as well. The root lock and *Pessimistic Offline Lock (426)* perhaps make an odd combination. By the time you navigate to the root and lock it you may need to reload a few objects to guarantee their freshness. And, as always, building a system against a legacy data store will place numerous constraints on your implementation choice. Locking implementations abound, and the subtleties are even more numerous. Be sure to arrive at an implementation that suits your needs.

When to Use It

The most obvious reason to use a *Coarse-Grained Lock* is to satisfy business requirements. This is the case when locking an aggregate. Consider a lease object that owns a collection of assets. It probably doesn't make business sense for one user to edit the lease and another user to simultaneously edit an asset. Locking either the asset or the lease ought to result in the lease and all of its assets being locked.

A very positive outcome of using *Coarse-Grained Locks* is that acquiring and releasing lock is cheaper. This is certainly a legitimate motivation for using them. The shared lock can be used beyond the concept of the [Evans] aggregate, but be careful when working from nonfunctional requirements such as performance. Beware of creating unnatural object relationships in order to facilitate *Coarse-Grained Lock*.

Example: Shared *Optimistic Offline Lock (416)* (Java)

For this example we have a domain model with *Layer Supertype (475)*, a relational database as our persistent store, and *Data Mappers (165)*.

The first thing to do is create a version class and table. To keep things simple we'll create a rather versatile version class that will not only store its value but

Coarse-
Grained
Lock

will also have a static finder method. Note that we're using an identity map to cache versions for a session. If objects share a version it's critical that they all point to the exact same instance of it. As the version class is a part of our domain model it's probably poor form to put database code in there, so I'll leave separating version database code into the mapper layer as an exercise for you.

table version...

```
create table version(id bigint primary key, value bigint,
    modifiedBy varchar, modified datetime)
```

class Version...

```
private Long id;
private long value;
private String modifiedBy;
private Timestamp modified;
private boolean locked;
private boolean isNew;
private static final String UPDATE_SQL =
        "UPDATE version SET VALUE = ?, modifiedBy = ?, modified = ? " +
        "WHERE id = ? and value = ?";
private static final String DELETE_SQL =
        "DELETE FROM version WHERE id = ? and value = ?";
private static final String INSERT_SQL =
        "INSERT INTO version VALUES (?, ?, ?, ?)";
private static final String LOAD_SQL =
        "SELECT id, value, modifiedBy, modified FROM version WHERE id = ?";
public static Version find(Long id) {
    Version version = AppSessionManager.getSession().getIdentityMap().getVersion(id);
    if (version == null) {
        version = load(id);
    }
    return version;
}
private static Version load(Long id) {
    ResultSet rs = null;
    Connection conn = null;
    PreparedStatement pstmt = null;
    Version version = null;
    try {
        conn = ConnectionManager.INSTANCE.getConnection();
        pstmt = conn.prepareStatement(LOAD_SQL);
        pstmt.setLong(1, id.longValue());
        rs = pstmt.executeQuery();
        if (rs.next()) {
            long value = rs.getLong(2);
            String modifiedBy = rs.getString(3);
            Timestamp modified = rs.getTimestamp(4);
            version = new Version(id, value, modifiedBy, modified);
            AppSessionManager.getSession().getIdentityMap().putVersion(version);
```

Coarse-Grained Lock

```
        } else {
            throw new ConcurrencyException("version " + id + " not found.");
        }
    } catch (SQLException sqlEx) {
        throw new SystemException("unexpected sql error loading version", sqlEx);
    } finally {
        cleanupDBResources(rs, conn, pstmt);
    }
    return version;
}
```

The version also knows how to create itself. The database insert is separated from the creation to allow deferment of insertion until at least one owner is inserted into the database. Each of our domain *Data Mappers (165)* can safely call insert on the version when inserting the corresponding domain object. The version tracks whether it's new to make sure it will only be inserted once.

class Version...

```
    public static Version create() {
        Version version = new Version(IdGenerator.INSTANCE.nextId(), 0,
                AppSessionManager.getSession().getUser(), now());
        version.isNew = true;
        return version;
    }
    public void insert() {
        if (isNew()) {
            Connection conn = null;
            PreparedStatement pstmt = null;
            try {
                conn = ConnectionManager.INSTANCE.getConnection();
                pstmt = conn.prepareStatement(INSERT_SQL);
                pstmt.setLong(1, this.getId().longValue());
                pstmt.setLong(2, this.getValue());
                pstmt.setString(3, this.getModifiedBy());
                pstmt.setTimestamp(4, this.getModified());
                pstmt.executeUpdate();
                AppSessionManager.getSession().getIdentityMap().putVersion(this);
                isNew = false;
            } catch (SQLException sqlEx) {
                throw new SystemException("unexpected sql error inserting version", sqlEx);
            } finally {
                cleanupDBResources(conn, pstmt);
            }
        }
    }
```

Next, we have an increment() method that increases the value of the version in the corresponding database row. It's likely that multiple objects in a change set will share the same version, so the version first makes sure it's not already locked before incrementing itself. After calling the database, the increment()

method must check that the version row was indeed updated. If it returns a row count of zero, it has detected a concurrency violation and throws an exception.

class Version...

```
public void increment() throws ConcurrencyException {
    if (!isLocked()) {
        Connection conn = null;
        PreparedStatement pstmt = null;
        try {
            conn = ConnectionManager.INSTANCE.getConnection();
            pstmt = conn.prepareStatement(UPDATE_SQL);
            pstmt.setLong(1, value + 1);
            pstmt.setString(2, getModifiedBy());
            pstmt.setTimestamp(3, getModified());
            pstmt.setLong(4, id.longValue());
            pstmt.setLong(5, value);
            int rowCount = pstmt.executeUpdate();
            if (rowCount == 0) {
                throwConcurrencyException();
            }
            value++;
            locked = true;
        } catch (SQLException sqlEx) {
            throw new SystemException("unexpected sql error incrementing version", sqlEx);
        } finally {
            cleanupDBResources(conn, pstmt);
        }
    }
}
private void throwConcurrencyException() {
    Version currentVersion = load(this.getId());
    throw new ConcurrencyException(
            "version modified by " + currentVersion.modifiedBy + " at " +
            DateFormat.getDateTimeInstance().format(currentVersion.getModified()));
}
```

Coarse-
Grained
Lock

With the code here be sure to invoke increment only in the system transaction in which you commit the business transaction. The isLocked flag makes it so that incrementing in earlier transactions will result in false lock acquisition during the commit transaction. This isn't a problem because the whole point of an optimistic lock is that you only get the lock when you commit.

When you use this pattern you may want to see if your data is still current with the database in an earlier system transaction. You can do this by adding a checkCurrent method to the version class that simply checks if an *Optimistic Offline Lock (416)* is available without updating.

Not shown is a delete method that executes the SQL to remove the version from the database. If the returned row count is zero, a concurrency exception is thrown. This is because the *Optimistic Offline Lock (416)* probably wasn't obtained when deleting the last of the objects using this version. That should never happen. The real trick is knowing when it's okay to delete a shared version. If you're sharing a version across an aggregate, simply delete it after you delete the aggregate root. Other scenarios make things much more problematic. One possibility is for the version object to keep a reference count of its owners and delete itself when the count reaches zero. Be warned that this could make for a version object that's rather sophisticated. Once your version gets complicated you might consider making it a full-blown domain object. This makes good sense, but, of course, it will be a special domain object without a version.

Now let's look at how we use the shared version. The domain *Layer Supertype (475)* contains a version object rather than a simple count. Each *Data Mapper (165)* can set the version when loading the domain object.

```
class DomainObject...

   private Long id;;
   private Timestamp modified;
   private String modifiedBy;
   private Version version;
   public void setSystemFields(Version version, Timestamp modified, String modifiedBy) {
      this.version = version;
      this.modified = modified;
      this.modifiedBy = modifiedBy;
   }
```

For creation, let's look at an aggregate consisting of a customer root and its addresses. The customer's create method will create the shared version. Customer will have an addAddress() method that creates an address, passing along the customer's version. Our abstract database mapper will insert the version before it inserts corresponding domain objects. Remember that the version will ensure that it's only inserted once.

```
class Customer extends DomainObject...

   public static Customer create(String name) {
      return new Customer(IdGenerator.INSTANCE.nextId(), Version.create(),
         name, new ArrayList());
   }
```

```
class Customer extends DomainObject...

   public Address addAddress(String line1, String city, String state) {
      Address address = Address.create(this, getVersion(), line1, city, state);
      addresses.add(address);
      return address;
   }
```

Coarse-Grained Lock

```
class Address extends DomainObject...

    public static Address create(Customer customer, Version version,
        String line1, String city, String state) {
        return new Address(IdGenerator.INSTANCE.nextId(), version, customer,
                    line1, city, state);
    }

class AbstractMapper...

    public void insert(DomainObject object) {
        object.getVersion().insert();
```

Increment should be called on a version by the *Data Mapper (165)* before it updates or deletes an object.

```
class AbstractMapper...

    public void update(DomainObject object) {
        object.getVersion().increment();
```

```
class AbstractMapper...

    public void delete(DomainObject object) {
        object.getVersion().increment();
```

As this is an aggregate, we delete the addresses when we delete the customer. This allows us to delete the version immediately after that.

```
class CustomerMapper extends AbstractMapper...

    public void delete(DomainObject object) {
        Customer cust = (Customer) object;
        for (Iterator iterator = cust.getAddresses().iterator(); iterator.hasNext();) {
            Address add = (Address) iterator.next();
            MapperRegistry.getMapper(Address.class).delete(add);
        }
        super.delete(object);
        cust.getVersion().delete();
    }
```

Example: Shared *Pessimistic Offline Lock (426)* (Java)

We need some sort of lockable token that we can associate with all objects in the related set. As discussed above we'll use *Pessimistic Offline Lock (426)* as a complement to *Optimistic Offline Lock (416)* so we can use as the lockable token the shared version. We'll use all of the same code to arrive at a shared version.

The only issue is that some of our data must be loaded in order to get the version. If we acquire the *Pessimistic Offline Lock (426)* after loading its data, how do we know that the data is current? Something we can easily do is increment the version within the system transaction where we obtained the *Pessimistic Offline Lock (426)*. Once that system transaction commits, our pessimistic lock is valid and we know that we have the latest copy of any data sharing that version, regardless of where we loaded within the system transaction.

```
class LoadCustomerCommand...

    try {
        Customer customer = (Customer) MapperRegistry.getMapper(Customer.class).find(id);
        ExclusiveReadLockManager.INSTANCE.acquireLock
            (customer.getId(), AppSessionManager.getSession().getId());
        customer.getVersion().increment();
        TransactionManager.INSTANCE.commit();
    } catch (Exception e) {
        TransactionManager.INSTANCE.rollback();
        throw e;
    }
```

You can see that the version increment might be something that you would want to build into your lock manager. At least you want to decorate [Gang of Four] your lock manager with code that increments the version. Your production code will, of course, require more robust exception handling and transaction control than the example shows.

Example: Root *Optimistic Offline Lock (416)* (Java)

This example makes most of the same assumptions as the previous examples, including a domain *Layer Supertype (475)* and *Data Mappers (165)*. There's a version object, but in this case it won't be shared. It simply provides a convenient **increment()** method to more easily allow acquisition of the *Optimistic Offline Lock (416)* outside of the *Data Mapper (165)*. We're also using a *Unit of Work (184)* to track our change set.

Our aggregate contains parent-child relationships, so we'll use child-to-parent navigation to find the root. We'll need to accommodate this in our domain and data models.

```
class DomainObject...

    private Long id;
    private DomainObject parent;
    public DomainObject(Long id, DomainObject parent) {
        this.id = id;
        this.parent = parent;
    }
```

Coarse-Grained Lock

Once we have our owners we can acquire our root locks before we commit the *Unit of Work*.

class UnitOfWork...

```
public void commit() throws SQLException {
    for (Iterator iterator = _modifiedObjects.iterator(); iterator.hasNext();) {
        DomainObject object = (DomainObject) iterator.next();
        for (DomainObject owner = object; owner != null; owner = owner.getParent()) {
            owner.getVersion().increment();
        }
    }
    for (Iterator iterator = _modifiedObjects.iterator(); iterator.hasNext();) {
        DomainObject object = (DomainObject) iterator.next();
        Mapper mapper = MapperRegistry.getMapper(object.getClass());
        mapper.update(object);
    }
}
```

Coarse-Grained Lock

Implicit Lock

by David Rice

Allows framework or layer supertype code to acquire offline locks.

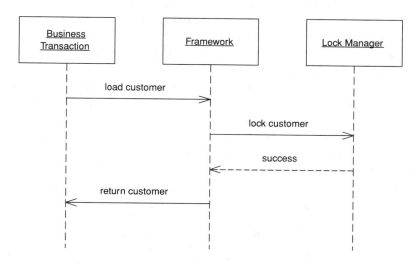

The key to any locking scheme is that there are no gaps in its use. Forgetting to write a single line of code that acquires a lock can render an entire offline locking scheme useless. Failing to retrieve a read lock where other transactions use write locks means you might not get up-to-date session data; failing to use a version count properly can result in unknowingly writing over someone's changes. Generally, if an item might be locked *anywhere* it must be locked *everywhere*. Ignoring its application's locking strategy allows a business transaction to create inconsistent data. Not releasing locks won't corrupt your record data, but it will eventually bring productivity to a halt. Because offline concurrency management is difficult to test, such errors might go undetected by all of your test suites.

One solution is to not allow developers to make such a mistake. Locking tasks that cannot be overlooked should be handled not explicitly by developers but implicitly by the application. The fact that most enterprise applications make use of some combination of framework, *Layer Supertypes (475)*, and code generation provides us with ample opportunity to facilitate *Implicit Lock*.

How It Works

Implementing *Implicit Lock* is a matter of factoring your code such that any locking mechanics that *absolutely cannot* be skipped can be carried out by your application framework. For lack of a better word we'll use "framework" to mean a combination of *Layer Supertypes (475)*, framework classes, and any other "plumbing" code. Code generation tools are another avenue to enforce proper locking. I realize this is by no means a ground-breaking idea. You're very likely to head down this path once you've coded the same locking mechanics a few times over in your application. Still, I've seen it done poorly often enough that it merits a quick look.

The first step is to assemble a list of what tasks are mandatory for a business transaction to work within your locking strategy. For *Optimistic Offline Lock (416)* that list will contain items such as storing a version count for each record, including the version in update SQL criteria, and storing an incremented version when changing the record. The *Pessimistic Offline Lock (426)* list will include items along the lines of acquiring any lock necessary to load a piece of data—typically the exclusive read lock or the read portion of the read/write lock—and releasing all locks when the business transaction or session completes.

Note that the *Pessimistic Offline Lock (426)* list doesn't include acquiring any lock necessary only for editing a piece of data—that is, exclusive write lock and the write portion of the read/write lock. Yes, these are mandatory if your business transaction wants to edit the data, but implicitly acquiring them presents, should the locks be unavailable, a couple of difficulties. First, the only points where we might implicitly acquire a write lock, such as the registration of a dirty object within a *Unit of Work (184)*, offer us no promise should the locks be unavailable, that the transaction will abort as soon as the user begins to work. The application can't figure out on its own when is a good time to acquire these locks. A transaction not failing rapidly conflicts with an intent of *Pessimistic Offline Lock (426)*—that a user not have to perform work twice.

Second, and just as important, is that these lock types most greatly limit system concurrency. Avoiding *Implicit Lock* here helps us think about how we impact concurrency by forcing the issue out of the technical arena and into the business domain. Still we have to make sure that locks necessary for writing are acquired before changes are committed. What your framework can do is ensure that a write lock has already been obtained before committing any changes. Not having acquired the lock by commit time is a programmer error and the code should at least throw an assertion failure. I advise skipping the assertion and throwing a concurrency exception here, as you really don't want any such errors in your production system when assertions are turned off.

A word of caution about using the *Implicit Lock*. While it allows developers to ignore much of the locking mechanics it doesn't allow them to ignore consequences. For example, if developers are using *Implicit Lock* with a pessimistic locking scheme that waits for locks, they still need to think about deadlock possibilities. The danger with *Implicit Lock* is that business transactions can fail in unexpected ways once developers stop thinking about locking.

Making locking work is a matter of determining the best way to get your framework to implicitly carry out the locking mechanics. See *Optimistic Offline Lock (416)* for samples of implicit handling of that lock type. The possibilities for a quality *Implicit Lock* implementation are far too numerous to demonstrate them all here.

When to Use It

Implicit Lock should be used in all but the simplest of applications that have no concept of framework. The risk of a single forgotten lock is too great.

Example: Implicit *Pessimistic Offline Lock (426)* (Java)

Let's consider a system that uses an exclusive read lock. Our architecture contains a *Domain Model (116)*, and we're using *Data Mappers (165)* to mediate between our domain objects and our relational database. With the exclusive read lock the framework must acquire a lock on a domain object before allowing a business transaction to do anything with it.

Implicit Lock

Any domain object used in a business transaction is located via the find() method on a mapper. This is true whether the business transaction uses the mapper directly by invoking find() or indirectly by navigating the object graph. Now it's possible for us to decorate [Gang of Four] our mappers with required locking functionality. We'll write a locking mapper that acquires a lock before attempting to find an object.

interface Mapper...

```
public DomainObject find(Long id);
public void insert(DomainObject obj);
public void update(DomainObject obj);
public void delete(DomainObject obj);
```

```
class LockingMapper implements Mapper...

    private Mapper impl;
    public LockingMapper(Mapper impl) {
        this.impl = impl;
    }
    public DomainObject find(Long id) {
        ExclusiveReadLockManager.INSTANCE.acquireLock(
            id, AppSessionManager.getSession().getId());
        return impl.find(id);
    }
    public void insert(DomainObject obj) {
        impl.insert(obj);
    }
    public void update(DomainObject obj) {
        impl.update(obj);
    }
    public void delete(DomainObject obj) {
        impl.delete(obj);
    }
```

Because it's quite common to look up an object more than once in a session, for the above code to work the lock manager must first check that the session doesn't already have a lock before it obtains one. If we were using an exclusive write lock rather than the exclusive read lock we'd write a mapper decorator that checked for previous lock acquisition on update and delete rather than actually acquiring a lock.

Implicit Lock

One of the nice things about decorators is that the object being wrapped doesn't even know that it's functionality is being enhanced. Here we can wrap the mappers in our registry:

```
LockingMapperRegistry implements MappingRegistry...

    private Map mappers = new HashMap();
    public void registerMapper(Class cls, Mapper mapper) {
        mappers.put(cls, new LockingMapper(mapper));
    }
    public Mapper getMapper(Class cls) {
        return (Mapper) mappers.get(cls);
    }
```

When the business transaction gets its hands on a mapper it thinks that it's about to invoke a standard update method, but what really happens is shown in Figure 16.5.

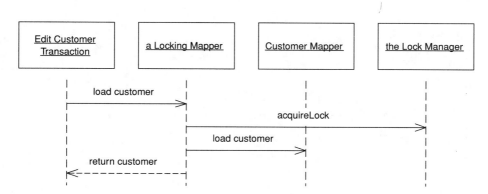

Figure 16.5 *Locking mapper.*

Implicit Lock

Chapter 17

Session State Patterns

Client Session State

Stores session state on the client.

How It Works

Even the most server-oriented designs need at least a little *Client Session State*, if only to hold a session identifier. With some applications you can consider putting all of the session data on the client, in which case the client sends the full set of session data with each request and the server sends back the full session state with each response. This allows the server to be completely stateless.

Most of the time you'll want to use *Data Transfer Object (401)* to handle the data transfer. The *Data Transfer Object (401)* can serialize itself over the wire and thus allow even complex data to be transmitted.

The client also needs to store the data. If it's a rich-client application it can do this within its own structures, such as the fields in its interface—although I would drink Budweiser rather than do that. A set of nonvisual objects often makes a better bet, such as the *Data Transfer Object (401)* itself or a domain model. Either way it's not usually a big problem.

With an HTML interface, things get a bit more complicated. There are three common ways to do client session state: URL parameters, hidden fields, and cookies.

URL parameters are the easiest to work with for a small amount of data. Essentially all URLs on any response page take the session state as a parameter. The clear limit to doing this is that the size of an URL is limited, but if you only have a couple of data items it works well, that's why it's a popular choice for something like a session ID. Some platforms will do automatic URL rewriting to add a session ID. Changing the URL may be a problem with bookmarks, so that's an argument against using URL parameters for consumer sites.

A hidden field is a field sent to the browser that isn't displayed on the Web page. You get it with a tag of the form <INPUT type = "hidden">. To make a hidden field work you serialize your session state into it when you make a response and read it back in on each request. You'll need a format for putting the data in the hidden field. XML is an obvious standard choice, but of course it's rather wordy. You can also encode the data in some text-based encoding scheme. Remember that a hidden field is only hidden from the displayed page; anyone can look at the data by looking at the page source.

Beware a mixed site that has older or fixed Web pages. You can lose all the session data if you navigate to them.

The last, and sometimes controversial, choice is cookies, which are sent back and forth automatically. Just like a hidden field you can use a cookie by serializing the session state into it. You're limited in how big the cookie can be. Also, many people don't like cookies and turn them off. If they do that, your site will stop working. However, more and more sites are dependent on cookies now, so that will happen less often, and certainly isn't a problem for a purely in-house system.

Realize that cookies are no more secure than anything else, so assume that prying of all kinds can happen. Cookies also work only within a single domain name, so if your site is separated into different domain names the cookies won't travel between them.

Some platforms can detect whether cookies are enabled; and if not, they can use URL rewriting. This can make client session state very easy for very small amounts of data.

When to Use It

Client Session State contains a number of advantages. In particular, it reacts well in supporting stateless server objects with maximal clustering and failover resiliency. Of course, if the client fails all is lost, but often the user expects that anyway.

The arguments against *Client Session State* vary exponentially with the amount of data involved. With just a few fields everything works nicely. With large amounts of data the issues of where to store the data and the time cost of transferring everything with every request become prohibitive. This is especially true if your stars include an http client.

There's also the security issue. Any data sent to the client is vulnerable to being looked at and altered. Encryption is the only way to stop this, but encrypting and decrypting with each request are a performance burden. Without encryption you have to be sure you aren't sending anything you would rather hide from prying eyes. Fingers can pry too, so don't assume that what got sent out is the same as what gets sent back. Any data coming back will need to be completely revalidated.

You almost always have to use *Client Session State* for session identification. Fortunately, this should be just one number, which won't burden any of the above schemes. You should still be concerned about session stealing, which is what happens when a malicious user changes his session ID to see if he can snag someone else's session. Most platforms come up with a random session ID to reduce this risk; if not run, a simple session ID through a hash.

Client
Session
State

Server Session State

Keeps the session state on a server system in a serialized form.

How It Works

In the simplest form of this pattern a session object is held in memory on an application server. You can have some kind of map in memory that holds these session objects keyed by a session ID; all the client needs to do is to give the session ID and the session object can be retrieved from the map to process the request.

This basic scenario assumes, of course, that the application server carries enough memory to perform this task. It also assumes that there's only one application server—that is, no clustering—and that, if the application server fails, it's appropriate for the session to be abandoned and all work done so far to be lost in the great bit-bucket in the sky.

For many applications this set of assumptions is actually not a problem. However, for others it may be problematic. There are ways of dealing with cases where the assumptions are no longer valid, and these introduce common variations that add complexity to an essentially simple pattern.

The first issue is that of dealing with memory resources held by the session objects. Indeed, this is the common objection to *Server Session State*. The answer, of course, is not to keep resources in memory but instead serialize all the session state to a memento [Gang of Four] for persistent storage. This presents two questions: In what form do you persist the *Server Session State,* and where do you persist it?

The form to use is usually as simple a form as possible, since the accent of *Server Session State* is its simplicity in programming. Several platforms provide a simple binary serialization mechanism that allows you to serialize a graph of objects quite easily. Another route is to serialize into another form, such as text—fashionably as an XML file.

The binary form is usually easier, since it requires little programming, while the textual form usually requires at least a little code. Binary serializations also require less disk space; although total disk space is rarely a concern, large serialized graphs will take longer to activate into memory.

There are two common issues with binary serialization. First, the serialized form is not human readable—which is a problem if humans want to read it. Second, there may be problems with versioning. If you modify a class by, say, adding a field after you've serialized it, you may not be able to read it back. Of course, not many sessions are likely to span an upgrade of the server software unless it's a 24/7 server where you may have a cluster of machines running, some upgraded and some not.

This brings us to the question of where to store the *Server Session State*. An obvious possibility is on the application server itself, either in the file system or in a local database. This is the simple route, but it may not support efficient clustering or failover. To support these the passivated *Server Session State* needs to be somewhere generally accessible, such as on shared server. This will support clustering and failover at the cost of a longer time to activate the server—although caching may well eliminate much of this cost.

This line of reasoning may lead, ironically to storing the serialized *Server Session State* in the database using a session table indexed by the session ID. This table would require a *Serialized LOB (272)* to hold the serialized *Server Session State*. Database performance varies when it comes to handling large objects, so the performance aspects of this one are very database dependent.

At this point we're right at the boundary between *Server Session State* and *Database Session State (462)*. This boundary is completely arbitrary, but I've drawn the line at the point where you convert the data in the *Server Session State* into tabular form.

If you're storing *Server Session State* in a database, you'll have to worry about handling sessions going away, especially in a consumer application. One route is to have a daemon that looks for aged sessions and deletes them, but this can lead to a lot of contention on the session table. Kai Yu told me about an approach he used with success: partitioning the session table into twelve database segments and every two hours rotating the segments, deleting everything in the oldest segment and then directing all inserts to it. While this meant that any session that was active for twenty-four hours got unceremoniously dumped, that would be sufficiently rare to not be a problem.

All these variations take more and more effort to do, but the good news is that application servers increasingly support these capabilities automatically. Thus, it may well be that application server vendors can worry their ugly little heads about them.

Java Implementation

The two most common techniques for *Server Session State* are using the http session and using a stateful session bean. The http session is the simple route and causes the session data to be stored by the Web server. In most cases this leads to server affinity and it can't cope with failover. Some vendors are implementing a shared http session capability that allows you to store http

Server
Session
State

session data in a database that's available to all application servers. (You can also do this manually, of course.)

The other common route is via a stateful session bean, which requires an EJB server. The EJB container handles all persistence and passivation, so this makes it very easy to program to. The main disadvantage is that the specification doesn't ask the application server to avoid server affinity. However, some application servers provide this capability. One, IBM's WebSphere, can serialize a stateful session bean into a BLOB in DB2, which allows multiple application servers to get at its state.

A lot of people say that, since stateless session beans perform better, you should *always* use them instead of stateful beans. Frankly, that's hogwash. Load-test with your environment first to see if you fall into the range of speed difference between stateful and stateless that makes any difference to your application. ThoughtWorks has load-tested apps with a couple of hundred of concurrent users and not found any performance problems due to stateful beans on that size of user load. If the performance advantage isn't significant for your loads, and stateful beans are easier, then you should use them. There are other reasons to be wary of stateful beans—failover may be more problematic depending on your vendor, but the performance difference only appears under a heavy load.

Another alternative is to use an entity bean. On the whole, I've been pretty dismissive of entity beans, but you can use one to store a *Serialized LOB (272)* of session data. This is pretty simple and less likely to raise many of the issues that usually surround entity beans.

.NET Implementation

Server Session State is easy to implement with the built-in session state capability. By default .NET stores session data in the server process itself. You can also adjust the storage using a state service, which can reside on the local machine or on any other machine on the network. With a separate state service you can reset the Web server and still retain the session state. You make the change between in-process state and a state service in the configuration file, so you don't have to change the application.

When to Use It

The great appeal of *Server Session State* is its simplicity. In a number of cases you don't have to do any programming at all to make this work. Whether you can get away with that depends on if you can get away with the in-memory implementation and, if not, how much help your application server platform gives you.

Even without that you may well find that the effort you do need is small. Serializing a BLOB to a database table may turn out to be much less effort than converting the server objects to tabular form.

Where the programming effort comes into play is in session maintenance, particularly if you have to roll your own support to enable clustering and failover. It may work out to be more trouble than your other options, especially if you don't have much session data to deal with or if your session data is easily converted to tabular form.

Server
Session
State

Database Session State

Stores session data as committed data in the database.

How It Works

When a call goes out from the client to the server, the server object first pulls the data required for the request from the database. Then it does the work it needs to do and saves back to the database all the data required.

In order to pull information from the database, the server object will need some information about the session, which requires at least a session ID number to be stored on the client. Usually, however, this information is nothing more than the appropriate set of keys needed to find the appropriate amount of data in the database.

The data involved is typically a mix of session data that's only local to the current interaction and committed data that's relevant to all interactions.

One of the key issues to consider here is the fact that session data is usually considered local to the session and shouldn't affect other parts of the system until the session as a whole is committed. Thus, if you're working on an order in a session and you want to save its intermediate state to the database, you usually need to handle it differently from an order that's confirmed at the end of a session. This is because you don't want pending orders to appear that often in queries run against the database for such things as book availability and daily revenue.

So how do you separate the session data? Adding a field to each database row that may have session data is one route.The simplest form of this just requires a Boolean isPending field. However, a better way is to store a session ID as a pending field, which makes it much easier to find all the data for a particular session. All queries that want only record data now need to be modified with a sessionID is not NULL clause, or need a view that filters out that data.

Using a session ID field is a very invasive solution because all applications that touch the record database need to know the field's meaning to avoid getting session data. Views will sometimes do the trick and remove the invasiveness, but they often impose costs of their own.

A second alternative is a separate set of pending tables. So if you have orders and order lines tables already in your database, you would add tables for pending orders and pending order lines. Pending session data you save to the pending table; when it becomes record data you save it to the real tables. This removes much of the invasiveness. However, you'll need to add the appropriate table selection logic to your database mapping code, which will certainly add some complications.

Often the record data will have integrity rules that don't apply to pending data. In this case the pending tables allow you to forgo the rules when you don't want them but to enforce them when you do. Validation rules as well typically aren't applied when saving pending data. You may face different validation rules depending on where you are in the session, but this usually appears in server object logic.

If you use pending tables, they should be exact clones of the real tables. That way you can keep your mapping logic as similar as possible. Use the same field names between the two tables, but add a session ID field to the pending tables so you can easily find all the data for a session.

You'll need a mechanism to clean out the session data if a session is canceled or abandoned. Using a session ID you can find all data with it and delete it. If users abandon the session without telling you, you'll need some kind of timeout mechanism. A daemon that runs every few minutes can look for old session data. This requires a table in the database that keeps track of the time of the last interaction with the session.

Rollback is made much more complicated by updates. If you update an existing order in a session that allows a rollback of the whole session, how do you perform the rollback? One option is not to allow cancellation of a session like this. Any updates to existing record data become part of the record data at the end of the request. This is simple and often fits the users' view of the world. The alternative is awkward whether you use pending fields or pending tables. It's easy to copy all the data that may be modified into pending tables, modify it there, and commit it back to the record tables at the end of the session. You can do this with a pending field, but only if the session ID becomes part of the key. In this way you can keep the old and new IDs in the same table at the same time, which can get very messy.

If you're going to use separate pending tables that are only read by objects that handle a session, then there may be little point in tabularizing the data. It's better to use a *Serialized LOB (272)*. At this point we've crossed the boundary into a *Server Session State (458)*.

You can avoid all of the hassles of pending data by not having any. That is, you design your system so that all data is considered record data. This isn't always possible, of course, and if it is it can be so awkward that designers would be better off thinking about explicit pending data. Still, if you have the option it makes *Database Session State* a lot easier to work with.

Database Session State

When to Use It

Database Session State is one alternative to handling session state; it should be compared with *Server Session State (458)* and *Client Session State (456)*.

The first aspect to consider with this pattern is performance. You'll gain by using stateless objects on the server, thus enabling pooling and easy clustering. However, you'll pay with the time needed to pull the data in and out of the database with each request. You can reduce this cost by caching the server object so you won't have to read the data out of the database whenever the cache is hit, but you'll still pay the write costs.

The second main issue is the programming effort, most of which centers around handling session state. If you have no session state and are able to save all your data as record data in each request, this pattern is an obvious choice because you lose nothing in either effort or performance (if you cache your server objects).

In a choice between *Database Session State* and *Server Session State (458)* the biggest issue may be how easy it is to support clustering and failover with *Server Session State (458)* in your particular application server. Clustering and failover with *Database Session State* are usually more straightforward, at least with the regular solutions.

**Database
Session
State**

Chapter 18

Base Patterns

Gateway

An object that encapsulates access to an external system or resource.

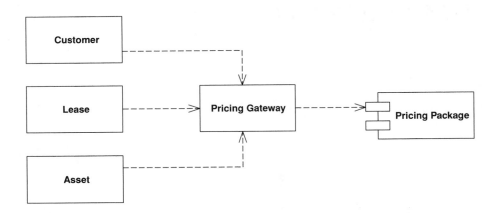

Interesting software rarely lives in isolation. Even the purest object-oriented system often has to deal with things that aren't objects, such as relational database tables, CICS transactions, and XML data structures.

When accessing external resources like this, you'll usually get APIs for them. However, these APIs are naturally going to be somewhat complicated because they take the nature of the resource into account. Anyone who needs to understand a resource needs to understand its API—whether JDBC and SQL for relational databases or W3C or JDOM for XML. Not only does this make the software harder to understand, it also makes it much harder to change should you shift some data from a relational database to an XML message at some point in the future.

The answer is so common that it's hardly worth stating. Wrap all the special API code into a class whose interface looks like a regular object. Other objects access the resource through this *Gateway*, which translates the simple method calls into the appropriate specialized API.

How It Works

In reality this is a very simple wrapper pattern. Take the external resource. What does the application need to do with it? Create a simple API for your usage and use the *Gateway* to translate to the external source.

One of the key uses for a *Gateway* is as a good point at which to apply a *Service Stub (504)*. You can often alter the design of the *Gateway* to make it easier to apply a *Service Stub (504)*. Don't be afraid to do this—well placed *Service Stubs (504)* can make a system much easier to test and thus much easier to write.

Keep a *Gateway* as simple as you can. Focus on the essential roles of adapting the external service and providing a good point for stubbing. The *Gateway* should be as minimal as possible and yet able to handle these tasks. Any more complex logic should be in the *Gateway's* clients.

Often it's a good idea to use code generation to create *Gateways*. By defining the structure of the external resource, you can generate a *Gateway* class to wrap it. You might use relational metadata to create a wrapper class for a relational table, or an XML schema or DTD to generate code for a *Gateway* for XML. The resulting *Gateways* are dumb but they do the trick. Other objects can carry out more complicated manipulations.

Sometimes a good strategy is to build the *Gateway* in terms of more than one object. The obvious form is to use two objects: a back end and a front end. The back end acts as a minimal overlay to the external resource and doesn't simplify the resource's API at all. The front end then transforms the awkward API into a more convenient one for your application to use. This approach is good if the wrapping of the external service and the adaptation to your needs are reasonably complicated, because each responsibility is handled by a single class. Conversely, if the wrapping of the external service is simple, one class can handle that and any adaptation that's needed.

When to Use It

You should consider *Gateway* whenever you have an awkward interface to something that feels external. Rather than let the awkwardness spread through the whole system, use a *Gateway* to contain it. There's hardly any downside to making the *Gateway*, and the code elsewhere in the system becomes much easier to read.

Gateway usually makes a system easier to test by giving you a clear point at which to deploy *Service Stubs (504)*. Even if the external system's interface is fine, a *Gateway* is useful as a first move in applying *Service Stub (504)*.

A clear benefit of *Gateway* is that it also makes it easier for you to swap out one kind of resource for another. Any change in resources means that you only have to alter the *Gateway* class—the change doesn't ripple through the rest of the system. *Gateway* is a simple and powerful form of protected variation. In many cases reasoning about this flexibility is the focus of debate about using

Gateway

Gateway. However, don't forget that even if you don't think the resource is ever going to change, you can benefit from the simplicity and testability *Gateway* gives you.

When you have a couple of subsystems like this, another choice for decoupling them is a *Mapper (473)*. However, *Mapper (473)* is more complicated than *Gateway*. As a result, I use *Gateway* for the majority of my external resource access.

I must admit that I've struggled a fair bit with whether to make this a new pattern as opposed to referencing existing patterns such as Facade and Adapter [Gang of Four]. I decided to separate it out from these other patterns because I think there's a useful distinction to be made.

• While *Facade* simplifies a more complex API, it's usually done by the writer of the service for general use. A *Gateway* is written by the client for its particular use. In addition, a Facade always implies a different interface to what it's covering, whereas a *Gateway* may copy the wrapped facade entirely, being used for substitution or testing purposes.

• *Adapter* alters an implementation's interface to match another interface you need to work with. With *Gateway* there usually isn't an existing interface, although you might use an adapter to map an implementation to a *Gateway* interface. In this case the adapter is part of the *Gateway* implementation.

• *Mediator* usually separates multiple objects so that they don't know about each other but do know about the mediator. With a *Gateway* there are usually only two objects involved and the resource that's being wrapped doesn't know about the *Gateway*.

Example: A Gateway to a Proprietary Messaging Service (Java)

I was talking about this pattern with my colleague, Mike Rettig, and he described how he's used it to handle interfaces with Enterprise Application Integration (EAI) software. We decided that this would be a good inspiration for a *Gateway* example.

To keep things at the usual level of ludicrous simplicity, we'll build a gateway to an interface that just sends a message using the message service. The interface is just a single method.

```
int send(String messageType, Object[] args);
```

The first argument is a string indicating the type of the message; the second is the arguments of the message. The messaging system allows you to send any kind of message, so it needs a generic interface like this. When you configure the message system you specify the types of message the system will send and the number and types of arguments for them. Thus, we might configure the confirm message with the string "CNFRM" and have arguments for an ID number as a string, an integer amount, and a string for the ticker code. The messaging system checks the types of the arguments for us and generates an error if we send a wrong message or the right message with the wrong arguments.

This is laudable, and necessary, flexibility, but the generic interface is awkward to use because it isn't explicit. You can't tell by looking at the interface what the legal message types are or what arguments are needed for a certain message type. What we need instead is an interface with methods like this:

```
public void sendConfirmation(String orderID, int amount, String symbol);
```

That way if we want a domain object to send a message, it can do so like this:

```
class Order...

    public void confirm() {
        if (isValid()) Environment.getMessageGateway().sendConfirmation(id, amount, symbol);
    }
```

Here the name of the method tells us what message we're sending, and the arguments are typed and given names. This is a much easier method to call than the generic method. It's the gateway's role to make a more convenient interface. It does mean, though, that every time we add or change a message type in the messaging system we need to change the gateway class, but we would have to change the calling code anyway. At least this way the compiler can help us find clients and check for errors.

There's another problem. When we get an error with this interface it tells us by giving us a return error code. Zero indicates success; anything else indicates failure, and different numbers indicate different errors. This is a natural way for a C programmer to work, but it isn't the way Java does things. In Java you throw an exception to indicate an error, so the *Gateway's* methods should throw exceptions rather than return error codes.

The full range of possible errors is something that we'll naturally ignore. I'll focus on just two: sending a message with an unknown message type and sending a message where one of the arguments is null. The return codes are defined in the messaging system's interface.

```
public static final int NULL_PARAMETER = -1;
public static final int UNKNOWN_MESSAGE_TYPE = -2;
public static final int SUCCESS = 0;
```

Gateway

The two errors have a significant difference. The unknown message type error indicates an error in the gateway class; since any client is only calling a fully explicit method, clients should never generate this error. They might pass in a null, however, and thus see the null parameter error. This error isn't a checked exception since it indicates a programmer error—not something that you would write a specific handler for. The gateway could actually check for nulls itself, but if the messaging system is going to raise the same error it probably isn't worth it.

For these reasons the gateway has to both translate from the explicit interface to the generic interface and translate the return codes into exceptions.

```
class MessageGateway...

    protected static final String CONFIRM = "CNFRM";
    private MessageSender sender;
    public void sendConfirmation(String orderID, int amount, String symbol) {
        Object[] args = new Object[]{orderID, new Integer(amount), symbol};
        send(CONFIRM, args);
    }
    private void send(String msg, Object[] args) {
        int returnCode = doSend(msg, args);
        if (returnCode == MessageSender.NULL_PARAMETER)
            throw new NullPointerException("Null Parameter bassed for msg type: " + msg);
        if (returnCode != MessageSender.SUCCESS)
            throw new IllegalStateException(
                    "Unexpected error from messaging system #:" + returnCode);
    }
    protected int doSend(String msg, Object[] args) {
        Assert.notNull(sender);
        return sender.send(msg, args);
    }
```

So far, it's hard to see the point of the doSend method, but it's there for another key role for a gateway—testing. We can test objects that use the gateway without the message-sending service being present. To do this we need to create a *Service Stub (504)*. In this case the gateway stub is a subclass of the real gateway and overrides doSend.

```
class MessageGatewayStub...

    protected int doSend(String messageType, Object[] args) {
        int returnCode = isMessageValid(messageType, args);
        if (returnCode == MessageSender.SUCCESS) {
            messagesSent++;
        }
        return returnCode;
    }
    private int isMessageValid(String messageType, Object[] args) {
        if (shouldFailAllMessages) return -999;
```

```
      if (!legalMessageTypes().contains(messageType))
         return MessageSender.UNKNOWN_MESSAGE_TYPE;
      for (int i = 0; i < args.length; i++) {
         Object arg = args[i];
         if (arg == null) {
            return MessageSender.NULL_PARAMETER;
         }
      }
      return MessageSender.SUCCESS;
   }
   public static List legalMessageTypes() {
      List result = new ArrayList();
      result.add(CONFIRM);
      return result;
   }
   private boolean shouldFailAllMessages = false;
   public void failAllMessages() {
      shouldFailAllMessages = true;
   }
   public int getNumberOfMessagesSent() {
      return messagesSent;
   }
```

Capturing the number of messages sent is a simple way of helping us test that the gateway works correctly with tests like these.

```
class GatewayTester...

   public void testSendNullArg() {
      try {
         gate().sendConfirmation(null, 5, "US");
         fail("Didn't detect null argument");
      } catch (NullPointerException expected) {
      }
      assertEquals(0, gate().getNumberOfMessagesSent());
   }
   private MessageGatewayStub gate() {
      return (MessageGatewayStub) Environment.getMessageGateway();
   }
   protected void setUp() throws Exception {
      Environment.testInit();
   }
```

You usually set up the *Gateway* so that classes can find it from a well-known place. Here I've used a static environment interface. You can switch between the real service and the stub at configuration time by using a *Plugin (499)*, or you can have the test setup routines initialize the environment to use the *Service Stub (504)*.

In this case I've used a subclass of the gateway to stub the messaging service. Another route is to subclass (or reimplement) the service itself. For testing you connect the gateway to the sending *Service Stub (504)*; it works if reimplementation of the service isn't too difficult. You always have the choice of stubbing the service or stubbing the gateway. In some cases it's even useful to stub both, using the stubbed gateway for testing clients of the gateway and the stubbed service to test the gateway itself.

Gateway

Mapper

*An object that sets up a communication
between two independent objects.*

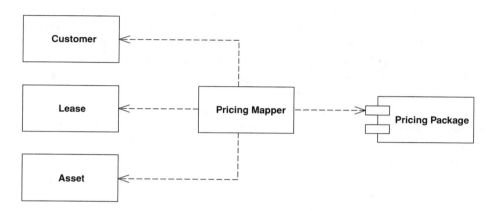

Sometimes you need to set up communications between two subsystems that still need to stay ignorant of each other. This may be because you can't modify them or you can but you don't want to create dependencies between the two or even between them and the isolating element.

How It Works

A mapper is an insulating layer between subsystems. It controls the details of the communication between them without either subsystem being aware of it.

A mapper often shuffles data from one layer to another. Once activated for this shuffling, it's fairly easy to see how it works. The complicated part of using a mapper is deciding how to invoke it, since it can't be directly invoked by either of the subsystems that it's mapping between. Sometimes a third subsystem drives the mapping and invokes the mapper as well. An alternative is to make the mapper an observer [Gang of Four] of one or the other subsystem. That way it can be invoked by listening to events in one of them.

How a mapper works depends on the kind of layers it's mapping. The most common case of a mapping layer that we run into is in a *Data Mapper (165)*, so look there for more details on how a *Mapper* is used.

Mapper

When to Use It

Essentially a *Mapper* decouples different parts of a system. When you want to do this you have a choice between *Mapper* and *Gateway (466)*. *Gateway (466)* is by far the most common choice because it's much simpler to use a *Gateway (466)* than a *Mapper* both in writing the code and in using it later.

As a result you should only use a *Mapper* when you need to ensure that neither subsystem has a dependency on this interaction. The only time this is really important is when the interaction between the subsystems is particularly complicated and somewhat independent to the main purpose of both subsystems. Thus, in enterprise applications we mostly find *Mapper* used for interactions with a database, as in *Data Mapper (165)*.

Mapper is similar to Mediator [Gang of Four] in that it's used to separate different elements. However, the objects that use a mediator are aware of it, even if they aren't aware of each other; the objects that a *Mapper* separates aren't even aware of the mapper.

Mapper

Layer Supertype

A type that acts as the supertype for all types in its layer.

It's not uncommon for all the objects in a layer to have methods you don't want to have duplicated throughout the system. You can move all of this behavior into a common *Layer Supertype*.

How It Works

Layer Supertype is a simple idea that leads to a very short pattern. All you need is a superclass for all the objects in a layer—for example, a Domain Object superclass for all the domain objects in a *Domain Model (116)*. Common features, such as the storage and handling of *Identity Fields (216)*, can go there. Similarly all *Data Mappers (165)* in the mapping layer can have a superclass that relies on the fact that all domain objects have a common superclass.

If you have more than one kind of object in a layer, it's useful to have more than one *Layer Supertype*.

When to Use It

Use *Layer Supertype* when you have common features from all objects in a layer. I Often do this automatically because I make a lot of use of common features.

Example: Domain Object (Java)

Domain objects can have a common superclass for ID handling.

```java
class DomainObject...

   private Long ID;
   public Long getID() {
      return ID;
   }
   public void setID(Long ID) {
      Assert.notNull("Cannot set a null ID", ID);
      this.ID = ID;
   }
   public DomainObject(Long ID) {
      this.ID = ID;
   }
   public DomainObject() {
   }
```

Layer
Supertype

Separated Interface

Defines an interface in a separate package from its implementation.

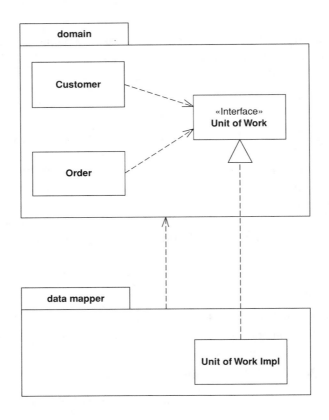

As you develop a system, you can improve the quality of its design by reducing the coupling between the system's parts. A good way to do this is to group the classes into packages and control the dependencies between them. You can then follow rules about how classes in one package can call classes in another—for example, one that says that classes in the domain layer may not call classes in the presentation package.

However, you might need to invoke methods that contradict the general dependency structure. If so, use *Separated Interface* to define an interface in one package but implement it in another. This way a client that needs the dependency to the interface can be completely unaware of the implementation. The *Separated Interface* provides a good plug point for *Gateway (466)*.

How It Works

This pattern is very simple to employ. Essentially it takes advantage of the fact that an implementation has a dependency to its interface but not vice versa. This means you can put the interface and the implementation in separate packages and the implementation package has a dependency to the interface package. Other packages can depend on the interface package without depending on the implementation package.

Of course, the software won't work at runtime without some implementation of the interface. This can be either at compile time using a separate package that ties the two together or at configuration time using *Plugin (499)*.

You can place the interface in the client's package (as in the sketch) or in a third package (Figure 18.1). If there's only one client for the implementation, or all the clients are in the same package, then you might as well put the interface in with the client. A good way of thinking about this is that the developers of the client package are responsible for defining the interface. Essentially the client package indicates that it will work with any other package that implements the interface it defines. If you have multiple client packages, a third interface package is better. It's also better if you want to show that the interface definition isn't

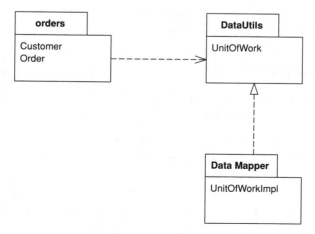

Figure 18.1 *Placing the* Separated Interface *in a third package.*

the responsibility of the client package developers. This would be the case if the developers of the implementation were responsible for it.

You have to consider what language feature to use for the interface. For languages that have an interface construct, such as Java and C#, the interface keyword is the obvious choice. However, it may not be the best. An abstract class can make a good interface because you can have common, but optional, implementation behavior in it.

One of the awkward things about separate interfaces is how to instantiate the implementation. It usually requires knowledge of the implementation class. The common approach is to use a separate factory object, where again there is a *Separated Interface* for the factory. You still have to bind an implementation to the factory, and *Plugin (499)* is a good way to do this. Not only does it mean there is no dependency, but it also defers the decision about implementation class to configuration time.

If you don't want to go all the way to *Plugin (499)*, a simpler alternative is to let yet another package that knows both the interface and the implementation instantiate the right objects at application startup. Any objects that use *Separated Interface* can either themselves be instantiated or have factories instantiated at startup.

When to Use It

You use *Separated Interface* when you need to break a dependency between two parts of the system. Here are some examples:

- You've built some abstract code for common cases into a framework package that needs to call some particular application code.

- You have some code in one layer that needs to call code in another layer that it shouldn't see, such as domain code calling a *Data Mapper (165)*.

- You need to call functions developed by another development group but don't want a dependency into their APIs.

I come across many developers who have separate interfaces for every class they write. I think this is excessive, especially for application development. Keeping separate interfaces and implementations is extra work, especially since you often need factory classes (with interfaces and implementations) as well. For applications I recommend using a separate interface only if you want to break a dependency or you want to have multiple independent implementations. If you put the interface and implementation together and need to separate them later, this is a simple refactoring that can be delayed until you need to do it.

There is a degree to where the determined management of dependencies in this way can get a little silly. Having only a dependency to create an object, and using the interface ever after, is usually enough. The trouble comes when you want to enforce dependency rules, such as by doing a dependency check at build time. Then all dependencies have to be removed. For a smaller system enforcing dependency rules is less of an issue, but for bigger systems it's a very worthwhile discipline.

Registry

*A well-known object that other objects can use
to find common objects and services.*

Registry	1
getPerson (id) addPerson (Person)	

When you want to find an object you usually start with another object that has an association to it, and use the association to navigate to it. Thus, if you want to find all the orders for a customer, you start with the customer object and use a method on it to get the orders. However, in some cases you won't have an appropriate object to start with. You may know the customer's ID number but not have a reference. In this case you need some kind of lookup method—a finder—but the question remains: How do you get to the finder?

A *Registry* is essentially a global object, or at least it looks like one—even if it isn't as global as it may appear.

How It Works

As with any object, you have to think about the design of a *Registry* in terms of interface and implementation. And like many objects, the two are quite different, although people often make the mistake of thinking they should be the same.

The first thing to think of is the interface, and for *Registries* my preferred interface is static methods. A static method on a class is easy to find anywhere in an application. Furthermore, you can encapsulate any logic you like within the static method, including delegation to other methods, either static or instance.

However, just because your methods are static doesn't mean that your data should be in static fields. Indeed, I almost never use static fields unless they're constants.

Before you decide on how to hold your data, think about the data's scope. The data for a *Registry* can vary with different execution contexts. Some of it is global across an entire process; some, global across a thread; and some, global across a session. Different scopes call for different implementations, but they don't call for different interfaces. The application programmer doesn't have to know whether a call to a static method yields process-scoped or thread-scoped data. You can have different *Registries* for different scopes, but you can also have a single *Registry* in which different methods are at different scopes.

If your data is common to a whole process, a static field is an option. However, I rarely use static mutable fields because they don't allow for substitution. It can be extremely useful to be able to substitute a *Registry* for a particular purpose, especially for testing (*Plugin (499)* is a good way to do this).

For a process-scoped *Registry*, then, the usual option is a singleton [Gang of Four]. The *Registry* class contains a single static field that holds a *Registry* instance. When people use a singleton they often make its caller explicitly access the underlying data (Registry.soleInstance.getFoo()), but I prefer a static method that hides the singleton object from me (Registry.getFoo()). This works particularly well since C-based languages allow static methods to access private instance data.

Singletons are widely used in single-threaded applications, but can be a problem for multi-threaded applications. This is because it's too easy for multiple threads to manipulate the same object in unpredictable ways. You may be able to solve this with synchronization, but the difficulty of writing the synchronization code is likely to drive you into an insane asylum before you get all the bugs out. For that reason I don't recommend using a singleton for mutable data in a multi-threaded environment. It does work well for immutable data, since anything that can't change isn't going to run into thread clash problems. Thus, something like a list of all states in the United States makes a good candidate for a process-scoped *Registry*. Such data can be loaded when a process starts up and never need changing, or it may be updated rarely with some kind of process interrupt.

A common kind of *Registry* data is thread scoped. A good example is a database connection. In this case many environments give you some form of thread-specific storage, such as Java's thread local. Another technique is a dictionary keyed by thread whose value is an appropriate data object. A request for a connection results in a lookup in that dictionary by the current thread.

The important thing to remember about thread-scoped data is that it looks no different from process-scoped data. I can still use a method such as Registry.getDbConnection(), which is the same form when I'm accessing process-scoped data.

A dictionary lookup is also a technique you can use for session-scoped data. Here you need a session ID, but it can be put into a thread-scoped registry when a request begins. Any subsequent accesses for session data can look up the data

Registry

in a map that's keyed by session using the session ID that's held in thread-specific storage.

If you're using a thread-scoped *Registry* with static methods, you may run into a performance issue with multiple threads going through them. In that case direct access to the thread's instance will avoid the bottleneck.

Some applications may have a single *Registry*; some may have several. *Registries* are usually divided up by system layer or by execution context. My preference is to divide them up by how they are used, rather than implementation.

When to Use It

Despite the encapsulation of a method, a *Registry* is still global data and as such is something I'm uncomfortable using. I almost always see some form of *Registry* in an application, but I always try to access objects through regular inter-object references instead. Basically, you should only use a *Registry* as a last resort.

There are alternatives to using a *Registry*. One is to pass around any widely needed data in parameters. The problem with this is that parameters are added to method calls where they aren't needed by the called method but only by some other method that's called several layers deep in the call tree. Passing a parameter around when it's not needed 90 percent of the time is what leads me to use a *Registry* instead.

Another alternative I've seen to a *Registry* is to add a reference to the common data to objects when they're created. Although this leads to an extra parameter in a constructor, at least it's only used by that constructor. It's still more trouble than it's often worth, but if you have data that's only used by a subset of classes, this technique allows you to restrict things that way.

One of the problems with a *Registry* is that it has to be modified every time you add a new piece of data. This is why some people prefer to use a map as their holder of global data. I prefer the explicit class because it keeps the methods explicit, so there's no confusion about what key you use to find something. With an explicit class you can just look at the source code or generated documentation to see what's available. With a map you have to find places in the system where data is read or written to the map to find out what key is used or to rely on documentation that quickly becomes stale. An explicit class also allows you to keep type safety in a statically typed language as well as to encapsulate the structure of the *Registry* so that you can refactor it as the system grows. A bare map also is unencapsulated, which makes it harder to hide the implementation. This is particularly awkward if you have to change the data's execution scope.

So there are times when it's right to use a *Registry*, but remember that any global data is always guilty until proven innocent.

Example: A Singleton Registry (Java)

Consider an application that reads data from a database and then munges on it to turn it into information. Well, imagine a fairly simple system that uses *Row Data Gateways (152)* for data access. This system has finder objects to encapsulate the database queries. The finders are best made as instances because that way we can substitute them to make a *Service Stub (504)* for testing. We need a place to put them; a *Registry* is the obvious choice.

A singleton registry is a very simple example of the Singleton pattern [Gang of Four]. You have a static variable for the single instance.

```
class Registry...

    private static Registry getInstance() {
        return soleInstance;
    }
    private static Registry soleInstance = new Registry();
```

Everything that's stored on the registry is stored on the instance.

```
class Registry...

    protected PersonFinder personFinder = new PersonFinder();
```

To make access easier, however, I make the public methods static.

```
class Registry...

    public static PersonFinder personFinder() {
        return getInstance().personFinder;
    }
```

I can reinitialize the registry simply by creating a new sole instance.

```
class Registry...

    public static void initialize() {
        soleInstance = new Registry();
    }
```

If I want to use *Service Stubs (504)* for testing, I use a subclass instead.

```
class RegistryStub extends Registry...

    public RegistryStub() {
        personFinder = new PersonFinderStub();
    }
```

Registry

The finder *Service Stub (504)* just returns hardcoded instances of the person *Row Data Gateway (152)*.

class PersonFinderStub...

```
public Person find(long id) {
   if (id == 1) {
      return new Person("Fowler", "Martin", 10);
   }
   throw new IllegalArgumentException("Can't find id: " + String.valueOf(id));
}
```

I put a method on the registry to initialize it in stub mode, but by keeping all the stub behavior in the subclass I can separate all the code required for testing.

class Registry...

```
public static void initializeStub() {
   soleInstance = new RegistryStub();
}
```

Example: Thread-Safe *Registry* (Java)

Matt Foemmel and Martin Fowler

The simple example above won't work for a multi-threaded application where different threads need their own registry. Java provides Thread Specific Storage variables [Schmidt] that are local to a thread, helpfully called thread local variables. You can use them to create a registry that's unique for a thread.

class ThreadLocalRegistry...

```
private static ThreadLocal instances = new ThreadLocal();
public static ThreadLocalRegistry getInstance() {
   return (ThreadLocalRegistry) instances.get();
}
```

Registry

The *Registry* needs to be set up with methods for acquiring and releasing it. You typically do this on a transaction or session call boundary.

class ThreadLocalRegistry...

```
public static void begin() {
   Assert.isTrue(instances.get() == null);
   instances.set(new ThreadLocalRegistry());
}
public static void end() {
   Assert.notNull(getInstance());
   instances.set(null);
}
```

You can then store person finders as before.

```
class ThreadLocalRegistry...

   private PersonFinder personFinder = new PersonFinder();;
   public static PersonFinder personFinder() {
      return getInstance().personFinder;
   }
```

Calls from the outside wrap their use of a registry in the begin and end methods.

```
      try {
         ThreadLocalRegistry.begin();
         PersonFinder f1 = ThreadLocalRegistry.personFinder();
         Person martin = Registry.personFinder().find(1);
         assertEquals("Fowler", martin.getLastName());
      } finally {ThreadLocalRegistry.end();
      }
```

Registry

Value Object

A small simple object, like money or a date
range, whose equality isn't based on identity.

With object systems of various kinds, I've found it useful to distinguish between reference objects and *Value Objects*. Of the two a *Value Object* is usually the smaller; it's similar to the primitive types present in many languages that aren't purely object-oriented.

How It Works

Defining the difference between a reference object and *Value Object* can be a tricky thing. In a broad sense we like to think that *Value Objects* are small objects, such as a money object or a date, while reference objects are large, such as an order or a customer. Such a definition is handy but annoyingly informal.

The key difference between reference and value objects lies in how they deal with equality. A reference object uses identity as the basis for equality—maybe the identity within the programming system, such as the built-in identity of OO programming languages, or maybe some kind of ID number, such as the primary key in a relational database. A *Value Object* bases its notion of equality on field values within the class. Thus, two date objects may be the same if their day, month, and year values are the same.

This difference manifests itself in how you deal with them. Since *Value Objects* are small and easily created, they're often passed around by value instead of by reference. You don't really care about how many March 18, 2001, objects there are in your system. Nor do you care if two objects share the same physical date object or whether they have different yet equal copies.

Most languages have no special facility for value objects. For value objects to work properly in these cases it's a very good idea to make them immutable—that is, once created none of their fields change. The reason for this is to avoid aliasing bugs. An aliasing bug occurs when two objects share the same value object and one of the owners changes the values in it. Thus, if Martin has a hire date of March 18 and we know that Cindy was hired on the same day, we may set Cindy's hire date to be the same as Martin's. If Martin then changes the month in his hire date to May, Cindy's hire date changes too. Whether it's correct or not, it isn't what people expect. Usually with small values like this people expect to change a hire date by replacing the existing date object with a new one. Making *Value Objects* immutable fulfills that expectation.

Value Objects shouldn't be persisted as complete records. Instead use *Embedded Value (268)* or *Serialized LOB (272)*. Since *Value Objects* are small, *Embedded Value (268)* is usually the best choice because it also allows SQL querying using the data in a *Value Object*.

If you're doing a lot of binary serializing, you may find that optimizing the serialization of *Value Objects* can improve performance, particularly in languages like Java that don't treat for *Value Objects* in a special way.

For an example of a *Value Object* see *Money (488)*.

.NET Implementation

.NET has a first-class treatment of *Value Object*. In C# an object is marked as a *Value Object* by declaring it as a struct instead as a class. The environment then treats it with value semantics.

When to Use It

Treat something as a *Value Object* when you're basing equality on something other than an identity. It's worth considering this for any small object that's easy to create.

Name Collisions I've seen the term *Value Object* used for this pattern for quite some time. Sadly recently I've seen the J2EE community [Alur et al.] use the term "value object" to mean *Data Transfer Object (401)*, which has caused a storm in the teacup of the patterns community. This is just one of those clashes over names that happen all the time in this business. Recently [Alur et al.] decided to use the term *transfer object* instead.

I continue to use *Value Object* in this way in this text. If nothing else it allows me to be consistent with my previous writings!

Value Object

Money

Represents a monetary value.

Money
amount currency
+, -, * allocate >, >, <=, >=, =

A large proportion of the computers in this world manipulate money, so it's always puzzled me that money isn't actually a first class data type in any mainstream programming language. The lack of a type causes problems, the most obvious surrounding currencies. If all your calculations are done in a single currency, this isn't a huge problem, but once you involve multiple currencies you want to avoid adding your dollars to your yen without taking the currency differences into account. The more subtle problem is with rounding. Monetary calculations are often rounded to the smallest currency unit. When you do this it's easy to lose pennies (or your local equivalent) because of rounding errors.

The good thing about object-oriented programming is that you can fix these problems by creating a Money class that handles them. Of course, it's still surprising that none of the mainstream base class libraries actually do this.

How It Works

Money

The basic idea is to have a Money class with fields for the numeric amount and the currency. You can store the amount as either an integral type or a fixed decimal type. The decimal type is easier for some manipulations, the integral for others. You should absolutely avoid any kind of floating point type, as that will introduce the kind of rounding problems that *Money* is intended to avoid. Most of the time people want monetary values rounded to the smallest complete unit, such as cents in the dollar. However, there are times when fractional units are needed. It's important to make it clear what kind of money you're working with, especially in an application that uses both kinds. It makes sense to have different types for the two cases as they behave quite differently under arithmetic.

Money is a *Value Object (486)*, so it should have its equality and hash code operations overridden to be based on the currency and amount.

Money needs arithmetic operations so that you can use money objects as easily as you use numbers. But arithmetic operations for money have some important differences to money operations in numbers. Most obviously, any addition or subtraction needs to be currency aware so you can react if you try to add together monies of different currencies. The simplest, and most common, response is to treat the adding together of disparate currencies as an error. In some more sophisticated situations you can use Ward Cunningham's idea of a money bag. This is an object that contains monies of multiple currencies together in one object. This object can then participate in calculations just like any money object. It can also be valued into a currency.

Multiplication and division end up being more complicated due to rounding problems. When you multiply money you do it with a scalar. If you want to add 5% tax to a bill you multiply by 0.05, so you see multiplication by regular numeric types.

The awkward complication comes with rounding, particularly when allocating money between different places. Here's Matt Foemmel's simple conundrum. Suppose I have a business rule that says that I have to allocate the whole amount of a sum of money to two accounts: 70% to one and 30% to another. I have 5 cents to allocate. If I do the math I end up with 3.5 cents and 1.5 cents. Whichever way I round these I get into trouble. If I do the usual rounding to nearest then 1.5 becomes 2 and 3.5 becomes 4. So I end up gaining a penny. Rounding down gives me 4 cents and rounding up gives me 6 cents. There's no general rounding scheme I can apply to both that will avoid losing or gaining a penny.

I've seen various solutions to this problem.

• Perhaps the most common is to ignore it—after all, it's only a penny here and there. However this tends to make accountants understandably nervous.

• When allocating you always do the last allocation by subtracting from what you've allocated so far. This avoids losing pennies, but you can get a cumulative amount of pennies on the last allocation.

Money

• Allow users of a Money class to declare the rounding scheme when they call the method. This permits a programmer to say that the 70% case rounds up and the 30% rounds down. Things can get complicated when you allocate across ten accounts instead of two. You also have to remember to round. To encourage people to remember I've seen some Money classes force a rounding parameter into the multiply operation. Not only does this force the programmer to think about what rounding she needs, it also might remind her of the tests to write. However, it gets messy if you have a lot of tax calculations that all round the same way.

• My favorite solution: have an allocator function on the money. The parameter to the allocator is a list of numbers, representing the ratio to be allocated (it would look something like aMoney.allocate([7,3])). The allocator returns a list of monies, guaranteeing that no pennies get dropped by scattering them across the allocated monies in a way that looks pseudo-random from the outside. The allocator has faults: You have to remember to use it and any precise rules about where the pennies go are difficult to enforce.

The fundamental issue here is between using multiplication to determine proportional charge (such as a tax) and using it to allocate a sum of money across multiple places. Multiplication works well for the former, but an allocator works better for the latter. The important thing is to consider your intent in using multiplication or division on a monetary value.

You may want to convert from one currency to another with a method like aMoney.convertTo(Currency.DOLLARS). The obvious way to do this is to look up an exchange rate and multiply by it. While this works in many situations, there are cases where it doesn't—again due to rounding. The conversion rules between the fixed euro currencies had specific roundings applied that made simple multiplication unworkable. Thus, it's wise to have a convertor object to encapsulate the algorithm.

Comparison operations allow you to sort monies. Like the addition operation, conversions need to be currency aware. You can either choose to throw an exception if you compare different currencies or do a conversion.

A *Money* can encapsulate the printing behavior. This makes it much easier to provide good display on user interfaces and reports. A Money class can also parse a string to provide a currency-aware input mechanism, which again is very useful for the user interface. This is where your platform's libraries can provide help. Increasingly platforms provide globalization support with specific number formatters for particular countries.

Storing a *Money* in a database always raises an issue, since databases also don't seem to understand that money is important (although their vendors do.) The obvious route to take is to use *Embedded Value (268)*, which results in storing a currency for every money. That can be overkill when, for instance, an account may have all its entries be in pounds. In this case you may store the currency on the account and alter the database mapping to pull the account's currency whenever you load entries.

When to Use It

I use *Money* for pretty much all numeric calculation in object-oriented environments. The primary reason is to encapsulate the handling of rounding behavior, which helps reduce the problems of rounding errors. Another reason to use *Money* is to make multi-currency work much easier. The most common objection to *Money* is performance, although I've only rarely heard of cases where it makes any noticeable difference, and even then the encapsulation often makes tuning easier.

Example: A Money Class (Java)

by Matt Foemmel and Martin Fowler

The first decision is what data type to use for the amount. If anyone needs convincing that a floating point number is a bad idea, ask them to run this code.

```
double val = 0.00;
for (int i = 0; i < 10; i++) val += 0.10;
System.out.println(val == 1.00);
```

With floats safely disposed of, the choice lies between fixed-point decimals and integers, which in Java boils down to BigDecimal, BigInteger and long. Using an integral value actually makes the internal math easier, and if we use long we can use primitives and thus have readable math expressions.

class Money...

```
private long amount;
private Currency currency;
```

I'm using an integral amount, that is, the amount of the smallest base unit, which I refer to as cents in the code because it's as good a name as any. With a long we get an overflow error if the number gets too big. If you give us $92,233,720,368,547,758.09 we'll write you a version that uses BigInteger.

It's useful to provide constructors from various numeric types.

```
public Money(double amount, Currency currency) {
   this.currency = currency;
   this.amount = Math.round(amount * centFactor());
}
public Money(long amount, Currency currency) {
   this.currency = currency;
   this.amount = amount * centFactor();
}
private static final int[] cents = new int[] { 1, 10, 100, 1000 };
private int centFactor() {
   return cents[currency.getDefaultFractionDigits()];
}
```

Money

Different currencies have different fractional amounts. The Java 1.4 Currency class will tell you the number of fractional digits in a class. We can determine how many minor units there are in a major unit by raising ten to the power, but that's such a pain in Java that the array is easier (and probably quicker). We're prepared to live with the fact that this code breaks if someone uses four fractional digits.

Although most of the time you'll want to use money operation directly, there are occasions when you'll need access to the underlying data.

class Money...

```
public BigDecimal amount() {
    return BigDecimal.valueOf(amount, currency.getDefaultFractionDigits());
}
public Currency currency() {
    return currency;
}
```

You should always question your use of accessors. There's almost always a better way that won't break encapsulation. One example that we couldn't avoid is database mapping, as in *Embedded Value (268)*.

If you use one currency very frequently for literal amounts, a helper constructor can be useful.

class Money...

```
public static Money dollars(double amount) {
    return new Money(amount, Currency.USD);
}
```

As *Money* is a *Value Object (486)* you'll need to define equals.

class Money...

```
public boolean equals(Object other) {
    return (other instanceof Money) && equals((Money)other);
}
public boolean equals(Money other) {
    return currency.equals(other.currency) && (amount == other.amount);
}
```

And wherever there's an equals there should be a hash.

class Money...

```
public int hashCode() {
    return (int) (amount ^ (amount >>> 32));
}
```

Money

We'll start going through the arithmetic with addition and subtraction.

class Money...

```java
public Money add(Money other) {
   assertSameCurrencyAs(other);
   return newMoney(amount + other.amount);
}
private void assertSameCurrencyAs(Money arg) {
   Assert.equals("money math mismatch", currency, arg.currency);
}
private Money newMoney(long amount) {
   Money money = new Money();
   money.currency = this.currency;
   money.amount = amount;
   return money;
}
```

Note the use of a private factory method here that doesn't do the usual conversion into the cent-based amount. We'll use that a few times inside the *Money* code itself.

With addition defined, subtraction is easy.

class Money...

```java
public Money subtract(Money other) {
   assertSameCurrencyAs(other);
   return newMoney(amount - other.amount);
}
```

The base method for comparison is compareTo.

class Money...

```java
public int compareTo(Object other) {
   return compareTo((Money)other);
}
public int compareTo(Money other) {
   assertSameCurrencyAs(other);
   if (amount < other.amount) return -1;
   else if (amount == other.amount) return 0;
   else return 1;
}
```

Money

Although that's all you get on most Java classes these days, we find code is more readable with the other comparison methods such as these.

class Money...

```java
public boolean greaterThan(Money other) {
   return (compareTo(other) > 0);
}
```

Now we're ready to look at multiplication. We're providing a default rounding mode but you can set one yourself as well.

class Money...

```
public Money multiply(double amount) {
    return multiply(new BigDecimal(amount));
}
public Money multiply(BigDecimal amount) {
    return multiply(amount, BigDecimal.ROUND_HALF_EVEN);
}
public Money multiply(BigDecimal amount, int roundingMode) {
    return new Money(amount().multiply(amount), currency, roundingMode);
}
```

If you want to allocate a sum of money among many targets and you don't want to lose cents, you'll want an allocation method. The simplest one allocates the same amount (almost) amongst a number of targets.

class Money...

```
public Money[] allocate(int n) {
    Money lowResult = newMoney(amount / n);
    Money highResult = newMoney(lowResult.amount + 1);
    Money[] results = new Money[n];
    int remainder = (int) amount % n;
    for (int i = 0; i < remainder; i++) results[i] = highResult;
    for (int i = remainder; i < n; i++) results[i] = lowResult;
    return results;
}
```

A more sophisticated allocation algorithm can handle any ratio.

class Money...

```
public Money[] allocate(long[] ratios) {
    long total = 0;
    for (int i = 0; i < ratios.length; i++) total += ratios[i];
    long remainder = amount;
    Money[] results = new Money[ratios.length];
    for (int i = 0; i < results.length; i++) {
        results[i] = newMoney(amount * ratios[i] / total);
        remainder -= results[i].amount;
    }
    for (int i = 0; i < remainder; i++) {
        results[i].amount++;
    }
    return results;
}
```

Money

You can use this to solve Foemmel's Conundrum.

class Money...

```
public void testAllocate2() {
    long[] allocation = {3,7};
    Money[] result = Money.dollars(0.05).allocate(allocation);
    assertEquals(Money.dollars(0.02), result[0]);
    assertEquals(Money.dollars(0.03), result[1]);
}
```

Special Case

A subclass that provides special behavior for particular cases.

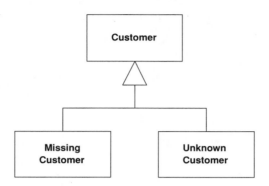

Nulls are awkward things in object-oriented programs because they defeat polymorphism. Usually you can invoke foo freely on a variable reference of a given type without worrying about whether the item is the exact type or a subclass. With a strongly typed language you can even have the compiler check that the call is correct. However, since a variable can contain null, you may run into a runtime error by invoking a message on null, which will get you a nice, friendly stack trace.

If it's possible for a variable to be null, you have to remember to surround it with null test code so you'll do the right thing if a null is present. Often the right thing is same in many contexts, so you end up writing similar code in lots of places—committing the sin of code duplication.

Nulls are a common example of such problems and others crop up regularly. In number systems you have to deal with infinity, which has special rules for things like addition that break the usual invariants of real numbers. One of my earliest experiences in business software was with a utility customer who wasn't fully known, referred to as "occupant." All of these imply altering the usual behavior of the type.

Instead of returning null, or some odd value, return a *Special Case* that has the same interface as what the caller expects.

How It Works

The basic idea is to create a subclass to handle the *Special Case*. Thus, if you have a customer object and you want to avoid null checks, you make a null customer object. Take all of the methods for customer and override them in the *Special Case* to provide some harmless behavior. Then, whenever you have a null, put in an instance of null customer instead.

There's usually no reason to distinguish between different instances of null customer, so you can often implement a *Special Case* with a flyweight [Gang of Four]. You can't do it all the time. For a utility you can accumulate charges against an occupant customer even you can't do much billing, so it's important to keep your occupants separate.

A null can mean different things. A null customer may mean no customer or it may mean that there's a customer but we don't know who it is. Rather than just using a null customer, consider having separate *Special Cases* for missing customer and unknown customer.

A common way for a *Special Case* to override methods is to return another *Special Case*, so if you ask an unknown customer for his last bill, you may well get an unknown bill.

IEEE 754 floating-point arithmetic offers good examples of *Special Case* with positive infinity, negative infinity, and not-a-number (NaN). If you divide by zero, instead of getting an exception that you have to deal with, the system just returns NaN, and NaN participates in arithmetic just like any other floating point number.

When to Use It

Use *Special Case* whenever you have multiple places in the system that have the same behavior after a conditional check for a particular class instance, or the same behavior after a null check.

Further Reading

I haven't seen *Special Case* written up as a pattern yet, but **Null Object** has been written up in [Woolf]. If you'll pardon the unresistable pun, I see Null Object as special case of *Special Case*.

Example: A Simple Null Object (C#)

Here's a simple example of *Special Case* used as a null object.

We have a regular employee.

class Employee...

```
    public virtual String Name {
       get {return _name;}
       set {_name = value;}
    }
    private String _name;
    public virtual Decimal GrossToDate {
       get {return calculateGrossFromPeriod(0);}
    }
    public virtual Contract Contract {
       get {return _contract;}
    }
    private Contract _contract;
```

The features of the class could be overridden by a null employee

class NullEmployee : Employee, INull...

```
    public override String Name {
       get {return "Null Employee";}
       set {}
    }
    public override Decimal GrossToDate {
       get {return 0m;}
    }
    public override Contract Contract {
       get {return Contract.NULL;}
    }
```

Notice that when you ask a null employee for its contract you get a null contract back.

The default values here avoid a lot of null tests if they end up with the same null values. The repeated null values are handled by the null object by default. You can also test for nullness explicitly either by giving the customer an isNull method or by using a type test for a marker interface.

Plugin

by David Rice and Matt Foemmel

Links classes during configuration rather than compilation.

Separated Interface (476) is often used when application code runs in multiple runtime environments, each requiring different implementations of particular behavior. Most developers supply the correct implementation by writing a factory method. Suppose you define your primary key generator with a *Separated Interface (476)* so that you can use a simple in-memory counter for unit testing but a database-managed sequence for production. Your factory method will most likely contain a conditional statement that looks at a local environment variable, determines if the system is in test mode, and returns the correct key generator. Once you have a few factories you have a mess on your hands. Establishing a new deployment configuration—say "execute unit tests against in-memory database without transaction control" or "execute in production mode against DB2 database with full transaction control"—requires editing conditional statements in a number of factories, rebuilding, and redeploying. Configuration shouldn't be scattered throughout your application, nor should it require a rebuild or redeployment. *Plugin* solves both problems by providing centralized, runtime configuration.

How It Works

The first thing to do is define with a *Separated Interface (476)* any behaviors that will have different implementations based on runtime environment. Beyond that, we use the basic factory pattern, only with a few special requirements. The *Plugin* factory requires its linking instructions to be stated at a single, external point in order that configuration can be easily managed. Additionally, the linking to implementations must occur dynamically at runtime rather than during compilation, so that reconfiguration won't require a rebuild.

Plugin

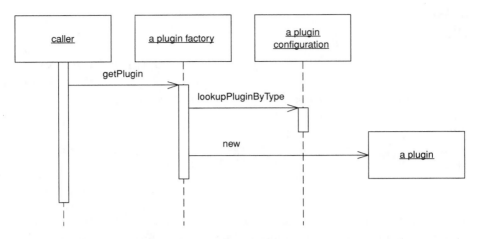

Figure 18.2 *A caller obtains a Plugin implementation of a separated interface.*

A text file works quite well as the means of stating linking rules. The *Plugin* factory will simply read the text file, look for an entry specifying the implementation of a requested interface, and return that implementation.

Plugin works best in a language that supports reflection because the factory can construct implementations without compile-time dependencies on them. When using reflection, the configuration file must contain mappings of interface names to implementation class names. The factory can sit independently in a framework package and needn't be changed when you add new implementations to your configuration options.

Even when not using a language that supports reflection it's still worthwhile to establish a central point of configuration. You can even use a text file to set up linking rules, with the only difference that your factory will use conditional logic to map an interface to the desired implementation. Each implementation type must be accounted for in the factory—not a big a deal in practice. Just add another option within the factory method whenever you add a new implementation to the code base. To enforce layer and package dependencies with a build-time check, place this factory in its own package to avoid breaking your build process.

Plugin

When to Use It

Use *Plugin* whenever you have behaviors that require different implementations based on runtime environment.

Example: An Id Generator (Java)

As discussed above, key, or ID, generation is a task whose implementation might vary between deployment environments (Figure 18.3).

First we'll write the IdGenerator *Separated Interface (476)* as well as any needed implementations.

```
interface IdGenerator...

    public Long nextId();
```

```
class OracleIdGenerator implements IdGenerator...

    public OracleIdGenerator() {
        this.sequence = Environment.getProperty("id.sequence");
        this.datasource = Environment.getProperty("id.source");
    }
```

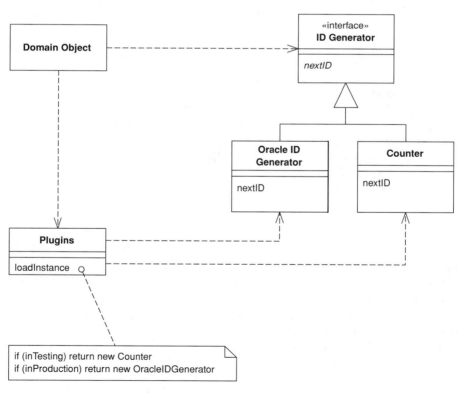

Figure 18.3 *Multiple ID generators.*

Plugin

In the OracleIdGenerator, nextId() select the next available number out of the defined sequence from the defined data source.

```
class Counter implements IdGenerator...

    private long count = 0;
    public synchronized Long nextId() {
        return new Long(count++);
    }
```

Now that we have something to construct, let's write the plugin factory that will realize the current interface-to-implementation mappings.

```
class PluginFactory...
    private static Properties props = new Properties();

    static {
        try {
            String propsFile = System.getProperty("plugins");
            props.load(new FileInputStream(propsFile));
        } catch (Exception ex) {
            throw new ExceptionInInitializerError(ex);
        }
    }

    public static Object getPlugin(Class iface) {

        String implName = props.getProperty(iface.getName());
        if (implName == null) {
            throw new RuntimeException("implementation not specified for " +
                                    iface.getName() + " in PluginFactory propeties.");
        }
        try {
            return Class.forName(implName).newInstance();
        } catch (Exception ex) {
            throw new RuntimeException("factory unable to construct instance of " +
                                    iface.getName());
        }
    }
}
```

Plugin

Note that we're loading the configuration by looking for a system property named plugins that will locate the file containing our linking instructions. Many options exist for defining and storing linking instructions, but we find a simple properties file the easiest. Using the system property to find the file rather then looking on the classpath makes it simple to specify a new configuration anywhere on your machine. This can be very convenient when moving builds between development, test, and production environments. Here's how two different configuration files, one for test and one for production, might look:

config file test.properties...

```
# test configuration
IdGenerator=TestIdGenerator
```

config file prod.properties...

```
# production configuration
IdGenerator=OracleIdGenerator
```

Let's go back to the IdGenerator interface and add a static INSTANCE member that's set by a call to the *Plugin* factory. It combines *Plugin* with the singleton pattern to provide an extremely simple, readable call to obtain an ID.

interface IdGenerator...

```
public static final IdGenerator INSTANCE =
    (IdGenerator) PluginFactory.getPlugin(IdGenerator.class);
```

We can now make that call knowing that we'll get the right ID for the right environment.

class Customer extends DomainObject...

```
private Customer(String name, Long id) {
    super(id);
    this.name = name;
}
public Customer create(String name) {
    Long newObjId = IdGenerator.INSTANCE.nextId();
    Customer obj = new Customer(name, newObjId);
    obj.markNew();
    return obj;
}
```

Plugin

Service Stub

by David Rice

Removes dependence upon problematic services during testing.

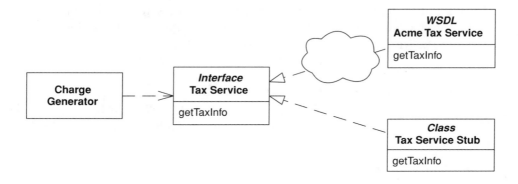

Enterprise systems often depend on access to third-party services such as credit scoring, tax rate lookups, and pricing engines. Any developer who has built such a system can speak to the frustration of being dependent on resources completely out of his control. Feature delivery is unpredictable, and as these services are often remote reliability and performance can suffer as well.

At the very least these problems slow the development process. Developers sit around waiting for the service to come back on line or maybe put some hacks into the code to compensate for yet to be delivered features. Much worse, and quite likely, such dependencies will lead to times when tests can't execute. When tests can't run the development process is broken.

Replacing the service during testing with a *Service Stub* that runs locally, fast, and in memory improves your development experience.

How It Works

The first step is to define access to the service with a *Gateway (466)*. The *Gateway (466)* should not be a class but rather a *Separated Interface (476)* so you can have one implementation that calls the real service and at least one that's only a *Service Stub*. The desired implementation of the *Gateway (466)* should be loaded using a *Plugin (499)*. The key to writing a *Service Stub* is that you keep it as simple as possible—complexity will defeat your purpose.

Let's walk through the process of stubbing a sales tax service that provides state sales tax amount and rate, given an address, product type, and sales amount. The simplest way to provide a *Service Stub* is to write two or three lines of code that use a flat tax rate to satisfy all requests.

Tax laws aren't that simple, of course. Certain products are exempt from taxation in certain states, so we rely on our real tax service to know which product and state combinations are tax exempt. However, a lot of our application functionality dependents on whether taxes are charged, so we need to accommodate tax exemption in our *Service Stub*. The simplest means of adding this behavior to the stub is via a conditional statement that exempt a specific combination of address and product and then uses that same data in any relevant test cases. The number of lines of code in our stub can still be counted on one hand.

A more dynamic *Service Stub* maintains a list of exempt product and state combinations, allowing test cases to add to it. Even here we're at about 10 lines of code. We're keeping things simple given our aim of speeding the development process.

The dynamic *Service Stub* brings up an interesting question regarding the dependency between it and test cases. The *Service Stub* relies on a setup method for adding exemptions that isn't in the original tax service *Gateway (466)* interface. To take advantage of a *Plugin (499)* to load the *Service Stub*, this method must be added to the *Gateway (466,* which is fine as it doesn't add much noise to your code and is done in the name of testing. Be sure that the *Gateway (466)* implementation that calls the real service throws assertion failures within any test methods.

When to Use It

Use *Service Stub* whenever you find that dependence on a particular service is hindering your development and testing.

Many practitioners of Extreme Programming use the term **Mock Object,** for a *Service Stub*. We've stuck with *Service Stub* because it's been around longer.

Example: Sales Tax Service (Java)

Our application uses a tax service that deployed as a Web service. The first item we'll take care of is defining a *Gateway (466)* so that our domain code isn't

Service Stub

forced to deal with the wonders of Web services. The *Gateway (466)* is defined as an interface to facilitate loading of any *Service Stubs* that we write. We'll use *Plugin (499)* to load the correct tax service implementation.

interface TaxService...

```
public static final TaxService INSTANCE =
    (TaxService) PluginFactory.getPlugin(TaxService.class);
public TaxInfo getSalesTaxInfo(String productCode, Address addr, Money saleAmount);
```

The simple flat rate *Service Stub* would look like this:

class FlatRateTaxService implements TaxService...

```
private static final BigDecimal FLAT_RATE = new BigDecimal("0.0500");
public TaxInfo getSalesTaxInfo(String productCode, Address addr, Money saleAmount) {
    return new TaxInfo(FLAT_RATE, saleAmount.multiply(FLAT_RATE));
}
```

Here's a *Service Stub* that provides tax exemptions for a particular address and product combination:

class ExemptProductTaxService implements TaxService...

```
private static final BigDecimal EXEMPT_RATE = new BigDecimal("0.0000");
private static final BigDecimal FLAT_RATE = new BigDecimal("0.0500");
private static final String EXEMPT_STATE = "IL";
private static final String EXEMPT_PRODUCT = "12300";
public TaxInfo getSalesTaxInfo(String productCode, Address addr, Money saleAmount) {
    if (productCode.equals(EXEMPT_PRODUCT) && addr.getStateCode().equals(EXEMPT_STATE)) {
        return new TaxInfo(EXEMPT_RATE, saleAmount.multiply(EXEMPT_RATE));
    } else {
        return new TaxInfo(FLAT_RATE, saleAmount.multiply(FLAT_RATE));
    }
}
```

Now here's a more dynamic *Service Stub* whose methods allow a test case to add and reset exemption combinations. Once we feel it necessary to add these test methods we need to go back and add these methods to our simpler *Service Stubs* as well as to the implementation that calls the actual tax Web service. The unused test methods should all throw assertion failures.

class TestTaxService implements TaxService...

```
private static Set exemptions = new HashSet();
public TaxInfo getSalesTaxInfo(String productCode, Address addr, Money saleAmount) {
    BigDecimal rate = getRate(productCode, addr);
    return new TaxInfo(rate, saleAmount.multiply(rate));
}
public static void addExemption(String productCode, String stateCode) {
    exemptions.add(getExemptionKey(productCode, stateCode));
}
```

Service Stub

```
    public static void reset() {
       exemptions.clear();
    }
    private static BigDecimal getRate(String productCode, Address addr) {
       if (exemptions.contains(getExemptionKey(productCode, addr.getStateCode()))) {
          return EXEMPT_RATE;
       } else {
          return FLAT_RATE;
       }
    }
}
```

Not shown is the implementation that calls the Web service providing our real tax data, to which our production *Plugin (499)* configuration would link the tax service interface. Our test *Plugin (499)* configurations would link to the appropriate *Service Stub* above.

Finally, any caller to the tax service must access the service via the *Gateway (466)*. We have a charge generator here that creates standard charges and then calls the tax service in order to create any corresponding taxes.

```
class ChargeGenerator...

    public Charge[] calculateCharges(BillingSchedule schedule) {
       List charges = new ArrayList();
       Charge baseCharge = new Charge(schedule.getBillingAmount(), false);
       charges.add(baseCharge);
       TaxInfo info = TaxService.INSTANCE.getSalesTaxInfo(
             schedule.getProduct(), schedule.getAddress(), schedule.getBillingAmount());
       if (info.getStateRate().compareTo(new BigDecimal(0)) > 0) {
          Charge taxCharge = new Charge(info.getStateAmount(), true);
          charges.add(taxCharge);
       }
       return (Charge[]) charges.toArray(new Charge[charges.size()]);
    }
```

Record Set

An in-memory representation of tabular data.

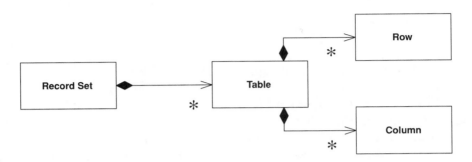

In the last twenty years, the dominant way to represent data in a database has been the tabular relational form. Backed by database companies big and small, and a fairly standard query language, almost every new development I see uses relational data.

On top of this has come a wealth of tools for building UI's quickly. These data-aware UI frameworks rely on the fact that the underlying data is relational, and they provide UI widgets of various kinds that make it easy to view and manipulate this data with almost no programming.

The dark side of these environments is that, while they make display and simple updates ridiculously easy, they have no real facilities in which to place business logic. Any validations beyond "is this a valid date," and any business rules or computations have no good place to go. Either they're jammed into the database as stored procedures or they're mingled with UI code.

The idea of the *Record Set* is to give you your cake and let you eat it, by providing an in-memory structure that looks exactly like the result of an SQL query but can be generated and manipulated by other parts of the system.

How It Works

A *Record Set* is usually something that you won't build yourself, provided by the vendor of the software platform you're working with. Examples include the data set of ADO.NET and the row set of JDBC 2.0.

The first essential element of a *Record Set* is that it looks exactly like the result of a database query. That means you can use the classical two-tier approach of issuing a query and throwing the data directly into a data-aware UI with all the ease that these two-tier tools give you. The second essential element is that you can easily build a *Record Set* yourself or take one that has resulted from a database query and easily manipulate it with domain logic code.

Although platforms often give you a *Record Set,* you can create one yourself. The problem is that there isn't that much point without the data-aware UI tools, which you would also need to create yourself. In any case it's fair to say that building a *Record Set* structure as a list of maps, which is common in dynamically typed scripting languages, is a good example of this pattern.

The ability to disconnect the *Record Set* from its link to the data source is very valuable. This allows you to pass the *Record Set* around a network without having to worry about database connections. Furthermore, if you can then easily serialize the *Record Set* it can also act as a *Data Transfer Object (401)* for an application.

Disconnection raises the question of what happens when you update the *Record Set.* Increasingly platforms are allowing the *Record Set* to be a form of *Unit of Work (184),* so you can modify it and then return it to the data source to be committed. A data source can typically use *Optimistic Offline Lock (416)* to see if there are any conflicts and, if not, write the changes out to the database.

Explicit Interface Most *Record Set* implementations use an **implicit interface.** This means that to get information out of the *Record Set* you invoke a generic method with an argument to indicate which field you want. For example, to get the passenger on an airline reservation you use an expression like aReservation["passenger"]. An explicit interface requires a real reservation class with defined methods and properties. With an explicit reservation the expression for a passenger might be aReservation.passenger.

Implicit interfaces are flexible in that you can use a generic *Record Set* for any kind of data. This saves you having to write a new class every time you define a new kind of *Record Set.* In general, however, I find implicit interfaces to be a Bad Thing. If I'm programming with a reservation, how do I know how to get the passenger? Is the appropriate string "passenger" or "guest" or "flyer"? The only way I can tell is to wander around the code base trying to find where reservations are created and used. If I have an explicit interface I can look at the definition of the reservation to see what property I need.

This problem is exacerbated with statically typed languages. If I want the last name of the passenger, I have to resort to some horrible expression such as ((Person)aReservation["passenger"]).lastName, but then the compiler loses all type information and I have to manually enter it in to get the information I want. An explicit interface can keep the type information so I can use aReservation.passenger.lastName.

For these reasons, I generally frown on implicit interfaces (and their evil cousin, passing data around in dictionaries). I'm also not too keen on them with *Record Sets*, but the saving grace here is that the *Record Set* usually carries information on the legal columns in it. Furthermore, the column names are defined by the SQL that creates the *Record Set*, so it's not too difficult to find the properties when you need them.

But it's nice to go further and have an explicit interface. ADO.NET provides this with its strongly typed data sets, generated classes that provide an explicit and fully typed interface for a *Record Set*. Since an ADO.NET data set can contain many tables and the relationships between them, strongly typed data sets also provide properties that can use that relationship information. The classes are generated from the XSD data set definition.

Implicit interfaces are more common, so I've used untyped data sets in my examples for this book. For production code in ADO.NET, however, I suggest using data sets that are typed. In a non-ADO.NET environment, I suggest using code generation for your own explicit *Record Sets*.

When to Use It

To my mind the value of *Record Set* comes from having an environment that relies on it as a common way of manipulating data. A lot of UI tools use *Record Set*, and a compelling reason to use them yourself. If you have such an environment, you should use *Table Module (125)* to organize your domain logic: Get a *Record Set* from the database; pass it to a *Table Module (125)* to calculate derived information; pass it to a UI for display and editing; and pass it back to a *Table Module (125)* for validation. Then commit the updates to the database.

In many ways the tools that make *Record Set* so valuable appeared because of the ever-presence of relational databases and SQL and the absence of any real alternative structure and query language. Now, of course, there's XML, which has a widely standardized structure and a query language in XPath, and I think it's likely that we'll see tools that use a hierarchic structure in the same way that current tools now use *Record Set*. Perhaps this is actually a particular case of a more generic pattern: something like *Generic Data Structure*. But I'll leave thinking about that pattern until then.

Record Set

References

[Alexander et al.]

Alexander, et al. *A Pattern Language*. Oxford, 1977.

> An inspiration for many people in the patterns movement. I'm less enamored of it than most, but it's worth looking at to understand an approach that so many draw so much from.

[Alpert et al.]

Alpert, Brown and Woolf. *Design Patterns Smalltalk Companion*. Addison-Wesley, 1998.

> Little known outside the Smalltalk community, this book expands and explains many of the classic patterns.

[Alur et al.]

Alur, Crupi, and Malks. *Core J2EE Patterns*: *Best Practices and Design Strategies*. Prentice Hall, 2001.

> One of the new wave of patterns books that put new life into the form. Although the patterns are expressed specifically for the J2EE platform, most also make sense in other places.

[Ambler]

http://www.ambysoft.com/mappingObjects.html

> A useful source of ideas on object-relational mapping.

[Beck XP 2000]

Beck, *Extreme Programming Explained*. Addison-Wesley, 2000.

> The manifesto for Extreme Programming. It should be read by anyone interested in software process.

[Beck Patterns]

Beck. *Smalltalk Best Practice Patterns*. Prentice Hall, 1997.

> Undeservedly little read because of its Smalltalk base. It has more good advice for other OO languages than most books that are specially written for them. The only downside is that you might realize how much we all miss by not programming in Smalltalk.

[Beck TDD]

Beck. *Test-Driven Development: By Example*. Addison-Wesley, 2003.

> Due to be out on the same day as this book. TDD is Kent's guide to the tight cycle of testing and refactoring that can evolve a design.

[Bernstein and Newcomer]

Bernstein and Newcomer. *Principles of Transaction Processing*. Morgan Kaufmann, 1997.

> An excellent introduction to the head-hurting world of transactions.

[Brown et al.]

Brown et al. *Enterprise Java Programming with IBM Websphere*. Addison-Wesley, 2001.

> Although two-thirds of this book is a software manual, the other third packs more good design advice than do most entire books devoted to the subject.

[Brown and Whitenack]

http://members.aol.com/kgb1001001/Chasms.htm

> One of the earliest, and best, papers on object-relational mapping.

[Cockburn UC]

Cockburn. *Writing Effective Use Cases*. Addison-Wesley, 2001.

> By far the best reference on use cases.

[Cockburn PloP]

Cockburn, "Prioritizing Forces in Software Design," in [PLoPD 2].

> A discussion of application boundaries.

[Coleman et al.]

Coleman, Arnold, and Bodoff. *Object-Oriented Development: The Fusion Method, Second Edition.* Prentice Hall, 2001.

Although much of this pre-UML book is primarily of historic interest, its discussion of the interface model is very helpful to those designing a service layer.

[Evans and Fowler]

http://martinfowler.com/apsupp/spec.pdf

A discussion of the Specification pattern.

[Evans]

Evans. *Domain Driven.* Addison Wesley, in preparation.

A book on developing domain models. Although I don't usually like to reference books not yet published, the manuscript promises a fascinating discussion of an important and difficult aspect of enterprise application developments.

[Fowler Temporal Patterns]

http://martinfowler.com/ap2/timeNarrative.html

Patterns dealing with object histories that change over time.

[Fowler AP]

Fowler. *Analysis Patterns.* Addison-Wesley, 1997.

Domain model patterns.

[Fowler Refactoring]

Fowler, *Refactoring.* Addison-Wesley, 1999.

A technique for improving the design of an existing code base.

[Fowler CI]

http://martinfowler.com/articles/continuousIntegration.html

An essay that explains how to automatically build software several times a day.

[Gang of Four]

Gamma, Helm, Johnson, and Vlissides. *Design Patterns*. Addison-Wesley, 1995.

    The seminal book on patterns.

[Hay]

Hay. *Data Model Patterns*. Dorset House, 1995.

    Patterns of conceptual models from a relational perspective.

[Jacobson et al.]

Jacobson et al. *Object-Oriented Software Engineering*. Addison-Wesley, 1992.

    An early book on OO design; introduces use cases and the interface-controller-entity approach to design.

[Keller and Coldewey]

http://www.objectarchitects.de/ObjectArchitects/orpatterns/index.htm

    An excellent resource for object-relational mapping.

[Kirtland]

Kirtland. *Designing Component-Based Applications*. Microsoft Press, 1998.

    Description of the DNA architecture.

[Knight and Dai]

Knight and Dai. "Objects and the Web." *IEEE Software*, March/April 2002.

    An excellent paper on model view controller, its evolution and use in Web applications.

[Larman]

Larman. *Applying UML and Patterns, Second Edition*. Prentice Hall, 2001.

    Currently my first-choice introduction to OO design.

[Lea]

Lea. *Concurrent Programming in Java, Second Edition*. Addison-Wesley, 2000.

    If you want to program with multiple threads, you need to understand this book first.

[Marinescu]

Marinescu. *EJB Design Patterns*. New York: John Wiley, 2002.

> Recent patterns book for Java's EJB.

[Martin and Odell]

Martin and Odell. *Object Oriented Methods: A Foundation (UML Edition)*. Prentice Hall, 1998.

> Object modeling from a conceptual perspective, as well as investigation into the foundations of what modeling is about.

[Nilsson]

Nilsson. *.NET Enterprise Design with Visual Basic .NET and SQL Server 2000*. Sams, 2002.

> A solid book on architecture for the Microsoft platform.

[Peckish]

two million (see page 79)

[PLoPD 2]

Vlissides, Coplien, and Kerth (eds.). *Pattern Languages of Program Design 2*. Addison-Wesley, 1996.

> Compendium of patterns papers.

[PLoPD 3]

Martin, Buschmann, and Rielhe (eds.). *Pattern Languages of Program Design 3*. Addison-Wesley, 1998.

> Compendium of patterns papers.

[POSA]

Buschmann et al. *Pattern-Oriented Software Architecture*. Wiley, 2000.

> The best book on broader architectural patterns.

[Riehle et al.]

Riehle, Siberski, Baumer, Megert, and Zullighoven. "Serializer," in [PLoPD 3].

> In-depth description of serialization of object structures, particularly when you need to serialize into different forms.

[Schmidt]

Schmidt, Stal, Rohnert, and Buschmann. *Pattern-Oriented Software Architecture, Volume 2.* New York: John Wiley, 2000.

> Patterns for concurrent and distributed systems. More for people who design application servers than for those who use application servers, but it's good to have some knowledge of these ideas when you use the results.

[Snodgrass]

Snodgrass. *Developing Time-Oriented Database Applications in SQL.* Morgan-Kaufmann, 1999.

> How to deal with tracking historic information in relational databases.

[Struts]

http://jakarta.apache.org/struts/

> A Web presentation framework for Java that's growing in popularity.

[Waldo et al.]

Waldo, Wyant, Wollrath, and Kendall. *A Note on Distributed Computing.* SMLI TR-94-29, *http://research.sun.com/technical-reports/1994/smli_tr-94-29.pdf,* Sun Microsystems, 1994.

> A classic paper on why "transparent distributed objects" is a dangerous oxymoron.

[wiki]

http://c2.com/cgi/wiki

> The original wiki web, developed by Ward Cunningham. A rambling but fascinating open Web site where all sorts of people share all sorts of ideas.

[Woolf]

Woolf. "Null Object," in [PLoPD 3].

> A description of the Null Object pattern.

[Yoder]

http://www.joeyoder.com/Research/objectmappings

> A good source of object-relational patterns.

Index

A Cheat Sheet

Warning: This discussion of issues is grossly simplified!

How do I structure my domain logic?
The logic is simple → *Transaction Script (110)*
The logic is complex → *Domain Model (116)*
The logic is moderate and there are good tools around Record Set (508) → *Table Module (125)*

How do I give my domain logic a distinct API?
→ *Service Layer (133)*

How do I structure a Web presentation?
→ *Model View Controller (330)*

How do I organize my processing of HTTP requests?
I have simple application flow with mostly direct-page URLs → *Page Controller (333)*
I have a complicated flow → *Front Controller (344)*
I have needs for internationalization or flexible security policies → *Front Controller (344)*

How do I control the formatting of my Web pages?
I like to edit the page and put hooks in for dynamic data → *Template View (350)*
I think of the page as a transform of domain data—probably in XML → *Transform View (361)*
I need to make general changes to my site's look and feel → *Two Step View (365)*
I need to multiple appearances for the same logical screen format → *Two Step View (365)*

How do I control complex application flow?
→ *Application Controller (379)*

How do I interact with the database?
I'm using Transaction Script (110) → *Row Data Gateway (152)*
I'm using Transaction Script (110) and my platform has good support for Record Set (508) → *Table Data Gateway (144)*
I have a Domain Model (116) that corresponds closely to my database tables → *Active Record (160)*
I have a rich Domain Model (116) → *Data Mapper (165)*
I'm using Table Module (125) → *Table Data Gateway (144)*

How do I ensure that I don't update the same database data in different places in memory?
→ *Identity Map (195)*

How do I keep my domain objects linked to database records?
→ *Identity Field (216)*

How do I minimize my code for mapping my domain data to the database?
→ *Metadata Mapping (306)*